EUROPEAN ENVIRONMENTAL LAW

CASEBOOK

AUSTRALIA

The Law Book Company
Brisbane • Sydney • Melbourne • Perth

CANADA

Carswell
Ottawa • Toronto • Calgary • Montreal • Vancouver

AGENTS

Steimatzky's Agency Ltd., Tel Aviv
N.M. Tripathi (Private) Ltd., Bombay
Eastern Law House (Private) Ltd., Calcutta
M.P.P. House, Bangalore
Universal Book Traders, Delhi
Aditya Books, Delhi
MacMillan Shuppan KK, Tokyo
Pakistan Law House, Karachi, Lahore

EUROPEAN ENVIRONMENTAL LAW

CASEBOOK

by

Dr Ludwig Krämer

Judge at Landgericht Kiel, LL.D.,
Head of Legal Matters and Application of Community Law,
DG XI of the E.C. Commission

LONDON
SWEET & MAXWELL
1993

Published in 1993 by Sweet & Maxwell Limited of
South Quay Plaza, 183 Marsh Wall, London E14 9FT.
Computerset by Interactive Sciences, Gloucester
Printed in England by Clays Ltd., St Ives plc

No natural forests were destroyed to make this product;
only farmed timber was used and re-planted

BRITISH LIBRARY CATALOGUING IN PUBLICATION DATA
A catalogue record for this book is available
from the British Library

ISBN 0 421 47310 X

INTRODUCTION

This book was written in order to stimulate discussion on Community environmental law. While it might be true to say that the more you are a lady the less you should be talked of, law and in particular environmental law, suffers and fades away where it is not discussed, argued about, critisised and defended. I still see as the main function of law, its task to protect the weak against the strong: any discussion on environmental law contributes, in my opinion, to such a "protection of the weak", *i.e.* the environment. This is particularly true of Community environmental law, which is all too often, in its making and in its application, exposed to political influences which do not necessarily consider environmental protection.

Since I am an E.C. official, the criticism of the potitical decisions which lead to the different rules of law or to its application, are obviously expressed with some reserve. But I do hope that nowhere is the reader left in ambiguity as to my own point of view. Of course, the decisions of the Court of Justice also need to be discussed and, where necessary, criticised. Only through an open discussion can progress towards better law and more environmental justice in our society be achieved. Any criticism of the Court's decisions does not take away the profound agreement with which I am following the Court's jurisprudence.

Being a judge myself and working in an administration which is exposed to hundred and one different influences, opinions, interests, pressures and considerations, I am deeply convinced that the only glue which can keep the European Community together is the law. Policy decides on the means, the speed and the direction. But the legal rule is the only way to reconcile the strong and the weak, the north and the south, the east and the west within the Community. And I am not afraid of a "gouvernement des juges": the E.C. suffers not so much from too many decisions taken by the Court, but rather from the weakness of the legal rules themselves as well as from the fact that even these rules are not properly applied.

This book tries to look at Community environmental law from a Community perspective. This perspective has also determined the choice of bibliographic references which have been kept to a minimum. My hope is that it will be used first of all by students. Until one or two years ago, environmental law was taught, for instance, in every law faculty in the Netherlands, but in no law faculty in Spain. Furthermore, in most Member States teaching and discussion of Community environmental law is still rather underdeveloped, though this law is often of considerable influence. When one realises that Portugal, when it joined the E.C. in 1986, did not have one single piece of national legislation which could legitimately be called "environmental law", one begins to appreciate the change which the incorporation of some 200 legal instruments of Community environmental law has had or could have on Portuguese economic agents, administrative attitudes, courts' decisions, public opinion—and on the Portuguese environment. Similar considerations might apply to other Member States.

The judgments which I have selected are my own choice. I stopped on June 30, 1993. Thus, the Court's judgment on the bathing water in Blackpool (C–56/90) is not commented on, though it is one of the first environmental cases in which the Commission has taken action against a Member State on the basis of an individual complaint: a lady had sent a postcard and asked the Commission to save the United Kingdom coastlines. Numerous other environmental cases are pending: on the interpretation of Article 100a(4); on environmental impact assessment questions; direct effects of environmental rules; and in particular several cases on waste issues, as well as cases which might be grouped under the heading of integrating environmental requirements into other policies. More comments will thus be necessary in future.

Indeed, it is my conviction that for the next 15 years waste issues will remain in the centre of general attention and also of the Court's activity regarding environmental law. This is due to two factors: *First*, I am not able to see a true internal market function—as the Court seems to imply (in Cases C–2/90 and C–155/91), where questions of waste are the primary responsibility of Member States. A free circulation of goods and a primarily national management of goods' residues (wastes) can hardly function in the long term. I remain of the opinion that the invention of the notion of "waste" by lawyers is quite frankly a bad one: waste are corporeal objects and should be treated as such. I fail to see that the Treaty provides for bans or restrictions of use of products to be regulated under internal market auspices (Article 100a), but that a rule on products which have ended their useful lifetime should not be based on that provision but on Article 130s. It is worthwhile mentioning that in the United States even air emissions are seen as "goods" and justify federal competence for air emissions under the commerce clause. Under environmental auspices, it is relatively unimportant whether the pollution comes from products, wastes or emissions: in all three cases the minimisation of environmental impairment is necessary and the splitting-up of pollutants into three different categories which follow three different sets of rules is only hiding this necessity.

Second: I am convinced that one of the main underlying features of the dispute on the legal basis for waste rules is not the issue of waste itself, but the eternal struggle between national (regional) power and Community power. Article 130s is preferred as a legal basis because it allows, by virtue of Article 130t, maintenance or introduction of more stringent rules at national level. Thus, the Community rule under Article 130s can be kept as minimal as possible, since any Member State which requests broader rules might be asked to adopt such measures at national level under Article 130t. It remains to be seen whether the Community will be stronger in the future and whether it will manage to set up appropriate standards for an integrated waste management for the whole of the Community.

I hope that this book shows how difficult it is to monitor the application of Community environmental law in practice—although obviously all the internal, political bargaining can not even be described. Community law is at the crossroads between national and public international law; its enforcement mechanisms are still in their infancy and one should be aware that this is not a coincidence. Indeed, where the Member States have given the Commission inspection functions for agriculture and fishery, slaughterhouses and competition, and in particular for the distribution of money by structured funds and other instruments, it is difficult to understand why there should be no environmental inspectors at Community level: where a company cheats with an illegal merger in order to increase its profits, the Commission may send its inspectors. Where the same company cheats and illegally discharges pollutants into the water in order to save money on treatment, the Commission sends a letter to the Member State's embassy: what an imbalance!

The environment needs a mechanism which ensures that environmental needs are effectively respected and safeguarded in daily life. At present, seen from a Community perspective and save for a few particular rules in specific areas, they are not. This casebook tries to illustrate the difficulties in collecting the facts of a case, in gathering evidence, the obstacles to administrative co-operation and the necessity for political will to ensure that environmental legislation does not remain a paper tiger but is applied in practice.

Of course, an enforcement mechanism cannot exist at Community level alone. The EEC cannot protect the environment against or without the will of the population concerned. However, this book is full of examples where no other action was taken by the Commission, though many local, regional or national persons, bodies, administrations, public prosecutors or courts could have intervened in order to ensure the respect of the law and the protection of the environment. Environmental law shares with human rights the problem that fundamental principles are pronounced every Sunday, but what really matters is the practical compliance with law, not the big words.

Thus, this casebook invites the examination of environmental case law. It does not convey the message that the law can, on its own, effectively protect the environment. Indeed, the E.C. Commission stated in 1992, after 20 years of Community environmental policy and law-making that "a new report on the State of the Environment . . . indicates a slow but relentless deterioration of the general state of the environment of the Community, notwithstanding the measures taken over the past two decades." This led the Council, in its resolution on the 5th Community environmental action programme to "agree that the achievement of sustainable development calls for significant changes in current patterns of development, production, consumption and behaviour."

Legal discussion, important and vital as it is, must not make us forget, that the European environment—no: the environment as such—is threatened and despite the legal efforts of the last 20 years, has got worse off. Hölderlin deplored his fate as being "a poet in difficult times." I hope that young lawyers will see this book as a stimulus to take up the challenge in order to create an order which is a bit less difficult.

Ludwig Krämer
Brussels
1993

CONTENTS

Part 3: SECTORS OF COMMUNITY ENVIRONMENTAL POLICY

Nature conservation

Table of Cases

ALPHABETICAL LIST

EUROPEAN COURT OF JUSTICE

NATIONAL CASES

Table of Legislation

TREATIES AND CONVENTIONS

REGULATIONS

DIRECTIVES

RESOLUTIONS, PROPOSALS, RECOMMENDATIONS, DECISIONS, GUIDELINES

RULES OF PROCEDURE

NATIONAL LEGISLATION

Part 1

The Principles of Environmental Protection in Community Law

1. THE PROTECTION OF THE ENVIRONMENT —A GENERAL INTEREST OF THE EEC

Judgment of the Court of February 7, 1985 in Case 240/83

Preliminary ruling in the proceedings pending before the Tribunal de grande instance, Créteil, between Procureur de la République and Association de défense des brûleurs d'huiles usagées

[1985] E.C.R. 531

FACTS AND PROCEDURE[1]

Directive 75/439 aims to protect the environment against the risks from waste oils. It provides that Member States must take the necessary measures to ensure the safe collection and disposal of waste oils preferably by recycling (regeneration and/or combustion). Undertakings which collect or dispose waste oils must have a permit for that purpose.

France implemented the Directive by legislation in 1979. That legislation provided in particular that the whole of France was to be partitioned in geographical zones; for each zone an approved waste oil collector was appointed by the government to be responsible for the collection of all waste oils produced in the zone. The approved collector had to deliver all waste oils to an approved disposal undertaking which had received a governmental approval for the disposal. The approved disposal undertakings had to treat the waste oils in their own plants.

In September 1981, a French Procureur de la République asked the Tribunal de grande instance, Créteil, France, to dissolve the Association de défense de brûleurs d'huiles usagées; an association created in 1980 to defend the interests of manufacturers, dealers and users of heating appliances designed to burn both fuel oil and waste oils. The Procureur was of the opinion that the Association's principal object was unlawful since it encouraged people to burn waste oils without approval.

In the procedures before the Tribunal de Créteil, the Association contested the validity of those provisions of Directive 75/439 which had regard to the principles of freedom of trade, the free movement of goods and free competition. The Tribunal referred the case to the European Court of Justice for a preliminary ruling where it was registered on October 24, 1984. During the procedure before the European Court, written statements were received by the Commission, the Council, and the French, German and Italian governments. At the oral procedure, arguments were presented by the Association de défense de brûleurs d'huiles usagées, the French and Italian governments, the Commission and the Council.

The Advocate General delivered his opinion on November 22, 1984.

---

[1] Summary by the author.

JUDGMENT

(1) By judgment of 23 March 1983, which was received at the Court on 24 October 1983, the Tribunal de Grande Instance [Regional Court], Créteil, referred to the Court for a preliminary ruling under Article 177 of the EEC Treaty two questions on the interpretation and validity of Council Directive No 75/439/EEC of 16 June 1975 on the disposal of waste oils (Official Journal 1975 L 194, p. 23), in order to ascertain whether French Decree No 79–981 of 21 November 1979 laying down rules for the recovery of waste oil (Journal Officiel de la République Francaise of 23 November 1979, p. 2900) and its implementing orders were compatible with Community legislation inasmuch as they contained provisions prohibiting the use of such oils as fuel.

(2) On the basis of those French provisions the Procureur de la République [Public Prosecutor] applied to the Tribunal de Grande Instance, Créteil, for the dissolution of the Association de défense des Brûleurs d'huiles usagées [Association for the defence of the interests of burners of waste oils, hereinafter referred to as 'the Association'], on the ground that its aim and objects were unlawful. The Association's object is to defend the interests of manufacturers, dealers and users of stoves and heating appliances which burn both fuel and waste oil, such burning being prohibited by the French legislation.

(3) Articles 2 to 4 of Directive No 75/439/EEC require Member States to take the necessary measures to ensure the safe collection and disposal of waste oils, preferably by recycling. Article 5 of the Directive provides as follows: 'Where the aims defined in Articles 2, 3 and 4 cannot otherwise be achieved, Member States shall take the necessary measures to ensure that one or more undertakings carry out the collection and/or disposal of the products offered to them by the holders, where appropriate in the zone assigned to them by the competent authorities.' Article 6(1) thereof further provides that 'any undertaking which disposes of waste oils must obtain a permit'. In addition, Articles 13 and 14 provide that an indemnity, financed in accordance with the 'polluter pays' principle and not exceeding the actual yearly costs, may be granted to undertakings collecting and/or disposing of waste oils, as compensation for the obligations imposed on them under Article 5.

(4) In pursuance of the directive, on 21 November 1979 the French Government adopted Decree No 79–981 laying down rules for the recovery of waste oils, together with the two above-mentioned implementing orders of the same date. Under those provisions French territory was divided into zones and a system was established for the approval both of waste-oil collectors and of the undertakings responsible for disposing of waste oils. Under Article 3 of Decree No 79–981, holders of waste oils must either deliver them to collectors approved pursuant to Article 4 thereof, or make them directly available to a disposal undertaking which has obtained the approval required by Article 8, or else perform the disposal themselves if they have been granted such an approval. Article 6 of the decree requires collectors to surrender the oils collected to approved disposal undertakings. Article 7 lays down that 'the only permitted methods for disposing of waste oils . . . are recycling or regeneration under economically acceptable conditions, or else industrial use as fuel'. With respect to such industrial use, the second paragraph of Article 2 of the implementing order on the conditions for the disposal of waste oils provides that disposal by

burning must take place 'in a plant which has been approved for the purposes of environmental protection'.

(5) Since the legislation in question was adopted pursuant to Directive No 75/439, the Association raised before the national court the question whether that directive could constitute a legal basis for the prohibition of the burning of waste oils. Furthermore, doubts were expressed as to the validity of the directive in the light of certain fundamental principles of Community law.

(6) In those circumstances, the Tribunal de Grande Instance, Créteil, stayed the proceedings and submitted to the Court a request for a preliminary ruling on the interpretation and validity of Directive No 75/439/EEC, in the following terms:

> "Is the directive in conformity with the principles of freedom of trade, free movement of goods and freedom of competition, established by the Treaty of Rome, in view of the fact that Articles 5 and 6 of the directive empower the administrative authorities of the States to draw up zones which are assigned to one or more undertakings approved by those authorities and charged by them with the collection and the disposal of waste, and the fact that Articles 13 and 14 authorize the granting of subsidies?
> In addition, does the directive provide legal grounds justifying the prohibition of the burning of waste oils?"

Validity of the directive

(7) The wording of the first question raises doubts as to the validity of the directive as a whole but the reason for those doubts relate more particularly to the provisions which envisage the possibility of exclusive zones being assigned to waste-oil collectors, the prior approval of undertakings responsible for disposal and the possibility of indemnities being granted to undertakings which collect and dispose of waste oils.

(8) In those circumstances it is appropriate to consider, first, the provisions of the directive relating to the system for the assignment of zones (Article 5) and for the prior issuing of permits to disposal undertakings (Article 6) and, secondly, the system for granting indemnities (Articles 13 and 14).

Articles 5 and 6 of the directive

(9) The national court asks whether the system of permits is compatible with the principles of free trade, free movement of goods and freedom of competition, but does not elaborate further. In that connection it should be borne in mind that the principles of free movement of goods and freedom of competition, together with freedom of trade as a fundamental right, are general principles of Community law of which the Court ensures observance. The above-mentioned provisions of the directive should therefore be reviewed in the light of those principles.

(10) As to whether the system of granting approvals by zones for the collection of

waste oils is consistent with the principle of free movement of goods, the Commission and the Council, and also the Italian Government, emphasize in their observations that, in the first place, Article 5 of the directive permits the creation of zones only in exceptional circumstances, in particular in cases where no other, less restrictive, system seems to be feasible. They go on to argue that, in conformity with the Treaty, the directive as a whole does not obstruct the free movement of waste oils.

(11) Whilst conceding that a system of approvals is bound to have a restrictive effect on freedom of trade, the Council and the Commission argue that the measure envisaged by Article 6 of the directive pursues an aim which is of general interest, by seeking to ensure that the disposal of waste oils is carried out in a way which avoids harm to the environment.

(12) In the first place it should be observed that the principle of freedom of trade is not to be viewed in absolute terms but is subject to certain limits justified by the objectives of general interest pursued by the Community provided that the rights in question are not substantively impaired.

(13) There is no reason to conclude that the directive has exceeded those limits. The directive must be seen in the perspective of environmental protection, which is one of the Community's essential objectives. It is evident, particularly from the third and seventh recitals in the preamble to the directive, that any legislation dealing with the disposal of waste oils must be designed to protect the environment from the harmful effects caused by the discharge, deposit or treatment of such products. It is also evident from the provisions of the directive as a whole that care has been taken to ensure that the principles of proportionality and non-discrimination will be observed if certain restrictions should prove necessary. In particular, Article 5 of the directive permits the creation of a system of zoning 'where the aims defined in Articles 2, 3 and 4 cannot otherwise be achieved'.

(14) In the second place, as far as the free movement of goods is concerned, it should be stressed that the directive must be construed in the light of the seventh recital in the preamble thereto, which states that the treatment of waste oils must not create barriers to intra-Community trade. As the Court has already ruled in its judgment of 10 March 1983 (Case 172/82, *Fabricants Raffineurs d'Huile de Graissage* v. *Inter-Huiles*, [1983] ECR 555) dealing with the same zoning scheme, an exclusive right of that kind does not automatically authorize the Governments of the Member States to establish barriers to trade. Indeed, such a partitioning of the markets is not provided for in the Council Directive and would be contrary to the objectives laid down therein.

(15) It follows from the foregoing that the measures prescribed by the directive do not create barriers to intra-Community trade, and that in so far as such measures, in particular the requirement that permits must be obtained in advance, have a restrictive effect on the freedom of trade and of competition, they must nevertheless neither be discriminatory nor go beyond the inevitable restrictions which are justified by the pursuit of the objective of environmental protection, which is in the general interest. That being so, Articles 5 and 6 cannot be regarded as incompatible with the fundamental principles of Community law mentioned above.

Articles 13 and 14 of the directive

(16) The articles in question provide for the possibility of undertakings being granted indemnities for the services which they perform in collecting and/or disposing of waste oils.

(17) It is apparent from the request for a preliminary ruling that the question to be answered is whether those indemnities are consistent with the requirements of free competition, and in particular with Articles 92 to 94 of the Treaty, which prohibit the granting of aid by Member States.

(18) In that respect the Commission and the Council, in their observations, rightly argue that the indemnities do not constitute aid within the meaning of Articles 92 et seq of the EEC Treaty, but rather consideration for the services performed by the collection or disposal undertakings.

(19) It is also important to note that according to the second paragraph of Article 13 of the directive. 'The amount of these indemnities must be such as not to cause any significant distortion of competition or to give rise to artificial patterns of trade in the products.'

(20) Articles 13 and 14 of the directive cannot therefore be considered to be contrary to the principle of free competition.

(21) In those circumstances, the reply to be given to the first part of the question is that consideration of Articles 5, 6, 13 and 14 of Council Directive No 75/439/EEC of 16 June 1975 has disclosed no factor of such a kind as to affect their validity.

Interpretation of the directive

(22) It is apparent from the request for a preliminary ruling and from the documents before the Court that the French legislation permits the burning of waste oils only in industrial installations, thereby prohibiting any other form of burning.

(23) In the second part of the question the national court enquiries whether Directive No 75/439, in implementation of which the French legislation was adopted, justifies the prohibition of the burning of waste oils.

(24) The German, French and Italian Governments and the Commission advocate an affirmative reply. They argue that the uncontrolled burning of waste oils contributes significantly to air pollution and, consequently, that a prohibition of oil-burning in any plant which does not incorporate adequate safeguards is in conformity with the objectives of the directive. The Italian Government adds that the disposal of waste oil by burning carried out by persons authorized for that purpose must be the subject of rules and inspections.

(25) As has already been emphasized, the main aim of the directive is the disposal of waste oil in a manner which is safe for the environment, and Article 2 makes it incumbent upon the Member States to pursue that aim.

(26) Article 3 of the directive provides that 'Member States shall take the necessary

measures to ensure that, as far as possible, the disposal of waste oils is carried out by recycling (regeneration and/or combustion other than for destruction)' and Article 4 provides that Member States must prohibit any deposit, discharge or processing of waste oils in such a way as to cause harmful effects on water, soil or air.

(27) In order to ensure compliance with those measures, Article 6 provides that any undertaking which disposes of waste oils must obtain a permit granted by the competent national authority, if necessary after an inspection of the installations, with a view to imposing the conditions required by the state of technical development.

(28) In addition to that prior inspection, subsequent checks are provided for by Articles 11 and 12, by virtue of which undertakings are required on the one hand to provide information concerning the disposal of deposit of waste oils or residues thereof, and, on the other, to be inspected periodically, particularly as regards their compliance with the conditions of their permits.

(29) It follows from those provisions that the directive requires Member States to prohibit any form of waste-oil disposal which has harmful effects on the environment. It is to that end that the directive compels Member States to set up an effective system of prior approval and subsequent inspections.

(30) The reply to be given to the second question must therefore be that the prohibition of the burning of waste oils in conditions other than those permitted under legislation such as the French legislation is not inconsistent with Directive No 75/439/EEC.

Costs

(31) The costs incurred by the German, French and Italian Governments, and by the Commission and the Council of the European Communities, which have submitted observations to the Court, are not recoverable. As these proceedings are, in so far as the parties to the main proceedings are concerned, in the nature of a step in the action pending before the national court, the decision on costs is a matter for that court.

On those grounds,

THE COURT

in answer to the questions referred to it by the Tribunal de Grande Instance, Créteil, by a judgment of 23 March 1983, hereby rules as follows:

(1) Consideration of Articles 5, 6, 13 and 14 of Council Directive No 75/439/EEC of 16 June 1975 has disclosed no factor of such a kind as to affect their validity.

(2) The prohibition of the burning of waste oils in conditions other than those permitted under legislation such as the French legislation is not inconsistent with Directive No 75/439/EEC.

COMMENTARY

(1) The present judgment[2] was one of four judgments which the European Court gave on the transposition of Directive 75/439 on waste oils[3] into French law. The judgment in Case 240/83 was preceded by a ruling in Case 172/82,[4] and followed by Cases 295/82[5] and 173/83.[6]

Only the last case was a decision which opposed the E.C. Commission and France, and where the action was brought under Article 169 of the EEC Treaty.[7] The other cases, including Case 240/83, were submitted to the European Court under Article 177 of the EEC Treaty[8] by several French courts.

Cases 172/82, 295/82 and 173/83 essentially all concerned the question whether the French legislation which implemented Directive 75/439 contained a prohibition of export of waste oils to other EEC Member States and whether such a prohibition was compatible with EEC law. This problem will be discussed, in short, below.

(2) In contrast to that, the judgment in Case 240/83 dealt with the question whether Directive 75/439 could rightly restrict the freedom of waste-oil generators, waste-oil collectors and others to trade freely with waste oils and to have them eliminated, or to eliminate them themselves in a way and by persons of their choice.

The national court, the Tribunal de grande instance, Créteil (France) had some doubts in this respect and had therefore asked whether Directive 75/439 was "in conformity with the principles of freedom of trade, free movement of goods and freedom of competition, established by the Treaty of Rome". The judgment partly took up this wording in talking of "the principles of free movement of goods and freedom of competition, together with freedom of trade as a fundamental right". The Court qualified these principles as "general principles of Community law of which the Court ensures observance".

(3) The formula of general principles of Community law is a rule which the

---

[2] Case 240/83, *Procureur de la République* v. *Association de défense des brûleurs d'huiles usagées*. [1985] E.C.R. 531–552.
[3] [1975] O.J. L194/23. Commission proposal, COM(74)334 of March 20, 1974; amended by COM(74)1667 of October 18, 1974; European Parliament opinion: [1974] O.J. C85/6; Economic and Social Committee Opinion: [1974] O.J. C125/33. The Commission had based its proposal on Art. 100 of the EEC Treaty; the Council changed the legal basis and retained Arts. 100 and 235.
[4] 172/82, *Syndicat national des fabricants raffineurs d'huile de graissage et autres* v. *Groupement d'interêt économique "inter-huiles" et autres*. [1983] E.C.R. 555, [1983] 3 C.M.L.R. 485.
[5] 295/82, *Groupement d'intérêt économique "Rhône Alpes Huiles" et autres* v. *Syndicat national des fabricants raffineurs d'huiles de graissage et autres*. [1984] E.C.R. 575.
[6] 173/83, *Commission* v. *France*. [1985] E.C.R. 491. A case is pending before the European Court, asking for a preliminary ruling on the question whether the French legislation reserves access to the used oil market *de facto* to French undertakings: [1992] O.J. C44/11.
[7] For more details on the procedure under Art. 169, see below, Cases 23 and 24, pp. 377 and 387.
[8] For more details on the procedure under Art. 177 and the difference to the procedure under Art. 169; see below, Case 26, p. 411.

Court has used since the late sixties in its discussion on fundamental rights.[9] The Court's reasoning on this question was as follows:[10] there are fundamental rights in existence in Member States, either in an unwritten form or laid down in constitutions, or which have been incorporated into national law by the ratification of international conventions. However, Community law is autonomous and cannot be interpreted by referring to principles or rules of national law. Therefore, national fundamental rights may not be invoked in order to question the validity of Community law.

As regards Community law, it contains general principles of which the Court ensures observance. These general principles include the respect of those fundamental rights which are protected by virtue of constitutional traditions of Member States. Also international conventions which have been concluded by Member States or to which Member States have adhered—in particular the European Convention on Human Rights which has been ratified by all 12 Member States[11]—may give indications as to which fundamental rights have to be protected.

The doctrine of general principles of Community law thus allows the Court to examine virtually every fundamental right which could be infringed by Community law, without being bound by any national or international catalogues of such rights. And since the national court in Case 240/83 had expressly questioned the validity of Directive 75/439 referring to fundamental freedoms established by the Treaty of Rome, the European Court found it appropriate to briefly recall its jurisprudence on the general principles.

(4) The Court went on to argue that the freedom of trade, which the Court qualified earlier as a fundamental right, "is not to be viewed in absolute terms but is subject to certain limits justified by the objectives of general interest pursued by the Community provided that the rights in question are not substantively impaired."

Again, this formula repeats numerous statements of the Court in previous judgments on general principles and fundamental rights.[12] Its general nature allows the Court to examine in detail the reasons which are given in the specific Community directive or regulation to limit a fundamental right or a general principle. Of particular importance in this examination is the proportionality principle, which provides that measures taken must not go beyond what is necessary for the pursuit of the objective of the measure. A second principle is that of non-discrimination, which provides that economic agents or persons in different Member States must not be treated differently.

---

[9] Beginning with Case 29/69, *Stauder.* [1969] E.C.R. 419, [1970] C.M.L.R. 112 and Case 11/70, *Internationale Handelsgesellschaft.* [1970] E.C.R. 1125, [1972] C.M.L.R. 255.

[10] See in particular Case 4/73, *Nold.* [1974] E.C.R. 491, [1978] 2 C.M.L.R. 183; Case 130/75, *Prais* [1976] E.C.R. 1589, [1976] 2 C.M.L.R. 708; Case 149/77, *Defrenne (No. 3):* [1978] E.C.R. 1365, [1978] 3 C.M.L.R. 312; Case 46/87, *Hoechst :* [1989] E.C.R. 2859, [1991] 4 C.M.L.R. 410.

[11] The Convention was first mentioned by the Court in Case 36/75, *Rutili:* [1975] E.C.R. 1219.

[12] For the first time in Case 4/73, *Nold,* n. 10 above.

(5) In order to determine the limits to the freedom of trade which Directive 75/439 contains, the Court examined the objectives of that Directive. It argued that the "directive must be seen in the perspective of environmental protection which is one of the Community's essential objectives"; in the same way the Court a moment later stated that "the objective of environmental protection . . . is in the general interest" pursued by the Community.

This reasoning was new. It was the first time that the Court declared environmental protection to be an essential objective pursued by the Community. This statement was all the more remarkable since the EEC Treaty did not contain, neither at the time of the adoption of Directive 75/439 nor at the time of the judgment, any reference to environmental protection as such. Nor could the Court's statement have been taken from a general view of several environmental directives or regulations, since Directive 75/439 was the very first environmental directive which the Community adopted.[13]

The Community is not a nation State. It has as its competence the pursuit of objectives which are laid down in the EEC Treaty. Since environmental protection was not laid down as an express objective of the EEC, in 1985, the only basis of the Court's statement could be that it was an implicit objective. The Court left open how it reached the conclusion that environmental protection is one of the Community's essential objectives.

(6) The Commission, in its submission to the Court stated that there could be "no doubt" that the protection of the environment against the risk of pollution constitutes an objective of general interest which the Community may legitimately pursue.[14] It then demonstrated the danger for the environment and human health created by the indiscriminate discharge of oils into the environment or their uncontrolled use. In the Commission's opinion, rules intended to control the use of waste oils with a view to protecting the environment correspond to an objective in the common interest.

The Council, in its submission to the Court, was of the opinion that there are potential risks for the environment and human life entailed by the discharge, deposit or processing of waste oils and that thus, restrictions by the Directive are necessary in the general interest.[15]

The Advocate General argued in very concrete terms. He did not look at the general problems of environmental protection, but referred to the Commission's submissions on the enormous problems which are caused by uncontrolled collection and elimination of waste oils. He thus concluded that uncontrolled dumping or burning of waste oils would lead to dangerous sub-

---

[13] There are earlier directives, such as Directive 67/548 on the classification, labelling and packaging of dangerous substances: [1967] O.J. Spec. Ed. 234; Directive 70/157 on noise emissions from cars: [1970] O.J. Spec. Ed. 111; Directive 70/220 on air emissions from motor vehicles: [1970] O.J. Spec. Ed. 171. However, these directives were adopted in order to ensure the free circulation of goods rather than to protect the environment.

[14] Case 240/83, n. 2 above, p. 542.

[15] *Ibid.* p. 544.

stances going into the soil, the water or the air, which would be contrary to the public interest.[16]

(7) There are thus only two "sources" for the Court's statement. The first is the declaration by Heads of State and Government of October 1972 in Paris, which stated:

> "Economic expansion is not an end in itself. Its first aim should be to enable disparities in living conditions to be reduced. It should result in an improvement in the quality of life as well as in standards of living. As befits the genius of Europe, particular attention will be given to intangible values and to protecting the environment, so that progress may really be put at the service of mankind."[17]

The Heads of State and Government underlined the importance of an environmental policy in the Community and called for an environmental action programme. As regards the means, they invited the Community institutions to make use "as largely as possible" of all Articles of the Treaty, "including Article 235."[18]

In essence this declaration stated that the objectives laid down in Article 2 of the EEC Treaty could not be reached without the pursuit of environmental objectives at Community level. This declaration thus led to the setting up of an environmental administration inside the Commission, the elaboration and adoption of Community environmental action programmes, and the adoption of numerous Community environmental directives and regulations.

The second is the Commission's 1974 guidelines for the application of Articles 92 *et seq.* of the EEC Treaty in respect of specific aids to the environment. These guidelines have not been published; however, extensive extracts were given in the Fourth Report on Competition Policy (1974).[19] In these guidelines, the Commission recognised that state aids to the environment could, under certain conditions, be recognised as aids to promote a "common European interest."[20] In its Fourth Report, the Commission considered that "environmental protection should be a priority Community objective."[21]

In 1980, the 1974 framework for state aids was prolonged, with some minor amendments,[22] for further six years. It may thus be safely argued that, as regards state aids, environmental protection has been, since the mid-seventies, a priority Community objective, and it might well be that the European Court saw no reason not to apply this consideration to other areas of primary and secondary Community law.

---

[16] *Ibid.* p. 534.
[17] Commission, 6th General Report (1972), p. 8.
[18] Declaration p. 17.
[19] Fourth Report on Competition Policy (1974). Brussels-Luxembourg, 1975.
[20] So the wording of Art. 92(3)(*b*) EEC.
[21] Fourth Report on Competition Policy, para. 176.
[22] Tenth Report on Competition Policy (1980). Brussels-Luxembourg, 1981.

(8) Even when one takes this background into consideration, the Court's statement that environmental protection is an essential objective of the Community remains remarkable. The Commission, the Council and the Advocate General, in their statements during the procedure, had all argued in no uncertain terms that uncontrolled discharge, deposit or treatment of waste oils could harm the environment. They had also expressly or implicitly referred to the effects on human health in order to justify restrictions on the freedom of trade.

The Court neither referred to the specific case of waste oils nor to the risks to human health. Its statement was general and unlimited and was even strengthened by the twofold reference to environmental protection being in the general interest. Thus the statement obtained an effect which goes far beyond the individual Case 240/83 and becomes a statement of principle for future cases.

The Court has used similar arguments since, in particular in Case 302/86.[23] The statement that there is a general interest of the Community and not only of Member States to have an appropriate environmental protection have influenced the discussion on Community competence versus national competence in environmental protection matters. Thus, Case 240/83 really was a landmark decision.

(9) Having reached the conclusion that the principle of freedom to trade—or more precisely, the fundamental right to pursue a professional or trade activity—may be limited by considerations of environmental protection, the Court went on to examine whether the restrictions provided for by Directive 75/439 did go too far. The Court, when addressing this question, did not sharply separate the questions of freedom of trade and free movement of goods, but found no element which would constitute an infringement on these principles.

(10) The Court admitted that the rule in Article 6 which requires disposal undertakings to obtain in advance a permit for their activity does have a restrictive effect on the freedom of trade and of competition. However, the Court is of the opinion that such a restriction is not discriminatory, since it is imposed on all undertakings. Nor is it disproportionate "since any legislation dealing with the disposal of waste oils must be designed to protect the environment from the harmful effects caused by the discharge, deposit or treatment of such products". The requirement of an advance permit was thus, in the Court's mind, an inevitable restriction, although it did not specify what the risk to the environment consisted of. The Court does not take up the reasoning of the Advocate General, who pointed out the risks coming from an uncontrolled disposal of waste oils. Also the Commission had stated in its sub-

---

[23] 302/86, *Commission* v. *Denmark* [1988] E.C.R. 4607, [1989] 1 C.M.L.R. 619; see p. 91 below.

mission that procedures for prior authorisation are customary in the legal system of all the Member States as safeguards on dangerous operations.

(11) More difficulties were caused by a rule in the French legislation implementing Directive 75/439 which, in simplified terms, requested holders of waste oils to deliver their waste oils to approved collectors; approved collectors were responsible for collecting all waste oils originating in the zone for which they had received an (exclusive) approval. They had to deliver the waste oils to an approved disposal undertaking, which had to treat the waste oils in its own plants.

In its judgment in Case 172/82, the Court stated[24] that the French rules contained an implicit export restriction, since they did not allow the export of waste oils to disposal undertakings in other Member States, even where these disposal undertakings were duly approved under Article 6 of Directive 75/439. The question was therefore, whether Directive 75/439 authorised France and other Member States to provide for such an export restriction and if yes, whether such a restriction was still compatible with the general principles of Community law and in particular freedom of trade and free movement of goods.

Case 240/83 contained only some marginal aspects of this discussion. The main arguments were discussed in Case 172/82. The problem for the Court was that although Article 34 of the EEC Treaty prohibits all export restrictions and measures of equivalent effect, the French Government based its argument expressly on Article 5 of Directive 75/439. This Article provides *inter alia*:

"where the aims defined in articles 2, 3 and 4 cannot otherwise be achieved, Member States shall take the necessary measures to ensure that one or more undertakings carry out the collection and/or disposal offered to them by holders, where appropriate in the zone assigned to them by the competent authorities."

(12) The Court argued in Case 172/82 that Article 5 of Directive 75/439 could be interpreted in such a way as to allow Member States to grant exclusive rights to undertakings as regards specific zones. However, it did not follow from that that Member States were entitled to erect export barriers. In particular the seventh recital of Directive 75/439 stated expressly that the exchange of goods within the Community should not be impeded. The Court went on to say that a rule which restricted exports to other Community countries, would also be contrary to Article 34 of the EEC Treaty.

The wording of Article 5 of the Directive[25] does seem to allow an export

---

[24] 172/82, n. 4 above, p. 564; in Case 173/83, n. 6 above, the Advocate General qualified this statement by the Court as an *obiter dictum*, since the Court does not have to interpret national law in a preliminary ruling under Art. 177 (p. 494).

[25] See the wording of Art. 5 in the Court's decision at p. 6 above, para. 3.

restriction. The Court could have examined whether the French rules were necessary, since the aims defined in Articles 2, 3 and 4 of the Directive could not be otherwise achieved. Arguments of such kind were developed in Case 172/82 by the "Syndicat national". This then, in turn, would have raised the question whether Directive 75/439 was itself compatible with Article 34 of the Treaty.

(13) The Court, as mentioned, avoided all these questions by interpreting Article 5 of the Directive as not containing an authorisation for Member States to provide for export restrictions. It found further, in the judgment in Case 173/83, which was pronounced the same day as the judgment in Case 240/83, that the export restriction provided under French law was incompatible with Article 34.

Since the Court interpreted Article 5 of Directive 75/439 by using the seventh recital of the Directive in a way that implied that there was no export restriction in Article 5, the question of whether this restriction could be justified to restrict the freedom of trade or the free movement of goods need not be discussed in detail in Case 240/83.

(14) As regards the restriction on freedom of competition the Court found that the Directive's rules on aids could not be considered to mean aids in the meaning of Articles 92 *et seq.* of the Treaty and thus rejected this argument.

2. ARTICLES 100A OR 130S AS A LEGAL BASIS FOR COMMUNITY MEASURES

**Judgment of the Court of June 11, 1991
in Case C–300/89**

E.C. Commission supported by the European Parliament v. *E.C. Council*

[1991] I E.C.R. 2867

FACTS AND PROCEDURE[1]

In 1978, the Council adopted Directive 78/176 on waste from the titanium dioxide industry.[2] Article 9 of that Directive requested Member States to set up
programmes for the reduction of waste discharges. These programmes were
to be submitted to the E.C. Commission which was to make proposals for a
harmonisation of these national programmes in order to reduce the pollution
of the environment and improve the conditions of competition.

In 1983, the Commission submitted a proposal for a directive on the harmonisation of programmes. The proposal was based on Articles 100 and 235.
After the entry into force of the Single European Act, the Commission
amended its proposal and based it on Article 100a. The Council adopted the
proposal in 1989 in form of Directive 89/428.[3] It fixed as a legal basis Article
130s.

The Commission applied to the Court and asked for an annulment of Directive 89/428 since it was based on the wrong legal basis.

Written submissions were made by the Commission, the European Parliament, which supported the Commission, and the Council. Oral hearings took
place on January 30, 1991.

The Advocate General delivered his opinion on March 13, 1991.

JUDGMENT

(1) By application lodged at the Court Registry on 28 September 1989, the Commission of the European Communities brought an action under the first paragraph of Article 173 of the EEC Treaty for the annulment of Council Directive 89/
428/EEC of 21 June 1989 on procedures for harmonizing the programmes for the
reduction and eventual elimination of pollution caused by waste from the titanium dioxide industry (Official Journal L 201, p. 56).

(2) That directive, which was unanimously adopted by the Council on the basis of
Article 130s of the EEC Treaty, "lays down ... procedures for harmonizing the
programmes for the reduction and eventual elimination of pollution from existing industrial establishments and is intended to improve the conditions of competition in the titanium dioxide industry" (Article 1). For that purpose, it

---

[1] Summary by the author.
[2] [1978] O.J. L54/19.
[3] [1989] O.J. L201/56.

establishes harmonized levels for the treatment of different kinds of waste from the titanium dioxide industry. Thus, for certain waste from existing establishments using particular processes, a total prohibition is imposed (Articles 3 and 4). On the other hand, for other waste from existing establishments, the directive lays down maximum values for harmful substances (Articles 6 and 9).

(3) It is apparent from the documents before the Court that the contested measure derived from a proposal for a directive presented by the Commission on 18 April 1983 on the basis of Articles 100 and 235 of the EEC Treaty. Following the entry into force of the Single European Act, the Commission changed the legal basis to Article 100a of the EEC Treaty, which had been inserted by the Single European Act. At its meeting of 24 and 25 November 1988, the Council nevertheless arrived at a common position whereby the directive would be based on Article 130s of the EEC Treaty. Despite the objections voiced by the European Parliament which, having been consulted by the Council pursuant to Article 130s, considered the legal basis proposed by the Commission to be appropriate, the Council adopted the directive at issue on the basis of Article 130s.

(4) Taking the view that Directive 89/428/EEC lacked a valid legal basis, in that it was based on Article 130s but should have been based on Article 100a, the Commission brought the present action for annulment.

(5) By order of 21 February 1990, the Parliament was granted leave to intervene in support of the applicant.

(6) Reference is made to the Report for the Hearing for a fuller account of the facts of the case, the course of the procedure and the pleas and arguments of the parties, which are mentioned or discussed hereinafter only in so far as is necessary for the reasoning of the Court.

(7) The Commission, supported by the Parliament, claims that the directive, although contributing to environmental protection, has as its "main purpose" or "centre of gravity" the improvement of conditions of competition in the titanium dioxide industry. It is therefore a measure concerning the establishment and functioning of the internal market, within the meaning of Article 100a, and should therefore have been based on the latter enabling provision.

(8) The Commission states that the very text of Articles 100a and 130s shows that the requirements of environmental protection form an integral part of the harmonizing action to be taken on the basis of Article 100a. It follows, according to the Commission, that Article 100a, which relates to the establishment and functioning of the internal market, constitutes a *lex specialis* in relation to Article 130s, the latter article not being intrinsically directed towards the attainment of that objective.

(9) The Council, for its part, contends that Article 130s is the correct legal basis for Directive 89/428/EEC. Whilst conceding that that directive is intended also to harmonize conditions of competition in the industrial sector concerned and thus to foster the establishment and functioning of the internal market, it considers that the "centre of gravity" of the contested measure is the elimination of the pollution caused by waste from the titanium dioxide manufacturing process. That objective is one of those referred to in Article 130r, which are pursued by means of measures adopted under Article 130s.

(10) It must first be observed that in the context of the organization of the powers of the Community the choice of the legal basis for a measure may not depend simply on an institution's conviction as to the objective pursued but must be based on objective factors which are amenable to judicial review (see the judgment in Case 45/86 *Commission* v. *Council* [1987] ECR 1493, paragraph 11). Those factors include in particular the aim and content of the measure.

(11) As regards the aim pursued, Article 1 of Directive 89/428/EEC indicates that it is intended, on the one hand, to harmonize the programmes for the reduction and ultimate elimination of pollution caused by waste from existing establishments in the titanium dioxide industry and, on the other, to improve the conditions of competition in that industry. It thus pursues the twofold aim of environmental protection and improvement of the conditions of competition.

(12) As regards its content, Directive 89/428/EEC prohibits, or, according to strict standards, requires reduction of the discharge of waste from existing establishments in the titanium dioxide industry and lays down time-limits for the implementation for the various provisions. By thus imposing obligations concerning the treatment of waste from the titanium dioxide production process, the directive conduces, at the same time, to the reduction of pollution and to the establishment of greater uniformity of production conditions and therefore of conditions of competition, since the national rules on the treatment of waste which the directive seeks to harmonize have an impact on production costs in the titanium dioxide industry.

(13) It follows that, according to its aim and content, as they appear from its actual wording, the directive is concerned, indissociably, with both the protection of the environment and the elimination of disparities in conditions of competition.

(14) Article 130s of the Treaty provides that the Council is to decide what action is to be taken by the Community concerning the environment. Article 100a(1), for its part, is concerned with the adoption by the Council of measures for the approximation of the provisions laid down by law, regulation or administrative action in Member States which have as their object the establishment and functioning of the internal market. According to the second paragraph of Article 8a of the EEC Treaty, that market is to comprise "an area without internal frontiers in which the free movement of goods, persons, services and capital is ensured". By virtue of Articles 2 and 3 of the Treaty, a precondition for such a market is the existence of conditions of competition which are not distorted.

(15) In order to give effect to the fundamental freedoms mentioned in Article 8a, harmonizing measures are necessary to deal with disparities between the laws of the Member States in areas where such disparities are liable to create or maintain distorted conditions of competition. For that reason, Article 100a empowers the Community to adopt measures for the approximation of the provisions laid down by law, regulation or administrative action in Member States and lays down the procedure to be followed for that purpose.

(16) It follows that, in view of its aim and content, the directive at issue displays the features both of action relating to the environment with which Article 130s of the Treaty is concerned and of a harmonizing measure which has as its object the establishment and functioning of the internal market, within the meaning of Article 100a of the Treaty.

(17) As the Court held in Case 165/87 *Commission* v. *Council* [1988] ECR 5545, paragraph 11, where an institution's power is based on two provisions of the Treaty, it is bound to adopt the relevant measures on the basis of the two relevant provisions. However, that ruling is not applicable to the present case.

(18) One of the enabling provisions at issue, Article 100a, requires recourse to the cooperation procedure provided for in Article 149(2) of the Treaty, whereas the other, Article 130s, requires the Council to act unanimously after merely consulting the European Parliament. As a result, use of both provisions as a joint legal basis would divest the cooperation procedure of its very substance.

(19) Under the cooperation procedure, the Council acts by a qualified majority where it intends accepting the amendments to its common position proposed by the Parliament and included by the Commission in its re-examined proposal, whereas it must secure unanimity if it intends taking a decision after its common position has been rejected by the Parliament or if it intends modifying the Commission's re-examined proposal. That essential element of the cooperation procedure would be undermined if, as a result of simultaneous reference to Articles 100a and 130s, the Council were required, in any event, to act unanimously.

(20) The very purpose of the cooperation procedure, which is to increase the involvement of the European Parliament in the legislative process of the Community, would thus be jeopardized. As the Court stated in its judgments in Case 138/79 *Roquette Frères* v. *Council* [1980] ECR 3333 and Case 139/79 *Maizena* v. *Council* [1980] ECR 3393, paragraph 34, that participation reflects a fundamental democratic principle that the peoples should take part in the exercise of power through the intermediary of a representation assembly.

(21) It follows that in the present case recourse to the dual legal basis of Articles 100a and 130s is excluded and that is necessary to determine which of those two provisions is the appropriate legal basis.

(22) It must be observed in the first place that, pursuant to the second sentence of Article 130r(2) of the Treaty, "environmental protection requirements shall be a component of the Community's other policies". That principle implies that a Community measure cannot be covered by Article 130s merely because it also pursues objectives of environmental protection.

(23) Secondly, as the Court held in its judgments in Cases 91/79 and 92/79 *Commission* v. *Italy* [1980] ECR 1099 (paragraph 8) and 1115 (paragraph 8), provisions which are made necessary by considerations relating to the environment and health may be a burden upon the undertakings to which they apply and, if there is no harmonization of national provisions on the matter, competition may be appreciably distorted. It follows that action intended to approximate national rules concerning production conditions in a given industrial sector with the aim of eliminating distortions of competition in that sector is conducive to the attainment of the internal market and thus falls within the scope of Article 100a, a provision which is particularly appropriate to the attainment of the internal market.

(24) Finally, it must be observed that Article 100a(3) requires the Commission, in its proposals for measures for the approximation of the laws of the Member States

which have as their object the establishment and functioning of the internal market, to take as a base a high level of protection in matters of environmental protection. That provision thus expressly indicates that the objectives of environmental protection referred to in Article 130r may be effectively pursued by means by harmonizing measures adopted on the basis of Article 100a.

(25) In view of all the foregoing considerations, the contested measure should have been based on Article 100a of the EEC Treaty and must therefore be annulled.

Costs

(26) Pursuant to Article 69(2) of the Rules of Procedure the unsuccessful party is to be ordered to pay the costs. Since the Council has failed in its submissions, it must be ordered to pay the costs, including those of the intervener.

On those grounds,

THE COURT

hereby:

1. Annuls Council Directive 89/428/EEC of 21 June 1989 on procedures for harmonizing the programmes for the reduction and eventual elimination of pollution caused by waste from the titanium dioxide industry;

2. Orders the Council to pay the costs, including those of the intervener.

COMMENTARY

(1) This judgment was the first in which the Court made the distinction between Article 100a and Article 130s of the EEC Treaty. Prior to the Court's decision, there was a certain disagreement between the Community Institutions over the proper legal basis for Community environmental legislation; and this disagreement only hid the disagreement between the Community, represented by the Commission, and the Member States as to the question of how far Community competence in environmental matters extends.

(2) The question of the legal basis for environmental legislation is by no means hypothetical. It has considerable impact on the law-making procedure, the content of the different environmental rules and on Member States' residual rights in environmental matters, once the Community has legislated. The following table illustrates the differences between the two articles:

	100a	**130s**
(1) Subject-matter of regulation	Measure which have as their object the establishment of the internal market	Actions relating to the environment, Art. 130r, para. 1
(2) Community competence	No express requirement; effect on the internal market (Art. 8a) is enough	Community can do better than Member States acting separately, Art. 130r, para. 4
(3) Commission proposal	Will take as a base a high level of environmental protection, Art. 100a, para. 3	No requirement fixed
(4) Decision-making procedure	Legislative co-operation with European Parliament, Art. 100a, para. 1 Art. 149, para. 2	Normal procedure (consultation of European Parliament), Art. 130s, para. 1
(5) Majority/Unanimity	Qualified majority	Unanimity
(6) Member Sates' rights after the adoption of the Community measure	In the case of a majority decision, a Member State may, for serious environmental reasons, continue to apply existing environmental legislation. Such measures must be notified and are subject to a Community control system. Art. 100a, para. 4[4]	Member States may maintain or introduce more stringent environmental measures, Art. 130t

(3) The Court started by mentioning its jurisprudence, according to which the choice of a legal basis for a Community measure does not depend on what a Community institution believes to be the aim of the measure, but rather on objective criteria, such as, in particular, the aim and the content of the specific measure in question.

As to the *aim* of Directive 89/428, the Court, by analysing Article 1, came to the conclusion that its aim is to protect the environment on the one hand and to improve the conditions for competition in the titanium dioxide sector of industry on the other hand. As to the *content* of Directive 89/428, the Court was of the opinion that the Directive aims at reducing pollution and at establishing more uniform rules of production and therefore also of competition. Indeed, as the Court found, the national rules on competition will inevitably influence

---

[4] There is a legal dispute on the meaning of Art. 100a, para. 4. Some authors are of the opinion that this article allows new measures to be taken at national level. This opinion is particularly widespread among German authors. Until mid-1993, only one case of practical application of Art. 100a had occurred which concerned a total ban of Pentachlorophenal in Germany. The Court of Justice has not yet given any interpretation of that article.

production costs, since the elimination of waste from the titanium dioxide industry is expensive.[5]

Thus the Court, in view of the aim and the content of Directive 89/428, came to the conclusion that Directive 89/428 deals with both environmental protection and the elimination of disparities in conditions of competition in such a way that the two cannot be separated.

(4) The Court did not try to elaborate on this point. It did not follow the Council, which was of the opinion that in such cases the "centre of gravity" or the "principal objective" of a Community measure should be determined. As a matter of fact, both the Commission and the Council had, during the procedure in this case, argued that the "centre of gravity" of a Community measure should be decisive for the determination of a legal basis. However, as regards Directive 89/428, the two institutions came to opposite results: while the Commission came to the conclusion that the centre of gravity of Directive 89/428 was the elimination of disparities of competition, the Council thought that the centre of gravity was the protection of the environment. The brilliant analysis of the Advocate General which is in all its parts a highly recommended read, rightly pointed to the fact that the opposite results show the uselessness, in practical terms, of the centre-of-gravity doctrine, since it opens the way to rather subjective and controversial results.[6]

The Court did not expressly reject this doctrine, but did not follow or even mention it in its reasoning.

(5) Nor did the Court follow the Commission's argument that Article 100a is *lex specialis* to Article 130s, again without rejecting it expressly. The Court limited itself to stating that Directive 89/428 is a measure which presents the characteristics of a measure to be adopted under Article 130s and at the same time as a measure to be adopted under Article 100a of the Treaty. Had the Court considered Article 100a to be *lex specialis* to Article 130s, this conclusion would have been sufficient to annul Directive 89/428 because it was based on Article 130s.

(6) Instead the Court turned to the question whether or not there should be two legal bases for the Directive, Article 100a and 130s. The Court mentioned prior decisions which had expressly indicated a double legal basis.[7] This jurisprudence, however, was inapplicable in the Court's opinion, since under Article 100a the procedure is that of a legislative co-operation with the European Parliament, while under Article 130s Parliament is only consulted. And

---

[5] The Advocate General quotes para. 7 figures from studies undertaken by the Commission which show that the different measures to reduce environmental pollution from titanium dioxide waste have an impact of 10 to 20 per cent. in the different Member States.

[6] Advocate General's opinion, para. 8. See also J.L. Dewost, "Rôle et position de la Commission dans le processus législatif" in J. Schwarze, *Legislation for Europe 1992* (Baden-Baden, 1989), pp. 85 *et seq.*.

[7] Case 165/87, *Commission* v. *Council* [1988] E.C.R. 5545, [1990] 1 C.M.L.R. 457.

the Court stated that the "essential" element of the co-operation procedure which is Parliament's co-operation and ability to influence the final (majority) decision on a directive would be lost, if by virtue of a double legal basis the Council would have to vote unanimously. The Court believed that Parliament's participation in the law-making procedure under the "legislative co-operation procedure" of Article 149 is the expression of a fundamental democratic principle under which people participate in the exercise of power by the intermediary of a representative assembly. This principle could not be set aside by a unanimous decision. Thus, the use of a double legal basis in the case of Directive 89/428 is excluded.

(7) These arguments are not entirely convincing. Even though the principle of democracy which finds its expression in the legislative co-operation with the European Parliament is fully agreed to, another solution would have been possible. The Court could have asked for both legal bases, Article 100a and 130s, to be applied—and the use of that decision-making procedure which is more "democratic", *i.e.* the procedure of Article 100a legislative co-operation and majority voting.

It is not clear from the Court's judgment whether the Court would have required a double legal basis to be used, if Article 130s had also allowed for the procedure of legislative co-operation. The Maastricht Treaty on European Union, which was agreed in December 1991, does provide for this co-operation procedure in Article 130s.[8] Decisions under Article 100a shall in future be taken by a joint decision between the European Parliament and the Council. Again, the procedures under Articles 100a and 130s are not the same. Nevertheless, it can not be excluded that the Court will come back to the problem of a double legal basis for environmental measures, though the consequences which follow from Article 100a, paragraph 4 and 130t respectively, are different and would need to be specified in such a case.

(8) Having excluded the possibility of a double legal basis, the Court was obliged to make a choice between the two articles. This final part of the judgment is short—three paragraphs only—and precise. The Court took three elements of Community law which, taken together, convinced it that Article 100a was the appropriate legal choice.

The first element is taken from Article 130r, paragraph 2, second sentence, according to which the requirements of environmental protection are a component of the Community's other policies. Here the Court repeated the formula which it had already used in Case C–62/88 (Impact of radioactive contaminated food)[9]: a Community measure cannot be part of Community

---

[8] Under the Maastricht Treaty, majority decisions adopted by way of legislative co-operation are the rule in environmental matters. However, Art. 130s, para. 2 provides for a number of areas where decisions are taken unanimously. Finally, general action programmes are adopted by way of joined decisions between the Parliament and the Council.

[9] C–62/88, *Greece* v. *Council* [1990] I E.C.R. 1527, [1991] 2 C.M.L.R. 649; see p. 39 below.

action on the environment—and thus be based on Article 130s—merely because it takes those requirements into account.

(9) The second argument used by the Court was less directly taken from the Treaty. The Court argued that measures which aim at the protection of the environment cost money and thus have an impact on companies. Without uniform measures taken at Community level such measures could and would be taken at national level and, being different from one Member State to the other, could distort competition considerably. However, Article 100a is particularly able to eliminate distortions of competition and thus contribute to the achievement of the internal market.

This seems to be the first case where the Court expressly recognised that measures which aim at the elimination of distortions of competition, but not of barriers to trade, may nevertheless come under Article 100a. The reasoning of the Court is convincing. Indeed, Articles 130r to 130t do not talk at all of "harmonisation" of "competition" or "trade", whereas the elements of "trade", "approximation" and "competition" are to be found in Articles 8, 100 and 100a, paragraphs 1 and 4.

Also, it is commonplace that environmental measures cost money. Different rules from one Member State to the other will, certainly in the market of titanium dioxide, influence the price and thus the competitive position of industry all the more since measures for waste elimination constitute up to 20 per cent. of the price of the titanium dioxide product.

(10) The third argument of the Court was taken from Article 100a, paragraph 3, which states that the Commission will base its proposals on environmental measures on a high level of protection. The Court took this paragraph as evidence that the objectives of Article 130r can be pursued efficiently by harmonisation measures which are based on Article 100a.

Implicitly the Court stated that the objectives of Article 100a cannot be pursued effectively under Article 130s, which is certainly correct. The reason for this "imperfection" of Article 130s is of course Article 130t which allows Member States to maintain or introduce more stringent rules. Article 130t demonstrates that measures adopted under Article 130s are not harmonisation measures.

However, the problem is that Article 100a, paragraph 3 only requires a high level of environmental protection for the Commission's proposal, but not for the Community environmental measure. Under Article 100a, it is perfectly possible that a measure adopted by the Council puts the emphasis on aspects of free circulation of goods or that it abstains from fixing a high level of protection for fear of high costs. In such a case, the environment in the Community— and thus also in the different Member States—might not be as effectively protected as the Commission had intended.

Had the Community measure been based on Article 130s, then each Member State would have the possibility to ensure, at least for its own territory, better—and thus more effective—protection of the environment. Such a possibility does not exist under Article 100a. Thus, the Court's argument that it follows from Article 100a, paragraph 3 that the environment can effectively be protected under measures which are adopted under Article 100a, is a possibility which rests, in the final instance, in the hands of the Council. In contrast, the possibility of effectively protecting the environment rests, under Article 130s, with the Council, with the possibility for Member States, however, to ensure an effective protection for their territory, should the Council's measure not be effective enough.

(11) It follows from this that an environmental measure which is based on Article 130s gives more room for manoeuvre to Member States whereas a measure that is based on Article 100a emphasises the Community-wide aspect: the uniformity of the measure. The interests of Member States as regards their national environmental policy and as regards questions of national sovereignty thus, plead in favour of Article 130s as legal basis of environmental measures. In contrast, the Community or those Member States who favour far-reaching integration would choose to have environmental measures based on Article 100a as often as possible.

(12) The Court's interpretation in the present case of Articles 100a and 130s and their relationship to each other will certainly help the Community institutions to better conceive, elaborate and adopt Community environmental measures. Of course, the judgment did not solve all questions. Some questions which still seem to be unresolved, are raised below.

(a) Does the decision in Case C–300/89 mean that in future a double or even a multiple legal basis is required whenever a Community measure pursues more than one aim?

The Court seems to be prepared to request such a double legal basis whenever two or more objectives are pursued. That solution is ruled out in Case C–300/89 because of the procedural reason that Article 100a provides for legislative co-operation with the European Parliament, while Article 130s only provides for consultation with the Parliament. However, it has already been pointed out that the Maastricht Treaty on European Union will amend Article 130s and provide, as a rule, majority voting and the legislative co-operation rule. Even though the Maastricht Treaty provides for a legislative joint decision procedure under Article 100a, and this does not ensure full parallelism in the procedures under Article 130s and 100a, it might nevertheless be that in the future, such a dual legal basis might be required more frequently.

(13) It would be possible to interpret the decision in Case C–300/89 in such a way that it only refers, as regards the dual legal basis, to cases where the two aims pursued—environmental protection and elimination of distortions of

competition—have the same weight. This would lead to other results where a Community measure has, as a principal objective (or the "centre of gravity") the pursuit of one aim, the other aim being of secondary importance.

However, the decision in Case C–300/89 did not examine the respective weight of the two aims pursued. Thus, it did not come to the conclusion that the two aims are of equal weight. It therefore seems that the doctrine of the principal objective of a measure has not been accepted by the Court and that therefore such an interpretation is not possible, unless the Court changes the approach adopted in Case C–300/89.

(14) In practice the doctrine of determining the principal objective of a measure cannot work. Suppose a Community measure fixed maximum levels for a substance contained in a product. There has never been a dispute in the past that such measures would have to be based on Article 100 or, since 1987, on Article 100a. However, the reason for limiting the presence of that dangerous substance may be the protection of the environment, or the protection of consumers or of producers of a competing substance, or the preservation of the unity of the Common Market, or even the protection against imports from third countries. Even where all these motivations and aims were expressly laid down in the measure and its preamble, it would be impossible to weigh them with precision, all the more since the wording of a measure and its preamble remains to some extent subject to drafting imponderabilities.

While it thus seems that the Court rejected the theory of "principal objective" of a measure, it remains to be seen whether the Court will confirm and refine its statements in Case C–300/89 and how the requirement of a double legal basis will be dealt with in future. In particular, there might be some doubt in cases where the primary objective of a Community measure is that of environmental protection (Article 130s) while there are secondary objectives (or mere effects) in the internal market in the form of barriers to trade or distortion of competition. The classification of waste measures might be a good example for this.

If the Court follows its own reasoning in Case C–300/89, such measures would also come under Article 100a of the Treaty.

(15)(b) Is the requirement of a double legal basis unnecessary, because Article 100a is a sort of *lex specialis* to Article 130s?

The Court has neither approved nor rejected the Commission's argument of Article 100a being a *lex specialis* to Article 130s. But its reasoning came close to that theory. Indeed the Court argued that Article 100a can effectively achieve the two objectives elimination of distortions of competition *and* protection of the environment. It has already been pointed out that Article 130s cannot achieve these two objectives, mainly because on the one hand, internal market requirements are not a component of environmental policy measures under Article 130s and, on the other hand, because the existence of

Article 130t leads to different environmental standards inside the Community; these, in turn, may influence—according to the Court's own findings—the competitive situation of economic agents. Furthermore, it seems that the Court decided in favour of Article 100a, just because that Article could achieve both objectives. This then is very close, if not equivalent, to the *lex specialis* doctrine. Again, more detailed consideration will undoubtedly be given to this question in future decisions.

(16)(c) Has the balance between Article 100a and 130s been struck once and for all?

The judgment in Case C–300/89 has been criticised in particular by Everling and Schröer.[10] Everling is of the opinion that the judgment restricts Articles 100 and 130r to 130t to a minimum. Such a decisive interpretation of the Treaty provisions would have needed a clearer expression in the Treaty. The Court went, in his opinion, rather far in developing the distribution of competence between the Community and Member States, a question which is first of all up to the political instances.

Schröer is of the opinion that the Court did not strike the right balance at all. His interpretation of the environmental Articles in the Treaty is that they are meant to ensure the optimal environmental protection. Consequently, almost all measures which affect the environment will have to be based on Article 130s rather than on Article 100a, since Article 130s allows Member States to introduce measures which are more protective [Art. 130t].

My own opinion is that a dual legal basis would have been possible. The procedural rights of the European Parliament would follow from the article which is more "democratic", *i.e.* Article 100a. Consequences of Article 100a, paragraph 4 on the one hand and Article 130t on the other hand would have to be approached as far as possible.

Apart from such a solution, which the Court rejected in Case C–300/89, I perceive the borderline between Articles 130s and 100a as being gradual. Indeed, hardly any measure which intends to protect the environment is without some economic consequence and thus, one way or another, the competitiveness of economic agents. Thus, where the economic impact is minimal, Article 130s applies, but the greater the impact of a measure on trade and economic competitiveness becomes, the more necessary is the use of Article 100a. In the present case, the cost of waste elimination was estimated to be up to 20 per cent. of the production costs.

This justifies the use of Article 100a. But if such costs were one to two per cent., or even one tenth of a per cent., it would be much less clear that Article 100a is the appropriate legal basis.

---

[10] U. Everling, "Abgrenzung der Rechtsangleichung zur Verwirklichung des Binnenmarktes nach Artikel 100a EWGV durch den Gerichtshof", *Europarecht* 1991, 179; U. Everling is a former judge of the Court of Justice. T. Schröer, Mehr Demokratie statts umweltpolitischer Subsidiarität?" *Europarecht* 1991, 356.

I do not share the opinion that the Treaty provides for the need to ensure the optimum environmental protection and that thus more or less all measures have to be based on Article 130s. This opinion neglects the wording of Article 100a and also of 130r, paragraph 2, second sentence, while clearly indicating that environmental measures can be based on other articles than 130s. The main objection, however, is that it omits to take into consideration the Community dimension of the protection of the environment. An optimum protection of the environment in one, two or three Member States is not the same as an optimum protection of the Community—or the global—environment. The plea for maximum competence in environmental matters for Member States is not convincing, because about half of the EEC Member States *de facto* do not have an active, coherent and consistent environmental policy. This situation neglects the need for European environmental integration.

(17)(d) Is the Council entitled to change the procedural rules during the law-making procedure?

As regards Directive 89/428, the Commission has, since 1987, based its proposal for a directive on Article 100a, which requires legislative co-operation with the European Parliament. The Council, being of the opinion that Article 130s should apply, did not use the procedure under Article 149 paragraph 2, but consulted the Parliament a second time, a procedure which is not envisaged in the EEC Treaty.

Though the Commission had expressly attacked this procedure in its application, the Court did not decide whether the Council's unilateral change of the rules of procedure was allowed.

In my opinion, the rules of procedure are fixed by the legal basis chosen by the Commission. During the law-making procedure, the Council has no right to change these rules, since there is no decision of the Council on the Commission's proposal. The "common position" of the Council, mentioned in Article 149, paragraph 2, is not an independent decision, which could be attacked in Court for instance by the Parliament. The only formal act which exists is the proposal of the Commission and it must be this proposal which determines the law-making procedure.

(18)(e) Will the rules fixed by the Court in Case C–300/89 also apply to decisions in the area of nature protection and waste?

In the past, all Community directives and regulations which concerned nature protection have been adopted, prior to 1987, on the basis of Article 235, and since 1987 on the basis of Article 130s.[11] This also applied to Regulation 3626/

---

[11] In particular, Dir. 79/409 on wild living birds: [1979] O.J. L103/1; Reg. 81/348 on cetacean products: [1981] O.J. L39/1; Reg. 3626/82 on trade with endangered species: [1982] O.J. L384/1; Dir. 83/129 on skins from seal-pups: [1983] O.J. L91/30; all texts with several subsequent amendments.

82[12] and its numerous amendments which concern the trade with endangered species of fauna and flora.

At the end of 1991, the Commission submitted a revised proposal for a regulation on the trade with endangered species. This proposal was based on Article 100a alone.[13]

This choice of a legal basis is a logical consequence of the judgment in Case C–300/89. Nevertheless it remains doubtful whether questions of nature protection do come under Treaty provisions which deal with the internal market. Plants and animals cannot be equated to products. This is also clear from the mention of animals and plants in Article 36, a provision designed to protect important non-economic values.

(19) Of particular interest will be the Court's attitude to the legal basis for waste regulation. Since the Single European Act of 1986, the Commission has based all its proposals for waste directives and regulations on Article 100a, with the one exception of air pollution from waste incineration plants where the proposals were based on Article 130s. The European Parliament has supported the Commission in this approach.

The Council is of the opinion that in principle, Article 130s should apply to waste legislation. Consequently, Directive 91/156 which amends Directive 75/442 on waste was based on Article 130s.[14] Also, Directive 91/689 which amends Directive 78/319 on toxic and dangerous waste was based on Article 130s.[15]

The Commission has applied to the Court against the Council, asking for an amendment to Directive 91/156, because it should have been based on Article 100a.[16] This application was rejected by the Court which considered that Article 130s was the appropriate legal basis for Directive 91/156.[17]

(20) All these legal theories should not make us forget the environment. The need to use Community measures in order to protect the environment and in particular the marine environment against waste from the titanium dioxide industry was already recognised as early as 1971.[18] The first Community action programme requested such a reduction.[19]

In 1975, the Commission made a proposal for a directive, asking *inter alia* for a reduction of discharges of waste into water and requesting Member

---

[12] See above n. 10.
[13] [1992] O.J. C26/1.
[14] [1991] O.J. L78/32.
[15] [1991] O.J. L377/20.
[16] [1991] O.J. C189/12.
[17] Case C–155/91, *Commission* v. *Council.* Judgment of March 17, 1993, not yet reported.
[18] See Commission, State of the Environment, First report 1977, pp. 50 *et seq.* Second report 1979, pp. 45 *et seq.*
[19] [1973] O.J. C112/1, Chapter 7.

States to submit programmes for gradually reducing those discharges over a period of eight to ten years.[20] The European Parliament criticised the proposal for allowing too much time for the submission of these programmes.[21] The Council adopted the proposal in 1978.[22] Directive 78/176 requested Member States to submit reduction programmes to the Commission before July 1, 1980. The programmes were to start on January 1, 1980 and should have achieved their objectives by 1987. The Commission was to submit to the Council, within six months after receipt of all national programmes, appropriate proposals for harmonising the programmes (Article 9) and the Council committed itself to decide on the harmonisation proposals within six months after publication of the opinions of Parliament and Economic and Social Committee.

On January 24, 1983 the deadline for the Commission to submit its proposals was put back to March 15, 1983.[23] In April 1983, the Commission submitted a proposal for a directive on the harmonisation of national programmes.[24] This proposal was adopted by the Council as Directive 89/428 in June 1989.[25] It provided, in principle, that discharges of waste into water should stop at the end of 1989. However, Member States were allowed, for "serious economic or technical reasons"—which were not specified further—to delay the ending of discharges until 1996. Directive 89/428 was annulled by the Court and only in 1992 did the Council adopt a new directive, based this time on Article 100a.[26] These rules are minimal rules and thus allow Member States to adopt more stringent provisions.

Thus, the Community has not managed to fix harmonised rules for the reduction of discharges of waste from the titanium dioxide industry despite twenty years of efforts and some Court decisions.[27]

This does not mean that nothing has been done to improve the protection of the environment, measures have been taken at national level in the absence of mutual control and of transparency and with a speed that was decided by each individual Member State according to its own political, economic and ecological decisions. The Community has not managed to set up an integrated approach for the protection of the environment. If and to what extent the environment is protected against waste from the titanium dioxide industry, is largely left to the discretion of Member States. The Community impact is small.

This is the story of but one branch of industry. No wonder that the intentions

---

[20] Commission, COM(75)339 final of July 18, 1975.
[21] [1976] O.J. C28/17.
[22] Dir. 78/176 (n. 2).
[23] Dir. 83/29: [1983] O.J. L32/28.
[24] [1983] O.J. C138/5.
[25] [1989] O.J. L201/56.
[26] Dir. 92/172: [1992] O.J. L409/11.
[27] Case 68/81, *Commission* v. *Belgium:* [1982] E.C.R. 153; Case 227–230/85, *Commission* v. *Belgium:* [1988] E.C.R. 1, [1989] 2 C.M.L.R. 797.

of the First Community Environmental Action Programme to tackle the most polluting industries one by one[28] and also the repetition of this intention in the Fourth Community Action Programme have not to date had any concrete results.[29]

---

[28] First Community Action Programme on the Environment (n. 19), Chap. 5 and Chap. 7.
[29] Fourth Community Action Programme on the Environment: [1987] O.J. C328/1, para. 3.4.2 where the experience with the titanium dioxide waste is qualified as not very encouraging.

3. THE INTEGRATION OF ENVIRONMENTAL
REQUIREMENTS INTO OTHER POLICIES

**Judgment of the Court of March 29, 1990
in Case C–62/88**

Greece v. *E.C. Council, supported by (1) United Kingdom, (2) E.C.
Commission*

[1990] I E.C.R. 1527, [1991] 2 C.M.L.R. 649

FACTS AND PROCEDURE[1]

On December 22, 1987, the Council adopted Regulation 3955/87 on the conditions governing imports of agricultural products originating in third countries following the accident at Chernobyl nuclear power-station in the U.S.S.R. The Regulation was adopted on the basis of Article 113 of the EEC Treaty by a qualified majority.

By an application received at the Court on February 26, 1988, the Greek government questioned that decision and asked the Court to cancel Regulation 3955/87; it was of the opinion that the Regulation was in particular based on the wrong legal basis.

The E.C. Commission and the United Kingdom intervened on the side of the Council. The applicant, the defendant and both intervenors submitted written statements to the Court. There was an oral procedure before the Court, but it is not stated who submitted statements to the Court.

The Advocate General delivered his opinion on February 14, 1990.

JUDGMENT

(1) By application lodged at the Court Registry on 26 February 1988, the Hellenic Republic brought an action under the first paragraph of Article 173 of the EEC Treaty for the annulment of Regulation (EEC) No 3955/87 of 22 December 1987 on the conditions governing imports of agricultural products originating in third countries following the accident at the Chernobyl nuclear power-station (Official Journal 1987, L 371, p. 14).

(2) That regulation, which was adopted by a qualified majority on the basis of Article 113 of the EEC Treaty, subjects the release for free circulation of certain agricultural products originating in non-member countries to compliance with maximum permitted levels of radioactive contamination. It requires the Member States to verify compliance with those levels and for that purpose provides for a system for the exchange of information centrally organized by the Commission. In the event of non-compliance with those maximum permitted levels, the regulation requires the requisite measures to be taken, which may include prohibition of the importation of the products in question.

(3) In support of its application the Hellenic Republic makes two submissions. The

---

[1] Summary by the author

first concerns infringement of the EEC and EAEC Treaties and misuse of powers by reason of the illegality of the legal basis of the contested regulation. The second submission is that the statement of the reasons on which the regulation is based is inadequate.

(4) Reference is made to the Report for the Hearing for a fuller account of the facts of the case, the course of the procedure and the submissions and arguments of the parties, which are mentioned or discussed hereinafter only in so far as is necessary for the reasoning of the Court.

The legal basis of the contested regulation

(5) The first submission, which has two limbs, concerns the legal basis of the contested regulation.

(6) In the first limb, the Hellenic Republic claims that, by basing Regulation No 3955/87 on Article 113 of the EEC Treaty, the Council infringed the EEC and EAEC Treaties. The Hellenic Republic states that the regulation is concerned exclusively with protection of the health of the general public in the Member States against the consequences of the Chernobyl nuclear accident and should therefore have been based on Article 31 of the EAEC Treaty or on Articles 130r and 130s of the EEC Treaty, possibly in conjunction with Article 235 of the EEC Treaty.

(7) The Council contends that the first limb of the first submission is inadmissible in so far as it relates to an infringement of the EAEC Treaty, on the ground that the applicant cannot claim an infringement of that Treaty in an action brought solely under the EEC Treaty.

(8) Pursuant to the first paragraph of Article 173 of the EEC Treaty 'the Court of Justice shall review the legality of acts of the Council and the Commission other than recommendations or opinions. It shall for this purpose have jurisdiction in actions brought ... on grounds of ... infringement of this Treaty or of any rule of law relating to its application ... '. The need for a complete and consistent review of legality requires that provision to be construed as not depriving the Court of jurisdiction to consider, in proceedings for the annulment of a measure based on a provision of the EEC Treaty, a submission concerning the infringement of a rule of the EAEC or ECSC Treaties.

(9) It follows that the Council's objection as to the partial inadmissibility of the first limb of the first submission must be dismissed.

(10) As regards the choice of legal basis, it must first be pointed out that that choice may influence the content of the contested measure in so far as the procedural requirements connected with the enabling provisions in question are not the same from one piece of legislation to the next.

(11) In the present case, Article 113(2) and (4) provide that in matters of common commercial policy the Council, on a proposal from the Commission, is to act by a qualified majority without the need for the Parliament or the Economic and Social Committee to be involved. By contrast, Article 31 of the EAEC Treaty,

although providing that the Commission is to have the right to make proposals and providing for the same majority in Council deliberations as Article 113, requires an opinion to be obtained from the Economic and Social Committee and the Parliament to be consulted. According to Article 130s of the EEC Treaty, the Council, acting unanimously on a proposal from the Commission and after consulting the Parliament and the Economic and Social Committee, is to decide what action is to be taken by the Community regarding environmental matters, subject to the Council being entitled to define those matters on which decisions are to be taken by a qualified majority. Article 235 of the EEC Treaty for its part provides that, if action by the Community should prove necessary to attain, in the course of the operation of the common market, one of the objectives of the Community and the Treaty has not provided the necessary powers, the Council, acting unanimously on a proposal from the Commission and after consulting the Parliament, is to take the appropriate measures.

(12) Since the procedural requirements of Article 113 of the EEC Treaty are thus different from those of Article 31 of the EAEC Treaty and from those of Articles 130s and 235 of the EEC Treaty, the Council's decision to adopt as the legal basis for the contested regulation Article 113 of the EEC Treaty rather than Article 31 of the EAEC Treaty or Article 130s of the EEC Treaty, possibly in conjunction with Article 235 of the latter Treaty, is capable of influencing the content of the measure. An incorrect choice of legal basis, if established, would not therefore constitute a purely formal defect. In those circumstances, it is necessary to decide whether the regulation in question could be validly adopted on the basis of Article 113 of the EEC Treaty.

(13) The Court held in its judgment of 26 March 1987 in Case 45/86 *Commission* v. *Council* [1987] ECR 1493, paragraph 11, that in the context of the organization of the powers of the Community the choice of the legal basis for a measure must be based on objective factors which are amenable to judicial review.

(14) As far as the objective pursued is concerned, the preamble to Regulation No 3955/87 indicates that 'the Community must continue to ensure that agricultural products and processed agricultural products intended for human consumption and likely to be contaminated are introduced into the Community only according to common arrangements' and that those 'common arrangements should safeguard the health of consumers, maintain, without having unduly adverse effects on trade between the Community and third countries, the unified nature of the market and prevent deflections of trade'.

(15) Regulation No 3955/87 establishes uniform rules regarding the conditions under which agricultural products likely to be contaminated may be imported into the Community from non-member countries.

(16) It follows that, according to its objective and its content, as they appear from the very terms of the regulation, the regulation is intended to regulate trade between the Community and non-member countries; accordingly it comes within the common commercial policy within the meaning of Article 113 of the EEC Treaty.

(17) Recourse to Article 113 as the legal basis for the contested regulation cannot be excluded on the ground that Article 30 *et seq.* of the EAEC Treaty lay down specific rules governing the basic standards for protection of the health of the

general public against the dangers arising from ionizing radiation. Those provisions, which appear in a chapter entitled 'Health and Safety', which forms part of the second title of the EAEC Treaty entitled 'Provisions for the encouragement of progress in the field of nuclear energy', are intended to provide for the protection of public health in the nuclear sector. They are not intended to regulate trade between the Community and non-member countries.

(18) The fact that maximum permitted levels of radioactive contamination are fixed in response to a concern to protect public health and that the protection of public health is also one of the objectives of Community action in environmental matters, in accordance with the Article 130r(1), likewise cannot remove Regulation No 3955/87 from the sphere of the common commercial policy.

(19) Articles 130r and 130s are intended to confer powers on the Community to undertake specific action on environmental matters. However, those articles leave intact the powers held by the Community under other provisions of the Treaty, even if the measures to be taken under the latter provisions pursue at the same time any of the objectives of environmental protection.

(20) Moreover, that interpretation is confirmed by the second sentence of Article 130r(2), pursuant to which 'environmental protection requirements shall be a component of the Community's other policies'. That provision, which reflects the principle whereby all Community measures must satisfy the requirements of environmental protection, implies that a Community measure cannot be part of Community action on environmental matters merely because it takes account of those requirements.

(21) As regards the Greek Government's reference to the need to base Regulation No 3955/87 also on Article 235, it need merely be stated that, as the Court has held, use of that article as the legal basis for a measure is justified only where no other provision of the Treaty gives the Community institutions the necessary power to adopt the measure in question (see most recently the judgment of 30 May 1989 in Case 242/87 *Commission* v. *Council* [1989] ECR 1425, paragraph 6).

(22) Since the contested regulation comes within the sphere of the common commercial policy and thus has an appropriate legal basis in Article 113, as is apparent from the foregoing, recourse to Article 235 is excluded.

(23) The first limb of the first submission must therefore be dismissed.

(24) In the second limb of the first submission, the Greek Government claims that the Council misused its powers by choosing Article 113 of the EEC Treaty as the legal basis for Regulation No 3955/87 solely in order to be able to decide by a qualified majority and thus avoid the unanimous decision required by Article 130s of the EEC Treaty.

(25) However, as stated above, Article 113 of the EEC Treaty is the appropriate legal basis for the contested regulation. The Council cannot therefore be accused of misusing its powers by following the procedure laid down in that article for the adoption of that regulation.

(26) Since the second limb of the first submission likewise cannot be upheld, the submission as to the illegality of the legal basis must be dismissed in its entirety.

The requirement to state reasons (Article 190 of the EEC Treaty)

(27) The second submission concerns an infringement of Article 190 of the EEC Treaty.

(28) The Hellenic Republic complains that the Council did not indicate in the contested regulation whether or not it was in conformity with the proposal from the Commission. That omission, it claims, infringes the principle of legal certainty since it deprives interested parties of the possibility of verifying whether the measure in question was adopted in accordance with Article 149(1) of the EEC Treaty. Pursuant to that provision, where an act of the Council is adopted on a proposal from the Commission, unanimity is required for the Council to adopt an act constituting an amendment to that proposal. The Greek Government does not claim, however, that the contested measure was adopted in breach of that procedure.

(29) Pursuant to Article 190 of the EEC Treaty, 'regulations, directives and decisions of the Council and of the Commission ... shall refer to any proposals or opinions which were required to be obtained pursuant to this Treaty'. The very terms of that provision show that, although it requires a reference to the Commission's proposal in measures which may be adopted only on a proposal from the Commission, it does not thereby impose the obligation to indicate whether or not the measure in question is in conformity with that proposal.

(30) The second submission thus likewise cannot be upheld.

(31) Since neither of the applicant's submissions has been successful, the action must be dismissed.

Costs

(32) Under Article 69(2) of the Rules of Procedure, the unsuccessful party is to be ordered to pay the costs. Since the Hellenic Republic has failed in its submissions, it must be ordered to pay the costs.

On those grounds,

THE COURT

hereby:

   (1) Dismisses the application;

   (2) Orders the Hellenic Republic to pay the costs.

COMMENTARY

(1) This case is one of a number of cases in which the European Court was asked, *inter alia*, to interpret the meaning of the environmental Articles which had been incorporated into the EEC Treaty by the Single European Act and had entered into effect in 1987.[2]

The Greek government asked for the annulment of Regulation 3955/87[3] which was one measure out of a package of directives and regulations adopted by the Community following the accident at the Chernobyl power-station in April 1986. Another regulation, Regulation (Euratom) 3954/87[4] laying down maximum permitted levels of radioactive contamination of foodstuffs and of feedingstuffs following a nuclear accident or any other case of radio-logical emergency, which had been adopted on the basis of Article 31 of the Euratom Treaty was tackled by the European Parliament.[5]

In the present Case C–62/88, the Greek government was of the opinion that Regulation 3955/87 should not have been based on Article 113 of the EEC Treaty as decided by the Council, but either on Article 31 of the Euratom Treaty or on Articles 130r and 130s, possibly in conjunction with Article 235 of the EEC Treaty. The Court came to the same conclusion as the Commission, the Council, the United Kingdom and the Advocate General and dismissed the application.

(2) When starting to examine the case, the Court was confronted with the diffi-culty that Greece had based its application on Article 173 of the EEC Treaty, but not on the corresponding Article of the Euratom Treaty, Article 146. The Council was therefore of the opinion, that the application was inadmissible insofar as an infringement of the Euratom Treaty was argued and the Com-mission and the Advocate General agreed with this opinion.

The Court held the application to be fully admissible. It justified this result with a "need for a complete and consistent review of legality" which is some-how laconic, while the result, *i.e.* to examine in detail Article 31 of the Euratom Treaty and Articles 130s, 113 and 235 of the EEC Treaty, is certainly desirable; it is questionable whether the text of Article 173 allows such an interpretation. It might be mentioned that in Case C–70/88, Parliament had argued in its application that, amongst others, the Council could only adopt directives under Article 31 of the Euratom Treaty. The Court did not examine this part of the Parliament's application, though such an examination might have been jus-tified by a "need for a complete and consistent review of legality", all the more since parts of Regulation 3954/87 were in fact examined by the Court.

---

[2] See also Case C–300/89, *Commission* v. *Council* [1991] I E.C.R. 2867; Case C–70/88, *European Parliament* v. *Council* [1990] I E.C.R. 2041, [1992] 1 C.M.L.R. 91.

[3] [1987] O.J. L371/14.

[4] [1987] O.J. L371/11.

[5] Case C–70/88 above.

(3) As regards the substance of the case, the Court did not have great difficulties in eliminating Article 235 as the appropriate legal basis for Regulation 3955/87. Indeed, the use of Article 235 is now quite clear. The Article applies when no other article gives a competence for action at Community level. The "use of that article as the legal basis for a measure is justified only where no other provision of the Treaty gives the Community institutions the necessary powers to adopt the measure in question." This doctrine was first expressed this clearly in Case 45/86[6] and repeated in Case 165/87.[7] It is thus now consistent court jurisprudence on this question; Article 235 expressly talks of the cases where no Community competence is provided for by the Treaty.

(4) In legal terms the only question for the choice of the legal basis was whether it was right to take Article 113 of the EEC Treaty or whether the Council should have taken either Article 31 of the Euratom Treaty or 130r and 130s of the EEC Treaty. Of course, the political aspect of the application was different: Greece opposed the content of Regulation 3955/87 since it considered the levels of Regulation 3955/87 to be too low. The choice of Articles 31 of the Euratom Treaty or 130r and 130s of the EEC Treaty which require unanimous decisions would have given Greece the possibility to block—to veto—any decision by the Council which it did not like.

The Court's decision had thus not only an important political impact. It also constituted a precedent for later cases and, indeed, for the interpretation of the EEC Treaty as amended by the Single European Act. This being so, it is useful to trace back how the Court reached its decision.

(5) The Commission argued[8] before the Court that the objectives laid down in Article 110 (113) of the Treaty are so general that they include objectives pursued by other policies, such as health protection or environmental policy. Article 130s merely gives the Community express powers for specific action for the environment which is not capable of being pursued by a "component" of other policies or by virtue of other spheres of competence provided in the Treaty. Article 130s was only introduced into the Treaty in 1987. It cannot result in any restriction of the competence of the Community already existing under the EEC Treaty. "The new area of competence does not enjoy primacy over the existing areas of competence". This last argument that the new Article 130s has not taken away or restricted competences which were provided for by other articles of the Treaty, is not very convincing. It should be noted that in Case 68/86[9] which dealt with hormones in meat, the Court, for the first time, stated that measures under Article 43 were possible even where questions of human health were also touched or affected by those measures.

---

[6] 45/86, *Commission* v. *Council* [1987] E.C.R. 1493, [1988] 2 C.M.L.R. 131.
[7] 165/87, *Commission* v. *Council* [1988] E.C.R. 5545, [1990] 1 C.M.L.R. 457.
[8] [1990] I E.C.R. 1527, 1534–1535, [1991] 2 C.M.L.R. 649, 652–654.
[9] 68/86, *United Kingdom* v. *Council* [1988] E.C.R. 855, [1988] 2 C.M.L.R. 543.

Even more illustrative is Article 130q of the Treaty. Since the entry into effect of Article 130q, all research measures are based on that article, though prior to 1987 agricultural research was based on Article 43. This shows that the 1987 amendment of the EEC Treaty did change the content of "old" articles in favour of "new" ones.

The Commission further argued that the objective of Regulation 3955/87 was not solely public health or the environment. It followed from Article 4 of the Regulation that it laid down rules on the external trade of the Community and was an instrument of commercial policy.

(6) The Council argued[10] that the legal basis of a measure is determined by the reasons on which it is based and not by its content. Regulation 3955/87 pursues a commercial objective, not the objective of protecting people's health, nor is it an action relating to the environment (Article 130r, paragraph 1). Moreover, it follows from Article 130r, paragraph 2, second sentence that environmental protection requirements are to be components of other policies, such as the common commercial policy.[11]

(7) The Advocate General started by examining earlier Court statements on the environment and by an examination of the different Treaty Articles. Environmental matters were the subject of Community measures before the entry into force of the Single European Act. Therefore, the "introduction into the Treaty of a new sphere of Community competence", could not have had the effect of transferring to that new field of action measures previously coming within areas of Community competence, such as those based on Articles 43, 100 or 113 the adoption of which may be governed by different rules. The position would be different only if Member States had expressly decided, by amending the Treaties, to restrict the Community's area of competence, and they did not do so by means of the Single European Act.[12]

This conclusion is then brought into line with previous judgments of the Court on commercial and agricultural policy in order to show that the Court had not, in the past, refused to allow the use of one specific Treaty article, where requirements of other interests were also involved.

(8) The Court started by pointing out that the choice of legal basis may influence the content of the Community measure in so far as the procedural requirements under Articles 113, 130s, 235 of the EEC Treaty and Article 31 of the Euratom Treaty are different. "An incorrect choice of legal basis would not therefore constitute a purely formal defect".

---

[10] [1990] I E.C.R. 1527, 1532–1533, [1991] 2 C.M.L.R. 649.
[11] *Ibid.* pp. 1539–1542 (E.C.R.), pp. 657–661 (C.M.L.R.).
[12] *Ibid.* p. 1540 (E.C.R.), pp. 658–659 (C.M.L.R.).

The procedural differences of the Articles can be seen in the table below:

	Art. 113	Art. 130s	Art. 235	Art. 31 (Euratom)
Majority/ Unanimity	Majority	Unanimity	Unanimity	Majority
Need to consult EP	No	Yes	Yes	Yes
Need to consult ECOSOC	No	Yes	No	Yes

The Court was thus of the opinion that the theoretical possibility of influencing the content of a measure must lead to an annulment of a measure where the correct legal basis was not chosen.[13]

(9) The Court then confirmed that the choice of the legal basis "must be based on objective factors which are amenable to judicial review". It examined the objectives of Regulation 3955/87 and its content by looking at the preamble and the different articles and concluded that it appeared "from the very terms of the regulation" that Regulation 3955/87 "is intended to regulate trade" between the Community and third countries and does therefore come under Article 113.

The wording cannot be understood to mean that the Court looked at the "intention" of the legislator. It follows instead from the context that the Court examined the (objective) content of the Regulation.

The Court has not yet had to decide on a case where the Council deliberately chose a specific legal basis which was later found by the Court to be incorrect, but where the preamble and the content follow the (incorrect) legal basis. Once the question whether waste legislation comes under Article 130s or 100a is decided, such a situation might well occur.[14]

---

[13] See as a consequence of this jurisprudence on the one hand European Court: Case C–70/88, interlocutory judgment of May 22, 1990, [1990] I E.C.R. 2041, [1992] 1 C.M.L.R. 91 where the Court recognises the right of the European Parliament to bring an action under Art. 173 of the EEC Treaty, in order to safeguard its institutional prerogatives. The Maastricht Treaty on European Union will amend Art. 173 of the Treaty in this sense.
See on the other hand Case C–300/89, n. 2 above, where Directive 89/428 was annulled.
[14] On March 17, 1993 the Court ruled that Art. 130s was the appropriate legal basis for Dir. 91/156, Case C–155/91, *Commission* v. *Belgium:* not yet reported. See Case 18 below p. 291.

(10) The Court then examined whether this result could be questioned by Articles 30 *et seq.* of the Euratom Treaty and the conclusion was negative. "Those provisions are intended to provide for the protection of public health in the nuclear sector. They are not intended to regulate trade between the Community and non-member countries".

Having thus eliminated Article 31 of the Euratom Treaty, the Court turned to Articles 130r and 130s. Its decisive phrase was that:

"those articles leave intact the powers held by the Community under other provisions of the Treaty, even if the measures to be taken under the latter provisions pursue at the same time any of the objectives of environmental protection."[15]

The Court took up the argument developed by the Commission and the Advocate General that the Single European Act had not touched on existing rules of competence under other provisions of the Treaty. It had already been suggested that in view of Article 130q and its interpretation, this argument is not entirely convincing. It leads to the result that only measures which were based on Article 235 before 1987, can now be based on Article 130s. This is indeed a theory which is argued by some authors. However the Council's and Commission's practice is different.

(11) The Court based its result on the objective of Article 130s on a second argument ("Moreover"), taken from Article 130r paragraph 2, second sentence. It sees that provision as a horizontal provision which requires that "all Community measures must satisfy the requirements of environmental protection". This being so, it concluded "that a Community measure cannot be part of Community action on environmental matters merely because it takes account of those requirements".[16]

Thus for both Article 31 of the Euratom Treaty and 130s of the EEC Treaty, the Court resorted to a systematic interpretation of the rules of the Treaties.[17] As regards Article 113, the Court instead examined the objective and content of Regulation 3955/87 in order to allow its classification as a commercial matter.

(12) The overall Court decision seems correct. It is very difficult to see how Regulation 3955/87 could have been based on Article 130s. Many Community measures in the food and agricultural sector, but also in the pharmaceutical area, contribute to public health and it would have stretched Articles 130r and 130s too far to try to subsume all these measures under the chapter of environmental protection.

(13) Two other aspects of the Court decision shall be commented upon here.

---

[15] Para. 19.
[16] Para. 20.
[17] For the different rules of interpretation see above. p. 27 *et seq.* and below p. 62 *et seq.*

The first one is the argument by the Greek government that the Council by adopting Regulation 3955/87 had not entirely respected Article 149 of the EEC Treaty, which requires that where "the Council acts on a proposal from the Commission, unanimity shall be required for an act constituting an amendment to that proposal". Neither the report of the Judge-Rapporteur nor the parties nor the Court itself seem, in my opinion, have fully measured the content of the Greek arguments. This is undoubtedly due to Greece's advocates who failed to express themselves with the necessary clarity or who did not correct the "Report for the Hearing" of the Judge-Rapporteur.[18]

In order to understand the problem, a short reminder of the history of Regulation 3955/87 is necessary. The Chernobyl nuclear accident occurred on April 26, 1986. The Council took provisional measures regarding the import of certain agricultural products from third countries.[19] These measures were replaced by Regulation 1707/86 which fixed the conditions under which imports of contaminated agricultural products from third countries were allowed.[20] The Regulation was to run to September 30, 1986. By Regulation 3020/86,[21] it was extended February 28, 1987 and by Regulation 624/87[22] to October 31, 1987.

On October 22, 1987, the Commission submitted a new proposal, suggesting a further extension to October 31, 1989.[23] However, the Council was unable to agree on that proposal before the end of October. Thus, Regulation 1707/86 expired. Therefore, when the Council adopted Regulation 3955/87 on December 22, 1987, there was only a Commission proposal to prolong the duration of Regulation 3955/87.

The Court could thus have raised the question whether the formalities of Article 149 were really respected, since the proposal of the Commission which provided, in more or less one article, for a prolongation of Regulation 1707/86, was in fact considerably "amended" by the Council which adopted Regulation 3955/87 with all its detailed provisions.

(14) However, in this case it should be pointed out that the substance of Regulation 3955/87 is not different from that of Regulation 1707/86. The maximum radioactive levels—370 Bq/kg for milk and 600 Bq/kg for all other products concerned—are the same and so are the provisions on the controls of compliance. The difference between the proposal to prolong Regulation 1707/86 and a proposal which would have taken up the content of that proposal in an express and detailed way are thus formal and it is unlikely that the Court would have reached any other result as regards Article 149.

Attention is drawn to this problem of Article 149 because the Commission

---

[18] See application by Greece, [1988] O.J. C91/4.
[19] Reg. 1388/86: [1986] O.J. L127/1.
[20] [1986] O.J. L146/89.
[21] [1986] O.J. L280/79.
[22] [1987] O.J. L58/101.
[23] Commission, COM(87)522 final of October 22, 1987; see [1987] 10 E.C. Bull no. 2.1.216.

not infrequently agrees, during the discussions in Council, to amendments of its own proposal without this agreement—which is also an amendment of its previous proposal!—being published. There are Commission rules that any agreement to a substantial change of the Commission's initial proposal should be the subject of a formal Commission decision, which is then published. The practice, however, does not always seem to respect these—admittedly vague—rules, which further contributes to the non-transparency of law-making procedures at Community level.

(15) The second point is that measures under Article 190 of the EEC Treaty have "to state the reasons on which they were based". Greece was of the opinion that the statement of reasons was inadequate. The Court is extremely short in its rejection of this argument which, again, was not clearly presented.

Article 190 is all the more important in the general context of the Treaty provisions, since—unlike legislative procedures in Member States—the discussion in Council, the EEC decision-making policy is not public. There are no "Council debates" equivalent to Parliamentary debates in Member States which are published. The non-public character of the debates is not requested by the EEC Treaty, but follows from the internal order of the Council.

This very serious democratic deficit in the law-making procedure is only partly filled by Article 190, all the more since the Court allows relatively short summary statements of reasons. The Maastricht Treaty has not changed Article 190 in substance, although it is true that the joined decision procedure will lead to a bit more transparency, since the European Parliament in some areas participates in the law-making and its debates are public.

(16) Underlying the Judgment in Case C–62/88 was the question whether the maximum levels of radioactivity fixed by Regulation 3955/87 were correct or more importantly environmentally sound. The Court did not pronounce on this question.

Also on December 22, 1987, the Council adopted Regulation 3954/87 (Euratom) laying down maximum permitted levels of radioactive contamination of foodstuffs and of feedingstuffs following a nuclear accident. This Regulation was adopted on the basis of Article 31 of the Euratom Treaty. The European Parliament tackled the Regulation by virtue of Article 173 of the EEC Treaty, arguing, *inter alia*, that the Regulation should have been based on Article 100a of the EEC Treaty.

The Court was of the opinion that the European Parliament had the right to base an action on Article 173 despite the wording of the Article.[24] In substance, however, the Court rejected the application, holding that Article 173 did constitute the appropriate legal basis. Also in that case no examination was made whether the levels of contamination were appropriate; indeed, the

---

[24] See n. 13 above.

European Parliament had asked for lower levels than the Commission's proposal.

(17) Thus, in both Cases C–62/88 and C–70/88, the environmental argument whether the levels fixed by the Council are really appropriate were turned, in the Court procedure, to procedural arguments and to arguments of legal basis. This is not surprising, since neither Article 113 of the EEC Treaty nor the Euratom Treaty provide for rules which indicate what is an appropriate level of health and/or environmental protection. The preamble of the Euratom Treaty only mentions the need to "create the conditions of safety necessary to eliminate hazards to the life and health of the public". At the same time, however, the preamble pleads for "the development and invigoration of industry". Thus, nobody could argue, under the Euratom Treaty that safety is the first and primary objective. This is confirmed by the articles on health and safety, Articles 30 *et seq.*, which do not say anything about the degree of safety to be achieved. In accordance with international nuclear energy practice, safety standards are fixed "as low as reasonably achievable" (ALARA-principle) and behind this word "reasonably" are hidden economic and social considerations.

Others argue that radioactive substances are generally admitted to be carcinogenic, teratogenic and mutagenic. Thus, the principle must be that any exposure to man must be kept as low as possible, all the more since nobody is really able to indicate from which level onwards a radioactive substance becomes harmless.

(18) To illustrate these indications it is interesting to note that after the Chernobyl accident, for milk France adopted levels of 3,700 Bq per litre and the United Kingdom 2,000 Bq per litre.[25] The original measures at Community level—including Regulation 3955/87—were 370 Bq per litre[26] and the experts consulted by the Commission under Article 31 of the Euratom Treaty after the Chernobyl accident, suggested, in December 1986, 20,000 Bq per litre of milk,[27]; while the European Environmental Bureau, the Community umbrella organisation of environmental groups, suggested 5 Bq per litre of milk.[28] The European Parliament suggested 100 Bq.[29] In Regulation 3954/87, the Council set the level at 1000 Bq per litre of milk.

This example shows that the question of "how safe is safe" is a political, rather than a legal question. Member States with strong nuclear interests might tend to favour higher levels and less public discussion on levels,

---

[25] According to Bureau Européen des Unions de Consommateurs (BEUC). Press release of October 29, 1987, no. 87/28. All figures here and hereafter refer to Cs-134 and Cs-137.
[26] See references in nn. 20 to 22.
[27] *Le Monde*, May 22, 1987: "La CEE préconise pour les aliments de nouvelles normes de radioactivité"—The report, including the figures, is published in Commission, COM(87)28 final of January 23, 1987, annex III.
[28] European Environmental Bureau, Press release of October 13, 1987, no. C123/87.
[29] [1987] O.J. C318/79.

whereas Member States with strong environmental movements might, under the pressure of public opinion, tend to set lower levels.

(19) Community nuclear energy policy cannot be described in detail here, not even in its relationship to the environment. But the fact that the fixing of Community emission standards for nuclear installations which set levels for maximum admissible emissions into the air, water or the soil, have never been suggested or seriously discussed at Community level, shows that the details of "nuclear energy and the environment" have not yet even begun to be discussed.

So, when looking into the legal formalities of the European Court's judgments, the reader should not forget that there is something of a legal policy which escapes the assessment by the Court and yet influences our environment very considerably.

4. THE EURATOM TREATY AND ENVIRONMENTAL PROTECTION

**Judgment of the Court of September 22, 1988
in Case 187/87**

Preliminary ruling in the proceedings pending before the Tribunal administratif, Strasbourg, between Saarland and Others and Minister for Industry, Post and Telecommunications and Tourism (France) and Others

[1988] E.C.R. 5013, [1989] 1 C.M.L.R. 529

FACTS AND PROCEDURE[1]

During the 1970s, France planned to construct a nuclear electricity-generating station at Cattenom, a place close to the German and Luxembourg frontiers. In October 1978, the construction was declared to be in the French public interest. Between 1979 and 1984, building permits were issued for four blocks of a capacity of 1,300 megawatt each. In July 1984, the owner of the power station asked for authorisation to discharge liquid and gaseous radioactive waste into the waters and the air. French authorities granted this authorisation on February 21, 1986.

On April 28, 1986, this authorisation order of February 21, 1986 was challenged before the Tribunal administratif of Strasbourg by the Land Saar, the "Association pour la sauvegarde de la vallée de la Moselle", several German and Luxembourg cities and bodies, and the City of Luxembourg. The application for an interim suspension of the work was dismissed by the Tribunal administratif. On April 29, 1986, the French government sought the opinion of the E.C. Commission under Article 37 of the Euratom Treaty. The Commission gave its opinion on October 22, 1986. On October 23, 1986, the French authorities authorised a nuclear reaction in the first block, which took place on October 25, 1986.

The Tribunal administratif voided the authorisation for discharges as regards two blocks. For the two other blocks it put a preliminary question to the European Court asking for the compatibility of the procedure with Article 37 of the Euratom Treaty. The case was registered with the Court on June 16, 1987.

Written submissions were made by the Land Saar, the City of Luxembourg, the "Association pour la sauvegarde de la vallée de la Moselle" and other persons, the governments of Ireland, Luxembourg, France and Portugal and the Commission. The Commission and France answered some written questions of the Court.

There were oral hearings. The judgment mentions that they took place on April 26, 1988. However, neither the judgment nor the report of the rapporteur indicate who gave oral argument.

The Advocate General delivered his opinion on June 8, 1988.

---

[1] Summary by the author

JUDGMENT

(1) By a judgment of 11 June 1987, which was received at the Court on 16 June 1987, the tribunal administratif, Strasbourg, referred to the Court for a preliminary ruling under Article 150 of the EAEC Treaty a question on the interpretation of Article 37 of that Treaty.

(2) The question was raised in proceedings brought by Saarland, a number of German local authorities, certain French and Luxembourg associations for the protection of the Moselle valley and of the environment and a number of private individuals against French inter-ministerial orders of 21 February 1986 authorizing the disposal of liquid radioactive waste and of gaseous radioactive waste from the four blocks of the Cattenom nuclear power-station, in the *département* of the Moselle.

(3) Those orders mark the conclusion of an administrative procedure which commenced on 11 October 1978 when the works necessary to establish a nuclear power-station at Cattenom comprising two 900-megawatt blocks and two 1 300-megawatt blocks were declared to be in the public interest ('d'utilité publique'), whereafter, between 6 July 1979 and 31 March 1982, building permits were issued for those blocks, and, between 24 June 1982 and 29 February 1984, decrees were adopted authorizing the installation at Cattenom of four blocks of 1 300 megawatts each.

(4) Before the tribunal administratif, Strasbourg, the plaintiffs in the main proceedings claimed, *inter alia*, that the French Government had infringed Article 37 of the EAEC Treaty by not providing the Commission with general data concerning the disposal of radioactive waste by the Cattenom nuclear power-station until 29 April 1986, that is to say after the adoption of the contested orders, whereas that article requires the Commission to be notified before disposals are authorized by the competent authorities.

(5) The defendants in the main proceedings contended that Article 37 of the EAEC Treaty must be interpreted as requiring consultation of the Commission before any disposal of waste is effected, notwithstanding the fact that such disposal might have been authorized before the Commission was notified.

(6) In those circumstances, the tribunal administratif, Strasbourg, raised the question whether Article 37 of the Treaty of 25 March 1957 establishing the European Atomic Energy Committee requires the Commission of the European Communities to be notified before the disposal of radioactive waste by nuclear power-stations is authorized by the competent authorities in the Member States, where a procedure for prior authorization is established, or before such disposal is effected by nuclear power-stations.

(7) Reference is made to the Report for the Hearing for a fuller account of the facts of the case, the procedure and the observations submitted to the Court, which are mentioned or discussed hereinafter only in so far as is necessary for the reasoning of the Court.

(8) Article 37 of the EAEC Treaty provides as follows:

"Each Member State shall provide the Commission with such general data relating to any plan for the disposal of radioactive waste in whatever form as will make it possible to determine whether the implementation of such plan is liable to result in the radioactive contamination of the water, soil or airspace of another Member State.

The Commission shall deliver its opinion within six months, after consulting the group of experts referred to in Article 31."

(9) For the interpretation of that provision, the French Government relied, in its observations, upon the Commission Recommendation of 3 February 1982 (Official Journal 1982, L 83, p. 15), according to which the general data for a plan like the one at issue should be submitted 'whenever possible one year but not less than six months before the planned date of commencement of disposal of radioactive waste'. That recommendation, which ranks lower than the Treaty, cannot, however, determine the interpretation to be given to Article 37 of the EAEC Treaty.

(10) The expression 'plan for the disposal of . . . waste' used in Article 37 appears to indicate that that article refers to a phase prior to any decision authorizing disposal. However, in order to define its terms with precision, it is necessary to interpret Article 37 in the light of its context and its purpose within the system of the EAEC Treaty.

(11) In that regard, it must be noted that the article appears in Chapter III of the EAEC Treaty, entitled 'Health and Safety', the provisions of which form a coherent whole conferring upon the Commission powers of some considerable scope in order to protect the population and the environment against the risks of nuclear contamination.

(12) Among the provisions of Chapter III of the EAEC Treaty, Article 37 appears as a provision to which recourse must be had in order to forestall any possibility of radioactive contamination, whereas other provisions, such as Article 38, are applicable where a risk of contamination is imminent or even where contamination has already occurred.

(13) In the light of that purpose of Article 37, the guidance which the Commission, assisted by highly qualified groups of experts, can give to the Member State concerned is of very great importance, owing, in particular, to the Commission's unique overview of developments in the nuclear power industry throughout the territory of the Community.

(14) In order to prevent the risk of radioactive contamination, it must therefore be possible for the Commission's opinion, particularly in those cases where it suggests a modification to the plan or the adoption of safety measures involving collaboration between two or more Member States, to be examined in detail by the Member State concerned, under conditions such that the Commission's suggestions can still be taken into account by that State, even if it is not legally obliged to conform with the opinion.

(15) That requirement is in no way put in doubt by the procedure for cases of urgency provided for in Article 38 of the Treaty, which must be reserved for exceptional circumstances and cannot relieve the Member States of their duty to comply scrupulously with their obligations under Article 37.

(16) Consequently, it must be acknowledged that, where a Member State makes the disposal of radioactive waste subject to authorization, the Commission's opinion must, in order to be rendered fully effective, be brought to the notice of that State before the issue of any such authorization.

(17) If a decision has already been adopted, it becomes more difficult to take account of an unfavourable Commission opinion, which would oblige the public authority to repudiate the action of the departments or bodies which inspired that decision. Furthermore, it is possible that, in certain Member States, an authorization for the disposal of radioactive waste might confer rights upon the person to whom it was granted and could not easily be withdrawn. Finally, knowledge of the Commission's opinion may be of use for the purpose of enabling any person concerned to assess the merits of a possible legal action against the decision granting authorization.

(18) All the foregoing factors lead to the view that the Commission's opinion has no real chance of being examined in detail and of having any effective influence on the attitude of the State concerned unless it is issued before the adoption of any decision definitively authorizing disposal, which *a fortiori* implies that the opinion must be sought before such authorization is granted.

(19) Only if Article 37 is interpreted as meaning that the Commission must be provided with general data relating to a plan for the disposal of radioactive waste before definitive authorization for such disposal is granted can that article achieve its purpose. It is to an interpretation to that effect, which is such as to ensure that the provision retains its effectiveness, that preference must be given, in accordance with a line of decided cases (judgment of 6 October 1970 in Case 9/70 *Grad* v. *Finanzamt Traunstein* [1970] ECR 825; judgment of 31 March 1971 in Case 22/70 *Commission* v. *Council* [1971] ECR 263; judgment of 5 May 1981 in Case 804/79 *Commission* v. *United Kingdom* [1981] ECR 1045).

(20) It must therefore be stated in reply to the question submitted by the national court that Article 37 of the Treaty of 25 March 1957 establishing the European Atomic Energy Community must be interpreted as meaning that the Commission of the European Communities must be provided with general data relating to any plan for the disposal of radioactive waste before such disposal is authorized by the competent authorities of the Member State concerned.

Costs

(21) The costs incurred by the governments of the French Republic, Ireland, the Grand Duchy of Luxembourg and the Portuguese Republic, and by the Commission of the European Communities, which have submitted observations to the Court, are not recoverable. Since these proceedings are, in so far as the parties to the main proceedings are concerned, in the nature of a step in the action pending before the national court, the decision on costs is a matter for that court.

On those grounds,

THE COURT,

in reply to the question submitted to it by the tribunal administratif, Strasbourg, by judgment of 11 June 1987, hereby rules:

Article 37 of the Treaty of 25 March 1957 establishing the European Atomic Energy Community must be interpreted as meaning that the Commission of the European Communities must be provided with general data relating to any plan for the disposal of radioactive waste before such disposal is authorized by the competent authorities of the Member State concerned.

COMMENTARY

(1) This case deals with legal problems concerning the construction of nuclear energy stations, an important environmental problem in several EEC Member States. It illustrates the possibilities, but also the limits of Community and national law in such cases.

Since nuclear energy questions are at stake, it is not the EEC Treaty, but the Treaty establishing the European Atomic Energy Community (Euratom Treaty) which applies. It is true that some environmental directives, adopted under the EEC Treaty, also refer to radioactive substances or waste or nuclear installations. They sometimes include rules for such installations or waste,[2] but most provide expressly that nuclear energy questions are not dealt with.[3]

(2) The Euratom Treaty provides that uniform safety standards to protect the health of workers and of the general public should be established.[4] Chapter III "Health and safety" deals in more detail with the protection against the dangers arising from ionising radiation. It provides that basic standards for such protection shall be laid down within the Community.[5] For "particularly dangerous experiments", Member States must take additional health and safety measures;[6] they must also set up monitoring facilities for measuring radioactivity in the air, water and soil and to ensure compliance with basic standards.[7] Article 37, which was in question in the present case, and Article

---

[2] See for instance Dir. 85/337: [1985] O.J. L175/40. This seems to be the only environmental directive where nuclear aspects are expressly included. However, other directives, such as 76/160 on the quality of bathing water: [1976] O.J. L31/1; 79/409 on the conservation of wild birds: [1979] O.J. L103/1; 90/313 on access to environmental information: [1990] O.J. L158/56 include the protection against radioactive radiation.

[3] See for instance Dir. 80/68 on groundwater pollution: [1980] O.J. L20/43; Dir. 84/360 on air pollution from industrial installations: [1984] O.J. L188/20; Dir. 75/442 on waste: [1975] O.J. L194/47; Dir. 78/319 on toxic and dangerous waste: [1978] O.J. L84/43; Dir. 82/501 on the prevention of industrial accidents: [1982] O.J. L230/1.

[4] Art. 2(*b*) Euratom

[5] Art. 30 Euratom

[6] Art. 34 Euratom

[7] Art. 35 Euratom

36 provide for some co-operation between the Commission and Member States. Article 38 allows the Commission to take recommendations concerning radioactivity in the air, water or soil or, in the cases of urgency, issue directives in the area of health and safety.

(3) The Euratom Treaty generally intends to create "the conditions necessary for the speedy establishment and growth of nuclear industries."[8] As early as the 1960s, however, it became clear that the leading role of Euratom in the development of nuclear energy could not be achieved. National nuclear industries developed in competition to each other. This situation still exists. No nuclear energy is produced in Denmark, Ireland, Greece, Portugal and— after a referendum took place in 1987—in Italy.

As regards health and safety, basic standards for radiation protection were developed which apply to the exposure of the general public during normal operations and to workers occupationally exposed to radiation. A considerable number of new basic standards were developed after the Chernobyl accident.[9]

Article 37 of the Euratom Treaty states that the Commission must be notified of nuclear plans in Member States that involve the discharge of radioactive substances. The Commission has to deliver an opinion on this within six months. Already this time-limit excludes comprehensive investigations on the project. Furthermore, an opinion has no binding force.[10]

(4) The Commission had already, in 1960, made a recommendation in respect of Article 37 in which it recommended that plans for the disposal of radioactive waste should be communicated to the Commission at least six months before the planned date for the execution of the waste disposal.[11] In 1980, the European Parliament adopted a resolution in which it called on the Commission to urge Member States to operate within time-scales sufficient to make the procedure of Article 37 an effective one.[12] Subsequent to that, a Commission Recommendation of 1982[13] which replaced the Recommendation of 1960, stated that plans in the context of Article 37 necessitated particular attention "prior to construction beginning". The Recommendation invited Member States to submit "general data" to the Commission "whenever possible one year but not less than six months before the planned date of commencement of disposal of radioactive waste."

(5) Furthermore, in 1976, the Commission presented to the Council a proposal

---

[8] Art. 1 Euratom
[9] See in particular Dir. 80/836/Euratom: [1980] O.J. L246/1; Dir. 84/467/Euratom: [1984] O.J. L265/4; Dir. 84/466/Euratom: [1984] O.J. L265/1; Reg. 3954/87: [1987] O.J. L371/1; Reg. 2218/89: [1989] O.J. L211/1; Dir. 89/618/Euratom: [1989] O.J. L357/31; Dir. 90/641/Euratom: [1990] O.J. L349/21.
[10] See Art. 161 Euratom.
[11] Recommendation of November 16, 1960: [1960] J.O. 1893.
[12] [1980] O.J. C327/34.
[13] Recommendation 82/181: [1982] O.J. L83/15.

for a regulation concerning the introduction of a Community consultation procedure in respect of power-stations likely to affect the territory of another Member State, based on Article 203 of the Euratom Treaty and Article 235 of the EEC Treaty.[14] The Council did not adopt this proposal. It did, however, adopt Directive 85/337,[15] which entered into force on July 3, 1988 and which provides for a detailed assessment of the direct and indirect environmental effects of, *inter alia*, nuclear power-stations. Directive 85/337 also contains rules on consultations which will be discussed below. At the time of the French decisions, which led to Case 187/87, that Directive was not yet in force.

(6) Before commenting on the Court's decision, some details of French law should be mentioned. French administrative law is not built on subjective rights. An administrative act, such as a permit to build, may be tackled on grounds that the act was illegal, in particular for reasons of excess of powers (excès de pouvoir) but generally not on grounds that a subjective right of somebody was affected.[16] This specific feature might explain why the building permits for the nuclear power plant at Cattenom, which were issued between 1979 and 1984, were not challenged in court. The authorisation to operate the plant, and thus to discharge radioactive waste into the environment, is in French law largely independent from the authorisation to build. Only in very exceptional circumstances, which were dismissed in the Cattenom power-plant case, can authorisation for building and authorisation to operate an installation be linked together.

(7) The case which was brought to the Strasbourg administrative court was thus threatened from the beginning to be limited to the challenge of the legality of the decision of February 21, 1986. The Strasbourg administrative court tried to link this authorisation to the construction authorisations of 1979 to 1984, but its decision on this was later reversed by the Conseil d'Etat.

(8) The European Court of Justice had to decide only on the question whether the French authorities should have requested—and received—the opinion of the E.C. Commission before giving the authorisation for discharges on February 21, 1986 or whether it was sufficient that the Commission's opinion was requested and received before the discharges of waste actually began, *i.e.* before October 25, 1986.

(9) The Court first eliminated reference to the Commission's Recommendation of 1982 as a possible means of interpretation. Its argument was that this recommendation "ranks lower than the Treaty" and thus is incapable of contributing to the interpretation of Article 37. This argument is obviously a strong one

---

[14] [1977] O.J. L31/3.
[15] See n. 2 above.
[16] It does not seem that an administrative act can be tackled on grounds that a fundamental or a human right of a particular person is affected—at least this does not seem to have been tried.

since a legal rule including a recommendation which is derived from Article 37 cannot really help to interpret the Article in the Treaty: the interpretation of the Treaty is, in the final instance, to be given by the Court of Justice, whereas the recommendation reflects the Commission's point of view.

It should be noted that the Recommendation of 1982 is relatively clear on when Member States shall request the opinion of the Commission under Article 37: by taking as a reference point the "date of commencement of disposal of radioactive waste" and not the date of the authorisation for such disposal, the recommendation is closer to the French point of view than to that of the Land Saar. This is the reason why the Commission's submissions to the Court during the procedure were remarkably unprecise on this point.

(10) The Court then went on to interpret Article 37 itself, starting with a literal interpretation. However, on that point the Court was extremely prudent. It stated that the wording of Article 37 "appears to indicate that that Article refers to a phase prior to any decision authorizing disposal". The Court did not explain how it got that impression. Indeed, the word "plan" in Article 37 is "Plan" in the German version, but it is "project" in the French version of the Euratom Treaty. Furthermore an understanding of "plan" in the sense of project seems rather to plead in favour of the opinion of the French government.

The literal interpretation of Article 37 does not help very much. This is a rather general feature of Community law. A German professor of law, who is a specialist in Community law and who acts at present as a judge at the European Court of Justice, put this problem into the following terms:

> "In the European Community the wording is also point of departure and limit of any interpretation. There can hardly ever be a question of clear wording, which would make superfluous any further attempts of interpretation, all the more since the Treaty is authentic in several official languages (Article 248 of the EEC Treaty)."[17]

(11) Having set aside the literal interpretation, the Court went on "in order to define its terms with precision" to interpret Article 37 "in the light of its context and its purpose within the system" of the Euratom Treaty. Thus, the Court did not refer to the intentions which Member States had when Article 37 was drafted. It is rare that the Court uses the history of a rule as a means for interpretation and even then only in support of other arguments.[18] In the same way, the Court did not refer to the function which a specific rule, at the time it was drafted, was intended to have.

(12) The Court's reference to the "context and purpose" of Article 37 refers to the systematic and teleological interpretation of the Article. The systematic

---

[17] M. Zuleeg, commenting on Art. 1 EEC, n. 30, in H. v. d. Groeben, J. Thiesing, C. D. Ehlermann, *Kommentar zum EWG-Vertrag* (4th edition) Baden-Baden, 1991.

[18] See, *e.g.* Case 81/72, *Commission* v. *Council* [1973] E.C.R. 575, [1973] C.M.L.R. 639.

interpretation places the individual rule into the general context of the Treaty or—in the case of secondary legislation—of the legal instrument and tries to interpret all rules against a coherent background and taking the legal order set up by Community law as a coherent system.

The teleological interpretation starts from the wording of a rule and tries to find out its meaning, its sense and its purpose within the Community legal order, taking into consideration the interests of Community institutions and Member States.

(13) In Case 187/87, the Court began by addressing the systematic interpretation. It found that Article 37 has a more general preventive effect, whereas Article 38 is applicable where a risk of contamination is imminent or even where contamination has already occurred; Article 38 is thus rather a rule for exceptional cases.

There seems to be little more said by the Court on the systematic interpretation of Article 37. In particular, the Court did not take up the argument of the French government, that Article 34 of the Euratom Treaty which states that a Member State shall *first* obtain the opinion of the Commission when particularly dangerous experiments are to take place in its territories. An *argumentum a contrario* could not too easily have been rejected.

(14) All the other arguments seem to be part of the teleological interpretation, though the decision does not sharply distinguish between these two lines. The Court's reasoning on the purpose of Article 37 was as follows:

  (a) the Commission has a unique overview of developments in the nuclear power industry throughout the Community;

  (b) thus its guidance under Article 37 is of very great importance to Member States;

  (c) the preventive purpose of Article 37 suggests that the Commission's opinion must be capable of being examined at a time where suggestions can still be taken into account;

  (d) if the opinion is given after the authorisation to discharge has been granted, it is more difficult to take into consideration in particular an unfavourable opinion; also authorisations may be difficult to withdraw once they have been granted;

  (e) therefore the Commission's opinion only has a real chance of being examined in detail and effectively influencing the Member State where it is issued *before* a decision to authorise the disposal of waste is taken.

(15) The Court concluded its reasoning by taking up the conclusions of the Advocate General and arguing that only with such an interpretation can Article 37 achieve its purpose. "It is to an interpretation to that effect, which is such as to ensure that the provision retains its effectiveness, that preference

must be given". This last statement refers to the *effet-utile* doctrine which the Court has occasionally applied.[19] In simplified terms, this doctrine states that a legal rule must be interpreted in a way which ensures its "effet utile", *i.e.* its effectiveness in the general context of Community law. Weighing the interests in an early communication of general data for the Commission, for the Community, the Member States, but also for third parties such as the applicants before the Tribunal administratif de Strasbourg, the Court found itself in favour of an interpretation which ensures the best protection of health, safety and the environment.

(16) The story of Cattenom does not end here. The Court's decision had a follow-up which is described below as regards the legal proceedings in France, the development of Cattenom and developments at Community level.

The preliminary ruling of the European Court went back to the Tribunal administratif de Strasbourg. However, the decision of the Tribunal of June 11, 1987 by which it had declared void under French law part of the authorisations of February 21, 1986 and had suspended further proceedings until the European Court had given its preliminary ruling, were tackled by the French government before the Conseil d'Etat. The judgment of the Conseil d'Etat of June 30, 1986 declared that French law had not been broken as regards the granting of building permits between 1979 and 1984.[20] Since this had been the grounds on which the Tribunal administratif de Strasbourg had based its judgment as regards French law and the authorisations of February 21, 1986, that decision was reversed. As regards European law, the Conseil d'Etat accepted the interpretation of the European Court on Article 37 and stated that the French decision of February 21, 1986 was *ultra vires* (*excés de pouvoir*), and therefore not valid.

(17) The nuclear power station of Cattenom was not too severely affected by all this. Indeed, the French government replaced the Decision of February 21, 1986 to authorise radioactive discharges into the environment by Decisions of October 21, 1988 and August 4, 1989.[21] Since it was aware at that time of the Commission's opinion under Article 37, no Community rule could be invoked. In February 1990, Cattenom started to work.

(18) At Community level, the Commission replaced its recommendation of 1982 with Recommendation 91/4/Euratom, where it referred expressly to the judgment in Case 187/87 and where it followed the interpretation of Article 37 given by the Court.[22]

On July 3, 1988 Directive 85/337[23] on the environmental impact of certain

---

[19] See for reference the cases quoted by the Court, in para. 19 of its decision, at p. 58 above.
[20] Conseil d'Etat, Judgment of June 30, 1989, (1990) *Revue Juridique de l'Environnement* 107 with note Colson; also (1989) *Revue française de droit administratif* 857 with note Dubouis.
[21] See Colson, n.20 above, p. 112.
[22] [1991] O.J. L6/16.
[23] [1985] O.J. L175/40.

public or private projects entered into force. Under this directive, nuclear power-stations must now undergo an environmental impact assessment before the authorisation "to proceed with the project" is given. The directive requests the consultation of the public concerned as well as the possibility for authorities which are likely to be concerned by the project by reason of their specific environmental responsibilities to express their opinion. Where a project is likely to have significant effects on the environment in another Member State, that other Member State shall receive appropriate information. "Such information shall serve as a basis for any consultations necessary in the framework of the bilateral relations between two Member States on a reciprocal and equivalent basis". At present, there is a dispute between the Commission and some Member States as to whether the requirements of consulting the public concerned and the information of other Member States are cumulative or alternative in border projects such as Cattenom.

This leads to the question whether Directive 85/337 would have led to different decisions as regards Cattenom, had it already been in existence 10 years ago. This question cannot be answered in detail. However, it should be kept in mind that Directive 85/337 only requests an environmental impact assessment to be made. It does not request Member States to abstain from carrying out a project where the environmental impact assessment reveals serious negative effects of the project on the environment. It is more than likely, therefore, that Cattenom would have been completed anyway.

Part 2

Community Law and National Law

5. WASTE DISPOSAL IN AN INTERNAL MARKET

Judgment of the Court of July 9, 1992
in Case C–2/90

E.C. Commission v. *Belgium*

[1992] I E.C.R. 4431, [1993] 1 C.M.L.R. 365

FACTS AND PROCEDURE[1]

In 1983, the regional government of Wallonia, Belgium, adopted a decree by which it prohibited the discharge or dumping of waste coming from another State or from another Belgian region than Wallonia; this decree was based on a Belgian law of 1976. In 1987, an almost identical decree was adopted, based this time on a Wallonian decree of July 5, 1985, but providing for the same prohibition to discharge or dump wastes in Wallonia. On request of a foreign state, exceptions may be granted from this general prohibition. They must, however, be limited in time and justified by serious and exceptional circumstances.

The Commission was of the opinion that these provisions were contrary to the requirements of Directives 75/442 on waste,[2] Directive 84/631 on the supervision and control within the Community of the transfrontier shipment of hazardous waste,[3] as well as to Articles 30 and 36 of the EEC Treaty. On February 29, 1988, the Commission sent a letter of formal notice to the Belgian Government under Article 169 of the EEC Treaty; on October 17, 1988 it sent a reasoned opinion. In both cases the Belgian Government did not answer.

The application to the Court was registered on January 3, 1990. The Commission and the Belgian Government presented observations. Oral hearings took place on November 28, 1990, July 4, 1991 and January 28, 1992. The Advocate General gave his opinions on January 10, 1991, September 19, 1991 and January 29, 1992.

JUDGMENT[4]

(1) By application received by the Court Registry on 3 January 1990 the E.C. Commission brought an action pursuant to Article 169 EEC for a declaration that, by prohibiting the storage, tipping or dumping and the procuring of the storage, tipping or dumping in the Region of Wallonia of waste from another Member State or a region other than Wallonia, Belgium has failed to fulfil its obligations under Council Directive 75/442 on waste,[5] Council Directive 84/361 on the

---

[1] Summary by the author.
[2] [1975] O.J. L194/47.
[3] [1984] O.J. L326/31.
[4] Publisher's translation.
[5] [1975] O.J. L194/39.

supervision and control within the European Community of the transfrontier shipment of hazardous waste[6] and Articles 30 and 36 EEC.

(2) It appears from the file that the basic instrument concerning the management of waste in the Region of Wallonia is the Decree of the Walloon Regional Council of 5 July 1985 on waste,[7] which aims to prevent waste from accumulating, to encourage recycling and the recovery of energy and materials and to organise the disposal of waste (Article 1).

(3) Pursuant to Article 19(6) of the same decree, empowering the Walloon Regional Executive to lay down special rules governing the use of supervised tips, depots and installations for processing waste from foreign States and other regions of Belgium, the Executive in question adopted the Decree of 19 March 1987 concerning the disposal of certain waste products in the Region of Wallonia.[8]

(4) Under Article 1 of that decree, as amended by the Decrees of 9 and 23 July 1987,

It shall be prohibited to store, tip or dump and to procure the storage, tipping or dumping of waste from a foreign State in depots, stores and tips subject to authorisation, ... with the exception of depots annexed to an installation for the destruction, neutralisation and disposal of toxic waste. Operators of the establishments referred to by paragraph 1 shall be prohibited from authorising or tolerating the tipping or dumping of waste from a foreign State in the establishments operated by them.

(5) Article 2 of the same decree provides that exceptions to Article 1 may be allowed on application by a foreign public authority. However, an exception may be allowed for a limited period and must be justified by serious and exceptional circumstances.

(6) Under Article 3, the prohibition laid down by Article 1 also applies to waste from a region of Belgium other than Wallonia. Exceptions may be allowed pursuant to agreements between Wallonia and other regions of Belgium.

(7) Article 5 of the decree is worded as follows:

Waste which is not produced in the Region of Wallonia shall be deemed to be from a foreign state or a region other than Wallonia.
If the waste is the result of a process involving two or more States or regions, it originates from the State or region where the last substantial, economically justified conversion took place in an enterprise equipped for that purpose. ...

(8) The Commission took the view that these Belgian provisions are contrary to the Community rules in so far as they prohibit the tipping in Wallonia of waste from other Member States and in so far as, by the combined effect of the abovementioned Articles 3 and 5 of the Decree of 19 March 1987, they prohibit the

[6] [1984] O.J. L326/31.
[7] *Moniteur Belge*, December 14, 1985.
[8] [1987] *Moniteur Belge* 4671.

disposal in Wallonia of waste from other Member States which has undergone substantial, economically justified conversion in another region of Belgium. The Commission therefore initiated against Belgium the procedure provided for by Article 169 EEC.

(9) Reference is made to the Report for the Hearing for a fuller account of the facts of the case, the pleas in law and arguments of the parties, which are mentioned or discussed hereinafter only in so far as is necessary for the reasoning of the Court.

(10) The Commission contends that the Belgian provisions are contrary, firstly, to the abovementioned Directives 75/442 and 84/631 and, secondly, Articles 30 and 36 EEC.

Directive 75/442

(11) The Commission contends that none of the provisions of Directive 75/442, which concerns waste, authorises a general prohibition of the kind contained in the Belgian measures. It adds that such a prohibition is contrary to the aims of the directive and the general structure of its provisions, which seek to ensure the free movement of waste under conditions which are not harmful to human health or the environment.

(12) It should be observed that Directive 75/442 sets out certain principles and contains general provisions concerning the disposal of waste.

(13) Thus it requires the Member States to take appropriate measures to encourage the prevention, recycling and processing of waste, and likewise the measures necessary to ensure that it is disposed of without endangering human health or harming the environment. The Member States are also to establish or designate the competent authorities to be responsible for the planning, organisation, authorisation and supervision of waste disposal operations, while enterprises transporting, collecting, storing, tipping or treating their own waste or that of third parties must obtain an authorisation for that purpose or are to be subject to supervision by the competent authorities.

(14) It follows from what has been said that there is no specific reference, either in the general framework laid down by the directive in question or in any of its provisions, to trade in waste between Member States, nor is there an express prohibition on adopting measures such as those laid down by the contested provisions. Therefore, it must be concluded that the violation of Directive 75/442 alleged by the Commission has not been established.

(15) Secondly, it should be observed that the contested provisions apply to waste in general, without distinguishing between hazardous and non-hazardous waste. However, as the category of hazardous waste is specifically regulated in Community law by the abovementioned Directive 84/631, it is necessary first to examine the arrangements set up by this directive.

Directive 84/631

(16) Directive 84/631 as amended by Council Directive 86/279[9] and adapted to technical progress by Commission Directive 87/112,[10] forms part, according to its first recital, of the programmes of Community action aiming to control the disposal of hazardous waste. The second recital points out that the Member States are required to take the necessary measures to dispose of toxic and hazardous waste without endangering human health or harming the environment. The third recital indicates that transfers of waste may be necessary between Member States in order to dispose of it under the best possible conditions, while the seventh recital points out the need for supervision and control of hazardous waste from the time it is formed until it is processed or disposed of under safe conditions.

(17) In the framework of these aims, with regard to the disposal of the waste in question the directive lays down conditions for ensuring that disposal does not endanger human health or harm the environment and provides for a system of authorisation for the storage, processing or dumping of such waste, and for communication to the Commission by the Member States of certain information concerning the installations, establishments or enterprises holding such authorisation.

(18) With regard to the transfrontier shipment of hazardous waste for the purpose of disposal, the directive provides that a holder of waste who intends to ship it from one Member State to another or to have it routed through one or more Member States must notify the competent authorities of the Member States concerned by means of a uniform consignment note containing information on the origin and composition of the waste, the proposed arrangements regarding the itinerary and insurance, and measures to be taken to ensure safety in transport (Article 3).

(19) A transfrontier shipment cannot be carried out before the competent authorities of the Member States concerned have acknowledged receipt of the notification. They may raise objections which must be substantiated on the basis of laws and regulations relating to environmental protection, safety and public policy or health protection which are in accordance with the directive and other Community instruments or relevant international conventions concluded by the Member State concerned (Article 4).

(20) It is clear from the foregoing that Directive 84/631 has set up a complete system relating to transfrontier shipments of hazardous waste for disposal in specified establishments and that it is based on the obligation of the holder of the waste to give prior detailed notification. The national authorities concerned have the option of raising objections and therefore prohibiting a particular transfer of dangerous waste (as opposed to transfers of such waste in general) in order to overcome problems relating to the protection of human health and the environment on the one hand and safety and public policy on the other. Consequently the system does not imply that the Member States have power to prohibit such transfers generally.

(21) It must therefore be concluded that in so far as the contested Belgian provisions

---

[9] [1986] O.J. L181/13.
[10] [1986] O.J. L48/31.

preclude the application of the procedure laid down by the directive and introduce an absolute ban on the importation of dangerous waste into Wallonia, even though they provide that certain exceptions may be allowed by the authorities concerned, those provisions are incompatible with the directive in question.

Articles 30 and 36 EEC

(22) It remains to examine the Belgian measures in question, in so far as they relate to waste which is outside the ambit of Directive 84/361, in the light of Articles 30 and 36 EEC.

(23) It is common ground that waste which can be recycled and re-used, after processing if necessary, has an intrinsic commercial value and therefore amounts to goods for the purpose of applying the Treaty, and that such waste is therefore within the ambit of Article 30 *et seq.*

(24) The question whether waste which is non-recyclable and cannot be re-used is also covered by Article 30 *et seq.* was argued before the Court.

(25) On this point the Belgian Government contended that such waste cannot be considered as goods within the meaning of Article 30 *et seq.* EEC because it has no intrinsic commercial value and could not therefore be sold. The Belgian Government adds that the operations for disposing of such waste are covered by the provisions of the Treaty relating to the freedom to supply services.

(26) In reply to these arguments it is sufficient to point out that objects which are transported over a frontier in order to give rise to commercial transactions are subject to Article 30, irrespective of the nature of those transactions.

(27) Secondly, it should be observed that the distinction between recyclable and non-recyclable waste raises a serious difficulty of practical application with regard to frontier controls, as was explained to the Court. Such a distinction is based on uncertain factors which may change in the course of time, depending on technical progress. Moreover, whether any particular waste is recyclable or not also depends on the cost of recycling and therefore the profitability of the proposed further use, so that a decision in this connection is necessarily subjective and depends on variable factors.

(28) Therefore it must be concluded that waste, whether recyclable or not, should be regarded as a product the movement of which must not in principle, pursuant to Article 30 EEC, be impeded.

(29) The defendant State contends that the obstacles to the movement of waste are justified on the grounds, firstly, that the contested provisions conform to mandatory requirements relating to the protection of the environment and the safeguarding of human health, which overrides the objective of the free movement of goods and, secondly, that those provisions are an exceptional, temporary measure to safeguard Wallonia from an influx of waste from neighbouring countries.

(30) So far as the environment is concerned, it should be observed that waste has a

special characteristic. The accumulation of waste, even before it becomes a health hazard, constitutes a threat to the environment because of the limited capacity of each region or locality for receiving it.

(31) In the present case the Belgian Government contended, and the Commission accepted, that an abnormal, massive influx of waste had taken place from other regions for the purpose of dumping in Wallonia, thus constituting a genuine threat to the environment in view of the Region's limited capacity.

(32) It follows that the argument that the contested measures are justified by mandatory requirements relating to the protection of the environment must be regarded as well-founded.

(33) However, the Commission contends that these mandatory requirements cannot be invoked in the present case because the measures in question discriminate against waste from other Member States which is no more harmful than the waste produced in Wallonia.

(34) It is true that the mandatory requirements are to be taken into account only with regard to measures which apply to national and imported products without distinction: see Case C–1/90, *Aragonesa de Publicidad*.[11] However, in order to determine whether the obstacle in question is discriminatory, the particular type of waste must be taken into account. The principle that environmental damage should as a priority be rectified at source—a principle laid down by Article 130r(2) EEC for action by the Community relating to the environment—means that it is for each region, commune or other local entity to take appropriate measures to receive, process and dispose of its own waste. Consequently waste should be disposed of as close as possible to the place where it is produced in order to keep the transport of waste to the minimum practicable.

(35) Furthermore this principle accords with the principles of self-sufficiency and proximity set out in the Basle Convention of 22 March 1989 on the control of transborder movements of hazardous waste and the disposal thereof, to which the Community is a party.[12]

(36) It follows that, having regard to the differences between waste produced in one place and that in another and its connection with the place where it is produced, the contested measures cannot be considered to be discriminatory.

(37) Therefore it must be concluded that the application should be dismissed in so far as it relates to waste which is not covered by Directive 84/631.

Costs

(38) Pursuant to Article 69(2) of the Rules of Procedure, the unsuccessful party is to be ordered to pay the costs if they have been applied for in the successful party's pleadings. As Belgium is only partly unsuccessful, each party should be ordered to bear its own costs pursuant to Article 69(3).

---

[11] Not yet reported.
[12] Kiss/Shelton, *International Environmental Law* (Kluwer, Deventer-Boston. 1991), p. 546.

On those grounds, THE COURT hereby:

(1) Declares that, by introducing an absolute prohibition on the storage, tipping or dumping in the Region of Wallonia of hazardous waste from another Member State, and by thus precluding the application of the procedure laid down by Council Directive 84/631 on the supervision and control within the Community of the transfrontier shipment of hazardous waste, Belgium has failed to fulfil its obligations under that directive.

(2) Dismissed the application in all other respects.

(3) Orders each party to pay its own costs.

COMMENTARY

(1) The fact that the Court thought it necessary to have three oral hearings instead of one clearly shows the importance of this decision.

It is the second decision where the Court had to deal in detail with the problem of a Member State adopting a measure which, in the eyes of the Commission, was not compatible with the requirements of Articles 30 and 36 of the EEC Treaty.[13] Also in this case, the Court, in substance, argued in favour of environmental requirements rather than of requirements on the free circulation of goods.

Apart from this, the judgment contains important orientations as regards national and Community requirements on waste. Since two further cases with potentially important consequences are pending before the Court,[14] it can be expected that Community-wide integrated waste management will be set up in some future, whatever the final borderline between national rules and Community rules will be.

(2) Before addressing the questions of Articles 30 and 36, the Court had to deal with two directives which the Commission claimed were applicable.

As regards Directive 75/442 on waste, the Court was rather short. It analysed the content of the Directive, concluded that it is of general nature and that none of its provisions specifically addressed exchanges between Mem-

---

[13] The first one was Case 302/86, *Commission* v. *Denmark* [1988] E.C.R. 4607, [1989] 1 C.M.L.R. 619; see p. 91 below.

[14] Case C–155/91, *Commission* v. *Council* [1991] O.J. C 189/12 and Case C–86/92, *Commission* v. *Council* [1992] O.J. C97/7. In Case C–155/91 the Court gave, on March 17, 1993, a judgment, stating that Art. 130s was the proper legal basis; see p. 291.

ber States.[15] Neither does Directive 75/442 prohibit national import restrictions. Thus, the Court stated that Directive 75/442 was not breached.

Adopted in 1975, Directive 75/442 was the third directive on environmental matters adopted at Community level under the First Environmental Action Programme of the EEC.[16] Since the EEC Treaty did not contain any express competence for environmental protection measures at the time, Articles 130r to 130t and 100a having only been introduced into the Treaty in 1987, the EEC based its directives on environmental issues on Articles 100 or 235 or both provisions of the Treaty, a practice which the Court has accepted.[17]

Directive 75/442 is based on Articles 100[18] and 235. The first and third recital state in this regard:

"Whereas any disparity between the provisions on waste disposal already applicable or in preparation in the various Member States may create unequal conditions of competition and thus directly affect the functioning of the common market; whereas it is therefore necessary to approximate laws in this field, as provided for in Article 100 of the Treaty;

Whereas the programme of action of the European Communities on the environment stresses the need for Community actions including the harmonisation of legislation;"

(3) These recitals clearly show that the general purpose of Directive 75/442 was also to avoid distortions of competition and to attain harmonisation of legislation. These general provisions, though, were obviously not enough for the Court to accept the Commission's point of view that Directive 75/442 was a directive on the approximation of legislation and thus prohibited national import bans. The Court came to its conclusion by examining the individual *articles* of Directive 75/442; and there is no provision in these articles which would take up the first or the fifth recital and specify Member States' obligations as to the free circulation of wastes. Indeed, most if not all product-related directives contain a provision stipulating:

"Member States may not, on grounds (regulated in this Directive) prohibit, restrict or impede the placing on the market of products which comply with the requirements of this Directive and the Annexes thereto."

---

[15] It should be noted that in Case C–33/90, *Commission* v. *Italy.* [1991] I E.C.R. 5987, [1992] 2 C.M.L.R. 353, the Court had argued that Directive 75/442 did also aim at the free circulation of wastes, see para. 1 of the judgment, p. 388 below.

[16] The first was Directive 75/439 on waste oils: [1975] O.J. L194/23, the second was Directive 75/440 on the quality of surface waters, [1975] O.J. L194/26.

[17] Case 91/79, *Commission* v. *Italy.* [1980] E.C.R. 1099 (as regards Art. 100).

[18] **Article 100** EEC: "The Council shall, acting unanimously on a proposal from the Commission, issue directives for the approximation of such provisions laid down by law, regulation or administrative action in Member States as directly affect the establishment or functioning of the common market ... "

Such a provision does not exist in Directive 75/442. It is true that most "environmental" directives adopted before 1987[19] contained a provision along the following lines:[20]

"This Directive shall not restrict the right of the Member States to apply or to adopt administrative or legislative measures ensuring greater protection of man and the environment than that which derives from the provisions of this Directive."

(4) Nevertheless, the Court was, in my opinion, right to consider the wording of Directive 75/442 rather than the recitals. Where the recitals of a Directive are not specifically reflected in the text, it will be possible only in very exceptional circumstances to derive, in the absence of a specific provision, an interpretation of the Directive only from its recitals.

The Court could, in order to support its findings have referred to the judgment of its Fifth Chamber in Case 380/87.[21] In that case, the Court was asked by a national court, whether the provisions of Directive 75/442 gave individuals the right to sell or use certain products. The Court answered this question in the negative[22] and thus indirectly confirmed that Directive 75/442 dealt with questions of waste disposal rather than with approximation of legislation.

(5) As regards Directive 84/631, the Court examined its recitals[23] and then, in detail, the system set up by the different provisions of the directive, in particular by Articles 3 and 4. The Court concluded that Directive 84/631 has set up a coherent system. Since the possibilities for Member States to object to a transfer of dangerous wastes are expressly enumerated in Articles 4(3)[24] and 4(4),[25] the Court concluded that there was no room for any national legislation to provide for a *general* ban on waste imports from other Member States. Thus, the Court found that the Wallonian decree, which provided for such a general ban on waste imports, was incompatible with the provisions of Direct-

---

[19] More precisely, before the entering into effect of the Single European Act, which introduced Art. 100a and 130s.

[20] Example from Dir. 82/501 on the major-accident hazards of certain industrial activities, Art. 17: [1982] O.J. L230/1.

[21] *Enichem*: [1989] E.C.R. 2491, [1991] 1 C.M.L.R. 313, see p. 131 below.

[22] See p. 134 below: "Directive 75/442, properly construed, does not give individuals the right to sell or use plastic bags and other non-biodegradable containers."

[23] The difference with the examination of Directive 75/442, where the recitals are not examined, is obvious.

[24] "Objections must be substantiated on the basis of laws and regulations relating to environmental protection, public policy and public security or health protection which are in conformity with this Directive, with other Community instruments or with international conventions on this subject concluded by the Member State concerned prior to notification of this Directive."

[25] "Not later than 20 days after receipt of the notification, the competent authorities of the Member State of dispatch may raise objections on the grounds that the shipment of waste adversely affects the implementation of plans drawn up pursuant to Article 12 of Directive 78/319/EEC or Article 6 of Directive 76/403/EEC . . . "

ive 84/631, and the possibility of granting an exception did not, in the opinion of the Court, change the nature of this total ban.

Directive 84/631 is based, as Directive 75/442, on Articles 100 and 235 of the EEC Treaty. Like Directive 75/442 it has two recitals which refer to the approximation of legislation and the free circulation of wastes, recitals 4 and 6.[26] However, in contrast to Directive 75/442, Directive 84/631 indicates in the different provisions themselves and in particular in Articles 3 and 4, the conditions for a transfrontier shipment of hazardous waste, and the limits in time and in substance as regards the possibility to object to such a transfer. There is thus nothing to oppose the Court's finding that Directive 84/631 has set up a complete system of rules on the transfrontier shipment of hazardous waste and that Member States are not allowed to interfere with this system by adopting different rules at national or regional level.

(6) Belgium was therefore by virtue of Directive 84/631 not entitled to provide for a total ban on imports of dangerous waste. Community secondary legislation contained no rules regarding ordinary waste. Therefore, the Court had to examine whether the Wallonian import ban was compatible with Articles 30 and 36 of the EEC Treaty, and the main importance of the judgment lies in these parts.

(7) The first question which the Court had to answer was whether waste came under the provisions of Articles 30 and 36 at all. The Belgian Government had argued before the Court that waste had a "negative" value: it is the seller who pays in order to get rid of it, whereas normally, in the area of products, it is the buyer who pays the purchase price.

In Case 7/68 the Court had already given an interpretation of goods.[27] In that case, the Italian Government argued that antique goods did not come under the provisions of the Treaty. The Court rejected that argument stating that such goods had an economic value and could thus be the object of commercial transaction. In the present case the Court rejected the Belgian defence which was based on the "economic-value" argument of Case 7/68 by stating that objects which are the subject-matter of commercial transactions come under Article 30 of the EEC Treaty, independent of the nature of such transactions.

This statement hopefully brought to an end a long controversy on the question whether waste with a "negative" economic value should be treated as goods, or whether the transaction should rather be seen as a service.[28] The

---

[26] As regards recital 4, it is identical to the first recital of Directive 75/442, see p. 78 above. Recital 6 reads: "Whereas an efficient and coherent system of supervision and control of the transfrontier shipment of hazardous waste should neither create barriers to inter-Community trade nor affect competition."

[27] 7/68, *Commission* v. *Italy*: [1968] E.C.R. 423, [1969] C.M.L.R. 1: "products which can be valued in money and which are capable, as such, of forming the subject of commercial transactions."

[28] The practical consequences might not, after all, be very different, since Art. 56 EEC would lead to similar results as Arts. 30 to 36.

opinion of Advocate General Jacobs of September 19, 1991 gave, in this regard, arguments which are convincing.[29]

(8) Indeed, independent from the "positive" or "negative" value of waste, waste remains a corporeal object. The notion of "negative" value comes from economic theory and might explain economic phenomena, but it is incapable of solving the legal problems linked to waste issues, such as for instance the mixing of waste of a negative value with waste of a positive value.

The next question which the Court had to address was whether a differentiation had to be made, as regards the legal assessment between wastes which are recyclable and those which are not.[30] This question is closely linked to the precedent one, since it is precisely the argument that non-recyclable waste has no "positive" value which led several authors to the conclusion that Articles 30 and 36 were not applicable to such waste.

(9) The Court was clear and outspoken in its judgment: in its opinion, such a differentiation is based on uncertain elements which change with time and technical progress; the question whether waste is recyclable or not also depends on the costs of the recycling process which makes the differentiation between recyclable and non-recyclable waste subjective and dependent on instable factors.[31] The conclusion that such a differentiation could not be made as regards the application of Article 30 to 36, was in line with the careful reasoning of the Advocate General.[32] Indeed, the fact that waste has in some cases a "negative economic value" is of economic, but not legal, significance. The economic value of waste changes, depending on recycling conditions, the market for raw materials, political circumstances, disposal problems, etc.; consequently it cannot be decisive for the legal evaluation.[33]

(10) Again it may be hoped that the Court's decision brings to an end a long-lasting discussion on the question of differentiating between non-recyclable and recyclable wastes. For the legal assessment, it is submitted, wastes are goods, though of a particular nature.

Having thus cleared the way for the application of Articles 30 and 36 of the EEC Treaty, the Court had to decide which article it wished to apply. As it has been explained elsewhere in this book,[34] the Court sees the enumeration of grounds in Article 36 which could justify national measures that restrict the

---

[29] Advocate General Jacobs, opinion of September 19, 1991. The Advocate General (a) referred to Case 7/68 which does not support the theory of a "service"; (b) mentioned that wastes are the subject of commercial transactions; and (c) pointed out that the notion of "negative value" is an economic notion.

[30] Paras. 27 and 28.

[31] *Ibid.* para. 27.

[32] Advocate General Jacobs, n. 20 above, paras. 14 to 17.

[33] See L. Krämer, *EEC Treaty and Environmental Protection* (London, 1990) p. 44.

[34] See above.

free circulation of goods, as exhaustive and therefore not capable of being prolonged.[35] The Belgian Government had also argued that the Wallonian ban on imports was justified on grounds of public policy.[36] The Court did not even discuss this provision of Article 36. Indeed, this general notion has been restricted by the jurisprudence of the Court to very fundamental political and social principles of a society. An import ban on goods, be they wastes, can obviously not be justified by reasons of public policy.

(11) The only justification which could be applicable in the present case was the protection of health and life of humans. And it was this argument, which the Belgian Government had raised, *inter alia*, in order to justify the Wallonian decree. It argued that the measure was a temporary safeguard taken with a view to master an exceptional situation.[37] The decree had already in large parts lost its *raison d'être* and would soon be replaced by a taxation system; the import restriction measures might be abolished by the end of 1990.[38]

The Court did not discuss in terms of "risk to health". It argued that before there could be a risk to the health of persons, wastes could become a risk to the environment, because they are of a specific nature which is revealed in particular when they accumulate, since regions or localities only have limited capacity to accept them.[39]

(12) This reasoning showed that the Court did not discuss the provision on "protection of health and life of humans" of Article 36, but rather the (unwritten) provision on "protection of the environment" of Article 30. Indeed, as explained elsewhere,[40] there is, since Case 120/78,[41] consistent ruling of the Court that national measures which create obstacles to the free movement of goods must be accepted under Article 30 insofar as such rules are necessary to satisfy mandatory requirements recognised by Community law; such national measures must be neither discriminatory nor disproportionate. The Court recognised in Case 302/86[42] that the protection of the environment is such a mandatory requirement recognised by Community law.[43] In the present case it did not expressly repeat its reasoning from previous cases, but took it as established that the need to protect the environment may restrict the free circulation of goods within the Community.

(13) The Court saw the risk for the environment in the Wallonian region in the

---

[35] See Krämer, *op. cit.*, p. 34.
[36] 2/90, Report for the Hearing, para. 40.
[37] Para. 29; Report for the Hearing, paras. 31, 32, 40.
[38] Report for the Hearing, para. 31.
[39] Para. 30.
[40] See below.
[41] 120/78, *Rewe* ("*Cassis de Dijon*"): [1979] E.C.R. 649, [1979] 3 C.M.L.R. 494.
[42] 302/86, see p. 91 below.
[43] *Ibid.* para. 8.

fact that there was an unforeseen and massive import of wastes into Wallonia which presented a real danger to the environment, since Wallonia had only limited capacity to dispose of these wastes. These arguments by the Belgian Government which had not, in the Court's opinion, been contradicted by the Commission, justified the import ban.

The Report for the Hearing does not mention that the Commission had contradicted the Belgian argument of an unforeseen and massive import of wastes. However, the Commission did contest the safeguard character and temporary nature of the decree of 1987, arguing that the import ban had been adopted already in 1983.[44] This argument ran contrary at least in substance to that put forward by Belgium; thus, the Court went rather far when it argued that there was "no contradiction" and claimed that the Wallonian import ban was taken in order to protect the environment against a massive and unforeseen import. Since between May 17, 1983 when the Wallonian import ban was first introduced by a decree, and July 9, 1992, the day of the Court's judgment, more than nine years had elapsed; it might not have been totally superfluous to consider when such safeguard measures would be repealed, all the more since Belgium had argued that they might be repealed by the end of 1990.[45] It is far-fetched to justify the maintenance of temporary safeguard measures on a massive and unforeseen import of wastes which took place nine years ago!

The very short reasoning of the Court which is mainly based on the fact that the Commission had not contested the facts described by Belgium, does not really allow to fully understand the underlying thinking of the Court.

(14) However, in my opinion the real problem is to be found elsewhere. Indeed, the Commission argued before the Court that Belgium could not invoke the protection of the environment in order to restrict the free circulation of waste under Article 30, because in order to be invoked the "mandatory requirements" have to be indistinctly applicable to wastes of national (regional) or foreign origin. Indeed, wastes were a risk to the environment whether they were generated in Wallonia or abroad. The Wallonian decree, the Commission concluded, discriminated against waste which was generated outside of Wallonia.[46]

The Court, however, was of the opinion that the Wallonian measure was not discriminatory. It argued that Article 130r, paragraph 2 of the EEC Treaty ("Action by the Community relating to the environment shall be based on the principles ... that environmental damage should as a priority be rectified at source ... ") implies, that wastes must be eliminated as closely as possible to the place where they are generated in order to limit the distance that they have to be transported as much as possible. The Court found similar principles in the principles of self-sufficiency and proximity of the Basle Conven-

---

[44] Report for the Hearing, para. 42.
[45] *Ibid.* para. 31.
[46] Para. 33.

tion on the control of transfrontier movements of dangerous wastes, which had been signed and ratified by the Community.[47]

(15) This reasoning practically leads to the conclusion that the Court has set up a rule of law according to which "waste must be eliminated as closely as possible to the place where it is generated." The Court derived this rule from Article 130r, paragraph 2 of the Treaty, but I have doubts whether it is possible to transform this loose *principle* of law into a *rule* of law. The Court did not explain either how the principle of Article 130r, paragraph 2, which clearly refers to actions by the Community, could be used to back a national measure. The Court did not even request, as the Advocate General did, that a national measure also applied the rule of law inside its own (national or regional or local) territory.[48] Furthermore, some products may be of a particular nature and, purely because of their accumulation in a region, present a risk to the environment; nuclear matters might come into this category, but also specific chemicals, genetically modified organisms and others. The principle of Article 130r, which was invoked by the Court, could easily be applied to products as well. Thus, there seems to be some political intention underlying the Court's decision. The Court's position can be summarised as follows: national or regional measures which ban the import of waste from other Member States are justified under Article 30 provided they contain the possibility of an exemption from the prohibition by way of derogations.

(16) The Court left only one way open to different results, though this way is, in my opinion, very small and might not exist at all: the Court has expressly based its judgment on the fact that the Wallonian measure was taken in order to face a massive and unforeseen import of waste from other Member States.[49] The Court might thus come to a different conclusion where such an "emergency" situation does not exist. As explained above,[50] however, this event is unlikely.

It is not clear how a rule which allows the adoption of legislation according to which waste must be eliminated as closely as possible to the place where it has been generated and which accordingly bans the (national or regional) import of waste, can be enforced. Since January 1, 1993, the internal market has been completed. National frontiers are no longer economic frontiers and border controls are prohibited. How could a national or regional import ban function in such circumstances?

(17) The "principle of proximity" mentioned in the Court's judgment as being part of the Basle Convention on the transfer of dangerous waste is hardly a

---

[47] Basle Convention on the Control of Transboundary Movements of Hazardous Wastes and their Disposal of March 22, 1989. The Convention was ratified by Council decision of February 12, 1993: [1993] O.J. L39/1.

[48] Advocate General Jacobs, see n. 20 above, para. 24.

[49] Report for the Hearing, paras. 29 and 31.

[50] Para. 13.

principle of Community law. In Community texts it first appeared in the communication from the Commission on a Community Strategy for Work Management[51] where it is stated:[52]

"The Commission thinks that provision must be made to ensure that as far as possible waste is disposed of in the nearest suitable units, making use of the most appropriate technologies to guarantee a high level of protection for the environment and public health.

The implementation of such a principle clearly must not lead to a monopoly situation.

Here 'the nearest' does not necessarily, in every case, mean close-by. To achieve the best possible distribution of installations, account must be taken of requirements and capacities for treatment. The distribution of plants for the reception of domestic refuse, for example, cannot be the same as for installations for disposing of halorganic chemical waste.

There will thus be a real need to monitor waste at Community level ... "

(18) In May 1990 the Council adopted a resolution on waste policy,[53] which broadly welcomed the Commission's communication and expressed the opinion that measures to eliminate waste in the nearest waste elimination installations should be promoted, but that this principle should not, in view of Articles 30, 36 and 8a, lead to the closure of national frontiers.

In 1991, the Council adopted Directive 91/156 on waste[54] which provided, among others, for a Community network of disposal installations. Article 5 stipulates:

"This network must enable the Community as a whole to become self-sufficient in waste disposal and the Member States to move towards that aim individually, taking into account geographical circumstances or the need for specialised installations for certain types of waste. The network must also enable waste to be disposed of in one of the nearest appropriate installations, by means of the most appropriate methods and technologies in order to ensure a high level of protection for the environment and public health."

It should be mentioned again that the Commission has tackled this directive before the European Court, arguing that it should have been based on Article 100a of the EEC Treaty, the provision which aims at the establishment of uniform rules in order to achieve the internal market by 1993. One of the implicit questions is also whether a Directive, which is based on Article 100a, could

---

[51] Commission, A Community Strategy for Waste Management, SEC(89)934 final of September 18, 1989.
[52] *Ibid.* p. 23s.
[53] [1990] O.J. C122/2.
[54] [1991] O.J. L78/32.

allow Member States to "move towards self-sufficiency individually."In March 1993, the Court held that Article 130s was the appropriate legal basis.[55]

(19) The difficulty with the Basle Convention on the Control of Transboundary Movements of Hazardous Wastes and their Disposal, from the Community point of view, is that, like many other international conventions, it was drafted with (national sovereign) states in view. A phenomenon such as the EEC is not really the model which the drafters of that convention had in mind. Thus, whether "self-sufficiency" and "proximity" in the Convention, which the Court expressly mentions in its decision,[56] mean self-sufficiency for the Community or for the individual Member States, is not clear from the text of the Convention. It might be appropriate to mention that the convention is not (yet) part of Community law, since the EEC has not yet adhered to it. Furthermore, the Convention is on hazardous waste, whereas the Court discusses other wastes than dangerous wastes.[57]

As regards Community law and policy it seems clear from the Commission's strategy paper[58] that the Commission had in mind a system of integrated waste management at Community level. Directive 91/156—which the Council based on Article 130s, whereas the Commission suggested Article 100a as the legal basis—provides for self-sufficiency of the Community, but also allows Member States to "move towards that aim individually". This can only mean, in particular in conjunction with Article 130t of the EEC Treaty[59] that Member States may introduce import bans on waste if they wish.

The Court's judgment in this case seems to confirm that, and the judgment does not seem to prejudge the question whether waste legislation is to be based on Article 100a or 130s.

(20) In my opinion Community legislation does allow for the establishment of a comprehensive system of waste management for both dangerous and non-dangerous wastes which would provide, in principle, for the circulation of domestic waste, and only allow exceptions in specifically enumerated cases. Since wastes are corporeal objects, nor can any principle of subsidiarity be invoked against it. Indeed, creating an internal market without frontiers and allowing each local authority and/or region to ban the (local or regional) import of non-dangerous waste is not far from squaring the circle; in the absence of Community rules, such a solution under Article 30 might be justified, as the Court has stated. But I do not see that the EEC Treaty in general, or Article 130r, paragraph 2 in particular, would prevent the Community legisla-

---

[55] Case C–155/91, Commission v. Council judgment of March 17, 1993, not yet reported; see p. 291 below.
[56] Para. 35; the Basle Convention does not seem to use these words at all.
[57] Para. 22 from which it becomes clear that hazardous wastes are not discussed under Art. 30.
[58] See n. 42 above.
[59] This article allows Member States to maintain or introduce stricter protection measures than those which were fixed at Community level.

tor from setting up a better system. The interests of Member States would be safeguarded by virtue of Article 100a, paragraph 4 or 130t of the EEC Treaty.

(21) If this judgment is confirmed by future Community legislation and jurisdiction which provides for such local and regional bans, this would mean an internal market without frontiers where goods (wastes) may not, in principle, be brought to installations in another Member State or region. Will this lead to price competition among installations which would grant derogations against payments? How will such a system of regional/national or a Community—originating ban be enforced in practice? Would a grey market in transport of waste and disposal of waste be created?

The discussion on waste management inside an internal market is bound to remain of interest for the decade to come—to say the least.

6. FIXING THE LEVEL OF PROTECTION BY MEMBER STATES

Judgment of the Court of September 20, 1988
in Case 302/86

E.C. Commission supported by the United Kingdom v. *Denmark*

[1988] E.C.R. 4607, [1989] 1 C.M.L.R. 619

FACTS AND PROCEDURE[1]

In 1981 Denmark introduced legislation for containers for beer and soft drinks. These drinks were only allowed to be marketed in returnable containers. Returnable containers were to be approved by the Danish authorities before they were allowed to be used. The use of metal cans was prohibited.

In 1984 Denmark amended its legislation. It allowed non-approved containers to be used either in limits of 3,000 hectolitre per producer per year in order to test the market. However, in such a case a deposit-and-return-system had to be set up. The prohibition of metal cans was upheld.

The Commission started proceedings under Article 169 in 1982. In 1986 it brought the action before the Court. In May 1987, the United Kingdom was allowed to intervene on the side of the Commission. Written submissions were made by the Commission, the United Kingdom and Denmark. The hearing took place on March 15, 1988.

The Advocate General delivered his opinion on May 24, 1988.

JUDGMENT

(1) By an application lodged at the Court Registry on 1 December 1986, the Commission of the European Communities brought an action under Article 169 of the EEC Treaty for a declaration that by introducing and applying by Order No 397 of 2 July 1981 a system under which all containers for beer and soft drinks must be returnable, the Kingdom of Denmark had failed to fulfil its obligations under Article 30 of the EEC Treaty.

(2) The main feature of the system which the Commission challenges as incompatible with Community law is that manufacturers must market beer and soft drinks only in re-usable containers. The containers must be approved by the National Agency for the Protection of the Environment, which may refuse approval of new kinds of container, especially if it considers that a container is not technically suitable for a system for returning containers or that the return system envisaged does not ensure that a sufficient proportion of containers are actually re-used or if a container of equal capacity, which is both available and suitable for the same use, has already been approved.

(3) Order No 95 of 16 March 1984 amended the aforementioned rules in such a way

---

[1] Summary by the author.

that, provided that a deposit-and-return system is established, non-approved containers, except for any form of metal container, may be used for quantities not exceeding 3 000 hectolitres a year per producer and for drinks which are sold by foreign producers in order to test the market.

(4) By order of 8 May 1987 the United Kingdom was granted leave to intervene in the case in support of the Commission's conclusions.

(5) Reference is made to the Report for the Hearing for a fuller account of the facts of the case, the course of the procedure and the submissions and arguments of the parties, which are mentioned or discussed hereinafter only in so far as is necessary for the reasoning of the Court.

(6) The first point which must be made in resolving this dispute is that, according to an established body of case-law of the Court (judgment of 20 February 1979 in Case 120/78 *Rewe-Zentral AG* v. *Bundesmonopolverwaltung für Branntwein* [1979] ECR 649; judgment of 10 November 1982 in Case 261/81 *Walter Rau Lebensmittelwerke* v *De Smedt PvbA* [1982] ECR 3961), in the absence of common rules relating to the marketing of the products in question, obstacles to free movement within the Community resulting from disparities between the national laws must be accepted in so far as such rules, applicable to domestic and imported products without distinction, may be recognized as being necessary in order to satisfy mandatory requirements recognized by Community law. Such rules must also be proportionate to the aim in view. If a Member State has a choice between various measures for achieving the same aim, it should choose the means which least restricts the free movement of goods.

(7) In the present case the Danish Government contends that the mandatory collection system for containers of beer and soft drinks applied in Denmark is justified by a mandatory requirement related to the protection of the environment.

(8) The Court has already held in its judgment of 7 February 1985 in Case 240/83 *Procureur de la République* v *Association de défense des brûleurs d'huiles usagées* [1985] ECR 531 that the protection of the environment is 'one of the Community's essential objectives', which may as such justify certain limitations of the principle of the free movement of goods. That view is moreover confirmed by the Single European Act.

(9) In view of the foregoing, it must therefore be stated that the protection of the environment is a mandatory requirement which may limit the application of Article 30 of the Treaty.

(10) The Commission submits that the Danish rules are contrary to the principle of proportionality in so far as the aim of the protection of the environment may be achieved by means less restrictive of intra-Community trade.

(11) In that regard, it must be pointed out that in its aforementioned judgment of 7 February 1985 the Court stated that measures adopted to protect the environment must no 'go beyond the inevitable restrictions which are justified by the pursuit of the objective of environmental protection'.

(12) It is therefore necessary to examine whether all the restrictions which the contested rules impose on the free movement of goods are necessary to achieve the objectives pursued by those rules.

(13) First of all, as regards the obligation to establish a deposit-and-return system for empty containers, it must be observed that this requirement is an indispensable element of a system intended to ensure the re-use of containers and therefore appears necessary to achieve the aims pursued by the contested rules. That being so, the restrictions which it imposes on the free movement of goods cannot be regarded as disproportionate.

(14) Next, it is necessary to consider the requirement that producers and importers must use only containers approved by the National Agency for the Protection of the Environment.

(15) The Danish Government stated in the proceedings before the Court that the present deposit-and-return system would not work if the number of approved containers were to exceed 30 or so, since the retailers taking part in the system would not be prepared to accept too many types of bottles owing to the higher handling costs and the need for more storage space. For that reason the Agency has hitherto followed the practice of ensuring that fresh approvals are normally accompanied by the withdrawal of existing approvals.

(16) Even though there is some force in that argument, it must nevertheless be observed that under the system at present in force in Denmark the Danish authorities may refuse approval to a foreign producer even if he is prepared to ensure that returned containers are re-used.

(17) In those circumstances, a foreign producer who still wished to sell his products in Denmark would be obliged to manufacture or purchase containers of a type already approved, which would involve substantial additional costs for that producer and therefore make the importation of his products into Denmark very difficult.

(18) To overcome that obstacle the Danish Government altered its rules by the aforementioned Order No 95 of 16 March 1984, which allows a producer to market up to 3 000 hectolitres of beer and soft drinks a year in non-approved containers, provided that a deposit-and-return system is established.

(19) The provision in Order No 95 restricting the quantity of beer and soft drinks which may be marketed by a producer in non-approved containers to 3 000 hectolitres a year is challenged by the Commission on the ground that it is unnecessary to achieve the objectives pursued by the system.

(20) It is undoubtedly true that the existing system for returning approved containers ensures a maximum rate of re-use and therefore a very considerable degree of protection of the environment since empty containers can be returned to any retailer of beverages. Non-approved containers, on the other hand, can be returned only to the retailer who sold the beverages, since it is impossible to set up such a comprehensive system for those containers as well.

(21) Nevertheless, the system for returning non-approved containers is capable of protecting the environment and, as far as imports are concerned, affects only limited quantities of beverages compared with the quantity of beverages consumed in Denmark owing to the restrictive effect which the requirement that containers should be returnable has on imports. In those circumstances, a restriction of the quantity of products which may be marketed by importers is disproportionate to the objective pursued.

(22) It must therefore be held that by restricting, by Order No 95 of 16 March 1984, the quantity of beer and soft drinks which may be marketed by a single producer in non-approved containers to 3 000 hectolitres a year, the Kingdom of Denmark has failed, as regards imports of those products from other Member States, to fulfil its obligations under Article 30 of the EEC Treaty.

(23) The remainder of the application must be dismissed.

Costs

(24) Under Article 69(2) of the Rules of Procedure, the unsuccessful party is to be ordered to pay the costs. However, under the first paragraph of Article 69(3), where each party succeeds on some and fails on other heads, the Court may order that the parties bear their own costs in whole or in part. Since the application has been successful only in part, the parties must be ordered to bear their own costs. The United Kingdom, which has intervened in the case, shall bear its own costs.

On those grounds,

THE COURT

hereby:

(1) Declares that by restricting, by Order No 95 of 16 March 1984, the quantity of beer and soft drinks which may be marketed by a single producer in non-approved containers to 3 000 hectolitres a year, the Kingdom of Denmark has failed, as regards imports of those products from other Member States, to fulfil its obligations under Article 30 of the EEC Treaty;

(2) Dismisses the remainder of the application;

(3) Orders the parties and the intervener to bear their own costs.

COMMENTARY

(1) This judgment is the first decision in which the European Court expressly[2] discussed the interrelationship between Article 30 of the EEC Treaty and the protection of the environment. Since the Court had to decide on the validity of a national measure, its decision is of great importance for the relationship between Member States' and the Community's competence in environmental

---

[2] 240/83: [1985] E.C.R. 531 (see p. 5 above) also discusses the interdependency between the free circulation of goods and the protection of the environment. However in that case, Directive 75/439 existed. In the present case, no Community directive existed.

matters. Hardly any author who writes about EEC environmental law omits to discuss this decision,[3] which is seen as a landmark decision in balancing environmental interests against the interest of free circulation of goods. When the case was registered with the Court, the Single European Act had not yet entered into force and when the Court gave its judgment the amended Treaty was about one year old. So the Court developed its arguments according to its previous jurisdiction, although it took care to point out that the amended EEC Treaty confirmed its findings.[4]

(2) Since no Community legislation existed on packages and packaging waste, the Court used Article 30 of the Treaty as the yardstick. In doing so, it had recourse to its "established body of case-law" as to the interpretations of that Article. This case law may be summarised as follows: Article 30 is of paramount importance to the free circulation of goods and thus to the establishment and functions of the internal market. Therefore, Article 36, which contains an exemption of the principle of free circulation of goods, must be interpreted restrictively. National measures which restrict the free circulation of goods must therefore be justified by the need to protect one of the non-economic values[5] enumerated in Article 36. The list in Article 36 cannot be extended.

However, Article 30 contains an inherent limitation. Indeed, national measures which create obstacles to the free movement of goods must be accepted under Article 30 in so far as such rules are necessary in order to satisfy mandatory requirements recognised by Community law. Such measures may be neither discriminating nor disproportionate[6] and the Court expressly recognises in this judgment that the protection of the environment is such a mandatory requirement recognised by Community law.

(3) I had myself examined the question of environmental protection under the amended EEC Treaty and had come to a slightly different wording. In my opinion, it follows from Article 130r to 130t and Article 100a that the environment cannot be left unprotected: if the Community fails to take action to protect it, any Member State can take measures on its own. Therefore, in the absence of Community provisions, a national measure to protect the environ-

---

[3] See J. H. Jans, *Europees Milieurecht in Nederland* (Groningen, 1991), p. 104; J. H. Jans, *Sociaal Economische Wetgeving* 1990, p. 482; J. H. Leopold and A. V. Van den Berg, *Milieu en Recht* 1989, p. 113; L. J. Vonhoff, *Tijdschrift voor Milieuaansprakelijkheid* 1989, p. 55; K. H. Kohlhepp, "Beschränkung des freien Warenverkehrs in der EG durch nationale Unweltschutzbestimmungen." *Der Betrieb* 1989, p. 1455; W. Schult and J. Steffens, "EuGH-Entscheidung zu Verpackungsvorschriften in Dänemark", *Recht der Internationalen Wirtschaft* 1989, 477; P. Kromarek, "Environmental Protection and Free Movement of Goods: The Danish Bottles Case," *Journal of Environmental Law* 1990, 89.
[4] Para. 8 of the Judgment, see p. 92 above.
[5] The expression "non-economic values" was developed by the Court, see Case 7/61, *Commission* v. *Italy*: [1961] E.C.R. 695, [1962] C.M.L.R. 39; Case 72/83, *Campus Oil*: [1984] E.C.R. 2727, [1984] 3 C.M.L.R. 544; now Art. 100a, para. 5 refers to non-economic values in Art. 36.
[6] See in particular Case 120/78, *Rewe* v. *Bundesmonopolverwaltung* ("*Cassis de Dijon*"): [1979] E.C.R. 649, [1979] 3 C.M.L.R. 494.

ment is permissible in so far as it is not discriminatory and that the pursued objective cannot be attained by less restrictive means.[7] This phrasing tries to avoid the reversal of a burden of proof which so easily slips into the reasoning under Article 30 and which requests Member States to justify their environmental measure. In my opinion, Article 30 does not contain such a reversal of the burden of proof.

(4) If one follows the Court's reasoning, the following points seem to have to be examined under Article 30 in an environmental case:

(1) Absence of Community rules.
(2) Was the measure taken to protect the environment?
(3) Was the measure necessary to protect the environment?
(4) Has the measure a discriminatory character?
(5) Was the measure proportionate to attain the aim?

These points are discussed below with regard to Case 302/86.

1. Absence of Community rules

(5) In 1985, Directive 85/339 on containers of liquids for human consumption was adopted, after almost ten years of discussion at Community level.[8] However, this Directive did not expressly address the question of refillable containers, deposit-and-return systems and so on. It mainly asked Member States to adopt and implement programmes for the reduction of waste. Deposit systems were mentioned as one possible measure, but all measures taken had to have due regard for the provisions of the Treaty on the free movement of goods.

Thus, although a general directive existed it did not address the question whether a system such as the Danish system was compatible with Community law. Therefore, the Court rightly does not even mention Directive 85/339.

2. Was the measure taken in order to protect the environment?

(6) This second question implies that principally environmental measures taken by Member States are capable of restricting the free movement of goods. In its decisions prior to Case 302/86, the Court had enumerated general interests which were capable of justifying such a restriction. In the landmark decision *Cassis de Dijon*,[9] the Court had mentioned "the effectiveness of fiscal supervision, the protection of public health, the fairness of commercial transactions and the defence of consumers". But the Court had always pointed out that this enumeration was not exhaustive.

---

[7] L. Krämer, *EEC Treaty and Environmental Protection* (London, 1990), pp. 39 and 84.
[8] [1985] O.J. L176/18.
[9] Above.

In Case 302/86, the Court expressly states that "the protection of the environment is a mandatory requirement which may limit the application of Article 30 of the Treaty." In doing so, the Court referred to Case 240/83 where it had found that the protection of the environment was one of the Community's essential objectives.[10]

(7) It is interesting to note that Case 240/83 had raised a similar problem without the Court addressing it under Article 30. One of the measures in question in that case was a rule in French legislation according to which waste oils had to be burnt in industrial installations; any other form of burning was prohibited. The Court examined Directive 75/439[11] but found no express rule on which French legislation would have been based. Thus the Court simply concluded "that the directive requires Member States to prohibit any form of waste oil disposal which has harmful effects on the environment." The Court does not even state that the burning of waste oils in other than industrial installations could be harmful to the environment but obviously implies it. The Court could also have stated that the restrictions to the free movement of goods inherent in the French rules was necessary for environmental reasons.

(8) In the present case, the Court did not examine whether the Danish legislation was taken in order to protect the environment. This question is not addressed in the judgment.

The Commission and the United Kingdom had argued before the Court that economic considerations were also at the basis of the Danish rules, since milk and wine were not submitted to the same system as beer and soft drinks, but rather to a much less restrictive system. This argument was further addressed by the United Kingdom government which indicated that the prohibition of metal containers put doubts on the sincerity of the ecological worries of Denmark. Similar words were used by the Commission.[12]

(9) Since these arguments were refuted by the Danish government, the Court did not seem to have any doubts about the environmental aim of the Danish measure, and quite rightly so. It is difficult to see in the Danish measure a disguised protectionist measure, which would be one of the cases where one could argue that a measure was not taken in order to protect the environment.

In 1987 the Commission had to deal with such a case. The Irish government notified its intention to prohibit the use of metal cans for beer. It expressly stated that the use of metal cans for other drinks would not be prohibited. The Commission objected to the Irish measure, arguing that from an environmental point of view, metal cans used for soft drinks and beer had the same effect.

---

[10] Above.
[11] [1975] O.J. L194/31.
[12] [1988] E.C.R. 4607, 4612 and 4614.

There was thus no environmental justification to limit the ban on beer containers.

The Irish government did not pursue its plans further.[13]

3. Was the measure necessary to protect the environment?

(10) Once more, the Court has not addressed this question. It started from the assumption that the measure was necessary.

The Commission had argued that the measures to protect the environment should not be at an exaggeratedly high level, giving absolute priority to the protection of the environment and almost totally neglecting the free movement of goods, but should rather offer a minimum level of protection for the environment sufficient to respect the principle of the free movement of goods.[14] The United Kingdom Government argued in a similar way that perfect protection went beyond the objective of environmental protection. "Measures intended to achieve extremely high aims" were to be seen either as a means of arbitrary discrimination or as a disguised restriction on trade.[15] Advocate General Slynn was also of that opinion:

> "There has to be a balancing of interests between the free movement of goods and environmental protection, even if in achieving the balance the high standard of the protection sought has to be reduced. The level of protection sought must be a reasonable level."[16]

All these arguments were not taken up by the Court, which did not question the Danish point of departure that there should be a system to ensure almost 100 per cent. of re-use of containers[17] and which considered then the legislation which introduced the deposit-and-return-system necessary in order to protect the environment.[18]

(11) In Case C–169/89[19] Advocate General Van Gerven expressed the opinion that when examining the necessity of a national measure, there was a need to check whether (a) the measure was adequate and pertinent to achieve the aim, and (b) whether there did not exist another measure which was less restrictive to the free movement of goods. Where these two conditions are not fulfilled, he considers the national measure as unnecessary.[20] This theory is, in my opinion, rather far fetched and one wonders, whether there would remain

---

[13] The case is not reported. See for some reference L. Krämer, *op. cit.*, p. 37.

[14] [1988] E.C.R. 4607, 4610–4612

[15] *Ibid.* 4612–4614.

[16] *Ibid. per* Advocate General Sir G. Slynn, 4626 (E.C.R.), p. 629 (C.M.L.R.).

[17] All parties in the case agreed that the Danish system ensured an almost 100 per cent. re-use of containers.

[18] This statement by the Court only refers to the deposit-and-return-system, not to the approval of containers.

[19] [1990] I E.C.R. 2143, see p. 149 below.

[20] *Ibid. per* Advocate General Van Gerven, paras. 8–10.

any cases where national environmental measures can be upheld against Article 30.

(12) The Court described the Danish measure as "a system intended to ensure the re-use of containers". The decision to set up such a system was a decision by Denmark alone. The Court did not question whether the protection of the environment made it necessary to set up such a system. It took that for granted. This can only mean that Member States are allowed to set themselves aims which they think appropriate to protect the environment.[21] If Denmark is of the opinion that the protection of the Danish environment needs a system to ensure the re-use of containers this is not to be questioned. This also implies that Denmark is free, in the Court's opinion, to decide whether it will give preference to the use of refillable containers over returnable or recyclable containers. It is the Member State which decides the aim of the environmental measure and national decisions cannot be challenged under Article 30.

(13) The Court's silence on the question of necessity was probably influenced by the statement of the Commission on a question put by the Court "that the Community has never itself attempted to lay down a particular level of protection of the environment and that the Member States are free to fix the level of protection which they consider appropriate".[22] The Commission also stated that the aim of its action was not to require the Danish government to replace the system at present in force by another system. Thus the Commission expressly indicated that it accepted the system set up by Denmark. But these statements were not, in my opinion, decisive.

(14) Furthermore, the general jurisprudence of the Court to Article 30 should be remembered. The Court had argued that national measures were to take care of scientific evidence as to the risk of substances or products. Where evidence was available that a specific substance was harmless a national measure prohibiting that substance or restricting its use was not considered necessary. Where no such evidence existed the decision could be different.[23]

In the case of environmental protection against packaging waste there is no scientific evidence as to the superiority of recycling systems over a re-use system. Ecological balances as to which container and which form of disposal is environmentally best and which are scientifically recognised, do not yet exist. And in the absence of sound scientific data nobody is capable of telling Denmark that its environment would be adequately protected by a less efficient system or a system which concentrated on the recycling of waste containers only.[24]

---

[21] See however below points 20 to 24 of this commentary.
[22] [1988] E.C.R. 4607, at p. 4617.
[23] In the same way Schult and Steffens (n. 3).
[24] See however below points 20 to 24 of this commentary.

4. Has the measure a discriminatory character?

(15) In its judgment the Court requested that the national rule must be "applicable to domestic and imported products without distinction." But it did not examine this criterion as regards the Danish legislation in general; only when the Court examined the 3,000 hectolitre clause—did it—under the examination of the proportionality of the measure—to some extent have a look at the differentiation between domestic and imported products.

As regards the requirement of the Danish legislation that containers must be returnable, the Court was aware of its restrictive effects on imports. Yet, this did not lead the Court to consider whether the measures distinguish between domestic and imported products. Procedurally, this is certainly correct since the Danish rules do not differentiate.

(16) However, in substance the Commission strongly argued that the Danish system "while formally applying to both domestic and imported products nevertheless puts imported products at a disadvantage in relation to domestic products"[25] and tried to demonstrate these effects by the description of the practical effects. The United Kingdom supported this view and Advocate General Slynn pointed out that the measures taken "must be indistinctly applicable in form and in substance to domestic producers and to producers from other Member States", quoting previous cases decided by the Court.[26] He concluded that "the Danish provisions in practice even if not in form are not indistinctly applicable".[27]

The fact that all these arguments and the accompanying evidence did not lead the Court to take up the argument means, in my opinion, that the Court accepts the discriminating *effect* of the Danish rule because it does not find any discriminating *intention* of the rules and rather sees the effect on imports inherently linked to the environmental intentions.

(17) This then would lead back to the discussion of the necessity of a measure: a Member State, as I understand the reasoning of the Court, is allowed to protect the environment where no Community rule ensures that protection. The Member State is free to decide which aim it wishes to achieve or at which level it wishes to ensure that protection. The chosen aim determines the instruments, the concrete measures which the Member State may choose. If these measures have the effect of placing a heavier burden on imports than on domestic products this must be accepted.

If this understanding is correct, the impact of the Court's judgment on future cases is and will be very considerable. However it will be seen later that such a conclusion could only apply to the Court's assessment on the use of refillable containers, not on the system of approval of containers. Thus, while the first

---

[25] [1988] E.C.R. 4607, 4610.
[26] *Ibid. per* Advocate General Slynn, pp. 4622 and 4623.
[27] *Ibid. per* Advocate General Slynn, p. 4625.

part of the judgment gives extensive discretion to a Member State, the second part takes that discretion away.

5. Is the measure proportionate to attain the aim?

(18) It was in this decision that the Court for the first time applied the principle of proportionality to an environmental case. The Court gave very large room to the examination of the principle of proportionality; in other words to the question whether the aim of the protection of the environment may be achieved by means less restrictive of intra-Community trade. The Court argued that the system intended to ensure the re-use of containers is necessary to protect the environment and that a deposit-and-return-system for empty containers is an "indispensable element" of the re-use of containers system. Therefore the restrictions which the deposit-and-return-system impose on the free movement of goods are not disproportionate.

No further explanation of how or why the deposit-and-return-system is an indispensable element of the re-use of containers, was given and why other, less restrictive means are not available.

(19) The Commission argued that the environment could also be protected by systems for recycling for containers and/or systems designed to encourage the selective collection of containers that are not re-usable. However, the Commission also answered the Court that it did not wish to see the system in force replaced by another system. In other terms, the Commission accepted that a system which required the re-use of containers was an appropriate means to protect the environment. This, however, makes it impossible to use a system for recycling of containers or a system of collection of non re-usable containers. Therefore the Court is right in stating that where a Member State establishes the rule that containers should be re-used—and a Member State is free to do so in order to protect the environment—a deposit-and-return-system is an indispensable element.

(20) The Court then examined jointly the requirement to use only approved containers and the possibility of using non-approved containers, where the quantity of the marketed drinks does not exceed 3,000 hectolitres per year, provided that a deposit-and-return-system is set up. In this respect the Court found the Danish system disproportionate. Its reasoning was as follows: a deposit-and-return-system is capable of protecting the environment; where approved containers are used, a higher degree of environmental protection can be ensured since empty containers can be returned to any retailer; whereas non-approved containers can only be returned to the retailer who originally sold the beverages. Nevertheless the system for non-approved containers is also capable of protecting the environment. Since there are only few imports, the limitation to 3,000 hectolitres or the requirement to use approved containers are excessive.

(21) Thus, one might try to set up a scheme of levels of protection of the environment.

(1) Obligation to use re-usable containers which are approved (this implies the use of approved containers and a deposit-and-return-system);
(2) Obligation to use re-usable containers (which implies a deposit-and-return-system);
(3) Obligation to use recyclable containers;
(4) Voluntary return system.

(22) The Court found that Member States may establish level 2 of environmental protection. The deposit-and-return-system which this system requires is necessary and must therefore be accepted, even though it creates more difficulties for imports than for domestic products.

The Court found that Member States may not establish level 1 of environmental protection. This is excessive, since level 2 is capable of protecting the environment.

The Court did not explain why it does not consider level 2 excessive, since there is a level 3. Level 2 is considered to be capable of protecting the environment. Does this mean that the Court considers that level 3 does not ensure an adequate protection? Why then does the Court not accept Denmark s conclusion that level 2 also does not ensure an adequate protection? In general, who decides on the level of protection?

It was said earlier that Member States decide on the level of protection. However, this affirmation has to be refined: Member States may decide on the level of protection to the extent that no other, less restrictive solution exists which is sufficient for the protection of the environment.

Therefore, Member States may adopt rules which are capable of protecting the environment. Where these rules affect the free movement of goods, these restrictions must be accepted as necessary. However, national rules which offer greater protection to the environment but which affect the free movement of goods more are not allowed.

(23) The Court did not answer the question of what criteria must be fulfilled by a rule in order to be capable of protecting the environment. In particular, why is level 1 excessive and thus disproportionate, but not level 2 since there is a level 3? Perhaps level 2 is considered to be a "reasonable" level, while level 1 which ensures a 99 per cent. return of containers is not. But obviously, opinions differ of what is "reasonable".

The Court did not discuss the Danish argument that a widespread use of non-approved containers would cause the whole deposit-and-return-system to break down. By allowing the unlimited use of unapproved containers it implicitly rejected this Danish argument.

(24) The Court did not discuss the prohibition of metal containers which the

United Kingdom had raised. In that context it should be noted that the Commission as the applicant had not asked for a Court decision on that question.[28] The Commission had accepted this prohibition as being a legitimate measure in order to protect the environment. The intervener could not introduce into the litigation a point that the applicant himself had not raised. So the Court was right not to discuss the metal can prohibition.

As regards the Commission's attitude to the prohibition of specific forms of containers, it appears from QE 2681/85[29] that the Commission has also accepted other prohibitions of specific containers, where environmental reasons appear to have caused this ban. The Irish can case, mentioned above, might be an example for weighing different interests as regards such bans.

(25) As regards questions which the Court left open, the following points seem relevant:

1. May Member States, in the absence of Community rules, fix the aim and degree of environmental protection?

I understand from the Court's decision that Member States may fix reasonable aims even where the measures to achieve these aims affect the free movement of goods. Aims which are unreasonably high and affect the free movement of goods are considered to be disproportionate. However, interpretations of the Court's decision differ and it must thus be left open whether the decision really does have this meaning.

It is my view that the case does not significantly contribute to answering this question.

2. What is a reasonable degree of protection of the environment?

The answer is relatively simple: we do not know. The weighing of interests between the environment and the free circulation of goods is to be decided on a case-by-case basis. However, since 1988 the Commission has not brought one single further case before the Court, where Article 30/environment questions were at stake.[30] And in the only case where a national court submitted such a case to the Court under Article 177 it forgot to ask for Article 30. So the Court did not deal with this problem.[31]

(26) Community legislation on packaging waste has a long history. Preparatory work for Directive 85/339[32] which only concerns waste from liquid beverage containers, took about ten years and very heavy intervention from vested interest groups in the seventies and the beginning of the eighties influenced

---

[28] For the background to this decision by the Commission see P. Kromarek, *op. cit.*, p. 97.
[29] [1986] O.J. C190/25.
[30] For examples see L. Krämer, *op. cit.* p. 36.
[31] Case 380/87, *Balsamo*: [1989] E.C.R. 2491, [1991] 1 C.M.L.R. 313. See p. 131 below.
[32] [1985] O.J. L176/18.

its final content, which is relatively weak. Confronted with growing problems of packaging wastes, some Member States—Denmark, the Netherlands, Germany, Italy—took initiatives at a national level. These measures created and continue to create a need for Community measures, since it is almost impossible for efficient environmental protection and efficient free circulation of goods to be ensured by national laws alone. Indeed, 12 sets of efficient national legislation in the environmental area may even create considerable problems for commerce within the Community.

(27) The Commission made a formal proposal on packaging early 1992.[33] The proposal is based on Article 100a and treats the re-use and the recycling of containers—which include the burning of packaging waste with recovery of energy—as equivalent. Non-recyclable waste shall gradually be phased out. No prohibition of specific containers—metal cans, non-biodegradable plastics, aerosols—is suggested. It remains to be seen whether the different national systems which have been set up, or are being set up in several Member States, will really be adapted to such a Community system should it ever be set up. It is obvious that the proposal does not go as far as the German, Dutch or Danish national systems in its environmental objectives. Whether in these circumstances it is really based on a high level of protection as required by Article 100a, paragraph 3 will hopefully be examined one day by the European Court. The only institution which could bring such a case would be the European Parliament. However the Court limited Parliament's rights to bring an action under Article 173 to cases where the prerogatives of Parliament are not respected.[34] In my opinion such a non-respect of Parliament's prerogatives exists where the Commission's proposal does not take as a basis a high level of protection, for the following reasons:

(28) Let us take as an example a situation where the European Parliament is in favour of the introduction of a deposit-and-return-system and Member State A opposes it.[35]

(a) Where the Commission's proposal takes up the requirement of a deposit-and-return-system, no particular problems arise. The Council can adopt the proposal by qualified majority once Parliament has approved the proposal with simple majority or has not taken position within three months. Member State A cannot stop the adoption of the proposal.

(b) Where the Commission does not propose a deposit-and-return-system, the Council's common position can only introduce such a requirement by unanimous decision since this decision amends the Commission's proposal. Thus Member State A can veto it. Parliament may ask for the

---

[33] [1992] O.J. C263/1.
[34] Case C–70/88, *Parliament* v. *Council* [1990] I E.C.R. 2041, [1992] 1 C.M.L.R. 91.
[35] See for the voting rules, etc. mentioned in the text, Art. 149 EEC.

introduction of the deposit-and-return-system; however for that it needs the absolute majority of its members. If then the Commission—in conformity with its own original proposal and Council's common position—does not incorporate these amendments the Council could again incorporate the deposit-and-return-system only by unanimous decision. Again Member State A can block the introduction of a deposit-and-return-system.

Thus, voting rules in the Parliament following the Council's common position—which in its turn is influenced, as far as voting is concerned, by the Commission's proposal—are different in case (a) and case (b). Also Council's decision-making procedures are different in both cases. I conclude that Parliament's prerogatives are affected where a proposal from the Commission is not based on a high level of protection.

7. CIRCULARS IN ENVIRONMENTAL LAW

**Judgment of the Court of February 28, 1991
in Case C–131/88**

E.C. Commission v. *Germany*

[1991] I E.C.R. 825

FACTS AND PROCEDURE[1]

Directive 80/68 on the protection of groundwater against pollution caused by certain dangerous substances[2] was adopted in December 1979. Its aim is to prevent the pollution of groundwater by certain substances and, as far as possible, reduce or eliminate the negative consequences of pollution which have already occurred. The Directive lays down different rules for direct and indirect discharges i.e., introduction of substances into groundwater without percolation through the ground (direct discharge) or with such percolation (indirect discharge) which it prohibits or regulates according to determined specifications.

The dangerous substances are divided into: a list (I) which contains particularly dangerous substances, selected on grounds of their toxicity, persistence and bioaccumulation, and a list (II) of substances which are not quite as dangerous, though they also have a harmful effect on groundwater. Furthermore the Directive contains a number of procedural provisions.

Member States had to implement the requirements of the Directive by mid 1981. Since the Commission was not convinced that the German legislation transmitted as implementing the Directive was fully in compliance with the Directive, it sent, on May 6, 1986, a letter of formal notice and, not being satisfied with the German answer, a reasoned opinion on August 6, 1987. Germany answered on September 25, 1987, November 23, 1987 and February 9, 1988.

The Commission was not satisfied with the German answers and made, on May 6, 1988, an application to the European Court. There was a written procedure. Oral hearings took place on June 19, 1990. The Advocate General delivered his opinion on September 25, 1990.

JUDGMENT

(1) By an application lodged at the Court Registry on 6 May 1988, the Commission of the European Communities brought an action under Article 169 of the EEC Treaty for a declaration that, by failing to adopt all the laws, regulations and administrative provisions necessary in order to comply with Council Directive 80/68/EEC of 17 December 1979 on the protection of groundwater against pollution caused by certain dangerous substances (Official Journal 1980 L 20, p. 43,

---

[1] Summary by the author.
[2] [1980] O.J. L20/43.

hereinafter referred to as "the directive"), the Federal Republic of Germany has failed to fulfil its obligations under the EEC Treaty.

(2) Reference is made to the Report for the Hearing for a fuller account of the facts of the case, the Community and national legislation relevant to the case, the course of the procedure and the submissions and arguments of the parties, which are mentioned or discussed hereinafter only in so far as is necessary for the reasoning of the Court.

General arguments

(3) The Federal Republic of Germany claims that the directive was correctly implemented in its national legal order by the Law on water (Wasserhaushalts-gesetz) of 1976, as amended on 23 September 1986 (BGB1. 1986, I, pp. 1529 and 1654), by the Law on the reduction and removal of waste (Gesetz über die Vermeidung und Entsorgung von Abfällen, Abfallgesetz, of 27 August 1986, BGB1. I, pp. 1410 and 1501), by the Federal law on administrative procedure (Verwaltungsverfahrensgesetz) and by a number of other laws, decrees and administrative provisions adopted by the *Länder*.

(4) The Federal Republic of Germany points out that even though the abovementioned laws were not adopted specifically in order to implement the directive, they are interpreted and applied in such a way as to achieve that result. According to the Federal Republic of Germany a directive must be considered to have been implemented if it is actually implemented, in a clear and precise manner, by national law. The Commission's claims are rather hypothetical because in practice there have been no cases in which the directive has been infringed.

(5) The Commission claims that the provisions relied on by the Federal Republic of Germany do not show clearly that the directive has been implemented because they do not fulfil the strict and rigorous conditions for implementation.

(6) It should be pointed out first of all that according to the case-law of the Court (see, in particular, the judgment in Case 363/85 *Commission* v *Italy* [1987] ECR 1733), the transposition of a directive into domestic law does not necessarily require that its provisions be incorporated formally and verbatim in express, specific legislation; a general legal context may, depending on the content of the directive, be adequate for the purpose provided that it does indeed guarantee the full application of the directive in a sufficiently clear and precise manner so that, where the directive is intended to create rights for individuals, the persons concerned can ascertain the full extent of their rights and, where appropriate, rely on them before the national courts.

(7) The directive at issue in the present case seeks to protect the Community's groundwater in an effective manner by laying down specific and detailed provisions requiring the Member States to adopt a series of prohibitions, authorization schemes and monitoring procedures in order to prevent or limit discharges of certain substances. The purpose of those provisions of the directive is thus to create rights and obligations for individuals.

(8) It should be pointed out that the fact that a practice is consistent with the protec-

tion afforded under a directive does not justify failure to implement that directive in the national legal order by means of provisions which are capable of creating a situation which is sufficiently precise, clear and open to permit individuals to be aware of and enforce their rights. As the Court held in its judgment in Case C–339/87 (*Commission* v *Netherlands* [1990] ECR I-851, paragraph 25), in order to secure full implementation of directives in law and not only in fact, Member States must establish a specific legal framework in the area in question.

(9) It follows from the foregoing that the argument of the Federal Republic of Germany that there has been no case in practice in which the directive was infringed cannot be accepted.

(10) It must therefore be considered whether the provisions relied on by the Federal Republic of Germany implement the directive correctly.

Discharges of substances in list I

1. The prohibition of direct discharges

(11) The Commission claims first that the Federal Republic of Germany has not implemented the first indent of Article 4(1) of the directive, which, in conjunction with Article 3(a), prohibits all direct discharges of substances in list I.

(12) The Federal Republic of Germany contends that the prohibition is not absolute but relative, and must be applied having regard to Article 2(b) of the directive, which provides for exceptions to the prohibitions where the competent authority of the Member State concerned finds that discharges contain substances in lists I or II in a quantity and concentration so small as to obviate any present or future danger of deterioration in the quality of the receiving groundwater. Article 2(b) therefore allows the Member State a discretion in the implementation of the directive.

(13) The Federal Republic of Germany contends that Paragraph 1a(1) Paragraph 2(1), Paragraph 3(1)(5) and in particular Paragraph 34(1) of the Wasserhaushaltsgesetz fully implement the prohibition at issue in its national legal order. Under the last-mentioned paragraph, authorization to introduce substances into groundwater may be granted only if there is no reason to fear detrimental effects on groundwater owing to pollution or impairment of the properties of the groundwater. The Federal Republic of Germany contends that those provisions mean that all discharges of substances are prohibited unless the conditions laid down in Paragraph 34(1) of the Wasserhaushaltsgesetz have been met.

(14) The prohibition laid down in the first indent of Article 4(1) is general and absolute and applies to discharges of substances in list I without distinguishing between the substances themselves and solutions thereof. That article does not empower the competent authorities of the Member States to determine, on a case-by-case basis and having regard to the circumstances, whether or not discharges have a detrimental effect. That interpretation results, moreover, from a comparison between the wording of the first indent of Article 4(1) and the wording of Article 5 of the directive, which does in fact introduce a system of authorization for discharges of substances in list II. It also results from the ninth recital

in the preamble to the directive, according to which, with the exception of direct discharges of substances in list I, which are automatically prohibited, all discharges must be made subject to an authorization scheme.

(15) Article 2(b) of the directive must be interpreted having regard to the fact that it is to be found in an article that specifies the cases to which the directive does not apply.

(16) Moreover, Article 2(b) of the directive does not refer to discharges of substances in list I or II, whether or not in solution, but to discharges of other substances that contain substances in those two lists.

(17) Substances in lists I or II contained in such discharges must be present in quantities sufficiently small as to obviate *prima facie*, without there even being a need for an evaluation, all risk of pollution of the groundwater. That is why Article 2(b) of the directive refers not to an evaluation by the competent authority of a Member State but to a simple finding.

(18) Thus the meaning of that provision is that if the quantity of substances in list I (or II) contained in discharges of other substances is such that the risk of pollution cannot be automatically excluded, the directive is applicable and, in that case, Article 2(b) cannot, contrary to what the Federal Republic of Germany claims, be taken in conjunction with the other provisions of the directive in order to interpret them. Consequently, it is not possible to refer to Article 2(b) of the directive in order to call into question the foregoing interpretation according to which the prohibition laid down by the first indent of Article 4(1) is absolute.

(19) In order to guarantee complete and effective protection of groundwater, it is vital that the prohibitions set out in the directive be expressly embodied in national law (see the judgment in Case 252/85 *Commission* v *France* [1988] ECR 2243, paragraph 19). Paragraph 34(1) of the Wasserhaushaltsgesetz, which is relied on by the Federal Republic of Germany, does not contain a general prohibition; it permits the competent authority to grant, subject to certain conditions, authorization to introduce substances into groundwater, on the basis, moreover, of rather vague criteria, such as "harmful pollution" and "detrimental effect on the properties" of the water.

(20) Consequently, the Commission's claim that the Federal Republic of Germany has failed to implement the first indent of Article 4(1) of the directive must be upheld.

2. Indirect discharges of substances in list I (second indent of Article 4(1))

(21) The Commission claims that the Federal Republic of Germany has not implemented the second indent of Article 4(1) of the directive, which makes disposal or tipping for the purpose of disposal which might lead to indirect discharge of substances in list I subject to a prior investigation in order to determine whether it should be prohibited or authorized.

(22) The Federal Republic of Germany cites various provisions of national law which, it claims, implement the second indent of Article 4(1) of the directive.

(23) Before those national provisions are considered, it should be stated that the second indent of Article 4(1), which must be read in conjunction with Article 3(a), may be analysed as follows:

    (a) it is intended to prevent any indirect discharge of substances in list I;

    (b) it applies to any disposal or tipping for the purpose of disposal;

    (c) it applies to all substances in list I;

    (d) it requires the Member States to make all such activities subject to a mandatory prior investigation;

    (e) it provides, finally, that the investigation must in all cases result in either a prohibition or an authorization, which may be granted only on condition that all the technical precautions necessary to prevent such discharge are observed.

The element referred to at (a)

(24) The first argument put forward by the Federal Republic of Germany is that having regard to Article 2(b) of the directive, the purpose of the second indent of Article 4(1) is not to prevent any indirect discharge of substances in list I, but only discharges in quantities which do not obviate any present or danger of deterioration in the quality of the receiving groundwater.

(25) On the basis of that interpretation, it refers to various provisions which, in its view, fulfil the requirements of the second indent of Article 4(1) of the directive.

(26) As has already been stated, the interpretation of Article 2(b) of the directive supported by the Federal Republic of Germany is not correct; consequently all the arguments which it bases on that interpretation cannot be upheld.

(27) That is sufficient ground for upholding the Commission's claim that the second indent of Article 4(1) of the directive has not been implemented. However, the following observations should be made concerning the national legislation which according to the Federal Republic of Germany has implemented that provision.

The element referred to at (b)

(28) As regards disposal or tipping for the purpose of disposal, the Federal Republic of Germany relies on a number of provisions contained in the Wasserhaushalts-gesetz and the Abfallgesetz. They are Paragraph 3(1)(5) and (2)(2), Paragraph 19a(1), 19b(2), 19g(1) et seq and Paragraph 34(1) and (2) of the former, and Paragraph 4(1) and (5) and Paragraph 7 of the latter. Each of those provisions refers to the disposal or tipping for the purpose of disposal of dangerous substances by a pipeline, by other facilities, without facilities and by final burial.

(29) The first remark that that calls for is that the provisions concern only certain

types of disposal or tipping for the purpose of disposal and in no way guarantee that every kind of disposal or tipping for the purpose of disposal capable of leading to indirect discharge of list 1 substances is covered by the German legislation.

(30) In that context the Federal Republic of Germany points out that under Paragraph 34 of the Wasserhaushaltsgesetz the introduction into groundwater, the storage and the burial of substances, and the transportation of liquids and gasses by pipeline, may be authorized only if there is no risk of harmful pollution of the groundwater or any other impairment of its properties, and that under Paragraph 3(2)(2) of the same law "introduction" of substances into the groundwater includes measures capable of affecting the physical, chemical, or biological properties of the water permanently or significantly. Consequently, the German legislation covers all possible modes of introduction into the groundwater.

(31) It also claims that the legislation does not enable authorization to be granted for activities which entail the risk of harmful pollution or impairment of the properties of the groundwater. Consequently, it is more strict than the directive, since the second indent of Article 4(1) of the directive provides that authorization may be granted provided that technical precautions are taken.

(32) Those arguments likewise cannot be upheld because they are based on the interpretation of Article 2(b) of the directive which has just been rejected.

The element referred to at (c)

(33) The Federal Republic of Germany claims that all list I substances are covered by the legislation referred to above, because they are mentioned in Paragraph 19a(2) of the Wasserhaushaltsgesetz, which must be read in conjunction with the Regulation of 19 December 1973 on the conveyance by pipeline of substances harmful to water (BGBl. I, p. 1946). It points out that list I substances are in any event covered by Paragraph 34, taken in conjunction with Paragraph 3(1)(5) and (2), which concern not only list I substances, but substances in general. As for the particular case of Paragraph 19g(5) of the Wasserhaushaltsgesetz, which lists only a number of dangerous substances, the Federal Republic of Germany emphasizes that they are merely examples, as is shown by the fact that they are introduced by the words "in particular".

(34) That argument cannot be upheld because the provisions relied on by the Federal Republic of Germany do not list the substances referred to in list I of the directive but rely on general and imprecise definitions.

The element referred to at (d)

(35) As far as the requisite prior investigation is concerned, the Federal Republic of Germany claims that Paragraphs 24 and 26 of the Federal Law on administrative procedure and the corresponding provisions adopted by the *Länder* require any authority before adopting any administrative act, as a general rule, to undertake automatically an inquiry as to the facts, collecting the evidence

which it considers necessary. That inquiry meets the requirements set out in the second indent of Article 4(1) of the directive.

(36) That argument must likewise be rejected because the provisions relied on by the Federal Republic of Germany apply to administrative procedure in general and do not implement the second indent of Article 4(1) of the directive in a manner which is sufficiently specific, precise and clear to satisfy fully the requirement of legal certainty. The second indent of Article 4(1) of the directive requires, in view of the specific purpose of the inquiry (the appraisal of the receiving environment) that the inquiry be conducted with specific reference to the hydrogeological conditions of the area concerned, the possible purifying powers of the soil and subsoil and other elements. That is why, moreover, Article 7 of the directive lays down precisely what elements are to be considered in the prior investigations.

The element referred to at (e)

(37) Lastly, as regards the result of the investigations, the Federal Republic of Germany maintains that if no authorization is granted, discharge is prohibited.

(38) That argument cannot be accepted because in view of the importance of the purpose of the investigation as regards the protection of the groundwater, the directive requires that after each investigation and in the light of the results thereof an express measure, either prohibition or authorization, must be adopted.

(39) As regards more particularly the case of authorization, the Federal Republic of Germany claims that it is self-evident that the administrative authorities would, if necessary, make the authorization subject to conditions.

(40) That argument cannot be accepted because the directive requires the authorization to be subject always to conditions regarding the observance of technical precautions in order to guarantee that all indirect discharges will be prevented.

(41) Consequently, the complaint regarding the failure to implement the second indent of Article 4(1) of the directive must be upheld.

3. Other indirect discharges of list I substances (third indent of Article 4(1))

(42) The Commission claims that the manner in which the third indent of Article 4(1) of the directive has been implemented is also inadequate.

(43) The purpose of that provision, which lays down details concerning the obligation provided for in Article 3(a), whereby the Member States are required to prevent indirect discharges of list I substances, is to prevent such discharges resulting from any activity other than those referred to in the second indent, and requires the Member States to take all appropriate measures to that end.

(44) The Federal Republic of Germany relies in that respect in the first place on Paragraphs 3(2), 19a, 19b, 19g et seq and Paragraph 34 of the Wasserhaushalts-

gesetz, that is to say the same provisions on which it has already relied as implementing the second indent of Article 4(1) of the directive.

(45) However, the considerations set out above as regards the failure to implement the latter provision, having regard to its purpose and the activities and substances covered, apply to the implementation of the third indent of Article 4(1) of the directive. It must therefore be held that Paragraphs 3(2), 19a, 19b, 19g, et seq and Paragraph 34 of the Wasserhaushaltsgesetz do not adequately implement the provision in question, interpreted correctly.

(46) The Federal Republic of Germany also relied on Paragraph 2 of the Wasserhaushaltsgesetz, which provides that use of water is subject to the authorization or approval of the administrative authorities, except where otherwise provided by that law or by the laws or regulations drawn up by the Länder pursuant thereto.

(47) The answer to that must be that although the paragraph it relies on makes all use of water subject to the authorization or approval of the national authorities, it does not provide that such an authorization or approval may be granted only if there is no question of indirect discharges of list I substances. On the contrary, it even permits the *Länder* to permit exceptions, without stating the restrictions which must apply to such exceptions.

(48) As regards Paragraph 3(2)(2) of the Wasserhaushaltsgesetz, which refers to measures capable of impairing the quality of water permanently or significantly, it must be stated that it relates to the introduction of substances into water, and to activities in the ground, but not to activities on the ground.

(49) As regards the provisions adopted by the *Länder*, the description of them in the application, which has not been challenged by the Federal Republic of Germany, shows that they make no provision for measures regarding activities other than those referred to in the second indent in order to prevent indirect discharges, and they do not cover all the substances mentioned in list I.

(50) Consideration of the provisions relied on by the Federal Republic of Germany shows, therefore, that the third indent of Article 4(1) of the directive has not been implemented in national law with the precision and clarity necessary in order to satisfy the requirement of legal certainty.

(51) Consequently, the Commission's complaint must be upheld.

Prevention of discharges of list II substances

(52) The Commission claims that the Federal Republic of Germany has not implemented Article 5 of the directive, which requires in the case of direct or indirect discharges of list II substances that the relevant Member State conduct a prior investigation and grant an authorization subject to conditions, and which requires the Member States to take the appropriate measures to limit indirect discharges of substances due to activities on or in the ground other than those mentioned in the first paragraph.

(53) It should be noted that the purpose of Article 5(1) of the directive, in conjunction

with Article 3(b), is to restrict the introduction of list II substances into ground-water. That is why it requires the Member States, on the one hand, to make all direct discharges and all activities capable of leading to indirect discharges of list II substances subject to a mandatory prior investigation and, on the other hand, not to grant an authorization for such discharges without requiring that all the technical precautions for preventing groundwater pollution are observed.

(54) It should also be noted that Article 5(2) of the directive requires the Member States to take the appropriate measures they deem necessary to limit all indir-ect discharge of list II substances due to activities on or in the ground other than those mentioned in the first paragraph.

(55) The Federal Republic of Germany maintains that the obligations imposed by Article 5 are to be interpreted in the light of Article 2(b) of the directive and that Paragraphs 2, 3(1)(5) and 34 of the Wasserhaushaltsgesetz prohibit all direct and indirect discharges of both list I and list II substances without distinction; the German legislation is thus more rigorous than the directive as regards list II substances.

(56) That argument cannot be accepted. It is based on an interpretation of Article 2(b) of the directive which has already been rejected; moreover, the provisions relied on by the Federal Republic of Germany do not provide for a mandatory and specific prior investigation and do not stipulate that the authorization may only be granted on condition that all the technical precautions are observed. Finally, they do not clearly state that any disposal or tipping for the purpose of disposal, and other activities on or in the grounds capable of leading to indirect discharges of list II substances, are covered.

(57) It follows that the requirements of Article 5 of the directive are not set out in German legislation with the precision and clarity required in order to satisfy fully the requirement of legal certainty.

(58) Consequently, the Commission's claim that Article 5 of the directive has not been implemented must be upheld.

The procedural provisions in the directive

General

(59) The Commission claims that Articles 7 to 11 and Article 13 of the directive, which concern the procedure for granting authorizations, have not been imple-mented, or adequately implemented, by the German legislation.

(60) The Federal Republic of Germany makes the preliminary point that the direct-ive's provisions are implemented by rules already in force, adopted at both federal and *Land* level, so that it is not necessary to adopt special legislation. It points out that in any event the framework provisions of the Federal Law on administrative procedure apply. It also claims that, as regards the detailed rules for applying the provisions, there are adequate administrative provisions which do not require publication because they do not impose substantive rules of law. The existence of an administrative practice or interpretation which complies with the directive is sufficient, consequently, to meet its requirements.

(61) It must be observed that the procedural provisions of the directive lay down, in order to guarantee effective protection of groundwater, precise and detailed rules which are intended to create rights and obligations for individuals. It follows that they must be incorporated into German law with the precision and clarity necessary in order to satisfy fully the requirement of legal certainty. Moreover, the Court has consistently held that mere administrative practices, which are alterable at the will of the administration and are not given adequate publicity, cannot be regarded as constituting adequate compliance with the obligation imposed on Member States to whom a directive is addressed by Article 189 of the EEC Treaty.

Article 7

(62) The Federal Republic of Germany maintains that Article 7 is implemented by Paragraphs 24 and 26 of the Federal Law on administrative procedure and the corresponding provisions of the *Länder* which require the competent authorities to conduct an investigation as a matter of course.

(63) It must be pointed out in that regard that Article 7 of the directive specifies in detail what matters are to be covered by the prior investigations referred to in Articles 4 and 5. Consequently, that provision cannot be regarded as having being implemented by the German legislation on general administrative procedure, in view of the fact that, as has been said, the legislation is not sufficiently specific, precise and clear to satisfy fully the requirements of legal certainty.

Article 8

(64) As far as the implementation of Article 8 of the directive is concerned, which provides that authorizations to discharge may not be issued by the competent authorities of the Member States until it has been ascertained that the groundwater, and in particular its quality, will undergo the requisite surveillance, the Federal Republic of Germany maintains that the substantive provisions concerning the conditions under which authorizations may be granted in Paragraphs 19a et seq, 19g and 34 of the Wasserhaushaltsgesetz, cited above, satisfy the requirements of Article 8 of the directive.

(65) It should be pointed out that Article 8 of the directive, which lays down a procedural rule, requires that it be ascertained beforehand, and specifically, that the groundwater, and in particular its quality, will undergo the requisite surveillance. Such a rule cannot be implemented by substantive provisions of national law of a general nature lacking the clarity and precision required in order to satisfy the requirements of legal certainty.

Articles 9 and 10

(66) As regards Articles 9 and 10 of the directive, which list the conditions which must be made in authorizations to discharge, the Federal Republic of Germany claims that under the Wasserhaushaltsgesetz the competent authorities may make those conditions in authorizations which they grant and that in addition

Article 37 of the Law on administrative procedure and the analogous provisions applicable in the *Länder* require generally that administrative acts be specific in content.

(67) However, the general obligation to which the competent national authorities are subject and the fact that they "may" stipulate the matters referred to in Articles 9 and 10 of the directive certainly do not satisfy the strict requirements of Articles 9 and 10.

Article 11

(68) As to Article 11 of the directive, which provides that authorizations may be granted for a limited period only and must be reviewed at least every four years, the Federal Republic of Germany claims that the administration is free to decide whether or not to limit the period of validity of an administrative act and to monitor compliance therewith.

(69) That argument cannot be upheld because Article 11 of the directive expressly requires that authorizations be granted for a limited period only and reviewed at least every four years. Consequently, the fact that the administrative authorities are free to decide whether or not to restrict the period of validity of the authorization cannot be sufficient to comply with Article 11 of the directive.

Article 13

(70) As regards Article 13 of the directive, which requires the Member States to monitor compliance with the conditions laid down in the authorizations and the effects of discharges on groundwater, the Federal Republic of Germany claims that Paragraph 21 of the Wasserhaushaltsgesetz requires users and owners of the land to permit monitoring by the authorities and that the way in which such monitoring is conducted need not be governed by primary legislation, but may be covered by internal measures or administrative provisions, such monitoring being the responsibility of the *Länder* which introduce such rules.

(71) The first remark which that calls for is that the Court has held, notably in Joined Cases 227 to 230/85 (*Commission* v *Belgium* [1988] ECR 1), that each Member State is free to delegate powers to its domestic authorities as it sees fit and to implement directives by means of measures adopted by regional or local authorities. That division of powers does not, however, release it from the obligation to ensure that the provisions of the directive are properly implemented in national law.

(72) Next, it should be noted that in the first place Paragraph 21 of the Wasserhaushaltsgesetz, which requires individuals to permit monitoring, does not itself impose an obligation to monitor compliance with the conditions laid down in the authorizations and that in the second place internal measures or administrative provisions which are by nature alterable and are not adequately publicized cannot satisfy the requirement laid down in Article 13 of the directive.

(73) Consequently, it must be held that the provisions contained in Articles 7 to 11

and Article 13 of the directive cannot be regarded as having been implemented in German legislation with the precision and clarity necessary in order to satisfy fully the requirement of legal certainty.

(74) In the light of all those considerations it must be held that by failing to adopt within the prescribed period all measures necessary to comply with Council Directive 80/68/EEC of 17 December 1979 on the protection of groundwater against pollution caused by dangerous substances the Federal Republic of Germany has failed to fulfil its obligations under the EEC Treaty.

Costs

(75) Under Article 69(2) of the Rules of Procedure the unsuccessful party is to be ordered to pay the costs. Since the Federal Republic of Germany has been unsuccessful, it must be ordered to pay the costs.

On those grounds,

THE COURT

hereby:

(1) Declares that the Federal Republic of Germany has failed to fulfil its obligations under the EEC Treaty by failing to adopt within the prescribed period all the measures necessary to comply with Council Directive 80/68/ EEC of 17 December 1979 on the protection of groundwater against pollution caused by certain dangerous substances.

(2) Orders the Federal Republic of Germany to pay the costs.

COMMENTARY

(1) This judgment, with its 74 paragraphs, is particularly long, compared to other judgments in environmental matters. The Court constructed it very carefully: after a short introduction (paragraphs 1 and 2), section A deals with general arguments (paragraphs 3 to 10), section B with discharges of substances on list I (paragraphs 11 to 51), section C with discharges of list II substances (paragraph 52 to 58) and section D with the procedural provisions in the Directive (paragraph 59 to 74).

In essence the Court had to address the question of the extent to which Community directives require Member States to adopt specific legislation or whether they could completely or partly rely on administrative circulars or administrative practice. Furthermore, the Court had to interpret the different provisions of Directive 80/68 and its meaning for national legislators.

(2) As regards the German legislation on groundwater it was not clear, from the report for the hearing, what the relevant legislation was. Indeed, in 1981, Germany had informed the Commission of implementing measures—orders—adopted by the Länder[3] and in 1982 it had sent a summary of legislative provisions on water at federal level.[4] In 1984, the Commission received a new series of laws,[5] while in 1986 Germany informed the Commission that the Directive had been implemented in full by the Wasserhaushaltsgesetz, a federal Act.

In its judgment, the Court passed elegantly over these factual aspects, mentioning that, according to the German authorities, the Directive had been implemented by those federal Acts and a number of Länder provisions.[6] Thus, the Court, rather than looking for the precise piece of legislation in national law which implemented the Directive, addressed the question, whether the German legislation in general implemented the Directive correctly.

(3) The Court has all rights to proceed in this way. However, it should be pointed out that where discussions take place between the Commission and a Member State, or between an individual and a national or regional administration, it is of vital importance to know with precision which Article of a Directive is transposed into national law by which legislative or administrative provisions. This is the reason why the Commission requires the Member States, after the adoption of a directive by the Council, to specify for each article and sub-article, the national provision which transposes its requirements into national law.[7] In the case of Directive 80/68 a precise knowledge of the national transposition measures is all the more important, since the Directive created, as the Court stated, "rights and obligations for individuals."[8] Therefore, national rules must be "sufficiently, precise, clear and open to permit individuals to be aware of and enforce their rights."[9]

(4) Germany had argued that in practice there had been no case in which the Directive was infringed.[10] The Court rejected this argument, as it had already done in previous judgments.[11]

This is logical. Indeed, implementation of Community directives is monitored by the Commission under three headings:

(a) Has a Member State taken measures to transpose the Directive and has it informed the Commission thereof?

---

[3] See the Report for the Hearing para. 13.
[4] *Ibid.* para. 14.
[5] *Ibid.*
[6] Para. 2 of the Judgment.
[7] See Commission, "Monitoring application of Community law, Eighth report": [1991] O.J. C338/1, Annex C, para. 8.
[8] Paras. 7 and 61.
[9] Para. 8: see also para. 6.
[10] Para. 4.
[11] See, Case 236/85, *Commission* v. *Netherlands*: [1987] E.C.R. 3989, paras. 18 and 23.

(b) Do the national implementation measures completely and correctly transpose the requirements of the Directive into national law?

(c) Is the Directive—or the national implementation measure—respected in practice?

The German argument refers to (c), whereas the Commission reproached Germany not having respected (b). This distinction is not merely theoretical: under Article 169 of the EEC Treaty, the Commission would have to prove any infringment under (c). Since Directive 80/68 does not provide for any reporting requirements to the Commission, it is more than difficult to prove that a Member State is not, in practice, respecting the requirements of the Directive, all the more since the Commission has no inspectors and no possibilities to take samples and have them analysed in laboratories. These difficulties do not exist, when compliance with (b) is examined, since the legal comparison between the Community Directive and the national implementation measures does not require the establishment of factual evidence.

In spite of this distinction, some authors have come out strongly against the attitude of the Court (and the Commission) which consists of examining the conformity of legal texts without considering the actual practice,[12] going even so far as to question whether this is compatible with Article 189 of the EEC Treaty:[13] if Member States were only obliged to achieve a result, how they achieve it would be irrelevant.

These arguments are not convincing. By asking Member States to prohibit direct discharges of list I substances into the groundwater (and this is only one example) Directive 80/68 creates obligations which at the end of the day, have to be complied with by actual or potential polluters. These persons or companies must know what their obligations are and it is appropriate therefore that the national law repeats the prohibition contained in the Directive. A national rule which provides that direct discharges of list I—substances may only take place when they are authorised, is simply not the same, even though in practice the administration might not authorise any direct discharge. Furthermore, the Commission would have to control administrative practice in all Member States to an extent which would require a considerable number of inspectors, laboratories, analyses, etc.

(5) When addressing the question of discharges of list I substances, the Court first addressed the prohibition of direct discharges. To that extent, Articles 3 and 4 of Directive 80/68 seemed to be clear and unambigious.[14] German law

---

[12] G. Lübbe-Wolff, "Die Bedeutung des EG-Rechts für den Grundwasserschutz," pp. 127 *et seq.* in P. Behrens & H.J. Koch (eds.), *Umweltschutz in der Europäischen Gemeinschaft* (Baden Baden, 1991).

[13] R. Breuer, "EG-Richtlinien und deutsches Wasserrecht," *Wirtschaft und Verwaltung* (1990), p. 79 *et seq.*; G. Lübbe-Wolff, *op cit.*, p. 148

[14] Article 34 German Wasserhaushaltsgesetz (translation from the Report for the Hearing, para. 34: "Authorisation to introduce substances into groundwater may be granted only if there is no risk of harmful pollution of the groundwater or any other impairment of its properties."

provided in article 34 of the Wasserhaushaltsgesetz a prohibition which was less outspoken.[15] The Court rejected the argument that this provision contained a general prohibition.[16]

However, Germany did not rely solely on the workings of article 34 of the Wasserhaushaltsgesetz. It argued that Directive 80/68 did not contain an absolute prohibition of direct discharges of list I substances into the groundwater, since Article 2(*b*) of the Directive exempted certain direct discharges from the field of application of the Directive.

The Court rejected this argument and declared that the prohibition was absolute, relying first on the wording of Article 4(1)[17] and, second, on the wording of Article 5 which introduces a system of authorisation for discharges of list II-substances, as well as on the ninth recital of the Directive.[18] In the Court's understanding, Article 2(*b*)[19] does not lead to different results, since it is a provision which deals with a case where the Directive is not applicable.[20] The wording and the fact that it is an exemption rule make it impossible to use it as an interpretation rule in cases where the Directive does apply.[21]

The German Government argued differently and saw its interpretation rejected by the Court, which considered it "vital" to see an express and absolute prohibition of direct discharges embodied in national law, in order "to guarantee complete and effective protection of groundwater."[22]

(6) As regards the indirect discharges of list I substances, the Court carefully examined the provisions of the German Act and concluded that it did not comply with Article 4(1), second indent.[23] The Court found that German provisions covered only certain types of disposal or tipping and "in no way guarantee that every kind of disposal ... is covered",[24] that the German provisions did not list the provisions of list I, but relied on general and imprecise defi-

---

[15] Para. 19.
[16] Paras. 12 and 13.
[17] Dir. 80/68, **Article 4(1)**: "To comply with the obligations referred to in Article 3(a), Member States ... shall prohibit all direct discharge of substances in list I ... " **Article 5(1)**: "To comply with the obligations referred to in Article 3(b), Member States shall make subject to prior investigation:—all direct discharge of substances in list II, so as to limit such discharges ... "
[18] "Whereas, with the exception of direct discharges of substances in list I, which are automatically prohibited, all discharges must be made subject to a system of authorisation; whereas such authorizations may only be delivered after a survey of the receiving environment."
[19] "This Directive shall not apply to discharges which are found by the competent authority of the Member State concerned to contain substances in list I or II in a quantity or concentration so small as to obviate any present or future danger of deterioration in the quality of the receiving groundwater."
[20] Paras. 15 to 18.
[21] Para. 19.
[22] Dir. 80/68, **Article 4(1)**, second indent: "To comply with the obligation referred to in Article 3(a), Member States ... shall subject to prior investigation any disposal or tipping for the purpose of disposal of these substances which might lead to indirect discharge. In the light of that investigation, Member States shall prohibit such activity or shall grant authorization provided that all the technical precautions necessary to prevent such discharge are observed."
[23] Para. 29.
[24] *Ibid.*

nitions"[25] that the prior investigation referred to in the Directive was not taken up specifically in German law "in a manner which was sufficiently specific, precise and clear"[26] and that authorisations under Article 4(1) second indent of the Directive may only be granted on condition whereas German law required such conditions only if—according to the assessment of the German local or regional authorities—they were considered to be necessary.[27]

Similar arguments were used by the Court to construe Article 4(1) third indent of Directive 80/68:[28] the German provisions do not have "the precision and clarity necessary in order to satisfy the requirement of legal certainty."[29]

(7) As regards discharges of list II substances (Article 5 of Directive 80/68) the Court first interpreted Article 5 and then pointed out that the German defence was based on an interpretation of Article 2(*b*) of the Directive which the Court had already rejected.[30] The Court added that the provisions in German law:

"do not provide for a mandatory and specific prior investigation and do not stipulate that the authorisation may only be granted on conditions that all the technical precautions are observed."[31]

Furthermore, the "clarity" argument was repeated which led the Court to the conclusion that the German rules on indirect discharges did not comply with the requirements of Directive 80/68.

Finally, the Court addressed the procedural rules of Directive 80/68.[32]

The Court did not follow the German defence in this area either, which had argued that the procedural provisions did not require more than a corresponding administrative practice or interpretation and, in particular, did not require publication, since they did not impose substantive rules of law.

The Court reiterated an argument which it has often used in environmental matters:[33]

"mere administrative practices, which are alterable at the will of the administration and are not given adequate publicity, cannot be regarded as con-

---

[25] Para. 34.
[26] Para. 36.
[27] Paras. 39 and 40.
[28] "To comply with the obligation referred to in Article 3(a), Member States ... shall take all appropriate measures they deem necessary to prevent any indirect discharge of substances in list I due to activities on or in the ground other than those mentioned in the second indent. They shall notify such measures to the Commission, which, in the light of this information, may submit proposals to the Council for revision of this Directive."
[29] Para. 50.
[30] Paras. 15 to 18.
[31] Para. 56.
[32] Arts. 7 to 11 and 13 of Dir. 80/68.
[33] See for instance Case 96/81, *Commission* v. *Netherlands* [1982] E.C.R. 1791; Case 236/85, *Commission* v. *Netherlands* [1987] E.C.R. 3989.

stituting adequate compliance with the obligation imposed on Member States to whom a Directive is addressed by Article 189 of the EEC Treaty."[34]

After these general observations, the Court found, after a detailed examination, that none of the procedural rules had been transposed into German law "with the precision and clarity necessary in order to satisfy fully the requirement of legal certainty."[35]

(8) The importance of this Court decision probably lies more in general considerations on Community environmental law and its transposition in the protection of groundwater. The judgment was given against a Member State with a very complex and sophisticated water legislation and administration at federal as well as at local level. The Court nevertheless accepted the Commission's argument that the national legislation was too general and imprecise to transpose correctly the requirements of Directive 80/68. Again the Court underlined that EEC environmental directives are not only orientations or guidelines for national administrations, but that they have to be taken seriously by the various national legislators. It is significant that the Court had already, in 1987, given a judgment against the Netherlands, another Member State with a rather vigorous environmental policy.[36] In that case also, the question was raised, whether existing Dutch water legislation ensured compliance with the requirements of Directive and to which extent provisions of Directive 80/68 had to be transposed at all into national law.

The present judgment clarified that, as a rule, administrative provisions, circulars or other practices are not sufficient to transpose an environmental directive into national law and that a specific legislative or regulatory measure is necessary. This applies in particular to all Community provisions which create rights or obligations for individuals. In such a case—and the Court made it clear that Directive 80/68 was such a case—individuals must be able to see, for reasons of legal certainty, with clarity and precision what rights and obligations flow out of the Community instrument; thus a clear and precise transposition in a legislative or regulatory instrument is necessary.

(9) The Court's formula on the creation of "rights and obligations for individuals" has been criticised for being too vague and should have been further clarified. However, although some clarification might have been desirable, the wording chosen by the Court seems to be clear, and the present case is a good illustration for it. Indeed, under article 34 of the German Wasserhaushaltsgesetz "authorization to introduce substances into groundwater may be granted if there is no risk of harmful pollution of the groundwater,"[37] whereas the Directive stipulates in Article 4 that Member States "shall prohibit all

---

[34] Para. 61.
[35] Para. 73.
[36] Case 291/84, *Commission* v. *Netherlands*. [1987] E.C.R. 3483, [1989] 1 C.M.L.R. 479.
[37] See the full text of that article in n. 14 above.

direct discharges of substances in list I." Where a company applies for an authorisation to discharge directly list I substances into the groundwater, it is not absolutely clear under the wording of article 34 of the Wasserhaushaltsgesetz that it would not get such an authorisation, as opposed to the total prohibition in Article 4 of Directive 80/68. The full legal meaning of article 34 of the Wasserhaushaltsgesetz becomes clear only when read against the Directive. But a company is not expected to do so and in order to create legal certainty for the company, the Court required that the transposing legislation precisely and clearly reflect the Directive's requirement.

A similar reasoning could also be made with other provisions. For example, a company wishing to obtain an authorisation for 15 years could apply for such an authorisation under German law[38] and thus argue for a long time with the administration whether or not this duration was adequate. However, under Article 11 of the Directive, the German administration was only allowed to grant authorisations for a limited period and had to review them at least every four years.

A precise formulation of the German rule would, in this example, have created legal certainty for the company.

(10) The main criticism against the judgment is based on the argument that German practice complied with the Directive and that the Community is unnecessarily formalistic, legalistic and meticulous in insisting on a precise transposition[39] all the more since German administrative practice would not change by virtue of the judgment.

The Community is based on law. Legal provisions which are—almost entirely by unanimity—adopted at Community level aim at creating an appropriate level of protection within the EEC and within the Community's ecosystem. The 12 different legal cultures of Member States contain so many factual divergencies and differences that it cannot always be possible to see a uniform text applied in the same way throughout the 12 Member States. Moreover it is important—if not vital—that the 12 different legal Acts which transpose a Community directive are as precise and clear as possible in this transposition: indeed, how can one expect uniform application, if already the legislation which is the basis for the application, is not a precise reflect of the Community's environmental instrument. It is the Commission's task under Article 155 of the EEC Treaty[40] to ensure that the transposing act is as faithful to the directive as any possible. And in case of a dispute with a Member State, the Court has to decide.

The argument that the practice of water management in Germany would

---

[38] See para. 68 of the judgement, according to which the German "administration is free to decide whether or not to limit the period of validity of an administrative act or to monitor compliance therewith."

[39] G. Lübbe-Wolff, *op. cit*, pp. 148 *et seq.*

[40] **Article 155** EEC: "In order to ensure the proper functioning and development of the common market, the Commission shall: ensure that the provisions of this Treaty and the measures taken by the institution pursuant thereto are applied; ... "

not change as a consequence of the judgment, might be correct. However, administrative practice was not at issue in the present case. The question which the Court had to decide, was only whether the German legislation had taken all measures necessary to transpose Directive 80/68 into German law. To answer that question, practice is irrelevant.

Officials of the Community are aware that Directive 80/68 has not really contributed to protect effectively groundwater in the Community. In February 1992, the Council adopted a resolution on future policy in the area of groundwater[41] asking the Commission to prepare an amendment to Directive 80/68. This proposal might be expected in 1993/94.

---

[41] Council resolution of February 25, 1992: [1992] O.J. C59/2.

8. LOCAL AUTHORITIES' MEASURES

**Judgment of the Court (Fifth Chamber) of July 13, 1989
in Case 380/87**

Preliminary ruling in the proceedings pending before the Tribunale
amministrativo regionale per la Lombardia between Enichem Base,
Montedipe, Solvay, SIPA Industriale Altene, Neophane and Polyflex Italiana
and Comune di Cinisello Balsamo

[1989] E.C.R. 2491, [1991] 1 C.M.L.R. 313

FACTS AND PROCEDURE[1]

By a decision of February 16, 1987, the Mayor of Cinisello Balsamo prohibited the supply to customers of non-biodegradable bags or other containers in which to carry away their purchases and also the sale or other distribution of plastic bags with the exception of those intended for the disposal of waste.

Enichem Base, Montedipe, Solvay, SIPA Industriale Altene, Neophane and Polyflex Italiana are companies which produce raw materials and process, market and distribute plastic containers, wrappings and bags. They brought an action against the decision of the Mayor before the Tribunale amministrativo regionale per la Lombardia in which they asked for the annulment of decision, because it contradicted Community law.

On November 30, 1987, the Tribunale decided, under Article 177 of the EEC Treaty, to submit four questions to the Court of Justice; this decision was registered on December 21, 1987.

During the procedure the Commission of the European Communities, the plaintiffs in the main proceedings, the Italian, United Kingdom and Portuguese Governments submitted written observations.

Oral hearings took place on March 2, 1989, but nothing further is known on the subject.

The Advocate General delivered his opinion on March 16, 1989.

JUDGMENT

(1) By order of 23 November 1987, which was received at the Court on 21 December 1987, the Tribunale amministrativo regionale per la Lombardia referred to the Court for a preliminary ruling under Article 177 of the EEC Treaty a number of questions on the interpretation of Council Directives 75/442 of 15 July 1975 on waste (Official Journal 1975, L 194, p. 39), 76/403 of 6 April 1976 on the disposal of polychlorinated biphenyls and polychlorinated terphenyls (Official Journal 1976, L 108, p. 41) and 78/319 of 20 March 1978 on toxic and dangerous waste (Official Journal 1978, L 84, p. 43), and on the determination of the principles applicable to compensation for loss caused by an administrative act contrary to Community law.

(2) The questions were raised in proceedings brought by several producers of

---

[1] Summary by the author.

plastic containers, wrappings and bags against the Municipality of Cinisello Balsamo concerning the decision of the Mayor of that municipality of 16 February prohibiting the supply to consumers of non-biodegradable bags and other containers in which to carry away their purchases and the sale or distribution of plastic bags, with the exception of those intended for the collection of waste.

(3) The companies Enichem Base, Montedipe, Solvay, SIPA Industriale, Altene, Neophane and Polyflex Italiana (hereinafter referred to as 'the plaintiffs') brought an action before the Tribunale amministrativo regionale for the annulment of that decision. They also asked that the operation of the decision be suspended. Since the plaintiffs had claimed in support of their applications for annulment that the decision in question was contrary to Community law, the national court stayed the proceedings and referred the following four questions to the Court for a preliminary ruling:

"(1) Do Council Directives 75/442 of 15 July 1975 on waste, 78/319/EEC of 20 March 1978 on toxic and dangerous waste and 76/403/EEC of 6 April 1976 on the disposal of polychlorinated biphenyls and polychlorinated terphenyls give EEC nationals the right under Community law, a right which national courts must uphold even as against Member States (and which Member States cannot therefore restrict), to sell or use the products concerned by those directives, since the directives provide for the observance of certain rules regarding the disposal of the products in question, not the prohibition of their sale or use?

(2) (a) Does it follow from the Community directives referred to or from Community law in general that any draft regulation or legislative measure (regarding the sale or use of the products in question) which may give rise to technical difficulties in their disposal or to excessive costs of disposal must be brought to the attention of the Commission before its adoption?

(b) Does that obligation bind the State and municipalities, with the result that they have no power to adopt provisions regarding the sale or use of products other than those included by Directive 76/403 in the exhaustive list of substances considered harmful unless it has first been determined at Community level that the measure does not create unequal conditions of competition?

(3) Having regard to the first recital in the preambles to the three directives referred to in the first question, in particular where it states that any disparity between the provisions on the disposal of the products in question applicable or in preparation in the various Member States may create unequal conditions of competition and thus directly affect the functioning of the common market:

(a) do that recital and the three directives in general give rise to a right (diritto soggettivo comunitario) on the part of EEC nationals, and a corresponding obligation on the part of all the Member States, under which any draft regulation regarding the use of the products in question which may result in technical difficulties in their disposal or excessive costs of disposal must be brought to the attention of the Commission before its adoption (Article 3(2) of Directive 75/442)?

(b) does that right (concerning the obligation to bring any draft regulation to the attention of the Commission before it is adopted, as set out in part (a)), if it exists, extend to *general* measures issued by municipalities, which are thus limited in their territorial application?

(4) Is the administration required under Community law to pay compensation where an unlawful administration measure taken by it infringes a right under Community law (diritto soggettivo comunitario) which upon its incorporation in the Italian legal system, whilst retaining its Community character, takes the form of a protected interest?"

(4) Reference is made to the Report for the Hearing for a fuller account of the facts of the case, the course of the procedure and the written observations submitted to the Court, which are mentioned or discussed hereinafter only in so far as is necessary for the reasoning of the Court.

(5) It is apparent from the order for reference that the proceedings before the national court concern products which do not come within the scope of Directives 76/403 and 78/319. Plastic bags contain neither polychlorobiphenyl nor polychloroterphenyl and do not in themselves constitute toxic or dangerous waste. Consequently, the questions submitted by the national court must be considered only in relation to Council Directive 75/442.

The first question

(6) The essential purpose of the first question is to determine whether Directive 75/442 gives individuals the right to sell or use plastic bags and other non-biodegradable containers.

(7) It must be borne in mind that the purpose of Directive 75/442 is to harmonize the legislation of the various Member States regarding the disposal of waste in order on the one hand to avoid barriers to intra-Community trade and inequality of conditions of competition resulting from disparities between such provisions and on the other to contribute to the attainment of Community objectives concerning protection of health and the environment. It does not prohibit the sale or use of any product whatsoever, but nor can it be inferred that it prevents Member States from imposing such prohibitions in order to protect the environment.

(8) There is no basis in the wording of the directive for a different interpretation, and in any case any different interpretation would conflict with its objectives. As is apparent from Article 3, the directive is intended *inter alia* to encourage national measures likely to prevent the production of waste. Limitation or prohibition of the sale or use of products such as non-biodegradable containers is conducive to the attainment of that objective.

(9) The plaintiffs have also claimed that an absolute prohibition of the marketing of the products in question constitutes a barrier to trade which cannot be justified by the need to protect the environment and is therefore incompatible with Article 30 of the Treaty.

(10) However, the national court has not submitted any question on Article 30 of the Treaty and accordingly there is no reason to interpret that provision.

(11) The reply to the first question must therefore be that Directive 75/442, properly construed, does not give individuals the right to sell or use plastic bags and other non-biodegradable containers.

The second question

(12) The essential purpose of the second question is to determine whether Article 3(2) of Directive 75/442 requires the Member States to inform the Commission of all draft rules of the kind at issue in the main proceedings before they are definitively adopted.

(13) It has been contended that the rules in question do not fall within the scope of Article 3 of the directive because they do not concern products whose disposal constitutes a source of technical difficulties or leads to excessive costs.

(14) It need merely be stated in that regard that Article 3(2) requires the Member States to inform the Commission in good time not only of draft rules concerning *inter alia* the use of products which might be a source of technical difficulties as regards disposal or lead to excessive disposal costs but also, by virtue of paragraph 1, of all draft rules designed to encourage *inter alia* the prevention, recycling and processing of waste.

(15) Consequently, even if the assertion that the products covered by the rules at issue are not a source of technical difficulties as regards disposal and do not lead to excessive disposal costs were substantiated, it would not follow that the draft rules in question fall outside the scope of Article 3(2) of the directive.

(16) It was also contended at the hearing that the obligation under Article 3(2) to inform the Commission beforehand related only to measures of a certain degree of importance and could not cover provisions whose practical effects are extremely limited, such as those adopted by a small municipality. It would not be practical, it was maintained, to inform the Commission of such draft rules.

(17) It need merely be stated that the directive does not provide for any derogation or limitation regarding the obligation to inform the Commission of the draft rules referred to in Article 3. Consequently, that obligation extends to draft rules drawn up by all authorities in the Member States, including decentralized authorities such as municipalities.

(18) It must therefore be stated in reply to the second question that Article 3(2) of Directive 75/442 must be interpreted as requiring Member States to inform the Commission of any draft rules such as those at issue in the main proceedings, prior to their final adoption.

The third question

(19) The purpose of the third question is to determine whether Article 3(2) of Directive 75/442 gives individuals a right which they may enforce before the national courts in order to obtain the annulment or suspension of national rules falling within the scope of that provision on the ground that those rules were adopted

without having previously been communicated to the Commission of the European Communities.

(20) Article 3(2) merely requires the Member States to inform the Commission in good time of any draft rules within the scope of that provision, without laying down any procedure for Community monitoring thereof or making implementation of the planned rules conditional upon agreement by the Commission or its failure to object.

(21) The obligation imposed on the Member States by Article 3(2) is intended to ensure that the Commission is informed of any plans for national measures regarding waste disposal so that it can consider whether Community harmonizing legislation is called for and whether the draft rules submitted to it are compatible with Community law, and take appropriate measures if necessary.

(22) Neither the wording nor the purpose of the provision in question provides any support for the view that failure by the Member States to observe their obligation to give prior notice in itself renders unlawful the rules thus adopted.

(23) It follows from the foregoing that the abovementioned provision concerns relations between the Member States and the Commission and does not give rise to any right for individuals which might be infringed by a Member State's breach of its obligation to inform the Commission in advance of draft rules.

(24) It must therefore be stated in reply to the third question that Article 3(2) of Directive 75/442, properly construed, does not give individuals any right which they may enforce before national courts in order to obtain the annulment or suspension of national rules falling within the scope of that provision on the ground that the rules were adopted without having been previously communicated to the Commission of the European Communities.

The fourth question

(25) In view of the answers given to the first three questions, there is no need to give a ruling on the fourth.

Costs

(26) The costs incurred by the United Kingdom, the Italian Government, the Portuguese Government and the Commission of the European Communities, which have submitted observations to the Court, are not recoverable. Since these proceedings are, in so far as the parties to the main proceedings are concerned, a step in the action pending before the national court, the decision on costs is a matter for that court.

On those grounds,

THE COURT (FIFTH CHAMBER),

in answer to the questions submitted to it by the Tribunale amministrativo regionale per la Lombardia, by order of 23 November 1987, hereby rules:

(1) Directive 75/442, properly construed, does not give individuals the right to sell or use plastic bags and other non-biodegradable containers.

(2) Article 3(2) of Directive 75/442 must be interpreted as requiring Member States to inform the Commission of any draft rules such as those at issue in the main proceedings, prior to their final adoption.

(3) Article 3(2) of Directive 75/442, properly construed, does not give individuals any right which they may enforce before national courts in order to obtain the annulment or suspension of national rules falling within the scope of that provision on the ground that the rules were adopted without having been previously communicated to the Commission of the European Communities.

COMMENTARY

(1) This judgment is remarkable because it touches on a series of very relevant issues of environmental law without contributing much to their solution; this is not due to an "omission" of the European Court, but rather—if not inherent in the case—to the questions which the Italian court had put.

Indeed, if one compares the questions laid before the European Court and the answers given, one wonders whether better questions could not have been asked. No attempt will be made hereafter to disentangle the Italian court's considerations in the case.[2]

(2) The plaintiffs in the main proceedings had opposed the prohibition to sell or use plastic bags and other non-biodegradable containers, because they considered such a prohibition to be incompatible with Community law. The Italian court did not put this question before the European Court, but rather a very sophisticated question on individuals' rights under Directives 75/442 on waste,[3] 78/319 on toxic and dangerous waste[4] and 76/403 on the disposal of polychlorinated biphenyles and polychlorinated terphenyls.[5] The most relevant question on the compatibility of the Italian measure with Article 30 was not posed and therefore not answered by the Court.

(3) The Court considered Directives 78/319 and 76/403 as not relevant to the case and thus only examined Directive 75/442. The Court examined the objective of Directive 75/442 and found that it aims at harmonising national legislation on the disposal of waste in order (a) to avoid trade barriers and inequalities of conditions of competition among Member States, and (b) "to

---

[2] See in this context N. Cerana-L. Gariboldi, "Sulla legitimitá del diritto di vendita e uso di sacchetti di plastica e altri contenitori non biodegradabili quale rimedio preventivo alla produzione di rifiuti", *Rivista Giuridica dell'Ambiente* 1989, 821.

[3] [1975] O.J. L194/39.

[4] [1978] O.J. L84/43 considerably amended by Directive 91/689: [1991] O.J. L337/20.

[5] [1976] O.J. L108/4.

contribute to the attainment of Community objectives concerning the protection of health and the environment". The Directive, the Court said, is silent on the question of prohibitions to sell or use certain products or of preventing Member States from making such prohibitions. The Court saw no difference to this teleological interpretation by giving a literal interpretation of Directive 75/442. Indeed, since Article 3 of the Directive encourages national measures intended to prevent the production of waste, a national measure which limits or bans the use of non-biodegradable containers may correctly be subsumed under this Article 3.

Since Directive 75/442 is silent on the position of the individual's right to sell plastic bags, the only relevant question was whether the Italian prohibition was compatible with Article 30 of the EEC Treaty. "However, the national court has not submitted any question on Article 30 of the Treaty and accordingly there is no reason to interpret that provision."[6]

(4) As if the Court ever had refrained from *obiter dicta*! The question of which national, regional or local measures are allowed in order to protect the environment is delicate and the Italian court is to be blamed for not having put the right question. However, the Dassonville-formula[7] or the Cassis-de-Dijon formula of the European Court[8] in order to explain the principles of free circulation of goods and the interpretation of Article 30, go far beyond the individual case and are thus *obiter dicta* in the classical sense. It would have been possible and helpful had the Court also given some environmental formula as regards the interpretation of Article 30.

There were good reasons to do so. Indeed, the United Kingdom stated[9] that the Directive 75/442 was not applicable in this case, since that Directive refers to waste, which, under Article 1 of that Directive, is "any substance which the holder disposes of or is required to dispose of pursuant to the provisions of national law in force." Plastic bags are not, in the view of the United Kingdom, waste within the meaning of Directive 75/442. Had the Court followed this line of thinking, it would have come directly into the interpretation of Article 30.

(5) The United Kingdom's point of view raises the general problem of differentiating between "waste" and "substance"/"product". The Italian prohibition is a measure related to products (plastic bags). These products will, at a later stage, be considered as "wastes", normally when they are thrown away. Their low costs make a deposit-and-return-system uneconomical; also recycling of plastic bags is probably not economical. Other products which are thrown away by some persons might be very useful for others, such as old furniture, used cars, and consumer durables in general. This shows that the classifica-

---

[6] 380/87: [1989] E.C.R. 2491, [1991] 1 C.M.L.R. 313, para. 10.
[7] Case 8/74, *Dassonville*: [1974] E.C.R. 837 [1974] 2 C.M.L.R. 436: Any measure by a Member State which is capable of affecting the free circulation of goods directly or indirectly, actually or potentially "was considered to be incompatible with Article 30".
[8] Case 120/78, *Rewe* v. *Bundesmonopolverwaltung*: [1979] E.C.R. 649, [1979] 3 C.M.L.R. 494.
[9] Case 380/87, above p. 2497.

tion of a physical object as "product" or "waste" is subjective and depends on subjective economic consideration rather than on objective criteria.

(6) My submission is that the distinction between "products" and "waste" in law has not been too helpful in the past. In the endless attempts to give precision to the definition of "waste" one easily overlooks the fact that from the environmental point of view "risk" or "damage" is the same thing, independent from the classification of the physical object. The criterion that "waste" has a negative economic value[10] is of limited use, since first it introduces an economic element into the legal definition and second, it cannot really help in cases of recyclable wastes which must be classified as "wastes" or "products" according to different economic, political or social situations.

Directive 91/156[11] defines waste as all substances or objects which come under Annex I and of which their owner disposes, wants to dispose or has to dispose. Since Annex I, number Q16 mentions as being wastes all substances or products not mentioned elsewhere in Annex I, the annex may, for the purpose of definition, be forgotten. The remaining definition does not, in my opinion, solve the problem of "waste" and "products". A returnable bottle or a recyclable product, *e.g.* old paper cannot really be considered as wastes.

This question cannot be discussed in all details here. It remains a surprising fact that a measure which prohibits the marketing of a product is purely examined under waste (prevention) aspects. Furthermore it is to be repeated that the Court, until now, has hardly ever discussed the compatibility of a national environmentally motivated prohibition or restriction with Article 30. Indeed:

— the French measure allowing the burning of used oils only in industrial, but not in other installations, was hardly discussed in Case 240/83;[12] and the Commission did not attack it in Case 173/83 which it brought against France;[13]
— the Danish prohibition of metal containers for beer and soft drinks was not attacked by the Commission in Case 302/86;[14]
— the Italian measure prohibiting the sale of non-biodegradable plastic bags was not submitted by the Commission to the Court in order to obtain a decision as to its compatibility with Article 30 in Case 380/87; neither has the Commission tackled it separately.[15]

At present, one may doubt whether much clarity will be gained from the Court's decision that under Article 30, waste is considered to be a product,

---

[10] This argument is the most often used in order to justify a distinct definition of waste.
[11] [1991] O.J. L78/32 amending Directive 75/442 mentioned above.
[12] Case 240/83, *ADBHU* [1985] E.C.R. 531; see pp. 5 *et seq.* above.
[13] Case 173/83, *Commission* v. *France:* [1985] E.C.R. 491.
[14] Case 302/86, *Commission* v. *Denmark:* [1988] E.C.R. 4607 [1989] 1 C.M.L.R. 619; see also pp. 91 *et seq.* above.
[15] Decreto Legge of September 9, 1988, n. 397; Legge of August 4, 1989; see also Cerana-Gariboldi (n. 2), p. 823.

whereas Community measures on waste are, normally, not to be based on Article 100n, but on Article 130s.

(7) Since the general possibility under Article 30 to take such measures is out of doubt, the question is only whether such measures are disproportionate.[16] In the present Case 380/87, the plaintiffs argued that an absolute prohibition of marketing cannot be justified, since it is always possible to attain the objective sought by less restrictive means. This again raises the question of how far national measures may go. I am of the opinion that such a decision is up to the national authorities and that, in particular, such measures do not undergo any test of "reasonableness". I understand the EEC Treaty in such a way that the environment must not remain unprotected and if there is no Community measure, Member States are entitled to protect it in the way they think fits the circumstances. This also follows from Article 100a which provides that a Member State may continue to apply, in the case of a Community measure adopted under Article 100a, more restrictive national environmental measures, provided that these measures are not a means of arbitrary discrimination or a disguised restriction on trade.

These limits are, in my opinion, also the only ones which apply to national measures taken in the absence of Community measures. In the long term, it would lead to severe discrepancies if national measures (in the absence of Community measures) could only be allowed if they are "reasonable" (Article 30) but would be allowed under Article 100a, paragraph 4 even if they are unreasonable but are neither discriminatory nor a disguised trade restriction. Rather, the measuring stick must be the same for both articles.

(8) Thus in my opinion, the measure of the Mayor of Cinisello Balsamo seems perfectly compatible with Article 30. It shows at the same time how far local authorities can go in protecting the environment. There is considerable scope for local authorities to take action: prohibiting (for environmental reasons) specific products or substances to be used in construction material; banning disposable bottles, cutlery, etc. at fairs or festivities; and, restricting transport for noise reasons. Of course, limits depend on national legislation[17] and on how much self-government is left for local authorities.

The Court requests Member States to inform the Commission of draft measures which prevent the generation of waste.[18] However, it is not clear how Member States would be able to fulfil the obligation of informing the Commission of draft local measures. Indeed, it is doubtful whether there is even a provision in all Member States which ensures that the central national

---

[16] See for further discussion of this question the commentary on Case 302/86, p. 91 above. Other examples in L. Krämer, *EEC Treaty and Environmental Protection* (London, 1990), p. 36.

[17] As an example, the local measure of Munich (Germany) may be cited which had forbidden all disposable plates, cups, knives, forks, etc. on fairs and public festivities. The measure was, end of 1991, held to be unlawful by the courts, because under German law, such measures have to be decided by the regional or national legislation and not by the local government.

[18] In practice very few notifications under Art. 3 have been and are being made to the Commission.

authorities are themselves informed of such local measures. As regards the Netherlands, Jans[19] raised this problem and suggested the introduction of such a rule at national level.

The situation might not be much different in other Member States. It should be noted that Directive 83/189,[20] which will be discussed below, expressly exempts the notification of local measures in draft form to the Commission. This might be due to the minimum effect on trade which such measures normally have.

(9) The Court then had to address the question of the obligation to notify the Commission of draft legislation in environmental matters. Directive 75/442, Article 3 provides:

> "1. Member States shall take appropriate steps to encourage the prevention, recycling and processing of waste, the extraction of raw materials and any other process for the re-use of waste.
> 2. They shall inform the Commission in good time of any draft rules to such effect and, in particular, ... "

As the Court considers the prohibition of plastic bags to be a measure encouraging the prevention of waste, it is therefore of the opinion that the Italian measure comes under Article 3 of Directive 75/442. The fact that it is a local and not a national measure is irrelevant since Article 3 does not differentiate between the two.

(10) The need for the Commission to be informed of draft environmental measures which Member States envisage to adopt, appeared very early. In fact the first measure of environmental policy, an agreement that the Commission should be informed of such draft measures was concluded in 1973.[21] Since at the time, there was a dispute among Member States whether environmental measures should be the subject of Community policy or of inter-governmental co-operation, the agreement was adopted by the Representatives of Member States in Council, not by the Council; furthermore it was called a "gentleman's agreement" in order to show its non-binding character. In the beginning the stand still agreement worked well and the Commission received a substantive amount of information. However, the Commission's reaction to this was limited, particularly due to staff shortage. Only in very exceptional cases was the Commission able to propose—within the time-limits of the agreement—a Community-wide measure in favour of the environ-

---

[19] J. H. Jans, *Europees Milieurecht in Nederland* (Groningen, 1991) p. 167.
[20] Laying down a procedure for the provision of information in the field of technical standards and regulations, [1983] O.J. L109/81.
[21] Agreement of the Representatives of the Governments of the Member States meeting in Council on March 5, 1973 on information for the Commission and for the Member States with a view to possible harmonisation throughout the Communities of urgent measures concerning the protection of the environment, [1973] O.J. C9/1, amended [1974] O.J. C86/2.

ment. Thus, the usefulness of informing the Commission was diminishing and gradually fewer and fewer draft measures were sent to the Commission, all the more since no "sanction" was foreseen in the stand still agreement for a breach of the obligations to communicate. Similar developments occurred in the area of Directives such as 75/442 or 85/339.[22]

(11) In 1983, Directive 83/189 concerning technical standards for industrial products was adopted[23] which provided, *inter alia*, for a compulsory notification to the Commission of all measures coming under that Directive; Member States were obliged to delay the adoption of national measures up to 12 months after notification, according to specific circumstances laid down in the Directive. Since the Commission gave a very wide interpretation of the notion of technical standard, most draft environmental measures came under Directive 83/189 so that the Commission in fact gave up monitoring the 1973 standstill agreement.[24]

It is questionable whether waste measures come under Directive 83/189 so that there is a mandatory standstill requirement for such measures.[25] In the present case, the Court was not asked such a question and thus did not have to answer it.

(12) The Court did not use the "effet utile" doctrine[26] to support the plaintiffs' argument that national measures which are adopted in draft form without the Commission being notified, are invalid. It is correct, as the Advocate General stated,[27] that nothing in Directive 75/442 provides for such a rule. However, it is also correct that the pure obligation of Article 3 without having any consequence, makes Article 3 ineffective. It is not realistic to expect the Commission to bring a case under Article 169 and receive, after several years, the Court's decision that a Member State has failed to notify a draft measure, without any consequences following from that failure. In practice, no such case has ever been brought before the Court by the Commission. The plaintiffs tried, though unsuccessfully, to make the Court apply an "effet utile" doctrine and thus to annul national measures which had been adopted without previously having been notified in draft form to the Commission. The Court found neither in the wording nor in the objective of Directive 75/442 any reason to provide for any legal sanction in case of non-respect of Article 3.

(13) One example, where the Court did refer to the "effet utile" doctrine was

---

[22] Directive 75/442, [1975] O.J. L194/39; Directive 85/339 on containers of liquids for human consumption, [1985] O.J. L176/18. Both directives contain an obligation to inform the Commission of draft measures by Member States.

[23] See n. 20 above.

[24] Commission, 21st General Report (1987), p. 221 and answer to Written Question 917/87, [1988] O.J. C86/26.

[25] The majority of national measures on waste is notified under that Directive.

[26] In this context, the "effet utile" doctrine might best be described as an interpretation of a Community rule which ensures that it has full and useful effect.

[27] Advocate General, p. 320 (C.M.L.R.). p. 2507 (E.C.R.)

given above. In Case 187/87, the Court referred to the "effet utile" doctrine in order to interpret the Euratom Treaty in a way that made it more effective.[28] Another environmental case where the Court, at least implicitly referred to that doctrine, is Case 322/86.[29] In that case the question arose whether Italy had fully complied with the requirements of Directive 78/659.[30] This Directive provides, *inter alia*, in Article 4:

> "1. Member States shall, initially within a two-year period following the notification of this Directive, designate salmonid waters and cyprinid waters.
> 2. Member States may subsequently make additional designations.
> 3. ..."

Italy had only designated waters capable of supporting freshwater fish in the province of Bolzano. The Court stated that "the transposition of Community Directives into national law must effectively and completely ensure their full application."

It concluded therefore that Italy had not respected its obligations under that Directive because it had only designated waters in the Bolzano region.

(14) Nothing in the wording of Directive 78/659 imposes a designation of waters capable of supporting freshwater fish all over the territory of a Member State and the Court's decision finds its justification in the attempt to give full effect to the Directive. Obviously, the purpose of Directive 78/659 is to improve the quality of waters and this objective might best be attained by the designation of as many waters as possible. However, the Directive leaves it to Member States to designate waters and does not ask for a nation-wide designation.

(15) In the present Case, one might argue that legal certainty for economic agents and the need to prevent the creation of barriers to trade, made it necessary to provide an effective dissuasion for Member States not to notify the Commission of draft measures.

It is clear from the Court's interpretation that the provisions of prior notification to the Commission of draft measures is almost of no practical value; and this conclusion is not changed by the fact that Directive 91/156 repeats the obligation—again without providing for any consequence in the case of non-compliance.[31]

(16) These considerations have an impact on the discussion of the third question put to the European Court, *i.e.* whether individuals have a right to take

---

[28] 187/87, *Saarland and others.* [1988] E.C.R. 5013, [1989] 1 C.M.L.R. 619, see p. 55 above.

[29] 322/86, *Commission* v. *Italy.* [1988] E.C.R. 3995.

[30] On the quality of fresh waters needing protection or improvement in order to support fish life, [1978] O.J. L222/1.

[31] Dir. 91/156 (n. 11 above), Art. 3, para. 2.

action before a national court in order to have national, regional or local measures annulled or suspended in those cases where these rules have not been notified (in draft form) to the Commission. The Court saw in Article 3 of Directive 75/442 (only) a means for the Commission to become informed of national measures in order to be able to consider whether Community-wide measures should be taken. Neither in the wording of Article 3 nor in its objective did the Court see any element to protect individuals and thus answered the question in the negative.

(17) The plaintiffs then invoked the direct-effect doctrine of the Court and tried to obtain another answer.[32] This doctrine, established by Court jurisdiction in a consistent line of decisions,[33] is layed down in Article 189 of the EEC Treaty. The article distinguishes between regulations and directives: while a regulation is directly applicable in all Member States, a directive is binding upon each Member State to which it is addressed. The European Court has developed the doctrine that directives which have not been transposed into national law, may nevertheless have some effects in the national legal order:

" . . . wherever the provisions of a Directive appear, as far as their subject-matter is concerned, to be unconditional and sufficiently precise, those provisions may, in the absence of implementing measures adopted within the prescribed period, be relied upon . . . in so far as the provisions define rights which individuals are able to assert against the State."[34]

Any other interpretation would mean, the Court said, that the Member State could rid a directive of its effect simply by failing to implement it completely or correctly. Such a consequence was not compatible with the wording of Article 189, paragraph 3.

(18) This doctrine requires that provisions of a directive be worded in a precise and unconditional way in order to have direct effect. In the present case, the Court did not find the wording of Directive 75/442 sufficiently precise and unconditional to give the individual the right to sell plastic bags (first preliminary question). Indeed, since the Directive is silent on this question, it would have been difficult to talk of a precise wording to that extent and the Court's statement that the Directive neither prohibits nor allows such sales is certainly closer to the text of the Directive than the interpretation given by the plaintiffs.

(19) The direct-effect doctrine reappeared in the plaintiffs arguments that the adoption of a national measure without notification to the Commission makes that national rule invalid and that this could be invoked before national courts.

---

[32] See p. 2499 (E.C.R.).
[33] Case 41/74, *Van Duyn*: [1974] E.C.R. 1337; Case 148/78, *Ratti*: [1979] E.C.R. 1629, [1980] 1 C.M.L.R. 96; Case 8/81, *Becker*. [1982] E.C.R. 53, [1982] 1 C.M.L.R. 499; Case 103/88, *Costanzo*: [1988] E.C.R. 339, [1990] 3 C.M.L.R. 239.
[34] Case 152/84, *Marshall*: [1986] E.C.R. 723, [1986] 1 C.M.L.R. 688.

However, again, the wording of Directive 75/442 does not state this. And it is not possible to interpret this silence to be a precise and unconditional statement that such consequences flow from the Directive. This follows in particular from a comparison of the wording of Directive 75/442 with that of Directive 83/189 which expressly states that the adoption of a draft national measure must be postponed for a certain period after the notification.[35]

(20) It should be noted that until now the Court has not yet applied the direct-effect doctrine to any environmental case and nor allowed individuals to invoke the direct and unconditional effect of a Directive.[36] In the present case, the Court rightly rejected the direct effect of Article 3 of Directive 75/442.

(21) I tried on another occasion[37] to list the provisions of environmental directives which, in my opinion, have a direct effect. These provisions normally concern:

(1) Provisions which fix maximum values, maximum concentrations and limit values;
(2) Provisions which contain a ban or a prohibition;
(3) Provisions which oblige to inform or consult the public, and which require an environment impact assessment to be made.

It is to be hoped that the Court of Justice soon finds occasion to apply the direct-effect doctrine to an environmental case. The effective enforcement at national level would be greatly promoted by such a step. The use of the direct-effect doctrine in environmental cases before national courts varies widely. Frequent use of the doctrine in the Netherlands[38] and no use of it in Portugal shows the two extreme positions.

(22) In the present case, Article 3 of Directive 75/442 seems well formulated in a precise, clear and unconditional way. However, it does not give, according to the Court's interpretation, any rights to individuals but merely deals with the relations between Member States and the Commission. Therefore, the Court rejected the direct-effect doctrine in this case.

(23) It was pointed out above that under the "effet-utile" doctrine another interpretation of Article 3 would have been possible, *i.e.* that non-notification of draft measures was sanctioned by the annulment or suspension of the national measure. In its communication of October 10, 1986 on Directive 83/189, the Commission itself concluded that the directive allows individuals to invoke in

---

[35] Directive 83/189 (n. 20 above), Art. 9.
[36] In the same sense, P. Kromarek, "La Cour de Justice des Communautés européennes et l'environnement", *Jurisclasseur Environnement*, Paris 1992, volume 240, n. 115.
[37] L. Krämer, The implementation of Community environmental directives within Member States: some implications of the direct effect doctrine. Journal of environmental law 1991, p. 39.
[38] See H. J. Jans, *op. cit.* pp. 71 *et seq.*

national courts the non-validity of national measures which were adopted without having been notified in draft form to the Commission.[39]

In that communication the Commission stated:

"The Commission considers that when a Member State enacts a technical regulation falling within the scope of Directive 83/189/EEC without notifying the draft to the Commission and respecting the standstill obligation, the regulation thus adopted is unenforceable against third parties in the legal system of the Member State in question. The Commission therefore considers that litigants have a right to expect national courts to refuse to enforce national regulations which have not been notified as required by Community law.[40]"

It must be added that until now the European Court has not confirmed the Commission's opinion.

(24) While I can understand the Commission's arguments, it seems going too far to deduce from a three-month-standstill obligation that a national measure, which was not notified, should be unenforceable even in cases where the three month standstill was *de facto* respected. The gravamen lies in the omission to notify the Commission which makes it impossible for the Commission to express an opinion and thus ensure that the Community dimension is taken into account by the national legislator. However, this element is also pertinent in the case of Directive 75/442. A difference of treatment in both cases is not justified.

(25) The Commission and the Advocate General had both concluded that—in contrast to Directive 83/189 which provided for an suspension of the draft measure—no rights were given to individuals by Article 3 of Directive 75/442, since this rule had no suspensory effect.

The Court concluded from the wording and the purpose of Article 3 that its non-respect did not make the national measure unlawful. From that it concluded that it did not give them rights. The Court could have given such a right to individuals; but it did not. The reason is probably that there is no mention of individuals' rights in Article 3 such as a right to health or a social right.

However, there is a general right to trade or to free exercise of economic activity which the Court itself mentioned in Case 240/83.[41] This right implies that—national or Community—measures which restrict it should be justified by, as the Court put in Case 240/83, essential objectives in the Community interest. The Court could have argued that the defense of the fundamental right to exercise an economic activity was ensured, *inter alia*, by the possi-

---

[39] [1986] O.J. C254/4; repeated in Commission, COM(88)722, final of December 1988, p. 66 (Report on the operation of Directive 83/189 between 1984 and 1987).

[40] *Ibid.*

[41] 240/83, [1985] E.C.R. 531, see also p. 5 above.

bility of taking into account the Community discussion of a local, regional or national measure; and that the guarantee for individuals to defend their fundamental rights was ensured by the non-enforceability of the national measure in the case of non-notification.

(26) This reasoning is even brought one step further if one applies the principles of Case C-106/89[42] to the present situation. In that case, the European Court could not apply the direct-effect doctrine, since the main case opposed two private companies and the Court has always argued that the direct effect can only be used against public authorities in cases where a Member State has not correctly and completely transposed Community law into national law.

The Court thus rejected the use of the direct-effect doctrine. But it stated that the national court was obliged to interpret the national law—even where it was clear and unambiguous—in a way that made it comply with Community law. The Court thus held that the national court in Case C-106/89 was not allowed to apply a rule of Spanish law, since Community law did not contain such a rule.

Since local authorities are obliged to apply Community law and to abstain from any measure which contradicts Community law, the Mayor of Cinisello Balsamo would only have been allowed to prohibit plastic bags where such a measure was compatible with Community law and in particular with Article 30. Otherwise he would not have been allowed to take such a measure. Individuals certainly have the right to invoke, before a national court, the incompatibility of a national measure with Article 30, as the Court has often enough recognised. This then would have led in this case to the examination whether a local prohibition of selling plastic bags is justified, under Article 30, by environmental reasons.

It is disappointing that the numerous lawyers from multinational companies and the national court managed to keep this question out of the discussion.

(27) The problem of litter, and of domestic waste in general, is causing more and more concern inside the Community. The Commission had already stated in the mid-seventies that it wanted to elaborate Community-wide rules for packaging and packaging waste. However, Directive 85/339[43] which was adopted in 1985 did not much contribute to solving the problems of domestic wastes since its provisions were not drastic enough. Several Member States thus adopted measures at national level which caused considerable concern for the packaging industry, for trade and for environmental groups. In 1992, the Commission made a proposal, based on Article 100a, for a directive on packaging and packaging waste.[44]

---

[42] C–106/89, *Marleasing* v. *la Comercial Internacional de Alimentacion* [1990] I E.C.R. 4135, [1992] 1 C.M.L.R. 305.
[43] Cited above.
[44] [1992] O.J. C263/1.

9. THE RIGHT TO TAKE STRICTER MEASURES AT NATIONAL LEVEL

**Judgment of the Court (Sixth Chamber) of May 23, 1990
in Case C–169/89**

Preliminary ruling in the criminal proceedings pending before the Hoge
Raad der Nederlanden against Gourmetterie Van den Burg

[1990] I E.C.R. 2143

FACTS AND PROCEDURE[1]

The Gourmetterie Van den Burg is a Dutch poultry and game undertaking. In 1984, Dutch inspectors found in its shop Red Grouse (Lagopus lagopus scoticus et hibernicus), a bird which is not a native of the Netherlands. It is mainly found in the United Kingdom where it is not considered to be an endangered species and where hunting and trading is permitted. Dutch law prohibits the trade in, *inter alia*, Red Grouse.

Dutch authorities started criminal proceedings against the Gourmetterie Van den Burg. In 1989, the Dutch Hoge Raad (the Supreme Court in criminal proceedings) submitted to the European Court of Justice the preliminary question whether the Dutch prohibition of the trade in Red Grouse was justified under Community law, in particular under Article 36 of the EEC Treaty and Directive 79/409[2] on the conservation of wild living birds.

The case was registered with the Court on May 16, 1989 and attributed to the Sixth Chamber. Written submissions were made by the Gourmetterie Van den Burg and the E.C. Commission. Oral hearings took place on February 7, 1990; only the Dutch government gave oral argument.

The Advocate General delivered his opinion on March 20, 1990.

JUDGMENT

(1) By judgment of 25 April 1989, which was received at the Court on 16 May 1989, the Hoge Raad der Nederlanden referred to the Court for a preliminary ruling under Article 177 of the EEC Treaty a question concerning the interpretation of Articles 30 and 36 of the Treaty. That question arose in criminal proceedings instituted against a trader in foodstuffs, Gourmetterie Van den Burg.

(2) In 1984 inspectors entrusted with ensuring compliance with the Netherlands Vogelwet (Law on Birds) confiscated a dead red grouse on the premises of Gourmetterie Van den Burg. The trader was subsequently prosecuted and convicted for infringing the provisions of the law in question, which is designed to protect birds occurring in the wild state in Europe. It appealed against that conviction on the ground that the confiscated red grouse had been lawfully killed in the United Kingdom, in accordance with the combined provisions of Article 6(2) and (3) and Annex III/1.2 of Council Directive 79/409/EEC of 2 April 1979 on the conservation of wild birds (Official Journal 1979, L 103, p. 1).

---

[1] Summary by the author.
[2] On the conservation of wild birds: [1979] O.J. L103/79, subsequently called "the Directive".

(3) The Hoge Raad, hearing the case at last instance, found that Article 7 of the Vogelwet precluded the bird in question from being bought or sold on the domestic market and that the application of that law hindered trade in a British game bird, lawfully shot and freely marketed in the country of origin. The Hoge Raad considered that, in so far as the prohibition laid down in the Vogelwet also extends to the importation and keeping of dead red grouse, it was in the nature of a measure having an effect equivalent to a quantitative restriction within the meaning of Article 30 of the Treaty. In its view, the assessment of the appeal depends on the question whether the prohibition in question may be considered justified under Article 36 of the Treaty on grounds of the protection of health and life of animals.

(4) The Hoge Raad accordingly referred the following question to the Court:

"May the prohibition applicable in the Netherlands by virtue of Article 7 of the Vogelwet (Law on Birds) on the importation and keeping of red grouse, shot and killed in the United Kingdom without any breach of the law applicable in that country, be regarded as a prohibition which is justified under Article 36 of the EEC Treaty on grounds of the protection of health and life of animals, regard being had to the fact that:

in the first place, the exception referred to in Article 6(2) of Directive 79/409/EEC applies to red grouse, which are referred to in Annex III/1 to the directive;

secondly, the purpose of the prohibition laid down in Article 7 of the Vogelwet is the preservation of wild birds and in particular the protection of all species of birds occurring in the wild state in Europe, subject to certain exceptions which do not, however, include the red grouse?"

(5) Reference is made to the Report for the Hearing for a fuller account of the legal background and the facts of the case, the course of the procedure and the written observations submitted to the Court which are mentioned or discussed hereinafter only in so far as is necessary for the reasoning of the Court.

(6) In its question, the national court raises in substance a problem concerning the interpretation of Article 36 of the Treaty, according to which the principle of the free movement of goods does not preclude prohibitions or restrictions on imports which are justified on grounds of the protection of health and life of animals.

(7) It is not disputed that the national measure in question constitutes a prohibition on imports and that the red grouse is a species which does not occur within the Netherlands.

(8) With regard to Article 36 of the Treaty, the Court has consistently held (see, most recently, the judgment of 14 June 1988 in Case 29/87 *Dansk Denkavit* v *Danish Ministry of Agriculture* [1988] ECR 2982) that a directive providing for full harmonization of national legislation deprives a Member State of recourse to that article.

(9) As regard the degree of harmonization brought about by Directive 79/409, it should be noted that, although the bird in question may, in accordance with Article 6(2) and (3) of the directive, be hunted within the Member State in which

it occurs, the fact remains that Article 14 authorizes the Member States to introduce stricter protective measures than those provided for under the directive. The directive has therefore regulated exhaustively the Member States' powers with regard to the conservation of wild birds.

(10) It is therefore appropriate to define the scope of the powers conferred on the Member States by Article 14 of the directive. In that regard, reference should be made to the principal criteria on which the Community legislature has relied in the matter.

(11) First of all, as the Court emphasized in its judgment of 27 April 1988 in Case 252/85 *Commission* v *France* [1988] ECR 2243, Directive 79/409 grants special protection to migratory species which constitute, according to the third recital in the preamble to the directive, a common heritage of the Community. Secondly, in the case of the most endangered birds, the directive provides that the species listed in Annex I must be the subject of special conservation measures in order to ensure their survival and reproduction.

(12) It follows from those general objectives laid down by Directive 79/409 for the protection of birds that the Member States are authorized, pursuant to Article 14 of the directive, to introduce stricter measures to ensure that the aforesaid species are protected even more effectively. With regard to the other bird species covered by Directive 79/409, the Member States are required to bring into force the laws, regulations and administrative provisions necessary to comply with the directive, but are not authorized to adopt stricter protective measures than those provided for under the directive, except as regards species occurring within their territory.

(13) Next, it should be noted that the red grouse is neither a migratory species nor a seriously endangered species set out in Annex I to the directive.

(14) Furthermore, Council Regulation (EEC) No 3626/82 of 3 December 1982 on the implementation in the Community of the Convention on international trade in endangered species of wild fauna and flora (Official Journal 1982, L 384, p. 1) does not refer to the red grouse as an endangered animal within the meaning of that Convention.

(15) It follows from the foregoing that Article 14 of the directive does not empower a Member State to afford a given species which is neither migratory nor endangered stricter protection, by means of a prohibition on importation and marketing, than that provided for by the legislation of the Member State on whose territory the bird in question occurs, where such legislation is in conformity with the provisions of Directive 79/409.

(16) The answer to the question submitted for a preliminary ruling must therefore be that Article 36 of the Treaty, read in conjunction with Council Directive 79/409 of 2 April 1979 on the conservation of wild birds, must be interpreted as meaning that a prohibition on importation and marketing cannot be justified in respect of a species of bird which does not occur in the territory of the legislating Member State but is found in another Member State where it may lawfully be hunted under the terms of that directive and under the legislation of that other State, and which is neither migratory nor endangered within the meaning of the directive.

Costs

The costs incurred by the Netherlands Government and the Commission of the European Communities, which have submitted observations to the Court, are not recoverable. Since these proceedings are, in so far as the parties to the main proceedings are concerned, in the nature of a step in the action pending before the national court, the decision on costs is a matter for that court.

On those grounds,

THE COURT (SIXTH CHAMBER),

in answer to the questions submitted to it by the Hoge Raad der Nederlanden, by judgment of 25 April 1989, hereby rules:

Article 36 of the Treaty, read in conjunction with Council Directive 79/409/EEC of 2 April 1979 on the conservation of wild birds, must be interpreted as meaning that a prohibition on importation and marketing cannot be justified in respect of a species of bird which does not occur in the territory of the legislating Member State but is found in another Member State where it may lawfully be hunted under the terms of that directive and under the legislation of that other State, and which is neither migratory nor endangered within the meaning of the directive.

COMMENTARY

(1) This judgment is one of the few which the Court has pronounced until now on the interdependency of the free circulation of goods, Articles 30 and 36, and the protection of the environment.[3] Since until this judgment, there had been only one other Court decision which expressly addressed this interdependency, one may regret that the Court transferred the case for decision to a chamber. Indeed, the importance of the case or the specific circumstances[4] might have required a plenary decision. This argument is further strengthened by the fact that in my opinion the present decision departed from the interpretation of Directive 79/409 which the Court (full sitting) had given on earlier occasions.[5]

---

[3] See also Case 302/86, *Commission* v. *Denmark:* [1988] E.C.R. 4607, [1989] 1 C.M.L.R. 619 (p. 91 above); one might also quote 380/87, *Enichem and others* v. *Cinisella Balsamo:* [1989] E.C.R. 2491, [1991] 1 C.M.L.R. 313 (p. 131 above).

[4] See Art. 95 *et seq.* rules of the procedure of the Court. Specific circumstances are in particular the relationship between environment protection and the free circulation of goods.

[5] Case 247/87, *Commission* v. *Belgium:* [1987] E.C.R. 3029, [1990] 1 C.M.L.R. 733; Case 262/85, *Commission* v. *Italy:* [1987] E.C.R. 3073; Case 412/85, *Commission* v. *Germany:* [1987] E.C.R. 3503; Case 236/85, *Commission* v. *the Netherlands:* [1987] E.C.R. 3989; Case 252/85, *Commission* v. *France:* [1988] E.C.R. 2243; Case 57/89R, *Commission* v. *Germany:* [1989] E.C.R. 2849; Case C–339/87, *Commission* v. *the Netherlands:* [1990] E.C.R. I 851; Case C–285/88, *Commission* v. *Germany:* [1990] I E.C.R. 2721.

(2) The reasoning of the Court is as follows: Article 36 of the EEC Treaty only applies in the absence of total harmonisation of a problem by secondary legislation. In the present case, Directive 79/409 contains such a total harmonisation.

Article 14 of Directive 79/409 allows Member States to introduce stricter protective measures than those provided for under Directive 79/409. However, this provision only applies either to migratory species, or to birds for which special conservation measures are necessary.[6]

The Red Grouse is neither a migratory bird nor a bird for which special conservation measures are required under the Directive nor is it an endangered species under Regulation 3626/82.[7] Therefore, Dutch legislation is not allowed to provide measures which go beyond those taken by the United Kingdom in conformity with Directive 79/409, as regards the protection of the Red Grouse.

(3) The Court's statement, that Article 36 only applies where a subject matter has not been regulated completely by Community legislation, conforms to a consistent line of decisions of the European Court of Justice[8] which seems to me correct and not questionable. A problem arises only, in general, when it has to be determined whether Community legislation does contain such a complete, exhaustive treatment of a specific problem. In the present case, the Court argued that Article 36 was excluded, since Article 14 of Directive 79/409 authorises Member States to introduce stricter protective measures than those provided for under Directive 79/409.[9] However, later in the decision, the Court argued that Article 14 only applies to measures concerning migratory species, particularly threatened species and species living on their territory.[10]

This seems a contradiction. Indeed, insofar as Article 14 does not apply, it cannot exclude the application of Article 36 of the EEC Treaty. Since the Court gives a limited field of application to Article 14, it cannot, at the same time, argue that Article 14 is of general application to all birds and thus exclude the application of Article 36 to any bird. It will be argued below that Article 14 does apply to all birds. Logically, the argument of the Court is, in my opinion, not acceptable.

(4) The arguments of the Court, as regards the field of application of Article 14 are not convincing. This Article reads:

---

[6] Para. 12.
[7] On the implementation in the Community of the Convention on international trade in endangered species of wild fauna and flora: [1982] O.J. L384/1.
[8] See Case 5/77, *Tedeschi* [1977] E.C.R. 1555, [1978] 1 C.M.L.R. 1; Case 148/78, *Ratti* [1979] E.C.R. 1629, [1980] 1 C.M.L.R. 96; Case 72/83, *Campus Oil* [1984] E.C.R. 2727, [1984] 3 C.M.L.R. 544; Case 251/78, *Denkavit* [1979] E.C.R. 3369, [1980] 3 C.M.L.R. 513.
[9] Para. 9.
[10] Para. 11.

"Member States may introduce stricter protective measures than those provided for under this Directive."

Nothing in the wording of this Article contains the slightest restriction as to which species of birds it covers. The Court did not refer to the wording, but took its arguments for a restrictive interpretation of Article 14 from the "principle criteria" which had inspired the Community legislator to take measures in favour of birds:

(5) The first argument is taken from the third recital of Directive 79/409 which reads:

"Whereas the species of wild birds naturally occurring in the European territory of the Member States are mainly migratory species; whereas such species constitute a common heritage and whereas effective bird protection is typically a transfrontier environment problem entailing common responsibilities."

The Court concluded from this wording that the Directive grants a special protection to migratory birds.

This however, is an obvious error. Indeed, Article 1 of Directive 79/409 states in all clarity:

"This Directive relates to the conservation of *all* species of naturally occurring birds in the wild state in the European territory of the Member States to which the Treaty applies. It covers the protection management and control of these species and lays down rules for their exploitation." (emphasis added).

There is not the slightest indication that its application should be limited to migratory birds. Nor can such a limitation be found in any other article of Directive 79/409.

By referring to Recital three of the Directive, the Court has omitted to take Recital two into consideration. This reads:

"Whereas a large number of species of wild birds naturally occurring in the European territory of the Member States are declining in number, very rapidly in some cases; whereas this decline represents a serious threat to the conservation of the natural environment, particularly because of the biological balances threatened thereby."

It is fair to say that this recital, which refers to all species and not just to migratory species, together with Article 1 introduces a general scheme of protection for all birds occurring within the Member States, as the Court itself has stated on earlier occasions.[11] It might well be possible to see a specific complementary scheme for migratory birds laid down in the directive and in particular in the third recital. But it does not seem possible to declare, without any further justification, that Article 14 only applies to the particular scheme for migratory birds, and not to the general protection scheme for all birds.

(6) The same reasoning applies to particularly threatened species of birds. The existence of a particular threat to some birds does not take away the general protection from which all birds benefit by virtue of Directive 79/409. This becomes clear, when one realises that the only supplementary protection which the Directive provides for particularly threatened birds is the protection of their habitats according to Article 4.[12] As regards hunting, marketing, sale and transport, no difference is made between particularly threatened birds and other birds.

(7) The Court allowed the application of Article 14 to cover one further category of birds: those which live in the territory of the Member State which takes the measure.[13] No justification was given to this argument. In my opinion the Court again failed to recognise that the Directive aims at the protection of all wild birds naturally occurring in the European territory of the Member States. This general protection system not only applies to birds which are alive but also to dead birds. The Directive itself defines and justifies this general protection status: the tenth recital reads:

> "Whereas, in order to prevent commercial interests from exerting a possible harmful pressure on exploitation levels it is necessary to impose a general ban on marketing and to restrict all derogation to those species whose biological status so permits, account being taken of the specific conditions obtaining in the different regions; ... "

Consequently, Article 6, paragraph 1 requires Member States to prohibit "for all the bird species referred to in Article 1, the sale, transport for sale, keeping for sale and the offering for sale of living or dead birds". Article 6, paragraph 2 continues:

> "The activities referred to in paragraph 1 shall not be prohibited in respect of the species referred to in Annex III/1, provided that the birds have been legally killed or captured or otherwise legally acquired."

The provision of Article 6, paragraph 2 is discussed below. At this point it should be made clear that the Directive provides for a general prohibition on

---

[11] Case 247/87, cited above, paras. 6, 7, 8, 22 and 52; Case 262/85, cited above, in particular paras. 6 and 18.
[12] See in particular Case–57/89, discussed at p. 219 below.
[13] Para. 12.

the sale of birds, dead or alive, which come under the Directive. Paragraph 2 of Article 6 contains an exception to this general prohibition. This exception would have to be weighed against the general possibility of Member States under Article 14, introducing stricter protective measures.

(8) All this is not even mentioned in the decision in Case C–169/89. This decision refers only once to another decision of the Court, indicating that migratory species benefit from a specific protection under Directive 79/409.[14] However, the decision omits to mention that the Court had already stated its position on the protection scheme set up under Directive 79/409 in no less than eight decisions[15] prior to C–169/89. The Court stated that the Directive protects all birds,[16] sets up a general protection scheme which protects all species and all birds,[17] and that the protection of the "common heritage"[18] of the birds is entrusted to the Member States. Of particular interest is the Court's statement in Case 262/85, *Commission* v. *Italy*, where the Court draws some conclusions on the issue of trading in birds between Member States.[19]

(9) In conclusion, it may be stated that contrary to the Court's opinion, Article 14 of the Directive does allow Member States to take stricter protective measures for all birds, not just for migratory species, particularly threatened species and species living in their territory.

The question remains whether this general possibility is restricted by the provision of Article 6, paragraph 2, mentioned above.[20] Case C–169/89 does not address this question; neither does it examine the meaning of Article 130t of the EEC Treaty, which contains, since July 1, 1987, a provision which is very similar to Article 14 of Directive 79/409.[21] Nor does it examine the question

---

[14] Para. 11, referring to Case 252/85, *Commission* v. *France*: [1988] E.C.R. 2243.
[15] See references cited above n. 5.
[16] See references cited above n. 11.
[17] Case 247/87, n. 5 above, para. 52; Case 262/85, n. 5 above, para. 6.
[18] The expression comes from Dir. 79/409, third recital. In Case 247/87, (cited above n. 5), the Court uses the expression for all birds (para. 9). This is almost word by word repeated in other decisions, see for instance Case 252/85, (cited above), para. 5. Furthermore, the French legislation which only protected "le patrimoine biologique national", was found incompatible with the general protection provided for under the Directive (para. 15), though it seems that the Court mainly referred to migratory birds.
[19] Case 262/85, *Commission* v. *Italy*: [1987] E.C.R. 3073, para. 18:
    "It should be borne in mind in this regard that Article 6(1) of the Directive requires the Member States to impose a general prohibition on the marketing of all the birds covered by the Directive, alive or dead, and of any readily recognizable parts or derivatives of such birds ... it is clear from the protection to be afforded under the Directive that it is intended to avoid a situation in which all the species that may be hunted may also be marketed because of the pressure which marketing may exert on hunting and consequently on the population level of the species in question ... "
[20] See p. 155 above.
[21] **Article 130t**:
    "The protective measures adopted in common pursuant to Article 130s shall not prevent any Member State from maintaining or introducing more stringent protective measures compatible with this Treaty."

whether Article 36 allows a Member State to protect the environment in another Member State.

(10) My own opinion is that the Directive sets up a general protection system for all wild birds. It tries to give them maximum protection by allowing, in particular, Member States to take stricter protective measures. It tries to reduce trade in birds in order to prevent commercial interests to exert harmful pressure on the hunting and killing of birds. Therefore, derogations from this general principle have to be interpreted narrowly. Article 6, paragraph 2 does allow birds which are killed legally in one Member State to be marketed, but it cannot restrict the general possibility for Member States under Article 14 of the Directive, not allowing such marketing, in order to prevent any harmful pressure on the population level of such birds. Indeed, it would just become a question of marketing that the Red Grouse could, if one were following the Court's decision, be marketed all over the EEC. Consequently, hunting and killing of that bird would considerably increase. That is exactly what the Directive tries to prevent.

This then is the main objection to the reasoning of the Court's decision in Case C–169/89. The Court treats birds which are not explicitly protected in the same way as any other movable goods without realising that the protection of birds is part of environmental protection, an important objective in the Community's general interest.[22] It does not see that the Directive creates a general protection scheme for birds and their habitats which makes it impossible to treat birds as movable goods. In other words: all birds,[23] not just especially threatened birds, are "threatened" in the sense of the Directive.

(11) Even if one were to follow the Court's interpretation of Directive 79/409 and in particular of Article 14, one problem remains. Indeed, the Court concluded in paragraphs 8 and 9 that Directive 79/409 is a measure of complete harmonisation of national rules and thus exclude any recourse to Article 36.[24] This seems logical and one wonders, why the Court in the present decision, argued so little on this question.[25]

The Court should have examined whether the Dutch measure could be jus-

---

[22] Case 240/83, *ADBHK* [1985] E.C.R. 531 (see p. 5 above); Case 302/86, *Commission* v. *Denmark* [1988] E.C.R. 4607, [1989] 1 C.M.L.R. 619 (see p. 91 above).

[23] The only explanation I can find for the Court's decision and its line of reasoning is the provenance of a thinking which finds its origin in the supremacy given to internal market requirements and to the idea of the dominance of free circulation of goods. To this line of thinking belongs the principle—which the decision in Case C–169/89 does not mention—that a product, which is lawfully produced and marketed in one Member State should be allowed to circulate everywhere within the Community. In my opinion, the interdependency between the free circulation of goods and the protection of the environment is to be seen in a much more nuanced way. The insertion of Articles 130r to 130t into the EEC Treaty have changed the balance which might have existed previously.

[24] See for this argument: Case 4/75, *Rewe* [1975] E.C.R. 843, [1977] 1 C.M.L.R. 599; Case 29/87, *Denkavit* [1988] E.C.R. 2965, [1990] 1 C.M.L.R. 203.

[25] J. Jans *Europees Milieurecht in Nederland*, (Groningen, 1991) talks on p. 182 of a "gebrekkig gemotiveerde uitspraak".

tified under Article 36. My own opinion is the same as for Article 14 of Directive 79/409. I consider the Dutch measure compatible with Article 36 and I am unable to see in it an arbitrary discrimination or a disguised restriction of trade between Member States. Neither can I consider the measures disproportionate, as will be explained below.

(12) Advocate General van Gerven followed a somewhat different line of argument. He considered the Dutch legislation a stricter measure under Article 14 of Directive 79/409. Furthermore, he stated—as did the Court—that Regulation 3626/82[26] did not consider Red Grouse an endangered species, but allowed, under Article 15, Member States to adopt stricter protective measures provided they were compatible with Article 36 of the EEC Treaty. He thus examined the Dutch legislation concerning Red Grouse for its compatibility with Article 36 of the EEC Treaty. He concluded that the Dutch measure was not compatible with Article 36, since it was disproportionate to the objective pursued.[27]

Since the Court did not agree with the Advocate General's reasoning, but followed a completely different reasoning, the argument of the Advocate General cannot be analysed and commented on in detail here. I am of the opinion that the Advocate General does not do justice to the fundamental objective of Directive 79/409 which aims at the protection, as far as possible, of all wild birds. Article 14 of directive aims at ensuring this optimal protection of birds as part of the environmental policy. It was the Member States themselves who wanted to prevent the pressure on species which could come from the sale of killed or hunted species. It is not clear why such a preventative measure[28] should be disproportionate.

The Advocate General argued that the Dutch Government had a less restrictive measure available to protect Red Grouse. He argued that it could have collected information on the status of Red Grouse via the reports mentioned in Article 12 of Directive 79/409[29] and, as appropriate, asked for measures to amend the Directive.[30]

It is interesting to note that the Member States have up to now been so remiss in sending their reports every three years to the Commission under Article 12 that the Commission has, between 1981 and 1992, not been able to produce one single composite report under that Article.[31] The alternative measure for the Dutch government is thus purely hypothetical. In practice, there is no less restrictive measure available.

---

[26] [1982] O.J. L384/1.
[27] Advocate General van Gerven, Case C–169/89: [1990] I E.C.R. 2151.
[28] Art. 130r EEC, para. 2 expressly requires that preventative action should be taken.
[29] [1979] O.J. L103/79 Art. 12: "Member States shall forward to the Commission every three years ... a report on the implementation of national provisions taken thereunder. The Commission shall prepare every three years a composite report."
[30] [1990] I E.C.R. 2143, 2151.
[31] The only report, which the Commission published so far has the title "Information sur l'application de la directive 79/409/CEE" Bruxelles—Luxembourg 1990, Rapport EUR 12835.

(13) Apart from these arguments, one basic question underlies all the dispute in the present case and has fundamental importance for the protection of the environment under the EEC Treaty: is a Member State entitled to protect the environment outside its own territory and how far does this right go?

Article 36 does not give an answer to this question. The Court has not yet expressly pronounced on it. Legal writers are divided and do not necessarily come to a clear answer. Elsewhere,[32] I argued that the environmental system set up under the EEC Treaty does allow the protection of the environment outside the national territory of the Member State, provided there is a threat to the environment, and that it is a question of protecting life or health of plants or animals or another specific part of the environment. This question will not be discussed here, since it does not directly relate to decisions by the European Court.

---

[32] L. Krämer, "The Protection of the Environment and Article 30 EEC Treaty", [1993] CMLRev. 111.

10. BIRD HUNTING: LEGAL RULES AND SOCIAL REALITY

**Judgment of the Court of April 27, 1988
in Case 252/85**

Commission v. *France*

[1988] E.C.R. 2243

FACTS AND PROCEDURE[1]

Directive 79/409 of April 2, 1979[2] provides for the conservation of all species of birds naturally occurring in the wild in the European territory of the Member States.[3]

Since the Commission claimed that the French legislation implementing the Directive was not in conformity with its requirements on six points, it opened proceedings against France under Article 169 of the EEC Treaty. The letter of formal notice was sent on February 22, 1984, the reasoned opinion on February 20, 1985. On August 13, 1985, the Commission's application to the Court was registered.

During the written proceedings, the Commission and the French Government submitted observations. Oral hearings took place on December 1, 1987. The Advocate General delivered his opinion on February 4, 1988.

JUDGMENT

(1) By an application lodged at the Court Registry on 13 August 1985, the Commission of the European Communities brought an action under Article 169 of the EEC Treaty for a declaration that by not adopting within the prescribed period all the laws, regulations and administrative provisions needed to comply with Council Directive 79/409/EEC of 2 April 1979 on the conservation of wild birds (Official Journal 1979, L 103, p. 1, hereinafter referred to as 'the Directive'), the French Republic has failed to fulfil its obligations under the EEC Treaty.

(2) Article 18 of the Directive provides that the Member States must implement the laws, regulations and administrative provisions needed to comply with the Directive within two years from its notification. Since the Directive had been notified on 6 April 1979, that period expired on 6 April 1981.

(3) After examining the provisions of the relevant French legislation and deciding that it was not in conformity with the Directive in a number of respects, the Commission commenced the procedure provided for in Article 169 of the Treaty. After giving formal notice to the French Republic to submit its observations, the Commission delivered a reasoned opinion on 20 February 1985. Since there was no response to the reasoned opinion, the Commission brought

---

[1] Summary by the author.
[2] [1979] O.J. L103/1.
[3] *Ibid.* Art. 1.

this action in which it has submitted six complaints against the French legislation concerning the protection of birds. Two of these complaints became devoid of purpose following the Commission's discontinuance of part of its action.

(4) Reference is made to the Report for the Hearing for the background to the case, the provisions of the French legislation in question, the course of the procedure and the submissions and arguments of the parties which are mentioned or discussed hereinafter only in so far as is necessary for the reasoning of the Court.

(5) Before examining the different complaints submitted by the Commission regarding the conformity of the French legislation with the Directive, it must be observed that the transposition of Community legislation into national law does not necessarily require the relevant provisions to be enacted in precisely the same words in a specific express legal provision; a general legal context may be sufficient if it actually ensures the full application of the directive in a sufficiently clear and precise manner (see the judgment of 23 May 1985 in Case 29/ 84 *Commission* v. *Federal Republic of Germany* [1985] ECR 1661). However, a faithful transposition becomes particularly important in a case such as this in which the management of the common heritage is entrusted to the Member States in their respective territories.

First complaint: Failure to transpose Article 5 (b) and (c) of the Directive

(6) The Commission considers that the French legislation is not in conformity with the abovementioned provision in two respects.

(7) First, the Commission alleges that, in the 10th paragraph of Article 372 and Article 374(4) of the code rural, the French Government has only provided for the protection of nests and eggs during the close season. Secondly, it complains that the nests and eggs of a certain number of birds are not protected since the provisions of Articles 1, 2 and 3 of the Ministerial Decree of 17 April 1981 taken in conjunction, exclude certain species from the scope of that Decree.

(8) The French Government considers that the objective set out in Article 5 of the Directive is achieved by the abovementioned provisions of the code rural. The protected species of birds in question do not nest during the hunting season and there would therefore be no real purpose in protecting their nests and eggs throughout the year. The possibility of destroying nests under Article 2 of the abovementioned decree is justified by the threat which the birds represent to mussel farming, other species of sea birds and air safety. The French Government states that Article 3 of that decree was repealed by a decree of 20 December 1983.

(9) As regards the first aspect of this complaint, it must be stressed that the prohibitions set out in Article 5 (b) and (c) of the Directive must apply without any limitation in time. An uninterrupted protection of the birds' habitat is necessary since many species re-use each year nests built in earlier years. To suspend that protection throughout a particular period of the year cannot be considered to be compatible with the abovementioned prohibition.

(10) As regards the second aspect of the Commission's first complaint, it must be

stated that even after Article 3 of the Decree of 17 April 1981 was repealed in 1983, the decree none the less excludes a certain number of protected birds from the scope of the prohibition on the destruction of nests and eggs.

(11) In determining whether this derogation is compatible with Article 9 of the Directive it should be noted that, as the Court held with regard to the Belgian rules in this field in its judgment of 8 July 1987 in Case 247/85 *Commission* v. *Belgium* [1987] ECR 3029, the French rules in question do not specify the reasons set out in Article 9(1) or the criteria and conditions referred to in Article 9(2), particularly as regards the circumstances of time and place in which a derogation may be granted. Consequently, the French legislation is not in conformity with Article 5 (b) and (c) of the Directive.

(12) The first complaint must therefore be upheld.

Second Complaint: The term 'national biological heritage'

(13) The Commission stresses that the protection provided for by the first paragraph of Article 3 of the Law of 10 July 1986 is limited to the preservation of the national biological heritage whereas Article 1 of the Directive extends the protection of the Directive to all species of naturally occurring birds in the wild state in the European territory of the Member States.

(14) The French Government contends that the list of species protected by virtue of the national rules contains numerous migratory species which nest in the other Member States but not in France.

(15) In this respect, it should be recalled, as the Court stated in its judgment of 8 July 1987 in Case 262/85 *Commission* v. *Italian Republic* [1987] ECR 3073, that, as is indicated by the third recital of the preamble to the Directive, the protection of migratory species is typically a transfrontier environment problem entailing common responsibilities for the Member States. The importance of complete and effective protection of wild birds throughout the Community, irrespective of the areas they stay in or pass through, causes any national legislation which delimits the protection of wild birds by reference to the concept of national heritage to be incompatible with the Directive.

(16) The second complaint must therefore be upheld.

Third complaint: Failure to transpose Article 5(e) of the Directive

(17) The Commission points out that French Law No 76/629 contains a general authorization concerning the keeping of protected birds. However, under Article 5(e) of the Directive Member States are obliged to prohibit the keeping of species of birds the hunting and capture of which is prohibited. Such a general prohibition on the keeping of birds other than species referred to in Annex III to the Directive, pursuant to Article 6(2) and (3), is not to be found in the French legislation which limits such protection to a restricted number of birds.

(18) While stating that the list of species protected by virtue of the Decree of 17

April 1981 is to be extended, the French Government considers that the French rules allow the result sought by the Directive to be achieved. The above-mentioned Decree prohibits the capture, the removal, the use and in particular the offering for sale or the purchase of those birds. Taken in conjunction, those prohibitions make the keeping of those protected species impossible.

(19) In this respect, it should be noted that in order to guarantee complete and effective protection of birds on the territory of all the Member States it is vital that the prohibitions set out in the Directive be expressly embodied in national law. However, the French rules contain no prohibition relating to the keeping of the protected birds, and thus allow the keeping of birds captured or obtained illegally, in particular those captured or obtained outside French territory. Furthermore, it should be stated that, as the French Government admitted, the list of birds which may be kept under the French rules does not correspond to the restricted number of birds species which may be kept under Annex III to the Directive.

(20) Consequently, the third complaint must be upheld.

Fourth complaint: Failure to transpose Article 7 of the Directive

(21) The Commission declared at the hearing that it considered that the fourth complaint, concerning the failure to implement Article 7 of the Directive, had become devoid of purpose following amendments to the French rules in 1987. In this respect, therefore, it must be held that the Commission has discontinued part of its action because of the conduct of the defendant.

Fifth complaint: Failure to implement Article 7(4) of the Directive

(22) At the hearing the Commission also indicated that the complaint relating to the hunting of turtle-doves in the Médoc region no longer formed part of the subject-matter of its action. The Commission has accepted that a judgment of the Conseil d'État annulling a number of decrees authorizing the hunting of turtle-doves in the Médoc region has brought the relevant national rules into conformity with the requirements of the Directive. Since that judgment of the Conseil d'État was given on 7 December 1984, that is to say before the delivery of the reasoned opinion on 20 February 1985, it must be held that by its partial discontinuance the Commission has acknowledged that its fifth complaint was unfounded.

Sixth complaint: Failure to comply with Article 8(1) of the directive

(23) The Commission points out that, as regards certain French *départements*, the Decree of 27 July 1982 authorizes the use of limes for the capture of thrushes and that the Decrees of 7 September 1982 and 15 October 1982 allow the capture of skylarks by means of horizontal nets known as 'pantes' or 'matoles'. However, the use of limes and horizontal nets is expressly forbidden by Article 8(1) of the Directive in conjunction with Annex IV (a) thereto.

(24) The Commission takes the view that the use of limes and horizontal nets cannot

be justified on the basis of Article 9(1)(c) of the Directive since those means of capture do not constitute selective methods and do not therefore allow 'judicious use of certain birds in small numbers' within the meaning of the Directive.

(25) The French Government considers that those measures, which were notified to the Commission on 25 May 1983, are justified under Article 9(1)(c) of the Directive because such capture is subject to strict territorial, temporal and personal controls in order to guarantee the selective nature of the capture.

(26) The French Government contends that the capture of birds with limes and horizontal nets is subject to an extremely strict and controlled system of individual authorizations. The decrees in question do not merely specify the places where and the period when such capture is permitted but also limit the number and the surface area of the means of capture as well as the maximum number of birds which may be captured. Furthermore, the competent authorities ensure that those conditions applying to such capture are complied with.

(27) It must be observed at the outset that under Article 9 of the Directive, in particular on the basis of Article 9(1)(c), Member States are authorized to provide for derogations from the prohibitions set out in Article 8(1) of the Directive.

(28) In order to establish whether national legislation complies with the various criteria of Article 9(1)(c) of the Directive it is necessary, as the Court stated in its judgment of 8 July 1987 (in Case 262/85 *Commission* v *Italy* [1987] ECR 3073), to examine whether the legislation guarantees that the derogation is applied on a strictly controlled and selective basis so that the birds in question are captured in only small numbers and in a judicious manner. In this respect, it is apparent from Article 2, in conjunction with the 11th recital of the preamble to the Directive, that the criterion of small quantities is not an absolute criterion but rather refers to the maintenance of the level of the total population and to the reproductive situation of the species concerned.

(29) It should be pointed out that the French rules concerning the capture of thrushes and skylarks in certain *départements* are very precise. The above-mentioned Decrees make the grant of authorizations to capture such birds subject to a considerable number of restrictive conditions.

(30) Furthermore, it should be noted that the Commission has not shown that the French rules permit the capture of birds in a manner incompatible with a judicious use of certain birds in small numbers. The Commission has not contested the defendant's argument that the number of birds captured constitutes a very small percentage of the population concerned.

(31) It should be added that the defendant notified the Commission of those derogations in accordance with Article 9(4) of the Directive and showed its willingness to reach agreement with the Commission regarding the detailed rules concerning those two hunting methods. However, the Commission did not respond to that initiative.

(32) In the light of the foregoing, the French provisions in question cannot, on the basis of the documents before the Court, be considered to be incompatible with the requirements of Article 9(1)(c) of the Directive.

(33) The sixth complaint must therefore be dismissed.

(34) It must therefore be held that by not adopting within the prescribed period all the laws, regulations and administrative provisions needed to comply with Council Directive 79/409/EEC of 2 April 1979 on the conservation of wild birds, the French Republic has failed to fulfil its obligations under the EEC Treaty.

Costs

(35) Under Article 69(2) of the Rules of Procedure the unsuccessful party is to be ordered to pay the costs. However under the first subparagraph of Article 69(3), the Court may order the parties to bear their costs in whole or in part if each party succeeds on some heads and fails on others. Since the Commission has succeeded in only some of its claims, each party should be ordered to pay its own costs.

On those grounds,

THE COURT

hereby:

(1) Declares that, by not adopting within the prescribed period all the laws, regulations and administrative provisions needed to comply with Council Directive 79/409/EEC of 2 April 1979 on the conservation of wild birds, the French Republic has failed to fulfil its obligations under the EEC Treaty;

(2) Orders each party to bear its own costs.

COMMENTARY

(1) The protection given by Directive 79/409[4] to wild birds has been the subject of a number of cases decided by the Court.[5] Most of these cases concern one of the following three areas:

– National hunting legislation;
– The protection of habitats;

---

[4] [1979] O.J. L103/1.
[5] Case 247/85, *Commission* v. *Belgium* [1987] E.C.R. 3029; Case 262/85, *Commission* v. *Italy* [1987] E.C.R. 3073 see p. 185 below; Case 412/85, *Commission* v. *Germany* [1987] E.C.R. 3503; Case 236/85, *Commission* v. *Netherlands* [1987] E.C.R. 3989. Subsequent to the decision in Case 252/85, the Court gave the following judgments: Case 57/89R, *Commission* v. *Germany* [1989] E.C.R. 2849, see p. 399 below; Case C–169/89, *Gourmetterie van den Burg* [1990] I E.C.R. 2143, see p. 149 above; Case C–288/88, *Commission* v. *Germany* [1990] I E.C.R. 2721; Case C–334/89, *Commission* v. *Italy* [1991] I E.C.R. 93; Case C–157/89, *Commission* v. *Italy* [1991] I E.C.R. 57; Case C–57/89, *Commission* v. *Germany* [1991] I E.C.R. 883, see p. 220 below.

– Derogations granted at national level from the provisions of the Directive.

Numerous other cases[6] were heard or are still pending under Article 169 of the EEC Treaty,[7] mainly following complaints from individuals or non-governmental organisations.[8]

Case 252/85 against France only deals with national legislation and derogations granted.

(2) In Cases 247/85 and 262/85 the Court stated:

"In order to institute an effective system of protection the directive lays down three types of provisions. First, it provides for general prohibitions against the killing, capturing, disturbing, keeping and marketing of birds and also against the destruction, damaging or removal of their nests and eggs (Article 5 and Article 6(1)). Furthermore, Article 8 prohibits the use of all means, arrangements or methods used for the large-scale or non-selective capture or killing of birds, in particular the use of those listed in Annex IV(a) to the directive. Secondly, the directive provides for derogations from those general prohibitions for the bird species listed in the annexes to the directive. Thus, provided that certain conditions and limits are laid down and respected, Member States may authorize the marketing of the species listed in Annex III and the hunting of the species listed in Annex II to the directive (Article 6(2) to (4) and Article 7). It follows that, for the bird species which are not listed in those annexes, or if the conditions and limits provided for in the abovementioned articles are not fulfilled, the general prohibitions remain applicable. Thirdly, Article 9 of the directive authorizes the Member States to derogate from the general prohibitions and from the provisions concerning marketing and hunting. However, this possibility is subject to three conditions: first, the Member State must restrict the derogation to cases in which there is no other satisfactory solution; secondly, the derogation must be based on at least one of the reasons listed exhaustively in Article 9(1)(*a*), (*b*) and (*c*); thirdly, the derogation must comply with the precise formal conditions set out in Article 9(2), which are intended to limit derogations to what is strictly necessary and to enable the

---

[6] By the end of 1990 there were 98 procedures pending under Article 169 which concerned "nature protection," the majority of which on Dir. 79/409; see Commission, *Monitoring the implementation of Community law*, 8th Report: [1991] O.J. C338/228; on March 15, 1990, 37 cases under Art. 169 were pending which concerned Art. 4 of Dir. 79/409. See also Case C–57/89: [1991] E.C.R. 3436.

[7] Art. 169 EEC: "If the Commission considers that a Member State has failed to fulfil an obligation under this Treaty, it shall deliver a reasoned opinion on that matter after giving the State concerned the opportunity to submit its observations. If the State concerned does not comply with the opinion within the period laid down by the Commission, the latter may bring the matter before the Court of Justice."

[8] The number of complaints to the Commission in environmental matters has developed from 10 in 1982 to 480 in 1990; Commission, n. 6 above, p. 226.

Commission to supervise them. Although Article 9 therefore authorizes wide derogations from the general system of protection, it must be applied appropriately in order to deal with precise requirements and specific situations".[9]

(3) First complaint: the destruction of nests and eggs.

Directive 79/409 prohibits the deliberate destruction of, or damage to nests and eggs or removal of nests as well as the taking of birds eggs in the wild and keeping these eggs even if empty.[10] French legislation[11] provides for such a prohibition "outside the hunting season". Furthermore, a Decree of April 17, 1981 prohibited, without restriction and at any time, the destruction or removal of eggs and nests of those birds which were listed in that decree.[12] At the request of the Court, the Commission submitted a list which included various species of birds which did not appear in the list of the decree, arguing that the French decree did not cover all birds.

The Court found that French law was incompatible with the requirements of Directive 79/409, because an uninterrupted protection of nests and birds was necessary[13] and because the Decree of April 17, 1981 did not list all the birds which were protected under the Directive.

Of particular interest is the Court's argument on the Decree of April 17, 1981. Indeed, that decree implicitly allowed, in its article 2, the destruction of nests and eggs of two species, the herring gull and the blackheaded gull. For these, France had asked for a derogation under Article 9 of the Directive.[14] The Court does not deal separately with article 2 of the Decree of April 17, 1981,[15] thus avoiding the question whether the conditions of form and procedure of Article 9 had been respected.[16] The relevance of this question will be examined below.

---

[9] 247/85, cited above, para. 7; 262/85, *ibid.* para. 7.
[10] [1979] O.J. L103/1, Art. 5(*b*) and (*c*).
[11] See the text of the French legislation on pp. 2246 *et seq.*
[12] *Ibid.* p. 2246; see also para. 24 of the Advocate General's opinion.
[13] See para. 9 of the judgment.
[14] See p. 2249.
[15] Paras. 9 and 10 of the judgment.
[16] Art. 9 of Dir. 79/409 reads as follows:
    1. Member States may derogate from the provisions of Articles 5, 6, 7 and 8, where there is no other satisfactory solution, for the following reasons:

        (a) — in the interests of public health and safety,
            — in the interests of air safety,
            — to prevent serious damage to crops, livestock, forests, fisheries and water,
            — for the protection of fauna and flora;
        (b) for the purposes of research and teaching, of re-population, of re-introduction and for the 2reeding necessary for these purposes;
        (c) to permit, under strictly supervised conditions and on a selective basis, the capture, keeping or other judicious use of certain birds in small numbers.

(4) Second complaint: the limitation of the protection to the "national biological heritage"

Directive 79/409 aims at the protection of all wild birds living in the European territories of Member States.[17] The French Act 76-629 of July 10, 1976 protects birds "where a specific scientific interest or the need to preserve the national biological heritage" so justifies.

The Court argued that effective protection of wild birds throughout the Community makes any concept which parts from a "national heritage" incompatible with the Directive and therefore upheld the complaint.[18]

While the result is fully approved of, it has to be pointed out that the Court's reasoning is not entirely precise: in the first sentence of paragraph 15, the Court argues that the protection of "*migratory species* is typically a transfrontier environment problem entailing common responsibilities for the Member States".[19] In the second sentence the Court underlines the "importance of complete and effective protection of *wild birds* throughout the Community"[20] without referring to migratory species. It is not clear from the Court's wording—nor from the wording of the Directive[21]—whether the "common responsibility" exists for all birds or only for migratory species, or, whether the "common heritage"[22] refers to migratory species only or to all birds. In earlier decisions, the Court has been more outspoken. In Case 247/85,[23] it indicated that the protective effect of the directive also covered species of wild birds occurring in the European territory of another Member State which are not found on Belgium territory but which are transported there, kept there or marketed there, whether alive or dead.[24] The Court therefore held the Belgian

---

2. The derogations must specify:
   —the species which are subject to the derogations,
   —the means, arrangements or methods authorized for capture or killing,
   —the conditions of risk and the circumstances of time and place under which such derogations may be granted,
   —the authority empowered to declare that the required conditions obtain and to decide what means, arrangements or methods may be used, within what limits and by whom.
   —   the controls which will be carried out.

3. . . .

4. . . .

[17] Art. 1.

[18] Para. 15

[19] Emphasis added.

[20] Emphasis added.

[21] Third recital: "whereas the species of wild birds naturally occurring in the European territory of the Member States are mainly migratory species; whereas such species constitute a common heritage and whereas effective bird protection is typically a transfrontier environment problem entailing common responsibilities;"

[22] Expression used in Case 262/85, *Commission* v. *Italy* [1987] E.C.R. 3073, para. 9. See p. 185 below.

[23] 247/85, *Commission* v. *Belgium* [1987] E.C.R. 3029.

[24] *Ibid.* para. 21 and 22.

legislation incompatible with the requirements of Directive 79/409, because it only protected Belgian birds.

In Case 262/85,[25] the Court indicated that Directive 79/409 aimed at a general prohibition on the marketing of all wild birds thus introducing a "general system of protection".[26]

The Directive's approach introduces a general system for all wild birds, not just for migratory species. The common responsibility to protect this common heritage is entrusted to the Member States. No differentiation is made between migratory species and other species.

The ambiguity in the Court's phrasing in Case 252/85 had considerable consequences. In Case C–169/89,[27] the Court (Sixth Chamber) derived from this wording that the possibility of granting more protection under Article 14 of the Directive only referred to migratory species, species enumerated in Annex I and to species living on the territory of the Member State which took specific measures.[28] This decision is discussed elsewhere in this book.[29]

Directive 79/409 is sometimes seen as protecting migratory species,[30] an interpretation which might not help to promote Community environmental law.

(5) Third complaint: the keeping of birds

Directive 79/409 prohibits in Article 5(e) the keeping of birds whose hunting and capture is prohibited. The French law 76–629 of July 10, 1976 establishes a general rule that "every person has the right to keep animals"[31] subject to certain specifications.

The Court was almost laconic in its judgment. It requested that "the prohibitions set out in the Directive be expressly embodied in national law"; the Court found no general prohibition for the keeping of birds in French law "in particular those captured or obtained outside French territory". It further stressed that the system where specific protected birds are enumerated, is incomplete.

(6) Fourth complaint: birds which may be hunted

The Commission argued, in its submission to the Court, that the directive allowed only those birds to be hunted which were listed in Annex II, whereas the French legislation allowed far more birds to be hunted.[32] On June 26, 1987, France adopted a decree by which it removed the birds which were not hun-

---

[25] 262/85, n. 22 below. See also p. 185 below.
[26] *Ibid.* paras. 7 and 18.
[27] C–169/89, Gourmetterie van den Burg: [1990] I E.C.R. 2143. See p. 149 above.
[28] Ibid. para. 14.
[29] See p. 149.
[30] See M. Prieur, *Droit de l'environnement*, (seconde édition) (Paris, 1991) pp. 329 *et seq.*, who lists Dir. 79/409 under "Le contrôle de la chasse maritime et des espéces migratrices" (p. 332).
[31] See the text of the French legislation, p. 2246.
[32] See p. 2250.

table under Directive 79/409, Annex II, from the national list of birds which may be hunted. In future derogations were to be made in accordance with Article 9 of Directive 79/409.[33]

In view of this development, the Commission did not continue its action.[34]

(7) Fifth complaint: the hunting of turtle-doves in the Médoc region

The Commission argued that French decrees allowed the hunting of turtle-doves in the Médoc region.[35] On December 7, 1984, the French Conseil d'État annulled these French decrees. Subsequent to this decision, the Commission discontinued its action.[36]

While it is thus clear that hunting of turtle-doves is not compatible with French law and thus illegal, this hunting nevertheless continues every year in the Médoc region, leading to considerable controversies between hunters and police forces which try to apply the law. Until now, 1993, France has not been able to bring the hunting of turtle doves to a halt, despite this decision of the French Supreme Court. The available space does not allow detailed examination here of the reasons for this situation.[37]

(8) Sixth complaint: Traditional hunting methods

The Directive expressly prohibits the use of limes and horizontal nets.[38] The French decree of July 27, 1982 provides:

"The use of limes for the capture of thrushes for personal purposes to act as call-birds is permitted from 10 October 1982 to 12 December 1982 inclusive."[39]

Article 1 of the Decree of September 7, 1982 provides as follows:

"The capture of skylarks by means of horizontal nets known as 'pantes' is

---

[33] See reasoning of the Advocate General, p. 2255.
[34] Para. 21 of the judgment.
[35] See p. 2252.
[36] Para. 22 of the judgment.
[37] See M. Prieur, *op. cit.*, p. 331; J. de Malafosse, *Nature et liberté; les acquis de la révolution française*, Revue du droit rural 1989, p. 486; J. de Malafosse, *Les usages français en matière de chasse et de pêche et le droit communautaire*, Environmental policy and law 1989, p. 11.
[38] Dir. 79/409, Art. 8:
  "1. In respect of the hunting, capture or killing of birds under this Directive, Member States shall prohibit the use of all means, arrangements or methods used for the large scale or non-selective capture or killing of birds or capable of causing the local disappearance of a species, in particular the use of those listed in Annex IV(a).
  2 . . .
  Annex IV:
  (a) — Snares, limes, hooks, live birds which are blind or mutilated used as decoys . . .
    — Nets, traps, poisoned or anaesthetic bait."
[39] See the text of the French legislation pp. 2246 *et seq.*

permitted from 8 a.m. on 1 October 1982, until the evening of 11 November 1982 . . . [40]

The Court argued as follows:[41]

1. The French rules concerning the capture of thrushes and skylarks are very precise.
2. The Commission has not shown that the French rules permit the capture of birds in a manner incompatible with a judicious use of certain birds in small numbers.
3. The Commission has not contested the French argument that there is only a small number of birds which are captured with limes and nets.
4. France had informed the Commission of the derogations, in accordance with Article 9(4) "and showed its willingness to reach agreement with the Commission regarding the detailed rules concerning those two hunting methods."
5. Thus, the French provisions "cannot, on the basis of the documents before the Court, be considered to be incompatible with the requirements of Article 9(1)(c) of the Directive."

It is therefore clear that the Court sees the French decrees as compatible with Article 9 of Directive 79/409[42] and in particular with Article 9(1)(c) which allows national derogations:

". . . to permit, under strictly supervised conditions and on a selective basis, the capture, keeping or other judicious use of certain birds in small quantities."

(9) As regards the general application of this Article 9, the Court had already, in previous judgments, indicated the conditions for its use. In Case 247/85,[43] the Court stated:

"a derogation under Article 9 must, according to Article 9(1) cover specific situations and, according to Article 9(2) comply with the requirements stated therein. The Belgian rules do not indicate the reasons regarding the protection of public health or the prevention of serious damage to crops or other fields mentioned in Article 9(1)(a) of the directive . . . Furthermore, the derogations do not comply with the criteria and conditions of Article 9(2) in so far as they mention neither the circumstances of time and place in which they may be granted nor the controls which will be carried out . . . "

---

[40] *Ibid.* p. 2247; see also the decree which gives the possibility to use "matoles", *ibid.*
[41] See also L. Krämer—P. Kromarek, *Droit communautaire de l'environnement* (1987–avril 1988), *Revue Juridique de l'Environnement* 1988, pp. 314 *et seq.*
[42] For the text of Art. 9, see n. 6 above.
[43] Case 247/85, n. 23 above, para. 34; similarly already in para. 28.

In Case 262/85,[44] the Italian government argued that the hunting of jays and magpies was allowed in Italy in compliance with Article 9(1)(a). The Court rejected that argument, though it considered that the protection of one of the reasons of Article 9(1)(a) could justify such a derogation. However, the Court argued that the Italian government had not indicated why the derogation was "the only satisfactory solution to prevent serious damage."[45]

The Court further ruled that since the Italian legislation providing for a derogation did not itself establish the criteria and conditions provided for in Article 9(2) of the Directive, it introduced an element of uncertainty. As there was no "guarantee" that the requirements of Article 9 were respected and the essential elements of Article 9 of the directive were not transposed completely clearly and unequivocally, Italy could not empower the regions to allow derogations.[46]

In Case 412/85, the Court argued that any derogation under Article 9 "must restrict the derogation to cases in which there is no other satisfactory solution", because the purpose of Article 9 was "to limit derogations to what is strictly necessary and to enable the Commission to supervise them."[47]

In Case 236/85, the Court held article 10 of the Dutch Vogelwet incompatible with Article 9(1) of Directive 79/409, because "the wording of Article 10 of the Vogelwet, does not make the grant of permits conditional upon the absence of any other satisfactory solution."[48]

For similar reasons, articles 18 to 20 of the Vogelwet were considered incompatible with Article 9 of the Directive.[49]

(10) It follows from the above that the Court allows national derogations in accordance with Article 9 of the Directive where the conditions of that provision are fulfilled and where, in particular, the wording of the national legislation indicates that any such derogation is only permitted where there is not other satisfactory solution.

The surprise in the present case is that the Court did not examine whether there was, in the French case, any other satisfactory solution. The Court was silent on this point.[50]

When the Court states that the French rules on hunting with limes and nets are "very precise" and that there is a considerable number of restrictive conditions to the capture of such birds, it is not clear to which rules the Court refers. Indeed, neither the Report for the Hearing nor any other statement

---

[44] 262/85, n. 22 above. See also p. 185 below.
[45] *Ibid.* para. 14.
[46] *Ibid.* para. 39.
[47] 412/85, *Commission* v. *Germany:* [1987] E.C.R. 3503, para. 18.
[48] 236/85, *Commission* v. *Netherlands:* [1987] E.C.R. 3989, para. 13.
[49] *Ibid.*, paras. 24 and 25.
[50] J. Untermaier, *Des petits oiseaux aux grands principes,* Revue Juridique de l'Environnement 1988, 460, talks on p. 465 of "Les chasses traditionnelles ou la clémence de la Cour" and later, p. 468, of a "mansuétude certaine".

within the decision indicate which these "very precise" and "restrictive conditions" to which the Court refers are. The judgment does not state this.[51]

The French legislation does not limit the number of birds to be captured. Since the legislation does not contain a limitation, it is irrelevant if in practice there is only a small quantity of birds captured. The Court stated in an earlier decision[52] that a factual practice is irrelevant where the legislation itself is not compatible with the requirements of the legislation.

(11) Apart from this, the figures about the actual number of birds captured with limes and nets vary between one and 15.[53] It is not clear, how the Commission, not having inspectors of its own, could find out about the exact number of birds captured.

The Advocate General held the French rules incompatible with Article 9 of the directive, because the capture with limes and nets was not selective.[54] The Court did not discuss this argument at all.

The Court's argument that France had notified its legislation to the Commission is not really a legal argument. If French legislation did not comply with Directive 79/409, one cannot see what kind of "agreement" there could have been with the Commission. Indeed, the Commission is at the service of Community law, but is not the master of it; thus it is not entitled to make "agreements."[55]

(12) If one looks into the Court's discussion of the sixth complaint, one has to come to the conclusion that the Court's decision seems to be based more on political considerations than on legal reasoning. The ongoing discussions in France between hunters and opponents to hunting; the emotive discussion on the "freedom to hunt" on the one side and ecological considerations on the other side; the creation of a political party "hunters and fishermen" which plays a role in local, regional, national and European elections, all this at one time led me to call the Court's decision "wise".[56] However, what kind of future is there in Europe if the law as the only instrument of reconciling different interests no longer has a role? Neither the decisions of the French Conseil

---

[51] In para. 4, the Court states: "Reference is made to the Report for the Hearing for the background to the case, the provisions of the French legislation in question, the course of the procedure and the submissions and arguments of the parties which are mentioned or discussed hereinafter only in so far as is necessary for the reasoning of the Court." However, the Report limits itself to quoting the texts of the French legislation. Untermaier, *op. cit.*, indicates that the French legislation fixes the number of sticks per hunter which support the lime, the length of those sticks, and limits the number of nets to three for each hunter. All these rules are not reproduced in the report for the Hearing.

[52] See in particular Case 236/85, n. 48 above, para. 12–13, 18 and 25.

[53] The French Government indicated in its defence that it estimated the number of thrushes captured by means of limes to be several thousands out of a total population of approximately 30 million; the number of skylarks was about 1 per cent. of some six millions: see p. 2253; Untermaier, *op. cit.*, quotes figures of one million skylarks per year (p. 469) which are captured.

[54] See p. 2259.

[55] See also Untermaier, p. 470.

[56] L. Krämer, *Focus on EEC Environmental Law* (London, 1992), p. 123.

d'Etat nor those of the European Court of Justice have brought peace to the regions where the traditional hunting is practised.

(13) Subsequent to the judgment in Case 252/85, France amended its legislation, by the Law of December 30, 1988. It is now the minister in charge who may authorise traditional hunting methods under the conditions of Article 9(1)(c) of Directive 79/409.[57] This kind of arrêtés is repeated on an annual basis. It is not clear, how Article 9 could justify a derogation which is repeated year by year, since Article 9 presupposes that there is "no other satisfactory solution". No other solution than capturing birds with limes and nets?

---

[57] See M. Prieur, *op. cit.*, p. 323.

Part 3

Sectors of Community Environmental Policy

Nature Conservation

11. CONSERVATION OF WILD BIRDS

**Judgment of the Court of July 8, 1987
in Case 262/85**

E.C. Commission v. *Italy*

[1987] E.C.R. 3073

FACTS AND PROCEDURE[1]

Directive 79/409 on the conservation of wild birds[2] was adopted on April 2, 1979 and entered into force on April 2, 1981. It was adapted consequent to the accession of Greece,[3] Spain and Portugal[4] and amended by Directives 85/411,[5] 90/656[6] and 91/244.[7]

Italian legislation on birds and their hunting from 1977 was amended several times in order to take into consideration the requirements of Directive 79/409. Since the Commission was of the opinion that this legislation was not fully in conformity with the requirements of the Directive, it sent, on February 22, 1984 a letter of formal notice to the Italian Government, under Article 169 of the EEC Treaty. No answer was received to that letter. Thus, the Commission issued, on October 16, 1984, a reasoned opinion, which again remained unanswered.

On August 20, 1985, the Commission applied to the Court. After the written procedure, the Court put some questions to the Commission and the Italian Government, which were answered in writing. Oral hearings took place on September 17, 1986. The Advocate General delivered his opinion on December 2, 1986.

JUDGMENT

(1) By an application lodged at the Court Registry on 20 August 1985, the Commission of the European Communities brought an action under Article 169 of the EEC Treaty for a declaration that, by not transposing into its internal legal order, fully and correctly, within the prescribed period Council Directive 79/409/EEC of 2 April 1979 on the conservation of wild birds (Official Journal 1979, L 103, p. 1) (hereinafter referred to as 'the directive'), the Italian Republic has failed to fulfil its obligations under the EEC Treaty.

(2) Article 18 of the directive provides that Member States are to bring into force

---

[1] Summary by the author.
[2] [1979] O.J. L103/1.
[3] [1979] O.J. L291/17, Annex I, Chap. XIII, point 1f.
[4] [1985] O.J. L302/9, Annex I, Chap. X, point 1h and 6.
[5] [1985] O.J. L233/33.
[6] [1990] O.J. L353/59.
[7] [1991] O.J. L115/41.

the laws, regulations and administrative provisions necessary to comply with the directive within two years of its notification. Since the directive was notified on 6 April 1979, the prescribed period expired on 6 April 1981.

(3) Having examined the provisions of the relevant Italian legislation and having formed the view that they did not wholly comply with the directive the Commission commenced the procedure provided for in Article 169 of the Treaty. After giving the Italian Republic formal notice to submit its observations, the Commission delivered a reasoned opinion on 16 October 1984. Having received no response to the reasoned opinion the Commission brought this action in which it raises six complaints against the Italian legislation in force.

(4) The case concerns three provisions of Law No 968 of 27 December 1977 (*Gazzetta Ufficiale della Repubblica Italiana* No 3 of 4. 1. 1978) as twice amended by Decrees of the President of the Council of Ministers of 20 December 1979 (*Gazzetta Ufficiale della Repubblica Italiana* No 1 of 2. 1. 1980) and 4 June 1982 (*Gazzetta Ufficiale della Repubblica Italiana* No 155 of 8. 6. 1982) (hereinafter referred to as 'the law'). It should be pointed out in this connection that, in Italian law, the regions have powers to adopt legislation and administrative measures concerning hunting within the limits arising from the principles established by the laws of the Italian State.

(5) Reference is made to the Report for the Hearing for the background to the case, the provisions of the Italian legislation in question, the course of the procedure and the submissions and arguments of the parties, which are mentioned or discussed hereinafter only in so far as is necessary for the reasoning of the Court.

The general obligations of the Member States under the directive

(6) Before examining the various complaints submitted by the Commission, the provisions of and the obligations arising under the directive should be recalled in so far as they are relevant to the present case. In this regard, it should be stated at the outset that, as stated in Article 1, the directive relates to the conservation of all species of naturally occurring birds in the wild state in the European territory of the Member States and covers the protection, management and control of those species and lays down rules for their exploitation. The directive is based on the consideration that effective bird protection, and in particular protection of migratory species, is typically a transfrontier environment problem entailing common responsibilities for the Member States (third recital in the preamble).

(7) In order to institute an effective system of protection the directive lays down three types of provisions. First, it provides for general prohibitions against the killing, capturing, disturbing, keeping and marketing of birds and also against the destruction, damaging or removal of their nests and eggs (Article 5 and Article 6(1)). Furthermore, Article 8 prohibits the use of all means, arrangements or methods used for the large-scale or non-selective capture or killing of birds, in particular the use of those listed in Annex IV(a) to the directive. Secondly, the directive provides for derogations from those general prohibitions for the bird species listed in the annexes to the directive. Thus, provided that certain conditions and limits are laid down and respected, Member States may authorize the marketing of the species listed in Annex III and the hunting of

the species listed in Annex II to the directive (Article 6(2) to (4) and Article 7). It follows that, for the bird species which are not listed in those annexes, or if the conditions and limits provided for in the abovementioned articles are not fulfilled, the general prohibitions remain applicable. Thirdly, Article 9 of the directive authorizes the Member States to derogate from the general prohibitions and from the provisions concerning marketing and hunting. However, this possibility is subject to three conditions: first, the Member State must restrict the derogation to cases in which there is no other satisfactory solution; secondly, the derogation must be based on at least one of the reasons listed exhaustively in Article 9(1)(a), (b) and (c); thirdly, the derogation must comply with the precise formal conditions set out in Article 9(2), which are intended to limit derogations to what is strictly necessary and to enable the Commission to supervise them. Although Article 9 therefore authorizes wide derogations from the general system of protection, it must be applied appropriately in order to deal with precise requirements and specific situations.

(8) In this context it is necessary to refer to Article 2 of the directive which requires the Member States to take the requisite measures to maintain the population of all bird species at a level, or to adapt it to a level, which corresponds in particular to ecological, scientific and cultural requirements, while taking account of economic and recreational requirements and from which it is therefore clear that the protection of birds must be balanced against other requirements. Therefore, although Article 2 does not constitute an autonomous derogation from the general system of protection, it none the less shows that the directive takes into consideration, on the one hand, the necessity for effective protection of birds and, on the other hand, the requirements of public health and safety, the economy, ecology, science, farming and recreation.

(9) As regards the transposition of the directive into national law, it must be observed that this does not necessarily require the provisions of the directive to be enacted in precisely the same words in a specific, express provision of national law; a general legal context may be sufficient if it actually ensures the full application of the directive in a sufficiently clear and precise manner (see the judgment of 23 May 1985 in Case 29/84 *Commission* v *Federal Republic of Germany* [1985] ECR 1661). However, a faithful transposition becomes particularly important in a case such as this in which the management of the common heritage is entrusted to the Member States in their respective territories.

First complaint: the list of birds which may be hunted

(10) The Commission notes that Article 11 of the law mentions 11 bird species, not listed in Annex II to the directive, which may be hunted. However, according to Article 7 of the directive, only the species listed in Annex II may be hunted.

(11) The Italian Government does not dispute that this complaint is well founded. It observes, however, that 2 of the 11 species in question (the jay and the magpie) were included in the list of birds which may be hunted because of their potentially harmful character. This derogation is therefore justified under the third indent of Article 9(1)(a) of the directive.

(12) In this regard, it should be stated that Article 7 of the directive authorizes Member States to allow hunting of the species listed in Annex II to the directive under certain conditions and within certain limits. It is clear from the general

scheme of protection provided for in the directive that national legislation may not extend the list contained in Annex II indicating the bird species which may be hunted.

(13) As regards the argument of the Italian Government concerning the third indent of Article 9(1)(a) of the directive, it should be noted that that provision does indeed allow Member States to derogate from the general scheme of protection in a way which goes further than is provided for in Article 7. However, as stated above, such a derogation must comply with the three abovementioned conditions of Article 9.

(14) In this regard the Italian Government has not put forward any evidence proving that it was necessary to include the jay and the magpie on the Italian list of birds which may be hunted in order to prevent serious damage to crops, livestock, forests, fisheries or water and that no other satisfactory solution existed. Neither has it indicated the reasons for which the listing of those species was, in its view, the only satisfactory solution to prevent serious damage. Finally, the provision in question does not specify the conditions of risk and the circumstances of time and place under which the derogation may be granted or the controls which will be carried out. Therefore, the inclusion of the jay and the magpie amongst the birds which may be hunted cannot be justified by the third indent of Article 9(1)(a) of the directive.

(15) It must therefore be held that the first complaint is well founded.

Second complaint: the marketing of birds

(16) The Commission points out that Article 11 of the law allows the marketing of all the species of birds which may be hunted. However, Article 6 of the directive prohibits trade in all live or dead birds or parts of such birds with the exception of the species listed in Annex III to the directive. Finally, the provisions of Article 6(2) to (4) of the directive are not to be found in the Italian legislation.

(17) The Italian Government does not dispute that the Italian rules are not entirely in accordance with the directive in this regard. It points out, however, that Article 20(t) of the law prohibits the sale of woodcock and of dead birds smaller than thrushes, except starlings, sparrows and skylarks, during the period when the hunting of those birds is allowed.

(18) It should be borne in mind in this regard that Article 6(1) of the directive requires the Member States to impose a general prohibition on the marketing of all the birds covered by the directive, alive or dead, and of any readily recognizable parts or derivatives of such birds. Article 6(2) provides that marketing is not to be prohibited in respect of the seven species referred to in Annex III/1, provided that the birds have been legally killed or captured or otherwise legally acquired. Since the list in Annex III/1 concerns only seven bird species, whereas the list of birds which may be hunted according to the national legislation includes 72 species, it is plain that the provision of Italian law in question does not comply with the requirements of the directive. Furthermore, it is clear from the protection to be afforded under the directive that it is intended to avoid a situation in which all the species that may be hunted may also be marketed because of the pressure which marketing may exert on hunting and consequently on the population level of the species in question. As regards the 10

species specified in Annex III/2, it is not disputed that the Italian legislation does not comply with the obligations arising under Article 6(3) of the directive.

(19) As far as concerns the reference by the Italian Government to Article 20(t) of the law, the Commission correctly notes that Article 6(1) of the directive prohibits the marketing of all species of birds irrespective of their size. Even if the Italian legislation does not therefore permit the marketing of all bird species which may be hunted, it must be held that Article 11, even in conjunction with Article 20(t) of the law, does not constitute a complete transposition of the directive.

(20) The second complaint must therefore be upheld.

Third complaint: hunting seasons

(21) The Commission complains that in Article 11 of the law the Italian Government fixes the dates when hunting may begin without taking account of the rearing season, the various stages of reproduction and, in the case of migratory species, the return to their rearing grounds, as required by Article 7(4) of the directive. In its reply to the defence the Commission has pointed out that the Italian legislation does not expressly prohibit hunting during the abovementioned periods. The hunting season begins on 18 August, a time when various species of nesting birds are either still in Italy or are traversing the Italian peninsula. In this respect the scientific community has proposed that the beginning of the hunting season should be fixed at a single date not earlier than the third Sunday in September. Hunting finishes on 10 March whereas migratory birds are still on their way to their rearing grounds from the first days of February. It has been requested that the closing of the hunting season should be fixed at a date not later than 31 January.

(22) The Italian Government has stated in reply that Article 7(4) of the directive does not specify particular dates on which the hunting season should begin or end. Article 11 of the law provides for different dates for the opening and closing of the hunting season for the various species precisely because their rearing seasons and stages of reproduction differ. As regards the birds' return to their rearing grounds, the abovementioned Decree of 20 September 1979 provided that the hunting of certain species of migratory birds was to end on 28 February and for other species on 10 March. The complaint is ill-founded because it does not address itself to the question whether the dates chosen for the opening and closing of the hunting season are appropriate.

(23) As regards the question whether the complaint made in the pre-litigation procedure and set out in the application is well founded, it must be noted first of all that, contrary to the Commission's contention, the Italian legislation takes account, in the provisions of Article 11 of the law and the Decree of 20 September 1979, of the various periods mentioned in Article 7(4) of the directive in which birds are to be protected. The Italian legislation does fix different dates for the opening and closing of the hunting season for the various species of birds having regard to their different rearing seasons and their different stages of reproduction and, in the case of migratory birds, their return to their rearing grounds. In this regard the Commission's complaint cannot be upheld.

(24) As regards the complaint that the dates chosen in the Italian legislation for the opening and closing of the hunting season for certain species of birds are not

appropriate, it must be noted that the Commission raised this point for the first time in its reply. Since this point extends the scope of the complaint made in the pre-litigation procedure and in the application, the question concerning the appropriateness of the dates chosen for the different hunting seasons must be disregarded.

(25) In those circumstances the Commission's third complaint must be dismissed.

Fourth complaint: use of automatic and semi-automatic weapons

(26) The Commission states that Article 9 of the law authorizes the use of repeating and semi-automatic weapons capable of firing three shots and that this provision of Italian law is not a correct application of Article 8(1) of the directive and Annex IV thereto.

(27) The Italian Government, on the other hand, contends that the provision in question provides for the fitting of a technical device in order to reduce the number of shots. That mechanism is intended to make it impossible to introduce more than two rounds of ammunition into the magazine whilst a third may be introduced directly into the firing chamber. The Italian rules are therefore not contrary to the provision in the directive.

(28) Given those two diverging views, the wording of the Italian provision and of the provision in the directive must first be recalled. Article 9 of the law provides that 'hunting with a repeating or semi-automatic rifle fitted with a device preventing more than three shots from being fired' is allowed. However, Article 8(1) of the directive, in conjunction with Annex IV(a) thereto, provides that Member States are to prohibit, in particular, semi-automatic or automatic weapons with a magazine capable of holding more than two rounds of ammunition.

(29) From a comparison of those provisions it may be concluded that Article 9 of the law does in fact prohibit weapons capable of discharging more than three rounds of ammunition. Moreover, it is undisputed that the directive does not prohibit the insertion of a third round of ammunition into the gun's firing chamber. Therefore, legislation authorizing weapons capable of firing three consecutive rounds is not contrary to the directive, provided that it is ensured that the magazines of those weapons can hold only two rounds of ammunition. It must be noted in this regard that the Italian provision clearly restricts the use of weapons to those which can discharge only three consecutive rounds. Since a round of ammunition may be in the gun's firing chamber, the reference in the Italian provision in question to a device preventing more than three shots from being fired is sufficient to guarantee that the magazine cannot hold more than two rounds of ammunition. In those circumstances, Article 9 of the law must be regarded as providing a proper guarantee of the full implementation of Article 8(1) of the directive.

(30) The fourth complaint of the Commission is therefore unfounded.

Fifth complaint: the powers given to the regions to permit the capture and sale of migratory birds

(31) According to the Commission, Article 18(2) of the law is incompatible with Articles 7 and 8 of the directive in so far as it confers on the Italian regions a

wide power to authorize the capture by any method and the sale of migratory birds even in the close season.

(32) The Italian Government denies that the provision in question confers a wide discretion on the regions and maintains that the regions may not depart from the wording of the law and of the directive. They must lay down precise rules governing arrangements for capturing migratory birds. The use of birds for recreational purposes at fairs and traditional markets is possible under Article 2 of the directive. Finally, migratory species may be captured only in limited numbers fixed in advance for each species. This provision is therefore a derogation provided for by Article 9(1) of the directive.

(33) That difference of view necessitates an initial clarification of the scope of the complaint, which must be understood as not objecting to the power to regulate hunting conferred on the regions or to the legislative and administrative provisions adopted by the regions. The complaint only concerns the fact that Article 18(2) of the law does not transpose, or require the regions to take into account, the obligations and requirements of the directive concerning methods of hunting migratory birds, the sale of migratory birds and hunting seasons for such birds.

(34) Article 18(2) of the law provides that, after consulting a particular scientific institute, the regions may operate, or authorize the operation, by means of specific regulations, of arrangements for capturing and selling migratory birds with a view to their being kept. To that end, they may authorize the use of means and arrangements for capturing birds, fix their own trapping seasons and draw up a list of birds which may be hunted even outside the periods when hunting is allowed under Article 11 of the law. However, Article 18 states that migratory birds may only be captured with a view to their being kept for use as live decoys in cover-shooting or for recreational purposes in traditional fairs and markets. Such species may be trapped in limited numbers previously fixed for each species.

(35) In this regard it must be noted that Article 18(2) gives the regions the power to regulate the hunting seasons for migratory birds and the means, arrangements or methods for their capture without taking into account the requirements of Articles 7 and 8 of the directive.

(36) The Italian Government puts forward three arguments on this point; first, that the rule-making power may only be exercised in consultation with a scientific institute; secondly, that the provisions of Article 18 of the law are justified under Article 2 of the directive; and thirdly that that provision could be authorized under Article 9(1)(c) of the directive.

(37) As regards the first argument, it must be stated that, even though the regions are obliged to consult a scientific institute before implementing their rules, the opinion of the institute is not binding and therefore that obligation does not guarantee that the requirements of the directive will be respected. As regards the second argument, it must be stressed that Article 2, as observed above, is not an independent derogation from the obligations and requirements of the directive.

(38) As regards the third argument concerning Article 9(1)(c) of the directive, that

provision authorizes Member States to derogate, *inter alia*, from Articles 7 and 8 in order to permit, under strictly supervised conditions and on a selective basis, the capture, keeping or other judicious use of certain birds in small numbers. It is clear that the capture and sale of birds, even outside the hunting season, with a view to keeping them for use as live decoys or for recreational purposes in fairs and markets may constitute judicious use authorized by Article 9(1)(c).

(39) However, it must be observed first of all that the provision concerned makes no reference to Article 9(1), which provides that a derogation from Articles 7 and 8 of the directive may be granted only if there is no other satisfactory solution. Secondly, Article 18 of the law, which authorizes the regions to permit the use of means and arrangements for capturing birds, to fix the periods in which capturing is permitted and to draw up the list of birds which may be hunted, does not, contrary to the requirements of Article 9(2) of the directive, specify the means, arrangements or methods authorized for the capture or killing of birds, the circumstances of time and place under which the derogations may be granted or the species covered by the derogations. Such criteria and conditions are necessary to ensure that the derogation is applied in a strictly controlled and selective manner. Since Article 18(2) of the law does not itself establish the criteria and conditions provided for in Article 9(2) of the directive or require the regions to take account of those criteria and conditions, it introduces an element of uncertainty as regards the obligations which the regions must observe when adopting their regulations. Therefore, there is no guarantee that the capture of certain species of birds will be limited to the strict minimum, that the period of capture will not coincide unnecessarily with periods in which the directive aims to provide particular protection or that the means, arrangements or methods for capture are not large-scale, non-selective or capable of causing the local disappearance of a species. It follows that the essential elements of Article 9 of the directive have not been transposed completely, clearly and unequivocally into the Italian rules.

(40) Therefore, the Commission's fifth complaint must be upheld.

Sixth complaint: the use of migratory birds as live decoys

(41) In the formal notice, the reasoned opinion and its application, the Commission complains that Article 18 of the law also authorizes the use of migratory birds as live decoys for hunting, in breach of Article 8 of the directive. In its reply it explained that the complaint was not that Article 18 authorizes the use of live decoys but that Article 18 does not prohibit the blinding and mutilation of birds used as decoys.

(42) In reply to that point the Italian Government has stated that Article 18(2) of the law only authorizes the use of migratory birds as live decoys but does not authorize the blinding or mutilation of those birds. Article 20(o) of the law expressly prohibits the use of blinded live decoys. The point made in the reply is, in its view, an inadmissible extension of the original complaint.

(43) As regards the argument of the Italian Government alleging an inadmissible extension of the complaint, it must be stated that, in its application, the Commission repeated verbatim the complaint which it had already made in the pre-litigation procedure, namely that Article 8 of the directive had not been transposed into the Italian rules. In its reply the Commission pointed out that, through

its reference to Annex IV to the directive, Article 8 of the directive prohibits the use not only of blinded live decoys but also of mutilated live decoys. Although the complaint formulated by the Commission in the pre-litigation procedure and in the application was unfortunately very brief, it nevertheless contains all the information which the Italian Government needed to understand the complaint made against it and to defend itself. All the information needed to assess the scope of the complaint is given: the provision infringed, namely Article 8 of the directive, the rule of national law considered to be contrary to that provision, namely Article 18 of the law, and the basis of the complaint, namely the granting of authorization contrary to the provisions of Article 8. The objection of inadmissibility raised by the Italian Government cannot therefore be upheld.

(44) As regards the substance of the complaint, it must be noted that Article 18(2) of the law allows the regions to authorize the use of migratory birds as live decoys in cover-shooting and Article 20(o) prohibits only the use of blinded live decoys. It therefore follows that Article 18(2) in conjunction with Article 20(o) of the law does not expressly prohibit the regions from authorizing the keeping and *a fortiori* the use of migratory species as mutilated live decoys in cover-shooting. Such use is prohibited by the directive.

(45) The Commission's complaint must therefore be upheld.

(46) It must therefore be held that, by not adopting within the prescribed period all the laws, regulations and administrative provisions needed to comply with Council Directive 79/409 of 2 April 1979 on the conservation of wild birds, the Italian Republic has failed to fulfil its obligations under the EEC Treaty.

Costs

(47) Under Article 69(2) of the Rules of Procedure, the unsuccessful party is to be ordered to pay the costs. However, according to the first subparagraph of Article 69(3), the Court may order the parties to bear their costs in whole or in part if each party succeeds on some heads and fails on others. Since the Commission has succeeded only in some of its claims, each party should be ordered to pay its own costs.

On those grounds,

THE COURT

hereby:

(1) Declares that, by not adopting within the prescribed period all the laws, regulations and administrative provisions needed to comply with Council Directive 79/409/EEC of 2 April 1979 on the conservation of wild birds, the Italian Republic has failed to fulfil its obligations under the EEC Treaty;

(2) Orders each party to bear its own costs.

COMMENTARY

(1) This judgment is one of numerous judgments which the Court has pronounced, at the request of the E.C. Commission, on the application of Directive 79/409 against a Member State.[8] Since all Member States had some legislation on birds (when Directive 79/409 was adopted)—be it on the hunting of birds—these cases normally did not concern the absence of communication of the national implementation measures. The one exception is Case C–334/89[9] where the Court decided that Italy had failed to adopt the necessary measures to comply with the requirements of Directive 85/411[10] which amended Directive 79/409.

(2) In the present case, the Italian Government had recognised that some more legislative measures were necessary in order to comply with the Directive and had indicated, prior to December 2, 1986, that "a draft law designed to implement the directive in full is now before Parliament."[11] This argument of defence was not considered relevant by the Advocate General[12] and not even taken up by the Court. It might be of interest to note that the new Italian legislation on the protection of birds was adopted on February 11, 1992.[13]

(3) Directive 79/409 sets up a comprehensive system of protection of wild birds and of their habitats. It restricts the killing, capturing, taking, marketing and hunting of birds and provides for protection of their biotopes and habitats. Several provisions ensure that the Commission receives information on the implementation and enforcement of the Directive as well as on its adaptation to scientific or technical requirements.[14] The Commission published one general report on its implementation.[15]

---

[8] Case 247/85, *Commission* v. *Belgium*: [1987] E.C.R. 3029; Case 412/85, *Commission* v. *Germany*: [1987] E.C.R. 3503; Case 236/85, *Commission* v. *Netherlands*: [1987] E.C.R. 3989; Case 252/85, *Commission* v. *France*: [1988] E.C.R. 2243, see p. 163 above; Case 57/89R, *Commission* v. *Germany*: [1989] E.C.R.; 2849; Case C–339/87, *Commission* v. *Netherlands*: [1990] I E.C.R. 851; Case C–169/89, *Gourmetterie Van den Berg*: [1990] E.C.R. 2143; Case C–288/88, *Commission* v. *Germany*: [1990] E.C.R. 2721; Case C–157/89, *Commission* v. *Italy*: [1991] E.C.R. 57; Case C–334/89, *Commission* v. *Italy*: [1991] E.C.R. 93; Case C–57/89, *Commission* v. *Germany* [1991] I E.C.R. 883; Case C–75/91, *Commission* v. *Netherlands*: judgment of February 6, 1992, not yet reported.
[9] Case C–334/89, n. 8 above.
[10] [1985] O.J. L233/33.
[11] See p. 3081.
[12] *Ibid.*
[13] Legge no. 157 of February 11, 1992 on "Norme per la protezione della fauna selvatica orneoterma e per il prelievo venatorio".
[14] In principle, only the lists of particularly endangered birds (Annex I) and of studies (Annex V) may be adapted to technical and scientific progress by majority voting in a Committee procedure, see Art. 15 of Dir. 79/409.
[15] Commission, *Information sur l'application de la directive*, 79/409/CEE. Bruxelles-Luxembourg 1990; environnement et qualité de la vie no. EUR 12835.

(4) The main problems which this Directive caused for Member States and which ultimately led to decisions of the European Court, were:

(a) *Hunting legislation*

All Member States had legislation which preceded the adoption of the Directive and which dealt with the hunting of birds. Member States did not always adapt this legislation to the requirements of the Directive which started from the principle that there should be no hunting of birds, except where an express derogation existed.[16]

(b) *Derogation clauses*

The Directive provided for general principles, but itself contained derogations to them. Since the wording of these derogations was sometimes relatively "vague",[17] the use which Member States made of those derogation possibilities, occasionally put into question the very principles of the Directive.

(c) *Habitat protection*

Article 4 of the Directive requested Member States to designate habitats for particularly threatened bird species, and to provide for special conservation measures within these habitats. The implementation of these provisions raised particular problems which will be commented in detail when the Court's decision in Case C–57/89 is discussed.[18]

(5) These problems are increased by a number of features which are specific to the protection of nature and more specifically to the protection of birds. In the first place one must stress the different nature of environmental problems from one Member State to the other. While the protection of nature and in particular the protection of animals plays an important role in countries such as the United Kingdom, the importance of protecting fauna and flora is perceived quite differently in the southern parts of the EEC. In some parts of the Community it is traditional to capture singing birds; in other parts hunting legislation has not really been adapted to the changed conditions for animals in Western Europe, or it is not felt that there is a need to provide for the protection of birds. Different perceptions of the need to properly implement and enforce Directive 79/409 inevitably lead to discrepancies and differences among the Member States.

In a number of Member States, Länder, regions or provinces are responsible for the protection of nature or hunting legislation (Spain, Italy, Germany, Belgium, United Kingdom) which increases complications. Indeed, traditional hunting rules or other practices with regard to birds may have, at regional

---

[16] Art. 7.

[17] See the opinion of Advocate General da Cruz Vilaça in Case 247/85, n. 8 above, p. 3043: "(the directive) contains both detailed framework provisions and vague expressions which are difficult to define."

[18] Case C–57/89, n. 8 above; see p. 219 below.

level, an even greater influence on the law-maker as well as on the daily practice.

As mentioned above, one element which contributes to the difficulties in
implementing and enforcing the Directive is, without doubt, the imprecise
wording of the Directive itself. To give but a few examples: Article 3 requests
Member States to "take the requisite measures to preserve, maintain or re-
establish a sufficient diversity and area of habitats for all the species of birds."
Article 7 provides for the hunting of some birds, but requests Member States
to "ensure that the hunting of these species does not jeopardize conservation
efforts in their distribution area." Article 9 allows for derogations from the provisions in Articles 5 to 8 "where there is no other satisfactory solution." One of
the reasons for which a derogation is allowed, reads as follows: "(c) to permit
under strictly supervised conditions and on a selective basis, the capture,
keeping or other judicious use of certain birds, in small numbers."[19]

Experience has shown that these rules are hardly enforceable, all the more
so because national courts have only very rarely directly relied on Directive
79/409 and because the decisions of the European Court of Justice are too rare
to influence the administrative practice at local or even regional level.

(6) Hunting legislation

There are mainly three sets of rules[20] where national legislation does not fully
comply with the requirements of Directive 79/409. All three aspects were discussed in Case 262/85.

(a) The opening and closing of the hunting season

Directive 79/409 lays down only general rules as regards the opening and
closure of the hunting season. Article 7(4) provides:

> "They (the Member States) shall see in particular that the species to which
> hunting laws apply are not hunted during the rearing season nor during the
> various stages of reproduction. In the case of migratory species, they shall
> see in particular that the species to which hunting regulations apply are not
> hunted during their period of reproduction or during their return to their
> rearing grounds."

The Italian legislation provided that, at least for some species, the hunting
season began on August 18 and ended on March 10. The Commission was of
the opinion, based on the opinion of the "scientific Community", that there
should be a single date for the opening of the hunting season which would be

---

[19] Art. 9(1)(c).
[20] The field of application of Dir. 79/409 is discussed in Case C–169/89, n. 8 above; see also p. 149
above.

no earlier than the third Sunday in September, and that the hunting season would be closed no later than January 31.[21]

(7) In the present case the Court stated that the Italian regulation rightly set different dates as regards the different birds and thus dismissed the Commission's complaint. The Court did not discuss the necessity of one single date. As regards the dates chosen in the Italian legislation, the Court rejected the Commission's complaint because the point had not been raised during the pre-litigation procedure under Article 169.[22]

The Commission thus restarted the procedure and obtained, on January 17, 1991, a decision from the European Court which stated that Italy had failed to comply with the requirements of Article 7(4) of Directive 79/409, by fixing the hunting season for birds at times of reproduction or return to rearing grounds.[23] This decision, however, also shows the limits of such a procedure. Indeed the Commission had to prove for each of the 23 species in question, when the reproduction or the return period started and when it ended. One can easily imagine that local, regional and national authorities are too overburdened to check whether the dates of the different hunting periods for different birds are respected; nor could the European Court be regularly seized with requests to control the hunting season. In France, such difficulties in monitoring compliance are complicated by the fact that the hunting season is fixed, for the different birds, at the level of the departments and on a yearly basis.

Under these circumstances a uniform hunting season would be more appropriate, in order to reflect the purpose of Directive 79/409 to set up a general system for the protection of all birds. However, the present wording of Article 7(4) does not require such a uniform hunting period.

(8) The Commission published, for all birds which are hunted, data on the opening and closing of the hunting season.[24]

It further indicated that for 49 species, the dates of opening or closing of the hunting season interfered with the reproduction period.[25] These findings have not lead to further complaints by the Commission to the European Court.

---

[21] Case 262/85, n. 8 above, para. 21.

[22] See on these questions also the Advocate General's opinion: [1987] E.C.R. pp. 3083 *et seq.*

[23] Case C–334/89, *Commission* v. *Italy*: [1991] E.C.R. 93.

[24] Commission, *op. cit.*, pp. 112 *et seq.* These dates go from mid-July til mid-March. Germany extends the hunting period for some birds until end of April. A number of birds may be hunted all year, see below.

[25] France (20 species for the opening of the hunting season, 22 for the closing of the hunting season), Italy (10 species for the opening, 12 for the closing), Greece (2 species for the opening, 18 for the closing), Portugal (3 species for the opening, 7 for the closing), Belgium (4 species for the opening), Germany (4 species for the opening, 11 for the closing), the Netherlands (5 species for the opening, 1 for the closing), Denmark (2 species for the opening, 2 for the closing), United Kingdom (3 species for the opening, 1 for the closing), Luxembourg and Ireland (each 1 species for the opening, 1 for the closing) are named. Figures for Spain were not available. Commission, *op. cit.*, pp. 137 and 138.

(9)(b) *The list of birds which may be hunted*

Directive 79/409 provides in Article 7(1):

"Owing to their population level, geographical distribution and reproductive rate throughout the Community, the species listed in Annex II may
be hunted under national legislation."

Annex II lists 72 species; 24 species may be hunted all over the Community,
the other 48 only within specific, expressly mentioned Member States.

In Case 262/85, the Commission was of the opinion that Italy had not respected the requirements of Directive 79/409, since Italian law allowed 11
species to be hunted, which were not listed in Annex II of Directive 79/409.
The Court confirmed, upon Italian request, that Article 9 of the Directive
allowed, in principle, to derogate from the requirements of Article 7 and thus
from Annex II, but stated that this would only be possible if the following three
conditions were fulfilled:[26]

(1) there must be no other satisfactory solution;
(2) the derogation must be based on at least one of the reasons listed
    exhaustively in Article 9(1);
(3) the derogation must comply with the precise formal conditions set out
    in Article 9(2).

As regards jays and magpies, birds which are not listed in Annex II but for
which Italy invoked Article 9, the Court stated that Italy had not put forward
any evidence supporting that either of these three conditions had been fulfilled and therefore held that the Commission's complaint was well founded.[27]

(10) The Court came to the same judgment as regards wood pigeons, carrion
crows, jackdaw magpies and jays hunted in the Netherlands;[28] the blackbirds,
jackdaws, magpies, house sparrows, sparrows and starlings hunted in Belgium;[29] and carrion crows, jays and magpies in parts of Germany.[30] The Court
saw the conditions of Article 9 fulfilled as regards the hunting of rooks in the
Netherlands.[31]

No other cases concerning other birds have been submitted to the Court.
The Commission lists in total 96 species which are being hunted within the
Community.[32] Since only 72 species are listed in Annex II of Directive 79/409,

---

[26] Para. 7.
[27] Paras. 10 to 15.
[28] Case C–339/87, *Commission* v. *Netherlands*: [1990] I E.C.R. 851, paras. 14, 15, 18 to 22.
[29] Case 247/85, *Commission* v. *Belgium*: [1987] E.C.R. 3029, paras. 10 to 16 and 30 to 34.
[30] Case C–288/88, *Commission* v. *Germany*: [1990] I E.C.R. 2721, para. 6.
[31] Case C–339/87, above, para. 16.
[32] Commission, n. 15 above, p. 112 *et seq.*

the rest must be subject to derogations under Article 9. Whether Article 9 does allow such derogations is discussed below.[33]

(11)(c) *Hunting methods*

Article 8 of Directive 79/409 provides:

> "1. In respect of the hunting, capture or killing of birds under this Direct-
>   ive, Member States shall prohibit the use of all means, arrangements or
>   methods used for the large-scale or non-selective capture or killing of
>   birds or capable of causing the local disappearance of a species, in
>   particular the use of those listed in Annex IV(a).
> 2. Moreover, Member States shall prohibit any hunting from the modes of
>   transport and under the conditions mentioned in Annex IV(b)."

Annex IV(a) lists snares, limes, hooks, live birds which are blind or muti-lated used as decoys, mirrors, explosives, nets, traps, weapons with a maga-zine capable of holding more than two rounds of ammunition and others; Annex IV(b) lists aircraft, motor vehicles and boats driven at a speed exceed-ing five kilometers per hour.

The Italian legislation authorised the use of weapons capable of firing three shots. The Court considered this provision compatible with the Directive since one round of ammunition was to be introduced directly into the firing chamber. In contrast, the Court held that Italian law, which did not prohibit the use of migratory birds as mutilated live decoys in cover-shooting, was con-trary to the requirements of the Directive.[34]

(12) The Commission had not attacked the use of nets, limes, traps and other hunting methods in Italy which were contrary to Annex IV of the Directive. Thus the Court did not have the opportunity to consider these methods. How-ever, the Court did give judgment on such hunting methods in a number of other judgments:

In Case 236/85, the Court was of the opinion that an express legal provision was necessary in order to transpose the provisions of Article 8 and Annex IV of the Directive into national law.[35] In Case 339/87, the Court confirmed that the fact that hunting from airplanes was not practised in a Member State, did not make it unnecessary to provide for an express prohibition of such a hunt-ing method.[36]

In Case 252/85, the Court considered the French "traditional hunting methods", which allowed the use of lime and nets, compatible with the

---

[33] See para. 15 below.
[34] Para. 44.
[35] Case 236/85, *Commission* v. *Netherlands* [1987] E.C.R. 3989, paras. 27 and 28.
[36] Case C–339/87, above, paras. 30 to 32.

requirements of the Directive, in particular Article 9 of Directive 79/409.[37] This decision is discussed elsewhere in this book.[38]

Hunting methods which are contrary to Article 8 and Annex IV of the Directive seem to be fairly common in some Member States, in particular in Belgium, France, Italy and Greece, possibly also in Spain and Portugal. After the decision of the Court in Case 252/85, it does not seem very likely that the Commission will take action against such hunting methods.

(13) Derogation clauses

Article 9 of Directive 79/409 provides:

> "1. Member States may derogate from the provision of Articles 5, 6, 7 and 8, where there is no other satisfactory solution, for the following reasons:
>   (a) — in the interests of public health and safety
>   — in the interests of air safety
>   — to prevent serious damage to crops, livestock, forests, fisheries and water
>   — for the protection of flora and fauna;
>   (b)   for the purposes of research and teaching, of re-population, of re-introduction and for the breeding necessary for these purposes;
>   (c)   to permit, under strictly supervised conditions and on a selective basis, the capture, keeping or other judicious use of certain birds in small numbers.
>
> 2. The derogations must specify:
>   — the species which are subject to the derogations;
>   — the means, arrangements or methods authorised for capture or killing;
>   — the conditions of risk and the circumstances of time and place under which such derogations may be granted;
>   — the authority empowered to declare that the required conditions obtain and to decide what means, arrangements or methods may be used, within what limits and by whom;
>   — the controls which will be carried out".

Article 5 of the Directive deals with the killing of birds, the taking of eggs and nests, etc. Article 6 concerns the marketing of birds, Article 7 is about those species which may be hunted under national law and Article 8 prohibits certain hunting methods.

In decision in Case 262/85, the Court stated, as mentioned above,[39] that Article 9 could only apply if three conditions were fulfilled:

---

[37] Case 252/85, see p. 163 above, paras. 23 to 32.
[38] See p. 163 above.
[39] See para. 9 at p. 198 above.

(a) no other satisfactory solution;

(b) invoke one of the reasons of Article 9(1); and

(c) respect the formalities of Article 9(2).

(14) These requirements led the Court to reject most of the derogations which Member States had made on the Articles 5 to 8 of the Directive. Thus the Court condemned national rules which allowed:

(a) the hunting of several birds which are not included in Annex II as described in detail above in paragraph 9;[40]

(b) Italian regions to permit the capture and sale of migratory birds;[41]

(c) Germany to not apply several rules of the Directive in the course of "the normal use of the land for agricultural, forestry or fishing purposes" or in the context of "the exploitation of the products obtained from such activities";[42] the Court did not think that this derogation could be subsumed under Article 9(1);

(d) the Netherlands to grant permits to kill or capture birds and to disturb their nests in cases where birds cause or are liable to cause damage or nuisance, since the Netherlands had not indicated that there was no other satisfactory solution;[43]

(e) the Netherlands to grant permits for trade in dead and stuffed birds, since the criteria of Article 9(1) were not satisfied;[43]

(f) the Netherlands to allow the collection of eggs and the disturbing of nests, since the Dutch provisions did not refer to the grounds for derogations from Article 9(1) and, furthermore, that there was no other satisfactory solution;[44]

(g) Belgium to provide for a general possibility to destroy nests built against houses, since this derogation was not sufficiently delimited and other satisfactory solution existed;[45]

(h) Belgium to set up a list of birds which may be kept as well as a list of birds which may be captured in small quantities, since such possibilities were not limited to cases in which there is no other satisfactory solution, the rules did not provide that only small quantities may be captured and they were in other aspects uncertain and ambiguous;[46]

(i) the Netherlands to allow land owners to hunt certain birds, since the Dutch legislation contained no precision to that extent;[47]

(j) the Netherlands to provide for derogations from hunting rules without the conditions of Article 9(1) being fulfilled; the Court held that simple

---

[40] See nn. 26 to 31.
[41] Paras. 31 to 40.
[42] Case 412/85, above, paras. 11 to 13.
[43] Case 236/85, n. 35 above, para. 17.
[44] *Ibid.* paras. 20 to 25.
[45] Case 247/85, n. 29 above, paras. 24 to 28.
[46] *Ibid.* paras. 36 to 42.
[47] Case C–339/87, *Commission* v. *Netherlands.* [1990] I E.C.R. 851, paras. 18 to 22.

administrative practices which complied with Article 9(1) were not sufficient.[48]

(15) Several problems as regards derogations were either not raised before
the Court or not discussed.

The first problem concerns the renewal of derogations. From the list which
the Commission published on derogations granted between 1981 and 1986,[49]
it seems that derogations are often granted for a year and then renewed.
Thus, in reality, the derogations are permanent deviations from the provisions
of the Directive.

This can be illustrated by derogations relating to the hunting of birds. The
Commission's report lists 14 species which may, in one or the other country,
be hunted throughout the year,[50] including during the reproduction time.
Where such derogations are—sometimes even by way of national regulation—permanently renewed, it is not clear how they can be justified as derogations from the general system of protection which the Directive has set up.
De facto, such repeated derogations are national deviations from the Directive; in my opinion, it follows from Article 9(2) that derogations under Article 9
must, in principle be limited locally and in time[51] and it is hardly imaginable
that there is no other satisfactory solution for regional or national derogations
which are renewed year after year.[52]

---

[48] *Ibid.* paras. 26 to 29.
[49] Commission, see n. 15 above, p. 137.
[50] *Ibid.* pp. 112 *et seq.* The following birds are concerned (Member States given in parenthesis):

Columba palumba (Netherlands, Belgium, United Kingdom, Ireland)
Larus fuscus (United Kingdom, Ireland)
Larus argentatus (United Kingdom, Ireland)
Larus marinus (United Kingdom, Ireland)
Streptopelia decaocto (United Kingdom)
Turdus mevulu (Germany)
Corvus corone (Germany, Netherlands, Belgium, United Kingdom, Ireland)
Corvus corone cornix (United Kingdom, Ireland)
Corvus frugilegus (Belgium, United Kingdom, Ireland)
Pica pica (Germany, Netherlands, Belgium, United Kingdom, Ireland, Denmark)
Garvulus glandiarius (Germany, Belgium, United Kingdom, Ireland)
Corvus moneclula (Netherlands, Belgium, United Kingdom, Ireland, Denmark)
Sturnus vulgaris (Belgium, Luxemburg, United Kingdom, Ireland, Denmark)
Passer domesticus (United Kingdom, Ireland, Denmark)

The English names of these birds cannot be given, since the Commission has published only
the Latin names.
[51] See in particular the requirement in Article 9(2) that there must be an authority which declares
that the required conditions obtain; since that also refers to "circumstances of time and place" a
general derogation seems always excessive.
[52] See also Case 247/85, *Commission* v. *Belgium* [1987] E.C.R. 3029, para. 41: "The general and
permanent rules laid down in the decrees do not guarantee that the number of birds which
may be captured is limited to small quantities, that the period during which their capture is
allowed does not coincide with periods in which the directive seeks to provide particular protection for birds (the nesting period and the various stage of breeding and rearing) or that capture and keeping are restricted to cases in which there is no other satisfactory solution, in
particular that the bird species concerned may reproduce in captivity."

(16) In Cases 262/85,[53] 236/85,[54] 247/85[55] and 252/85,[56] the Italian, Dutch, Belgian and French governments had justified derogations under Article 9 of the Directive as a cultural tradition or a recreational requirement. The Court did not discuss this argument in detail. In Case 236/85, it rejected the Dutch national provision because it did not refer to the grounds for derogations under Article 9(1) of the Directive.[57] In Case 262/85, the Court stated that Article 9(1)(c) would allow derogations for the capture or sale of birds "for recreational purposes in fairs and markets", but rejected the Italian provision because it was not limited to the strict minimum and had not transposed Article 9 "completely, clearly and unequivocally" into Italian law.[58] The Belgian rules were rejected because, again, the Court was of the opinion that "they [were] not sufficiently precise and limitative as requested by Article 9(1)(c)" and because Article 2 of the Directive[59] [did] not give an independent ground for derogation.[60] The French rules were accepted as valid derogations, since the Commission had not proven a breach of Article 9.[61]

It might be concluded from this case law that derogations for traditional reasons may come under Article 9(1)(c), but that such derogations must guarantee that killing or capture of birds is kept to the strict minimum.

(17) Particularly difficult is the situation where national legislation authorises regions or local authorities to pronounce derogations under Article 9. In Case 262/85, the Court held that the enabling legislation must refer to Article 9 and the requirement that there be no other satisfactory solution, and that the reasons for derogations, *i.e.* the conditions in Article 9(1) and (2) must be mentioned. Otherwise, the enabling legislation "introduces an element of uncertainty as regards the obligations which the regions must observe when adopting their regulation."[62] This strong emphasis on formal requirements in the enabling legislation and the obligation under Article 9(3) of the Directive to report annually to the Commission on derogations granted, give, in theory, some guarantee for a prudent use of this provision. Whether in practice the Commission is really regularly informed of all derogations granted may well be doubted.

These comments show how difficult and complicated it may be to secure

---

[53] Para. 36.
[54] Case 236/85, *Commission* v. *Netherlands:* [1987] E.C.R. 3989, para. 21: "the collecting of lapwing eggs is a historical and cultural tradition" (in Friesland).
[55] Case 247/85, above, para. 38: "capture is justified by recreational requirements".
[56] Case 252/85, *Commission* v. *France:* [1988] E.C.R. 2243, Advocate General's opinion, para. 39.
[57] Case 236/85, above, para. 23.
[58] Paras. 38 and 39.
[59] Dir. 79/409, Art. 2: "Member States shall take the requisite measures to maintain the population of the species referred to in Article 1 at a level which corresponds in particular to ecological, scientific and cultural requirements, while taking account of economic and recreational requirement, or to adapt the population of these species to that level."
[60] Case 247/85, n. 52 above, para. 41.
[61] See comments on this decision on pp. 163 *et seq.* above.
[62] Para. 39.

legal implementation and practical compliance with Directive 79/409. Pressure from hunters is very strong in all Member States and a fair balance of the diverging interests may sometimes be difficult to find.

(18) In 1991, the Commission proposed an amendment to the Directive in order to allow certain birds to be hunted or captured all year round.[63] Ironically, the Commission had already made such a proposal in 1976 when it submitted its proposal for what later became Directive 79/409.[64] At that time the Council unanimously agreed that the system of protection should apply to all birds.

---

[63] [1991] O.J. C255/1.
[64] [1977] O.J. C24/3.

12. PROTECTION OF ENDANGERED SPECIES

Judgment of the Court of November 29, 1990
in Case C–182/89

E.C. Commission v. *France*

[1990] I E.C.R. 4337

FACTS AND PROCEDURE[1]

Under Regulation 3626/82,[2] wild cats of the *Felis geoffroyi* and *Felis wiedii* species can only be imported into the Community after an import permit has been issued. In 1985, it appeared doubtful whether Bolivia assured sufficient protection to the wild cats living on its territory. On February 6, 1986 the French authorities issued import permits for some 6,000 skins of these two species originating in Bolivia. Subsequently, the owner of the skins, a French company, exported the skins to Germany where they were seized by the German authorities at Munich airport. An action against that seizure was filed before German courts.

The Commission sent, on July 30, 1986, a letter of formal notice to France, arguing that France should not have issued the import permits. Having received the French answer of December 3, 1986, the Commission issued, on November 4, 1987 a reasoned opinion, and, as it was not satisfied with the French answer of May 25, 1988, filed the application to the Court on May 25, 1989.

The Commission and the French Government made written submissions. The oral hearing took place on October 9, 1990. The Advocate General gave his opinion on October 18, 1990.

JUDGMENT

(1) By an application lodged at the Court Registry on 25 May 1989, the Commission brought an action under Article 169 of the Treaty for a declaration that by issuing in February 1986 import permits for more than 6000 wild-cat skins of the *Felis geoffroyi* and *Felis wiedii* species originating in Bolivia, the French Republic had failed to fulfil its obligations under Article 10(1)(b) of Council Regulation (EEC) No 3626/82 of 3 December 1982 on the implementation in the Community of the Convention on international trade in endangered species of wild fauna and flora (Official Journal 1982 L 384, p. 1) and Articles 5 and 189 of the Treaty. At the hearing the Commission withdrew the submission alleging infringement of Articles 5 and 189 of the Treaty.

(2) The Convention on international trade in endangered species of wild fauna and

---

[1] Summary by the author
[2] [1982] O.J. L384/1; this regulation was amended 16 times; the CITES Convention of March 3, 1973 is Annex A of Reg. 3626/82.

flora of 3 March 1973 (Official Journal 1982 L 384, p. 7, hereinafter referred to as 'the Convention') regulates international trade in animals and plants of certain species and in readily recognizable parts and derivatives thereof. During the period concerned in these proceedings, wild cats of the *Felis geoffroyi* and *Felis wiedii* species were listed in Appendix II to the Convention. This appendix includes species which might become threatened with extinction unless trade in such species is subject to strict regulation in order to avoid utilization incompatible with their survival.

(3) Regulation No 3626/82, cited above, was adopted in order to ensure the uniform application of the measures of commercial policy which implement the provisions of the Convention. For certain species, including the wild cats in question, the regulation provides for stricter protective measures than those provided for by the Convention. At the material time, the importation of *Felis geoffroyi* and *Felis wiedii* into the Community was subject, by virtue of Article 3(2) of the regulation, to the presentation of an import permit issued in accordance with the conditions laid down in Article 10(1)(b) of the regulation.

(4) The first indent of Article 10(1)(b) of the regulation provides as follows:

'The import permit referred to in Article 3(2) shall be issued only where:

(i) it is clear, or where the applicant presents trustworthy evidence, that the capture or collection of the specimen in the wild will not have a harmful effect on the conservation of species or on the extent of the territory occupied by the populations in question of the species ... '

(5) On 6 February 1986, the competent French authorities issued import permits for wild-cat skins of the species in question. These permits refer to export permits issued by the Bolivian authorities on 5 August 1985. The Commission considers that the import permits were wrongly issued on the ground that the conditions laid down in Article 10(1)(b) were not satisfied.

(6) Reference is made to the Report for the Hearing for a fuller account of the facts and background to the dispute and the submissions and arguments of the parties, which are mentioned or discussed hereinafter only in so far as is necessary for the reasoning of the Court.

(7) In support of its view, the Commission refers to the factual context in which the decision of the French authorities was adopted. According to the Commission, the facts are essentially as follows:

(i) the application of the Convention in Bolivia was the subject of discussions at the Conference of the contracting parties to the Convention which took place in Buenos Aires between 22 April and 3 May 1985. The contracting parties found that there was substantial illegal trade in products covered by the Convention originating in Bolivia and that there were a large number of false export or re-export permits. The recitals to the resolution dated 30 April 1985, to which those discussions led, refer to the concern expressed by certain countries, in particular countries bordering on Bolivia whose wild fauna and flora are directly threatened. The same resolution therefore recommended that the contracting parties should no longer accept shipments of specimens covered by the Convention accompanied by Bolivian documents or declared to originate in Bolivia until the Bolivian Government had demonstrated to the Conference of the Parties to the Convention or to its Standing Committee that it had adopted all the measures within its power properly to apply the Convention. At its meeting between 28 October and 1 November 1985 the Standing Committee stated that the measures subsequently adopted by the Bolivian Government were significant. Accordingly, it requested the Convention Secretariat to recommend that the contracting parties which had imposed an import ban on specimens from Bolivia should consider suspending it;

(ii) following the adoption of the aforesaid resolution of 30 April 1985, the Commission had on the same date sent to the Convention management authorities in the Member States a telex message which stated that import permits should no longer be issued for the Bolivian specimens concerned;

(iii) imports of those specimens were then placed on the agenda of a meeting of the Community's Committee on the Convention, which took place between 12 and 14 November 1985. It is clear from a draft opinion drawn up by that meeting that, according to the information available to the Committee at that time, Bolivia would no longer issue export permits for the wild-cat skins concerned as long as the scientific and trade data necessary for establishing export quotas and for implementing other measures agreed between the Bolivian Government and the Convention Secretariat were unavailable.

(8) According to the Commission, it follows from all those facts that, when the import permits concerned were issued in February 1986, the French authorities were not entitled to consider that the conditions imposed by Article 10(1)(b) of Regulation No 3626/82 were satisfied.

(9) The French Government challenges this view by putting forward a number of arguments which appear in the Report for the Hearing and the Opinion of the Advocate General of 18 October 1990. Those arguments are for the most part based on a misinterpretation of the Commission's claim, which relates solely to the incorrect application of Article 10(1)(b) of the regulation in question.

(10) On this point, the French Government contends that the only decisive factor as regards the granting of import permits is the favourable opinion of the national scientific authority in the importing country which was obtained in this case.

(11) This argument must be rejected. There is no provision of the regulation which subjects the issue of import permits to the opinion of such an authority, which can therefore constitute only one of the factors for determining whether the criteria laid down in Article 10(1)(b) are satisfied.

(12) Under Article 10(1)(b), there are two cases in which the competent authorities may issue import permits, namely where it is clear that the capture of the specimen will not have a harmful effect on the conservation of the species or on the extent of the territory occupied by the populations in question of the species, or where the applicant presents trustworthy evidence that this is the case.

(13) In the light of all the abovementioned factors which were known to the French authorities, it must be accepted that they could not reasonably have reached

the conclusion that it was clear that the capture of the wild cats in question would not have a harmful effect on their conservation or on the extent of the territory occupied by them.

(14) Furthermore, it is clear from the documents before the Court that the only export permits submitted to the French authorities by the applicant were issued by the Bolivian authorities on 5 August 1985, that is to say during the period in which the application of the Convention in Bolivia was giving rise to serious problems. Therefore the French authorities could reasonably have considered that the applicant had presented trustworthy evidence that the aforesaid requirements were satisfied.

(15) Lastly, it should be stated that the opinion of the French scientific authority is not sufficiently clear and favourable to form a valid basis of assessment.

(16) It must therefore be held that by issuing in February 1986 import permits for more than 6 000 skins of the *Felis geoffroyi* and *Felis wiedii* species originating in Bolivia, the French Republic failed to fulfil its obligations under Article 10(1)(b) of Regulation No 3626/82.

Costs

(17) Under Article 69(2) of the Rules of Procedure, the unsuccessful party is to be ordered to pay the costs. Since the French Republic has failed in its submissions, it must be ordered to pay the costs.

On those grounds,

THE COURT

hereby:

(1) Declares that, by issuing in February 1986 import permits for more than 6 000 skins of the *Felis geoffroyi* and *Felis wiedii* species originating in Bolivia, the French Republic failed to fulfil its obligations under Article 10(1)(b) of Council Regulation (EEC) No 3626/82 of 3 December 1982 on the implementation in the Community of the Convention on international trade in endangered species of wild fauna and flora;

(2) Orders the French Republic to pay the costs.

COMMENTARY

(1) This judgment interprets Regulation 3626/82 on the implementation in the Community of the Convention on international trade in endangered species of wild fauna and flora. It is until now, mid 1993, the only judgment as regards that Regulation and I will try to demonstrate that this is no coincidence.

The Convention on International Trade in Endangered Species of wild fauna and flora (CITES) was concluded on March 3, 1973 in Washington. Only sovereign states were allowed to be parties to the Convention. The conference of the contracting parties adopted on April 30, 1983 in Gabarone, Botswana, an amendment to the Convention in order to allow accession to the Convention by regional economic integration organisations, such as the EEC. The amendment will enter into force after ratification by 54 contracting parties, which is not yet the case.

(2) Since the EEC could thus not become a contracting party to the CITES Convention, it had to find other means of dealing with the problem of trade in endangered species, all the more since two of its Member States, Ireland and Greece, are not party to the Convention[3] and because the achievement of the EEC internal market aims at the disappearance of national frontiers as economic barriers. For these reasons, Regulation 3626/82 was adopted in 1982, and is based on Article 235 of the EEC Treaty. Article 1 of the Regulation provides:

"The Convention, as set out in Annex A, shall apply throughout the Community under the conditions laid down in the following Articles.
The objectives and principles of the Convention shall be respected in the application of this Regulation."

This provision, while clear in its intention, has not prevented problems of interpretation regarding the application of the Convention in the Member States, the obligation for Member States to adopt supplementary provisions to the Regulation in order to comply with the requirements of the Convention,[4] and the interdependency of provisions of the Convention and the Regulation.[5]

(3) Since the Convention is not part of Community law, the Court of Justice could only interpret the provisions of Regulation 3626/82, and more precisely Article 10(1)(b). However, in construing the words "it is clear, or where the applicant presents trustworthy evidence", the Court had very largely recourse to the discussion which took place within the framework of the Convention.[6]

The words "clear" or "trustworthy evidence" are not really capable of a precise linguistic interpretation, since much, if not all, depends on the specific circumstances at the moment of application for an import permit. As regards

---

[3] See W. Wijnstekers, *The Evolution of CITES* (Lausanne, 1988).
[4] See, *e.g.* Art. VIII(1) of the Convention: "The parties shall take appropriate measures to enforce the provisions of the present Convention and to prohibit trade in specimens in violation thereof. These shall include measures:
(a) to penalize trade in, or possession of, such specimens, or both; and
(b) to provide for the confiscation or return to the State of export of such specimens".
Reg. 3626/82 does not contain rules on sanctions. It is submitted, that by virtue of the Convention EEC Member States are under an obligation to introduce criminal sanctions for cases as of (a).
[5] See below, n. 8.
[6] Para. 7 of the judgment. See also the Report for the Hearing, paras. 8 to 10.

the notion of "trustworthy evidence", the Court was furthermore confronted with the problem that the Report for the Hearing did not indicate any substantive element as regards the evidence which the applicant for the import permit had submitted.[7]

As a consequence the Court rightly relied on the only means available, namely the careful examination of the facts which were known at the moment of issuing the import permit.[8] These facts were not at all contested by the French Government[9] which only gave a different evaluation of these facts.

(4) In this respect the French Government's argument that it had based its decision to issue import permits on the favourable opinion of its national scientific authority is clearly based on an error. The Advocate General had already pointed out[10] that such an opinion of a national scientific authority is needed for an import permit under the Convention,[11] but not under Regulation 3626/82.[12]

France had ratified the CITES Convention and therefore one might argue that the scientific statement was required under French national law. However, such reasoning is not possible:

(a) the two species of wild cats in question were, in 1985/86, listed in Appendix II to the Convention. According to article IV(4) of the Convention, the import of skins thus did not require a permit but took place upon presentation of either an export permit or a re-export certificate;[13]

(b) the Convention expressly allows parties to adopt stricter domestic measures.[14] By requiring an import permit for the species of wild cat in question, Regulation 3626/82 is stricter than the Convention. Since it is directly applicable in France[15] it is, in the sense of the Convention, a stricter domestic measure which thus prevails over the general rules of the Convention.

It remains surprising that in its own defence the French Government argued that it had been mistaken in the interpretation of the provisions of the Conven-

---

[7] *Ibid.* p. 4338 *et seq.*
[8] The Court carefully underlines, para. 13, that "all the above mentioned factors . . . were known to the French authorities."
[9] *Ibid.* para. 9.
[10] Para. 25.
[11] Convention, **article III(3)**: "An import permit shall only be granted when the following conditions have been met: (a) a scientific authority of the State of import has advised that the import will be for purposes which are not detrimental to the survival of the species involved . . . "
[12] Reg. 3626/82, Art. 10(1)(*b*).
[13] Convention, **article IV(4)**: "The import of any specimen of a species included in Appendix II shall require the prior presentation of either an export permit or a re-export certificate."
[14] Convention, **article XIV(1)**: "The provision of the present Convention shall in no way affect the right of parties to adopt: (a) stricter domestic measures . . . "
[15] See Art. 189, para. 2 EEC: "A regulation shall have general application. It shall be binding in its entirety and directly applicable in all Member States".

tion and the Regulation. The Court rejected the argument by referring to the wording of Article 10(1)(*b*) which did not mention a scientific authority.

(5) The Court is also rather laconic in its evaluation of the facts which preceded the issuing of import permits. Having pointed out that all facts were known to the French authorities, the Court simply stated:

  (a) "the French authorities ... could not reasonably have reached the conclusion that it was clear ... "[16]
  (b) "the French authorities could not reasonably have considered that the applicant had presented trustworthy evidence ... "[17]

The Court also argued that the opinion of the French scientific authority was not sufficiently clear and favourable to form a valid basis of assessment whether the requirements of Article 10 were fulfilled.[18] This statement cannot be checked, since neither the report for the hearing nor the opinion of the Advocate General give any detail about the content of the French scientific authority's opinion.

(6) While the judgment is precise, clear and convincing, attention should be drawn to some other aspects of the case. Between the time when the import permits were issued and the judgment, more than 57 months elapsed; between the opening of formal proceedings under Article 169 and the judgment, 52 months. This time-span is extremely long.

The case presents the specificity that the cat skins were seized in Germany and that presumably, the question of damages was raised before the national court. The judgment of the European Court might have contributed to solve that dispute between the interested parties.

However, had the Commission heard about the issuing of import permits by the French authorities without such a seizure having taken place, the proceedings under Article 169 would have taken too much time to have any effect on the protection of this sort of endangered species. Instead, since the procedure under Article 169 has no suspensive effect, the skins would have been sold and/or manufactured.

This case clearly shows the limits of the Article 169—procedure for individual administrative acts which concern movable objects. The procedure might have, at best, a certain preventive effect for future cases; it seems hardly appropriate to be effective in repairing "wrong" decisions under Regulation 3626/82.

(7) Turning now to Regulation 3626/82, its provisions set up a Community-wide system of monitoring. Goods are controlled when they enter or leave the

---

[16] Para. 13.
[17] Para. 14.
[18] Para. 15.

territory of the Community; internally, however, the philosophy is that no further import controls take place. The British Royal Society for the Protection of Birds (RSPB) commented recently[19] in the following terms:

"As an example of drafting difficulties, we believe that the International Trade in Endangered Species Regulation (3626/82), as drawn, has been founded on the incorrect premise that wildlife trade is inherently capable of being regulated in detail. This was apparent to us at the time of its inception, and should have been seen as such by the regulation. In practice, it is the easiest of all wildlife laws to circumvent, particularly as regards birds. Enforcement requires that all points of entry into the Community have on hand inspectors capable of recognizing some 9,000 bird species (each in their various forms and plumages). Successful enforcement requires knowledge of country of origin (not just export) for each specimen, which is very often impossible to ascertain. The substantial problem of smuggling wild birds is clear evidence of its unenforceability. The Regulation is so ineffective that the RSPB has called for a radical change. We are promoting the concept that other than in certain prescribed and exceptional circumstances, imports of wild-caught birds into the Community are banned altogether."

(8) This might be seen by some as a relatively strong criticism, which illustrates, however, some of the problems of Regulation 3626/82. Wijnstekers reports that already at international level, in the context of the CITES Convention, 135 resolutions were adopted between 1976 and 1987 and that the proceedings of the meetings of the conference of the parties to CITES count some 6,000 pages;[20] and the understanding of lawyers, students, environmentalists, but also of border control people, administrations and others is certainly not increased by the fact that Regulation 3626/82 reproduces in its annexes only the latin names of endangered species.[21]

In 1991, the Commission submitted a proposal for a Regulation to the Council, with the aim to completely revise Regulation 3626/82. This proposal[22] is at present being discussed by the Council and the European Parliament. It is based on Article 100a of the Treaty. As regards the deficiencies of Regulation 3626/82 the explanatory memorandum identifies three series of problems:[23]

(a) only those provisions of the CITES Convention which have been

---

[19] House of Lords, Select Committee on the European Communities: *Implementation and Enforcement of Environmental Legislation* (London, 1992) Vol. II, p. 147, no. 72.

[20] W. Wijnstekers, *op. cit.* p. 9.

[21] It is true, that the names of most species which appear in the appendices of the Convention, are reproduced in the Community languages. But not all are reproduced: for instance, the two species of wildcat which are dealt with in Case C–182/89 are not. However, these names are to be found in Regulation 1970/92 of the Commission: [1992] O.J. L201/1 (p. 15) which replaces part of the Annexes of Regulation 3626/82.

[22] [1991] O.J. C–26/1.

[23] Commission COM(91)448 final of December 6, 1991, No. 3.

amended in order to be applied within the Community have been incorporated into the Regulation.

(b) only those species which were included in the CITES Convention appendices were listed in the annexes of the Regulation.

(c) difficulties to change the status of species by transferring it from one annex to the other.

All names of endangered species are given only in latin. It is submitted that this is not appropriate for Community legislation.

(9) Finally, the substantive question of law should not be forgotten. Indeed, Community law tried to protect the environment in Bolivia, by providing stricter protection for the two species of wildcats of Bolivia and of other countries than provided by the CITES Conventions, and by suspending imports. Trade problems likely to arise because of the existence of such a protection in a third country are discussed elsewhere in this book.[24] While, as stated, the Court's decision in the present case is fully approved, one should not forget that the rule itself demonstrates that the protection of the environment is not in all circumstances a purely national problem and cannot easily be solved by relying on the idea that measures to protect the environment in another country are allowed once there is an international agreement. The protection of fauna and flora, and also, for instance, of the ozone layer, is a general interest which must not be, normally, subordinated to free trade requirements.[25]

---

[24] See comments on Case C–169/89, above p. 149.
[25] For more details see comments on Case C–169/89.

13. PROTECTION OF HABITATS

Judgment of the Court of February 28, 1991
in Case C–57/89

E.C. Commission v. *Germany*
supported by the United Kingdom

[1991] I E.C.R. 883

FACTS AND PROCEDURE[1]

Germany had declared the Ostfriesische Wattenmeer, situated in the Land Niedersachsen by the North Sea, wetland of international importance under the Ramsar Convention on international wetlands.[2] In 1983, Germany indicated to the Commission that the Ostfriesische Wattenmeer was a protected area under Article 4 of Directive 79/409.[3] In 1985 it declared the Wattenmeer national park under German law[4] and informed the Commission of this decision in 1988, within the context of discussions on the designation of birds' habitats under Directive 79/409 on the conservation of wild birds.[5]

In the area of Rysumer Nacken, Germany disposed of dredged material from the Ems, thus increasing the height of the area. As for the Leybucht, a bay of some 2,800 hectars within the Wattenmeer, Germany decided, in 1985, to increase the existing dyke in that area. For geographic and other considerations, it was decided to give that dyke the form of a nose. Work started in 1986.

Having received complaints in respect of both areas, the Commission objected to the work in the Rysumer Nacken, because it was of the opinion that the dredged sludge would lead to the disappearance of parts of a birds' habitat. It sent Germany a letter of formal notice on May 11, 1987 and, not having received an answer, a reasoned opinion on August 11, 1988.

As regards the Leybucht, the Commission was of the opinion that measures of coastal protection could exceptionally be considered necessary even in an area designated as birds' habitat under Article 4 of Directive 79/409,[6] but had to be limited to the strict minimum; the German measures, however, went beyond this minimum.

On August 7, 1987 the Commission sent a letter of formal notice and, not having received an answer, on July 4, 1988 a reasoned opinion. Germany answered to both the Rysumer Nacken and the Leybucht on September 6, 1988, adding maps on the Wattenmeer.

On July 14, 1989 the Commission applied to the Court. On July 28, 1989 the United Kingdom intervened on the side of Germany. Oral hearings took place

---

[1] Summary by the author.
[2] Convention on international wetlands of Ramsar (Iran) of February 2, 1971. Germany has ratified the Convention, but the EEC has not.
[3] Dir. 79/409 on the conservation of wild birds: [1979] O.J. L103/1. The text of Art. 4 is reproduced in the Court's judgment, para. 2 below.
[4] See Report for the Hearing.
[5] See Report for the Hearing.
[6] See n.3 above.

on October 16, 1990 during which the Commission withdrew its complaint as
regards the Rysumer Nacken.

The Advocate General gave his opinion on December 5, 1990.

JUDGMENT

(1) By application lodged at the Court Registry on 28 February 1989, the Commission of the European Communities brought an action under Article 169 of the
EEC Treaty for a declaration that by planning or undertaking works detrimental
to the habitat of protected birds in special protection areas, contrary to Article 4
of Council Directive 79/409/EEC of 2 April 1979 on the conservation of wild birds
(Official Journal 1979 L 103, p. 1, hereinafter referred to as "the directive"), the
Federal Republic of Germany has failed to fulfil its obligations under the EEC
Treaty.

(2) Article 4 of the directive is worded as follows:

"1. The species mentioned in Annex I shall be the subject of special conservation measures concerning their habitat in order to ensure their survival
and reproduction in their area of distribution.
(Omissis)
Member States shall classify in particular the most suitable territories in
number and size as special protection areas for the conservation of these
species, taking into account their protection requirements in the geographical sea and land area where this Directive applies.
2. Member States shall take similar measures for regularly occurring migratory species not listed in Annex I, bearing in mind their need for protection
in the geographical sea and land area where this Directive applies, as
regards their breeding, moulting and wintering areas and staging posts
along their migration routes. To this end, Member States shall pay particular
attention to the protection of wetlands and particularly to wetlands of international importance.
3. Member States shall send the Commission all relevant information so that it
may take appropriate initiatives with a view to the coordination necessary to
ensure that the areas provided for in paragraphs 1 and 2 above form a
coherent whole which meets the protection requirements of these species
in the geographical sea and land area where this Directive applies.
4. In respect of the protection areas referred to in paragraphs 1 and 2 above,
Member States shall take appropriate steps to avoid pollution or deterioration of habitats or any disturbances affecting the birds, in so far as these
would be significant having regard to the objectives of this Article. Outside
these protection areas, Member States shall also strive to avoid pollution or
deterioration of habitats."

(3) The application initially comprised two claims, the first concerning dredging
and filling operations in the *Rysumer Nacken*, and the second concerning dyke-
building operations carried out in the *Leybucht*.

(4) With regard to the first claim, the Commission, at the hearing, formally acknow-

ledged that the Rysumer Nacken is not covered by the regulation of the *Land* of
Lower Saxony of 13 December 1985 creating the Niedersächisches Wattenmeer National Park and that, consequently, the Rysumer Nacken is not designated as a special protection area. However, the Commission argues that that is
a new argument put forward by the defendant in its rejoinder, so that the
defendant must bear the costs relating to that point.

(5) The German Government replies that the Commission was aware, even before
the commencement of proceedings before the Court, of all the information concerning the legal status of the Rysumer Nacken, in particular of maps showing
the boundaries of the national park. It is clear from those maps that the Rysumer
Nacken is not designated as a special protection area. According to the German Government, the details it provided in its rejoinder do not therefore constitute a new argument.

(6) The information regarding the extent of the protected areas in the Wattenmeer
was supplied by the German Government in its letter of 6 September 1988 sent
pursuant to Article 4(3) of the directive. At the time it lodged its application, the
Commission had at its disposal *inter alia* the maps appended to the abovementioned regulation, defining the boundaries of the protected area. It is evident
from that information that the Rysumer Nacken is not one of the sites designated
as a special protection area. Consequently, since the withdrawal of this part of
the application is not the consequence of the conduct of the German Government, the Commission must bear the costs relating thereto.

(7) With regard to the dyke-building operations in the Leybucht, the Commission
claims that they disturb birds which enjoy special protection under the provisions of Article 4(1) of the directive, in conjunction with Annex I, and damage
the habitat of the birds, which is designated as a special protection area. The
Commission emphasizes that the first sentence of Article 4(4) of the directive
requires Member States to take positive steps to avoid any deterioration or pollution of habitats as part of the management of special protection areas.

(8) The Commission states that coastal defence measures such as the strengthening of a dyke are acceptable in the case of a threat to human life, but only on
condition that the necessary measures are restricted to those which cause only
the minimum necessary deterioration of the special protection area in question.

(9) According to the Commission, those conditions have not been fulfilled in the
present case. It is of the opinion that both the construction work in the Leybucht
and its results entail deterioration in the living conditions of protected birds and
the loss of land areas of considerable ecological importance, thereby leading to
lower population densities for some of the species of birds listed in Annex I to
the directive, in particular the avocet.

(10) The German Government observes that according to the information sent to the
Commission pursuant to Article 4(3) of the directive, the new line of the dyke in
the Leybucht and the areas located on the landward side of the dyke are
excluded from the special protection area. It states that the boundaries of the
area in question are defined in the regulation creating the national park in such
a way that the protected area extends only to the foot of the dyke, in the form it
will have once the construction work in question has been completed.

(11) According to the German Government, the sole purpose of the operations is to

secure the safety of the dyke. It emphasizes that during the planning stage of the project at issue the competent authorities took account of all bird conservation requirements and balanced them against the requirements of coastal protection. The German Government states that the new line of the dyke and the temporary disturbances caused by the works constitute the smallest possible interference for bird life in the Leybucht. It adds that the Commission has not furnished any evidence at all that the measures at issue significantly impair the protection of those birds.

(12) With regard to the interpretation of Article 4(4) of the directive, the German Government claims that that provision requires a balance to be struck between the various public interests likely to be affected by the management of a special protection area, so that the Member States must have a wide discretionary power in this field.

(13) The United Kingdom considers that the Commission has not established that the project at issue has a significant effect within the meaning of the first sentence of Article 4(4) of the directive. It states that that condition must be interpreted as meaning that the deterioration of a special protection area must be such as to threaten the survival or reproduction of protected species within their area of distribution. In the United Kingdom's view, the material supplied by the Commission does not appear sufficient to support the conclusion that the operations in the Leybucht involve such deterioration.

(14) The United Kingdom emphasizes the importance of the evidence supplied by the defendant which shows that the works at issue will significantly improve ecological conditions in the Leybucht. It considers that it is legitimate, when assessing whether a particular project will cause deterioration to a special protection area and whether any such deterioration will be significant, to consider whether the works will at the same time bring compensatory ecological improvements.

(15) In the submission of the United Kingdom, within the context of Article 4(4) of the directive account can be taken of other important public interest considerations, including those referred to in Article 2 of the directive. It considers that the Member States must be able to take into account the interests of persons living in or around a special protection area.

(16) Reference is made to the Report for the Hearing for a fuller account of the facts of the case, the course of the procedure and the submissions and arguments of the parties, which are mentioned or discussed hereinafter only in so far as is necessary for the reasoning of the Court.

(17) With regard to the boundaries of the special protection area in question, it must be pointed out that the boundary of the Leybucht is defined by the regulation creating the national park and the maps appended thereto. Although the plan of the area does include a reference to the regional planning scheme, the legal measure designating the special protection area nevertheless sets out its precise territorial delimitation, constituted by the present line of the dyke. The displacement of the dyke towards the sea as part of the coastal defence project thus entails a reduction in the protected area.

(18) Consequently, in order to resolve this dispute it is necessary to settle a number of questions of principle concerning the obligations of the Member States under

Article 4(4) of the directive in relation to the management of the special protection areas. It must be determined whether—and if so, under what conditions—the Member States are authorized to reduce the size of a special protection area and to what extent other interests may be taken into account.

(19) With regard to the powers of the Member States to review in that way a decision to classify an area as a special protection area, it must be stated that a reduction in the geographical extent of a protected area is not expressly envisaged by the terms of the directive.

(20) Although the Member States do have a certain discretion with regard to the choice of the territories which are most suitable for classification as special protection areas pursuant to Article 4(1) of the directive, they do not have the same discretion under Article 4(4) of the directive in modifying or reducing the extent of the areas, since they have themselves acknowledged in their declarations that those areas contain the most suitable environments for the species listed in Annex I to the directive. If that were not so, the Member States could unilaterally escape from the obligations imposed on them by Article 4(4) of the directive with regard to special protection areas.

(21) That interpretation of Article 4(4) of the directive is borne out, moreover, by the ninth recital in the preamble, which underlines the special importance which the directive attaches to special conservation measures concerning the habitats of the birds listed in Annex I in order to ensure their survival and reproduction in their area of distribution. It follows that the power of the Member States to reduce the extent of a special protection area can be justified only on exceptional grounds.

(22) Those grounds must correspond to a general interest which is superior to the general interest represented by the ecological objective of the directive. In that context the interests referred to in Article 2 of the directive, namely economic and recreational requirements, do not enter into consideration. As the Court pointed out in its judgments in Case 247/85 (*Commission* v *Belgium* [1987] ECR 3029) and Case 262/85 (*Commission* v *Italy* [1987] ECR 3073), that provision does not constitute an autonomous derogation from the general system of protection established by the directive.

(23) With regard to the reason put forward in this case, it must be stated that the danger of flooding and the protection of the coast constitute sufficiently serious reasons to justify the dyke works and the strengthening of coastal structures as long as those measures are confined to a strict minimum and involve only the smallest possible reduction of the special protection area.

(24) With regard to the part of the project concerning the Leyhörn area, the line of the dyke was influenced by considerations relating not only to coastal protection but also to the concern to ensure that fishing vessels from Greetsiel had access to the harbour. In the light of the principles for the interpretation of Article 4(4) of the directive set out above, to take account of such an interest is in principle incompatible with the requirements of the provision.

(25) However, that part of the project has at the same time specific positive consequences for the habitat of birds. Once the works are completed it will be possible to close two navigation channels which cross the Leybucht, with the result that the Leybucht will be left in absolute peace. Moreover, the decision approv-

ing the proposed works envisages a strict protection scheme for the Leyhörn area. The dyke which previously protected the Hauener Hooge site will be opened, thus once more exposing an extensive area to tidal movements and allowing the formation of salt meadows of considerable ecological importance.

(26) The desire to ensure the survival of the fishing port of Greetsiel could thus be taken into account in order to justify the decision on the line of the new dyke because there were the abovementioned offsetting ecological benefits, and solely for that reason.

(27) Finally, the disturbance arising from the construction work itself does not exceed what is necessary to carry it out. The information concerning the number of avocets in that sector of the Wattenmeer shows, moreover, that during the period in question there was no significant change, within the meaning of Article 4(4) of the directive, in population trends for that species. Furthermore, the Commission has not supplied any other evidence relating to population trends for protected species.

(28) It follows from the foregoing that the application must be dismissed.

Costs

(29) Under Article 69(2) of the Rules of Procedure, the unsuccessful party is to be ordered to pay the costs. Since the Commission has failed in its submissions, it must be ordered to pay the costs, including the costs of the intervener and those relating to the application for interim measures.

On those grounds,

THE COURT

hereby:

(1) Dismisses the application;

(2) Orders the Commission to pay the costs, including the costs of the intervener and those relating to the application for interim measures.

COMMENTARY

(1) This is the first decision of Court on habitat protection and both the Court and the Advocate General seem to have considered the case, if not as a test case, at least as a leading case.[7] Due to legislative developments, this will

---

[7] See opinion of the Advocate General, pp. 903 *et seq.* He indicates (p. 904) that on March 15, 1990, the Commission had started 37 proceedings against Member States under Art. 169 EEC, based on Art. 4 of Dir. 79/409.
As to the Court's attitude see for instance para. 18—"it is necessary to answer a number of questions of principle"—and 26—"because there were the ... compensations *and only for that reason.*" (emphasis added)

most likely not be so, and commentators who welcomed the Court's decision because it ensured a satisfactory degree of environmental protection, will probably be disappointed.[8]

(2) The first problem which the Court had to address was the question whether the areas of Rysumer Nacken and Leybucht were habitats under Article 4 of Directive 79/409.[9] With regard to the Rysumer Nacken, the Court concluded from the maps which Germany had submitted in its answer to the reasoned opinion on September 6, 1988[10] that the Commission should have known, when applying to the Court that this area was not part of the Wattenmeer. The Court's reasoning shall not be disputed. Instead, attention should be drawn to the difficulties of the Commission in obtaining information. Indeed, the Commission received the first complaints in 1985. In 1987 the letter of formal notice was sent and in 1988 this was followed by the reasoned opinion. Only in answer to the latter were the relevant maps transmitted to the Commission. The Commission had to work for about three years without reliable factual knowledge. As a number of cases on habitat protection occur all over the Community, one can imagine the difficulties in collecting factual information on complaints brought to the knowledge of the Commission.[11]

(3) The Court did not need to raise the question whether the Leybucht was a habitat under Article 4, since Germany had recognised this fact.[12] However, in this case as well, the letter of formal notice and the reasoned opinion had to be based on the legal reasoning that either the Leybucht was a designated habitat or the omission to designate it was, in view of the importance of the area for birds, a breach of the obligations under Article 4.

This raises the general problem of the designation of habitats under Article 4. There is no doubt that it is the Member States who have to designate the habitats.[13] Under Article 18(1) of Directive 79/409, Member States had to designate the "most suitable territories in number and size as special protection areas" within two years, *i.e.* until 1981.[14]

(4) The Commission made an inventory of those areas, which were candidates for designation under ecological and scientific criteria.[15] However, since

---

[8] See G. Winter, "Der Säbelschnäbler als Teil fürs Ganze," *Natur und Recht* (1992), p. 21; more nuanced D. Baldock, "The Status of Special Protection Areas for the Protection of Wild Birds," *Journal of Environmental Law* (1992), p. 139.

[9] See the wording of Art. 4 in para. 2 of the judgment above.

[10] See para. 6.

[11] Apart from the 37 cases mentioned in n. 7 there are numerous complaints as regards Art. 4 where the instruction is ongoing, but where the Commission has not yet taken a decision.

[12] See para. 17 and the report of the hearing, p. 885.

[13] See Art. 4(1), second para. of Dir. 79/409.

[14] *Ibid.* **Article 18(1)**: "Member States shall bring into force the laws, regulations and administrative provisions necessary to comply with this Directive within two years of its notification. They shall forthwith inform the Commission thereof."

[15] See Commission, Information sur l'application de la directive 79/409/CEE. Rapport EUR 12835, Bruxelles-Luxembourg 1990, no. 4. 3, p. 41.

other criteria such as economic, social and political criteria play a role in the designation of an area, no direct conclusion can be drawn from such a list. Nevertheless, more than 13 years after the adoption of Directive 79/409 (at mid 1993) out of more than 1,600 candidate areas, only 600 to 700 have been designated. In view of this gap in the implementation, the Commission attempted a number of mechanisms in order to persuade Member States to designate more areas. Apart from bilateral and multilateral discussions with Member States, the Commission tried to assist with financial help in the acquisition of land, conservation measures or other actions. The legal framework for these activities was Regulation 1872/84,[16] and Regulation 2247/87[17] which was replaced later by Regulation 3907/91;[18] since 1992 this financial assistance is channeled through the environmental fund LIFE, set up by Regulation 1973/92.[19] One of the conditions for granting money is that at the latest at the end of the contract period, the area must be designated under Article 4 of Directive 79/409. None of the decisions to give financial assistance have been published yet.[20]

(5) The Commission is not empowered to designate areas under Article 4 of Directive 79/409. This follows first of all from the wording of Article 4 which gives, as the Court stated, "a certain margin of discretion" in selecting areas.[21] However in specific cases it has started proceedings against a Member State because a specific area had not been designated.[22] But such cases remain very exceptional and in practice limited to situations where the environmental evidence is such that no other solution than their designation could be envisaged.

Directive 79/409 is drafted in a rather vague way. Even areas which Member States have designated as "wetland of international importance" under the Ramsar Convention[23] do not automatically qualify as areas under Article 4(1), but need another designation under Directive 79/409.

(6) Difficulties in setting up a coherent network throughout the Community are, in my opinion, increased by the fact that the Commission monitors more than one list of designated areas under Article 4; the published lists on the network include

(a) designated areas under Article 4 of Directive 79/409;

---

[16] [1984] O.J. L176/1.
[17] [1987] O.J. L207/8.
[18] [1991] O.J. L370/17.
[19] [1992] O.J. L206/1.
[20] The monthly "Bulletin of the European Community" publishes, however, general information. See for an example [1991] 12 E.C. Bull. 1.2.311 where it is indicated that the Commission approved financial assistance of an amount of 980,000 ECU. The individual habitats are not indicated.
[21] See para. 20.
[22] See, *e.g.* Case C–355/90, *Commission* v. *Spain*: pending.
[23] Convention on international wetlands, see n.2 above.

(b) wetlands of international importance "which make part of the network";
(c) areas which have a specific status under national law and are submitted "to an equivalent protection scheme."[24]

This joint list diffuses the legal responsibilities. Indeed, while the obligations as regards designated areas are laid down in Directive 79/409, the obligations as regards international wetlands an areas under national law flow entirely from national law.

(7) Under Article 4(1) Member States are obliged to take, for species which are listed in Annex I to the Directive[25] "special conservation measures concerning their habitat in order to ensure their survival and reproduction in this area of designation."

Thus, the mere designation of a birds' habitat is not sufficient. Instead, Member States have to take positive steps in favour of the threatened birds. The Commission has started a number of proceedings under Article 169 of the EEC Treaty, where the designation of a habitat was not, during several years, accompanied by positive steps in favour of the birds. It seems obvious, though, that the very general wording of Article 4(1) does not easily lend itself to legal monitoring. Most habitats are thus exclusively managed by national measures and legal steps taken at Community level do not significantly change this situation. In the context of financial assistance, management plans for designated areas are sometimes being discussed between national authorities and the Commission.

(8) In the present case, the Court had to decide on the interpretation of Article 4(4) of Directive 79/409, and in particular, whether the construction of a dyke, which reduced the Leybucht habitat by about 25 per cent.[26] was allowed. Article 4(4) requests Member States to "avoid ... any disturbances affecting the birds, insofar as these would be significant."

The Court started by pointing out that the wording of Directive 79/409 contains no such indication.[27] The Court further argued that if Member States were allowed to alter or to reduce the size of designated areas, they could unilaterally change their obligations for these areas, which the Court considers incompatible with Community law.[28]

Nevertheless, the Court did not conclude that the reduction of the size of a special protection area was totally prohibited; on the contrary, it argued that this was allowed "only in exceptional circumstances", which "must relate to a

---

[24] Commission, Information sur l'application de la directive 79/409, (n. 15) No. 4.4, pp. 46 *et seq.* The Commission justifies this by reference to Council resolution of April 2, 1979: [1979] O.J. C103/6.

[25] Annex I of Dir. 79/409 lists at present 175 species of birds.

[26] See the report for the hearing, pp. 886 *et seq.*; Opinion of the Advocate General, pp. 903 *et seq.*, paras. 19 *et seq.*; G. Winter, n. 8 above p. 21.

[27] See para. 19.

[28] See para. 20.

public interest which is greater than the ecological interest covered by the Directive."[29] The Court sees such public interests in the protection against "the danger of flood and protection of the coastline."[30]

(9) Up to this point, the decision was in agreement with the arguments of the Commission and Germany, and the United Kingdom as intervener. The Commission had not objected to the strengthening of the dykes as protection against flood,[31] but had argued that the measures were not kept to the strict minimum, since agricultural, fishery, tourist interest had also influenced the line of the dyke. Indeed, it would be difficult to imagine that a risk of flooding and inundations should have to be accepted because of the existence of a birds' habitat. The Court was thus quite right in introducing an unwritten justification for "disturbance affecting the birds" into Article 4(4). In that context it is remarkable that the Court expressly repeated statements from earlier judgments[32] that economic and recreational reasons—mentioned in Article 2 of Directive 79/409[33]—cannot be such "exceptional circumstances". Both the United Kingdom and Germany had pleaded in favour of consideration of Article 2.[34]

(10) The Court then had to discuss the specific form of the dyke which was influenced by, as stated, agricultural, tourist and fishery considerations. Out of these considerations, only the fishery problem was taken up by the Court, *i.e.* the attempt to provide access to the port of Greetsiel for fishing vessels.[35] First the Court stated that "in principle" taking such an interest into account is incompatible with Article 4(4). However, the Court found that giving the dyke such a shape as to assist fishing vessels bore "positive effects for the birds' habitats"—the calming down of the Leybucht and the possibility to allow the formations of salt water meadows. Thus it was possible to take into account the wish to "ensure the survival of the fishing port of Greetsiel in order to justify the decision regarding the line of the new dyke because there were the above mentioned offsetting ecological benefits and solely for that reason."[36]

---

[29] See paras. 21 and 22.

[30] See para. 23.

[31] The judgment itself does not make this clear beyond any doubt, see paras. 8 and 9. See, however, the opinion of the Advocate General, pp. 916 and 919, paras. 31 and 37.

[32] Case 247/85, *Commission* v. *Belgium:* [1987] E.C.R. 3029; Case 262/85, *Commission* v. *Italy,* [1987] E.C.R. 3073, see pp. 185–204 above.

[33] Dir. 79/409, **Article 2**: "Member States shall take the requisite measures to maintain population of the species referred to in Article 1 at a level which corresponds in particular to ecological, scientific and cultural requirements while taking account of economic and recreational requirements, or to adapt the population of these species to that level."

[34] See para. 15.

[35] See para. 24. The Advocate General had agreed on grounds of fishery and agriculture, see pp. 919 and 920, para. 37 and 40. G. Winter, (n. 8 above) mentions rightly on p. 22 (no. 2) that the true reasons for giving a nose to the line of the dyke was the creation of an artificial lake which was to serve agricultural—and one day also touristic—purposes.

[36] Para. 26.

(11) These arguments of the Court follow relatively closely those of Advocate General van Gerven.[37] The line of argument is as follows:

(a) Article 4(4) provides for unrestricted protection of designated habitats.
(b) There are unwritten limits to this protection which may be justified by a higher public interest. Economic and recreational reasons are no justification.
(c) Protection against flooding and protection of the coastline are such higher interests which justify the construction of a dyke, and make acceptable the reduction of the size of habitat.
(d) Where the reduction of the size of the habitat is justified, economic interests such as access to the port of Greetsiel may be taken into account when considering the extent of the reduction, provided that there are ecological compensations.

(12) It is obvious that ecological compensations will almost never be capable of being checked by the Commission as to size, reasonableness and ecological results.[38] As a result the Court does not require the strict minimum of measures under Article 4(4), but allows for larger steps to be taken. In making this statement, I am of course aware that the question of habitat protection as part of nature conservation policy would not have been better answered had the Court prohibited to take the Greetsiel port into consideration. Indeed, the stricter the requirements for habitat protection, the greater the objection of local or regional populations, economic agents and others to see parts of their environment transformed into a museum. This, in turn, would reduce the number of designations.

Legal considerations, therefore, quickly reach their limits and one has to rely on nature conservation policy and management. Such policy considerations depend on environmental awareness, administrative infrastructure,[39] political priorities and other considerations which are not to be discussed here.

(13) The monitoring by the Commission of Article 4 and of Community environmental law has certainly not become easier. The Court indicated directly or indirectly, a number of points where the Commission has not produced enough facts or where the Court took over facts presented by the German Government, such as:

(a) the dyke ensures the "survival" of Greetsiel port[40]

---

[37] See opinion of the Advocate General pp. 919 *et seq*, paras. 37 to 42.
[38] See also D. Baldock, (n. 8 above) p. 143.
[39] See D. Baldock, I. Holzner, G. Bennett, *The organization of nature conservation in selected EC countries* (London, 1987).
[40] Para. 26.

(b) the Commission has not provided material regarding the evolution of populations of protected species[41]

(c) the measures involve only the smallest possible reduction in the size of the area[42]

(d) the line of the dyke was (only) influenced by the desire to give access to Greetsiel port[43]

(e) the compensation measures have specific positive effects on the birds' habitats[44]

It is submitted that without an environmental Inspectorate of its own, the Commission is just not equipped to handle such factual circumstances.

(14) All in all the judgment is certainly a useful and positive contribution to environmental protection via Community law. Member States considered the judgment to be going too far.[45] Therefore, when adopting Directive 92/43[46] on natural habitats which also applies to birds' habitats, they introduced the following provision into Article 6(4) which replaces the first sentence of Article 4(4) of Directive 79/409:

"If, in spite of a negative assessment of the implications for the site and in the absence of alternative solutions, a plan or project must nevertheless be carried out for imperative reasons of public interest, including those of a social or *economic matter*, the Member State shall take all compensatory measures necessary to ensure that the overall coherence of Nature 2000 is protected. It shall inform the Commission of the compensatory measures adopted." (emphasis added)

(15) Directive 79/409 and its Article 4 only concern the protection of birds' habitats. Directive 78/659[47] requested Member States to designate habitats for fish and to take appropriate measures against the pollution of waters. However, since Member States were entirely free to designate fresh fish water to which Directive 78/659 applied, that Directive had a very limited effect.

The EEC has also ratified the Convention on the conservation of European wildlife and natural habitats of September 19, 1979.[48] This Convention requests contracting parties to "take appropriate measures to ensure the conservation of the habitats of the wild flora and fauna species . . . and conser-

---

[41] Para. 27.
[42] Para. 23.
[43] Para. 24.
[44] Para. 25.
[45] See D. Baldock, (n. 8 above) p. 144.
[46] Dir. 92/43 on the conservation of natural habitats and of wild fauna and flora: [1992] O.J. L206/7.
[47] Dir. 78/659 on the quality of the fresh waters needing protection or improvement in order to support fish life: [1978] O.J. L222/1.
[48] Decision 82/72 concerning the conclusion of the Convention on the conservation of European wildlife and natural habitats: [1982] O.J. L38/1. The Convention is annexed to that decision.

vation of endangered natural habitats."[49] However, the EEC does not monitor compliance with and enforcement of this Convention.

In 1992, the EEC adopted Directive 92/43 on the protection of natural habitats and of wild fauna and flora.[50] This Directive provides for a comprehensive system of habitat conservation which is to be set up within the next 15 years. It is to be hoped that nature in Western Europe will survive until then.

---

[49] Art. 4 of the Convention.
[50] Dir. 92/43.

Water

14. THE QUALITY OF DRINKING WATER

**Judgment of the Court of July 5, 1990
in Case C–42/89**

E.C. Commission v. *Belgium*

[1990] I E.C.R. 2821, [1992] 1 C.M.L.R. 22

FACTS AND PROCEDURE[1]

Directive 80/778 relating to the quality of water intended for human consumption[2] was adopted on July 15, 1980 and notified to Member States on July 18, 1980. It provides in Article 18 that Member States shall bring into force the national legal provisions necessary to comply with Directive 80/778 within two years following its notification and that Member States shall take the necessary measures to ensure that the quality of drinking water complies with the Directive within five years of its notification. In exceptional cases Member States have the possibility to request, under certain conditions, for a longer period for compliance.[3]

Belgium transmitted a Royal Decree of April 27, 1984 on drinking water to the Commission. This Decree was annulled by a Belgian Court end 1988. At the end 1989, Belgium transmitted drinking water legislation adopted by the Flanders, Brussels and Walloon Regions.

On August 4, 1986, the Commission sent a letter of formal notice to the Belgian Government, raising in particular[4] that drinking water in the town of Verviers was not, in view of its lead content, in compliance with the requirements of the Directive. A second letter of formal notice was sent to the Belgian Government on December 15, 1987, arguing that water drawn by private individuals for household use was not covered by the Belgian legislation.

Belgium answered by letter of February 25, 1988 and requested, amongst others, a delay in the application of the Directive until January 1, 1991 as regards the Verviers drinking water, referring to Article 20 of the Directive.[5]

The Commission issued a reasoned opinion on May 16, 1988. On January 17,

---

[1] Summary by the author.

[2] [1980] O.J. L229/11.

[3] Arts. 19 and 20 read as follows:

Article 19: "The Member States shall take the necessary measures to ensure that the quality of water intended for human consumption complies with this Directive within five years of its notification."

Article 20: "Member States may, in exceptional cases and for geographically defined population groups, submit a special request to the Commission for a longer period for complying with Annex I.

This request, for which grounds must be duly put forward, shall set out the difficulties experienced and must propose an action programme with an appropriate timetable to be undertaken for the improvement of the quality of water intended for human consumption.

The Commission shall examine these programmes, including the timetables. In the case of disagreement with the Member State concerned, the Commission shall submit appropriate proposals to the Council."

[4] The letter also contained arguments on lack of compliance with Art. 9, which were later remedied by the Belgian legislation, see Report for the Hearing: [1990] I E.C.R. 2823.

[5] See the wording of Art. 20 in n. 3 above.

1989, Belgium asked again for additional time in respect of the Verviers drinking water. The Commission considered that this request did not fulfil the requirements of Article 20 and lodged its application to the Court on February 20, 1989.

Oral hearings took place on December 6, 1989. The Advocate General delivered his opinion on December 14, 1989.

JUDGMENT

(1) By an application lodged at the Court Registry on 20 February 1989, the Commission of the European Communities brought an action under Article 169 of the EEC Treaty for a declaration that by not adopting within the prescribed period the laws, regulations and administrative provisions necessary to comply with the provisions of Council Directive 80/778/EEC of 15 July 1980 relating to the quality of water intended for human consumption (Official Journal 1980 L 229, p. 11), and in particular Articles 1, 2, 9, 18, 19 and 20 thereof, the Kingdom of Belgium has failed to fulfil its obligations under the EEC Treaty.

(2) The action in this case has its origin in the finding by the Commission, in the first place, that the Royal Decree of 27 April 1984 transposing the directive into Belgian law (*Moniteur belge* 1984, p. 9860) is not in conformity with Article 9(1)(b) and (3) of that directive inasmuch as it allows derogations from the provisions of the directive under conditions which are less stringent than those prescribed by the directive (Article 5 of the Royal Decree) and excludes from its scope water drawn by private individuals for household use (Article 1 of the Royal Decree), and, secondly, that the water supplied to the town of Verviers does not, in view of its lead content, comply with the requirements set out in the directive.

(3) On 4 August 1986, the Commission, pursuant to the first paragraph of Article 169 of the Treaty, issued a formal notice to the Belgian Government mentioning the infringement of the provisions of the directive prohibiting certain derogations and the infringement relating to the inadequate quality of the water in Verviers. On 15 December 1987 the Commission issued a further notice to the Belgian Government concerning the exclusion from the measures transposing the directive of water drawn by private individuals for household use. Since it considered that the Belgian Government's reply was not such as to cause it to withdraw those objections, the Commission on 16 May 1988 issued a reasoned opinion giving the Belgian Government a period of two months within which to take the measures necessary to comply therewith.

(4) By letter of 17 January 1989, the Belgian Government first requested additional time under Article 20 of the directive in order to comply with its obligations under Annex 1 to the directive in respect of the water at Verviers. It then replied to the reasoned opinion by letter of 1 March 1989 in which it claimed, first, that it was the acidity level of the water supplied to the population of Verviers, in respect of which no rule is laid down in the annexes to the directive, which was the cause of the pollution in houses still equipped with lead conduits.

It considered that, inasmuch as Article 12 of the directive provided for monitoring only at the point where the water was made available to the user, that is to say its supply by the water company, the water supplied in Verviers must be deemed to be in compliance with the requirements of the directive. It added that in any event the pollution in question affected only a small number of inhabitants (10 000).

(5) Secondly, the Belgian Government claimed that the drawing of water by individuals did not fall within the scope of the directive. In support of that contention it referred not only to the first indent of Article 2 and to Article 12(2) of the directive, but also to the practical difficulties in monitoring individual wells and to the purpose of the directive which, according to the second recital in its preamble, was to prevent differences in the conditions of competition and, as a result, was concerned only with water supplied commercially.

(6) Since it considered that the Belgian Government's reply to the reasoned opinion was not satisfactory, the Commission brought the present action.

(7) Reference is made to the Report for the Hearing for a fuller account of the facts of the case, the course of the procedure and the pleas in law and arguments of the parties, which are mentioned or discussed hereinafter only in so far as is necessary for the reasoning of the Court.

The claims concerning the non-compliance of the Royal Decree of 27 April 1984 with the provisions of the directive

(8) It should, first of all, be pointed out that, by a judgment of 14 December 1988, the Belgian Conseil d'État (Council of State) annulled the Royal Decree of 27 April 1984 on the ground that the Regional Executives had not been associated in the drawing-up of that decree, as required by Article 6(4) of the Law of 8 August 1980 on institutional reforms (*Moniteur belge* 1980, p. 9434).

(9) Following the institution of the proceedings before the Court, measures transposing the directive into national law were adopted by the three Regions. Taking the view that those adopted by the Flemish Region were in compliance with the directive, the Commission withdrew its application to that extent. The Commission found that the situation was different in the case of the Royal Decree of 19 June 1989 adopted for the Brussels Region (*Moniteur belge* 1989, p. 11895), inasmuch as water drawn by private individuals continued to be excluded from the scope of that decree, and in the case of the Decree of the Walloon Executive of 20 July 1989 (*Moniteur belge* 1990, p. 3052) in respect of which all the claims already formulated with regard to the Royal Decree of 27 April 1984 applied.

(10) It is a fact that Article 5 of the Decree of the Walloon Executive reproduces Article 5 of the aforementioned Royal Decree as regards the rules on derogations and the Decree of the Walloon Executive and the Royal Decree adopted for the Brussels Region exclude from their scope water drawn by private individuals.

(11) In those circumstances, the Commission has not altered the subject-matter of the dispute by imputing, in the course of the proceedings, its claims concerning

the Royal Decree of 27 April 1984 to the regional legislation which replaced that decree.

(12) It is therefore appropriate to examine the Commission's claims concerning the derogations permitted by the national legislation as compared with those provided for by the directive, and those concerning the exclusion of private water supplies from its scope.

(13) On that point the Commission submits in the first place that the power conferred by Article 5 of the Decree of the Walloon Regional Executive on the minister responsible for local authorities, subsidized works and water, to authorize maximum permissible concentrations to be exceeded in the event of serious accidental circumstances or situations resulting from exceptional meteorological conditions, 'in so far as the excess amount does not entail any unacceptable risk to public health and the network distribution cannot be assured in any other manner', is incompatible with Article 9(3) of the directive.

(14) The decree in question in no way excludes derogations relating to toxic or microbiological factors, although that is an express requirement of the aforementioned provision of the directive. The claim, to that effect, which moreover is not contested by the Belgian Government, must therefore be upheld.

(15) The Commission submits, in the second place, that the exclusion of private water supplies from the scope of the legislation applicable to the Walloon and Brussels Regions is incompatible with Article 1 of the directive according to which the directive applies to all water regardless of its origin, intended for human consumption.

(16) In that connection it should be borne in mind that according to Article 2 of the directive 'water intended for human consumption shall mean all water for that purpose, either in its original state or after treatment, regardless of origin,

  (i) whether supplied for consumption, or
  (ii) whether

  (a) used in a food production undertaking for the manufacture, processing, preservation or marketing of products or substances intended for human consumption, and
  (b) affecting the wholesomeness of the foodstuff in its finished form'.

(17) It follows from that provision that the directive applies only to water supplied for human consumption and to water used in foodstuffs by a food production undertaking and that water from private sources of supply is excluded from its scope.

(18) That interpretation is confirmed by Article 12(2) by virtue of which the monitoring prescribed by the directive applies to water intended for human consumption at the point where it is made available to the user. It follows that only water supplied for human consumption is subject to monitoring and, consequently, to the regime laid down by the directive.

(19) That interpretation is also confirmed by Annex II to the directive. With regard, on the one hand, to the parameters to be taken into consideration for the pur-

poses of periodic monitoring, note 4 to Section A of that annex states that those parameters 'will be determined by the competent national authority, taking account of all factors which might affect the quality of drinking water supplied to users and which could enable the ionic balance of the constituents to be assessed'. With regard, on the other hand, to occasional monitoring in special situations or in case of accidents, it is stated in Section A of that same annex that 'the competent national authority of the Member State will determine the parameters according to circumstances, taking account of all factors which might have an adverse affect on the quality of drinking water supplied to consumers'. Those provisions therefore only concern water supplied to consumers and not water from private sources of supply.

(20) It follows that the claim based on the exclusion of private water supplies from the measures transposing the directive which relate to the Walloon and Brussels Regions must be rejected.

The claim concerning the conformity of drinking water in Verviers with the requirements laid down in the directive

(21) It should first be observed that, contrary to the Belgian Government's contention in its reply to the reasoned opinion, the Verviers drinking water which comes from the Eupen treatment station and supplies a part of the town pending the completion of works at the Gileppe treatment station, is not in conformity with the requirements of the directive. In accordance with Section D of Annex I, the lead content, where lead pipes are present, is evaluated on the basis of samples taken directly after the passage of water and, if the lead content, either frequently or to an appreciable extent, exceeds 100 μg/l, suitable measures must be taken to reduce consumer exposure to lead. It is not disputed that the Verviers drinking water supplied by the Eupen treatment station exceeds that parameter and that no suitable measure has been adopted.

(22) The Belgian Government contended before the Court that owing to the cost and complexity of the construction works at the water treatment station which were needed in order that the town of Verviers might be supplied with water in conformity with the requirements of the directive, it will be possible to comply with those requirements only towards the end of 1990. That situation underlies the request made by the Belgian Government on 17 January 1989 under Article 20 of the directive for a longer period for complying with Annex I to the directive.

(23) It should be observed in that connection that a request for a longer period for complying with Annex 1 must, in accordance with Article 20 of the directive, be made within the period laid down in Article 19 for the transposition of the directive into national law. After the expiry of that period derogations are permissible only in the case of serious accidents and under the conditions laid down in Article 10 of the directive. The request by the Belgian Government was made more than four years after expiry of the abovementioned period.

(24) As regards, finally, the difficulties, pleaded by the Belgian Government, in ensuring that the water supplied to the town of Verviers is in conformity with the directive, it should be borne in mind that, according to the case-law of the Court, a Member State may not plead practical or administrative difficulties in order to justify non-compliance with the obligations and time-limits laid down in

Community directives. The same holds true of financial difficulties, which it is for the Member States to overcome by adopting appropriate measures.

(25) It follows that the Commission's claim that the Verviers drinking-water supply is not in confirmity with the requirements set out in the directive is well founded.

(26) It must therefore be held that by permitting the Walloon Region to allow the maximum admissible concentrations set out in Annex 1 to Council Directive 80/778 of 15 July 1980 relating to the quality of water intended for human consumption to be exceeded in circumstances other than those provided for in that directive, and the supply to Verviers of drinking water not in conformity with the requirements laid down in the same directive, the Kingdom of Belgium has failed to fulfil its obligations under the Treaty.

Costs

(27) Under Article 69(2) of the Rules of Procedure, the unsuccessful party is to be ordered to pay the costs. However, the first subparagraph of Article 69(3) provides that the Court may order the parties to bear their own costs in whole or in part if each party succeeds on some and fails on other heads, or where the circumstances are exceptional.

(28) Since the parties have been partially unsuccessful in their submissions, they should bear their own costs.

On those grounds,

THE COURT

hereby declares that:

(1) By permitting the Walloon Region to allow the maximum admissible concentrations listed in Annex I to Council Directive 80/778/EEC of 15 July 1980 relating to the quality of water intended for human consumption to be exceeded in circumstances other than those provided for in the directive, and the supply to Verviers of drinking water not in conformity with the requirements laid down in the same directive, the Kingdom of Belgium has failed to fulfil its obligations under the Treaty.

(2) The remainder of the application is dismissed.

(3) The parties shall bear their own costs.

COMMENTARY

(1) Directive 80/778 on the quality of drinking water was adopted in 1980 after five years discussion at Community level.[6] The compliance with its require-

---

[6] Commission proposal: [1975] O.J. C214/2.

ments raises considerable problems in almost all Member States. Drinking water is produced either from surface water[7] or from ground water[8] and where these waters are polluted it is sometimes difficult to respect the rather strict requirements of Directive 80/778; furthermore, the cleaning of surface or ground water is more and more often done with the help of chemicals which, in turn, influence the quality of drinking water.

Directive 75/440 on the quality required of surface water intended for the abstraction of drinking water,[9] tried to make Member States draw up systematic clean-up plans for surface waters and thus generally lead to improvements. Directive 80/68 on the quality of ground water tried to reduce ground water pollution in particular by prohibiting or limiting the direct or indirect discharge of dangerous substances into the groundwater.[10] Both directives had only limited success, a situation which certainly contributed to the difficulties to comply with Directive 80/778 on drinking water.

(2) After having shortly discussed the question whether the changes in Belgian legislation did not require a new procedure to be started, the Court first addressed the problem whether or not Directive 80/778 applied to drinking water drawn from private sources. The Court answered this question in the negative, arguing from the wording of Article 2 of the Directive as well as from the monitoring provisions of Article 12 and Annex.[11] This reasoning was based on the interpretation that the words "supplied for consumption" in Article 2 only applies to public supplies. The Court does not explain how it comes to this conclusion. Arguments for a different interpretation may be based on the wording of Article 2 and on the teleological interpretation of the purpose of the Directive:

(3) Article 2 aims to cover "*all* water" intended for human consumption, "regardless of origin". This text seems to request a wide interpretation. The following qualification "whether supplied for consumption" is not, in my opinion, a restriction. Indeed, in paragraph 17 of its judgment, the Court itself used the word "private source of supply". Thus, also water from private sources is "supplied," and the question whether private sources of supply are excluded depends on the emphasis which is laid on the words "all water" in Article 2.

It should be stressed that the Court did not use the words "public supply" and "private supply". Instead, it starts from the assumption that water from private sources of supply is not "supplied" in the sense of the Directive. However, are the members of the family of the owner of a private source not "supplied"

---

[7] See also Dir. 75/440 concerning the quality required of surface water intended for the abstraction of drinking water in the Member States: [1975] O.J. L194/26.
[8] See also Dir. 80/86 on the protection of groundwater against pollution caused by certain dangerous substances: [1980] O.J. L20/43.
[9] Dir. 75/440, above.
[10] Dir. 80/68, above.
[11] Paras. 14 to 19.

with water? What if pipes are laid between the source and the place where the water is taken? In the new German Länder, private sources sometimes serve to bring water to several co-operatives of up to a hundred people.

(4) The interpretation that water from private sources is included in Directive 80/778 is confirmed by its purposes. Indeed, the first recital of the Directive states:

> "Whereas, in view of the importance for public health of water for human consumption, it is necessary to lay down quality standards with which such waters must comply."

The aim of Directive 80/778 is therefore to ensure a good quality of drinking water in order to protect public health. Now, public health is also affected where drinking water is used from private sources. And since private sources are not mentioned anywhere in the Directive or its recitals, it is not entirely convincing to limit the words "supplied for consumption" to public supplies only. In practice, private supplies are mainly used in rural areas and the possibility that private supplies do not comply with the requirements of the Directive might well lead to an increase in the difference of standards of living in urban and rural areas.

(5) The second argument used by the Court is taken from the monitoring provisions. Here the same arguments in favour of the inclusion of private sources may be raised. This is further confirmed by Annex II to the Directive, where a note in IIA states: "An initial analysis, to be carried out before a source is exploited, should be added." Again, no differentiation is made between private and public supply—which makes sense if one thinks of protecting public health. The Court's understanding that "supplied to consumers" only refers to public supplies as well as the inherent doubts on such an interpretation appears very clearly in the phrase:

> "Those provisions (of Annex II) therefore only concern water *supplied* to consumers and not water from private sources of *supply*."[12]

Politically it should be made clear that since the decision of the Court, the discussion whether private sources of supply are also covered by Directive 80/778 has come to an end. Member States are completely free, under Community law, to set standards for private sources of supply.

(6) The second question which the Court had to address concerned the quality of drinking water in Verviers,[13] which contained too much lead. This fact was out of dispute and the Court had just to address the question, whether

---

[12] *Ibid.* para. 19, last phrase (emphasis added).
[13] *Ibid.* paras. 21 to 26. The drinking water with too much lead content was supplied to approximately 10,000 people, *ibid.* para. 4.

Belgium could invoke one of the Articles of the Directive which allowed Member States to derogate from its provisions.

Directive 80/778 contains three possibilities to derogate, laid down in Articles 9,[14] 10[15] and 20.[16]

(7) Article 9 allows derogations in order to take account of situations which are due to the nature and structure of the ground or to exceptional meteorological conditions. Geological conditions are of a permanent nature and therefore derogations under Article 9(1)(a) are of a permanent nature. In view of this permanent situation it seems appropriate to limit the possibility to have recourse to this provision to cases, where "without human intervention, a given body of water receives from the soil certain substances contained therein."[17] Thus, where agricultural activity causes the pollution of the supply in question, it is not possible to invoke Article 9(1)(*a*), because the pollution of the drinking water is man-made. This interpretation of Article 9 which has not yet been confirmed by the Court of Justice,[18] also follows from comparing the possibility of derogation in Article 9 with those in Articles 10 and 20.

(8) Article 10 allows derogations "in the event of emergencies". The wording of this provision is not quite clear:[19] while the English version talks of emergencies, the French and the Italian text talks of "serious accidental circumstances", while the German version is close to the English text.[20]

---

[14] **Article 9**: "(1) Member States may make provision for derogations from this Directive in order to take account of:
    (a) situations arising from the nature and structure of the ground in the area from which the supply in question emanates . . .
    (b) situations arising from exceptional meteorological conditions . . .
    (c) In no case shall the derogations made by virtue of this Article relate to toxic or microbiological factors or constitute a public health hazard."

[15] **Article 10**: "(1) In the event of emergencies, the competent national authorities may, for a limited period of time and up to a maximum value to be determined by them, allow the maximum admissible concentration shown in Annex I to be exceeded, provided that this does not constitute an unacceptable risk to public health and provided that the supply of water for human consumption cannot be maintained in any other way . . . "

[16] Art. 20, see n.3 above.

[17] Dir. 75/440, Art. 8, para. 2, see n. 7 above.

[18] By end 1992, Directive 80/778 was on four occasions the subject matter of Court decisions; besides the present case, see Case 228/87, *Pretura di Torino* v. *X*: [1988] E.C.R. 5099; Case C–237/90, *Commission* v. *Germany*: judgment of November 24, 1992, not yet reported; Case C–337/89, *Commission* v. *United Kingdom*; judgment of November 25, 1992, not yet reported.

[19] Case 228/87, cited above, para. 14. This case is commented on by L. Salazow, *Rivista Giuridica dell'Ambiente* 1988, p. 669 and by N. Cerano, *ibid.* p. 811.

[20] The different versions read as follows:
    French: *circonstances accidentelles graves*
    Italian: *in caso di circonstanze accidentali gravi*
    German: *in Notfällen*
    Dutch: *in noodgevallen*
    Danish: *tilfælde af alvorlige hændelser*
    Spanish: *en el caso de circumstancias accidentales graves*
    Portuguese: *em caso de grave emergência*

(9) In Case 228/87, the Court (third chamber) gave an interpretation of that provision; the underlying case illustrates well the practical difficulties of Member States.[21] An Italian Decree of 1985 had set the maximum concentrations of pesticides in drinking water in conformity with the Directive.[22] Later, in several regions drinking water was found to contain more than 0.1 microgram of pesticides, in particular of atrazine and molinate. Thus, the Italian Health Department adopted decrees which derogated from the Decree of 1985 and thus also from the Directive and allowed concentrations of atrazine and molinate in drinking water which were 17 and 60 times higher than those allowed under the Directive. An Italian court, to whom this case was brought asked the European Court for an interpretation of Article 10.

(10) The European Court ruled that the notion of "emergency" had to be understood to cover an urgency situation, where the public authorities suddenly have to face supply difficulties. This situation allows for derogations only for a time span which is normally necessary to re-establish the necessary water quality.[23]

This ruling has led to different interpretations. In particular it continues to be argued that agricultural activity which leads to concentrations of pesticides or nitrates in drinking water above the maximal admissible concentrations[24] creates an emergency situation within the meaning of Article 10, and thus allows a derogation under that provision.[25]

(11) In my understanding of the Court's ruling in Case 228/87, such an interpretation is not possible. Indeed, the contamination and pollution of surface or ground water by agricultural activity resulting later in the pollution of drinking water is not a sudden event. Agricultural pollutants accumulate in the soil and in the water; they gradually increase over time and it is thus easily foreseeable if and when the concentration of pesticides and nitrates in drinking water are exceeded. It would mean giving a premium to Member States if they were allowed to derogate in such circumstances, even though they did not take enough measures to prevent the pollution of the drinking water, for instance by limiting the use of fertilizers or pesticides or by changing specific agricultural practices.

---

[21] Cited above.
[22] Dir. 80/778 provides in Annex I, number 55 for "pesticides and related products": For substances considered separately a maximum admissible concentration in drinking water of 0.1 microgram per litre; for the total of substances 0.5 microgram per litre. "Pesticides and related products" mean: (a) Insecticides:–persistent organochlorine compounds; –organophosphorous compounds; –carbamates, (b) Herbicides, (c) Fungicides, (d) PCBs and PCTs.
[23] Case 228/87, see n. 18 above, paras. 14 to 17.
[24] Dir. 80/778, see n. 2 above, provides in Annex I, number 20, for nitrates a maximum admissible concentration of 50 milligrams per litre. The guide value is 25 milligrams per litre. Guide values shall be taken as a basis for the setting of national values, Art. 7(3) of Dir. 80/778.
[25] This was the position of the Italian government in Case 228/87; a number of Member States which expressly or implicitly allow the maximum admissible concentrations of Dir. 80/778 to be exceeded—either by way of legislation such as Germany, Italy, Belgium (Flanders) or by individual decision (United Kingdom, France, the Netherlands)—invoke Art. 10.

In my opinion, the Italian derogations of the Directive were not capable of being justified by Article 10 of the Directive.

The Court seems to follow this interpretation since it mentioned in Case C–42/89 that Article 10 only applies "in the case of serious accidents."[26] Apart from this *obiter dictum*, the question of applying Article 10 was not raised in this case and therefore Court did not have to discuss it in detail.

(12) The third possibility for a "derogation" under the Directive is contained in Article 20, and in this case, the Belgian Government expressly invoked this provision. Here, the Court's reasoning was very short: it follows from the wording of Article 20 that the request for a longer period to comply with the requirements of the Directive must be made within the period of Article 19, *i.e.* before Member States actually have to comply with the Directive. Indeed, it is obvious that the words "for a longer period for complying . . . " only make sense where the period for compliance is still running. Therefore it is in fact not quite precise as regards Article 20, to talk of derogations; more appropriately, it concerns the possible prolongation of the compliance period.

(13) Since Belgium had introduced its request for a prolongation under Article 20 only in 1989, more than four years after expiring of the period of Article 19, the Court did not accept this request. It also rejected Belgium's argument that the clean-up measures for Verviers waters—the construction of a water treatment work—were expensive, arguing that a Member State was not allowed to plead financial difficulties in order to justify non-compliance with Community law.

(14) The Verviers water is particularly aggressive and absorbs lead from lead pipes which is then found back in the drinking water of some 10,000 persons in Verviers.[27] This environmental pollution was already the subject of Court decisions in 1938.[28] Again in 1963 and 1968 local authorities were held responsible for intoxications of victims. But it was only in 1984 that the responsible authorities began to construct a water treatment station[29] which was put into service in spring 1992. It may be hoped that Directive 80/778 and the procedure which the Commission had started under Article 169, contributed a little to repair this situation.

(15) Directive 80/778 is under considerable attack for being too severe, in particular as regards the pesticides parameter.[30] In this regard, it should be pointed out that Member States unanimously agreed the Directive's

---

[26] Para. 23.

[27] *Ibid.* para. 4, and the Opinion of the Advocate General.

[28] See B. Jadot, "Remous juridiques autour de la qualité de l'eau en Europe, en Belgique et a Verviers, Amènagement" *Environnement* 1990, p. 153.

[29] Report for the Hearing, p. 2824 and the Opinion of the Advocate General, *ibid.* para. 21.

[30] See n. 22 for the pesticide parameter.

standards, after five years discussions at Council level.[31] Since it is estimated that there are some 600 different effective substances for pesticides in circulation within the EEC, it does not seem reasonable to set different concentration levels for each individual pesticide, because any analysis would be virtually impossible.

Member States have not made use of Article 20 to ask for a prolonged delay for compliance.[32] However, it is a fact that in many regions of the Community the quality of drinking water is not yet in conformity with Directive 80/778, pesticides and nitrates being the biggest problems. Member States might not always analyse the drinking water quality, nor publish the results. And the Directive does not oblige Member States to inform the Commission or the public in general of the quality of drinking water. For both these reasons, Directive 80/778 has been amended in 1991 in order to provide for requirement to the report to the Commission.[33] The Commission will have to publish a comprehensive report on drinking water; the first report of this kind is scheduled for 1997.

(16) From a legal point of view, there is a real dilemma: Directive 80/778 allows Member States to exceed the maximum admissible concentrations in drinking water only under the conditions of Articles 9 and 10. However, in reality the concentrations are also exceeded in many other cases, as a result of agricultural activity in particular. Until now, the Commission and the Court have resisted all attempts to either change the text of Directive 80/778 in order to "legalise" the existing pollution or to interpret Directive 80/778 in a different way, allowing such excesses to be subsumed under Articles 9 or 10.[34] From the environmental point of view, it is obviously necessary to do more in order to prevent pollutants from entering the waters. The Commission might well be able to consider not to submit a case to the European Court, where a Member State submits clean-up programmes which allow the polluted drinking water to be cleaned up as quickly as technically possible. Hopefully the Community institutions will be able to resist any attempt to adapt the law to reality—adopting the approach "business as usual" as regards water pollution is not a progressive environmental solution.

---

[31] See Commission proposal of July 31, 1975; [1975] O.J. L214/2.

[32] Commission, answer to Written Question 1091/85 (Kuipers), [1985] O.J. C341/27; in answer to Written Question 2811/85 (Collins) it is stated that one Member State has requested the application of Art. 20: [1986] O.J. C156/27. It may be deduced from the two answers that the request was made after the time-limit contained in Art. 20 had elapsed; see also answer to Written Question 223/90 (Mr. Hughes): [1990] O.J. C303/16.

[33] See Dir. 91/692 standardising and rationalising reports on the implementation of certain Directives relating to the environment: [1991] O.J. L377/48, Art. 2(2) and Annex II(*b*).

[34] See as an example Case 228/87, n. 18 above, pp. 5110 to 5116 (E.C.R.), pp. 722 to 728 (C.M.L.R.).

15. NITRATE AND LEAD IN DRINKING WATER

**Judgment of the Court of November 25, 1992
in Case C—337/89**

E.C. Commission v. *United Kingdom*

[1992] I E.C.R. 6103

FACTS AND PROCEDURE[1]

Directive 80/778 relating to the quality of water intended for human consumption[2] was adopted on July 15, 1980. Articles 18 and 19 of the Directive provide that Member States must adopt the necessary legislative measures in order to comply with the requirements of the Directive within two years and that they take the necessary measures in order to ensure that the quality of drinking water complied with the provisions of the Directive within five years.[3]

The Commission was not satisfied that the United Kingdom had taken all the necessary legislative measures in order to comply with the Directive. Furthermore, it was of the opinion that drinking water in parts of the United Kingdom contained too high levels of nitrate and lead. For these reasons, the Commission sent, on August 11, 1987, a letter of formal notice, followed by a reasoned opinion on April 14, 1989 after an unsatisfactory reply by the United Kingdom. The United Kingdom's answer was followed by "several discussions between Ministers and officials of the United Kingdom and the Commission."[4] Finally, on October 31, 1989, the Commission had its application to the Court registered.

There was a written procedure before the Court. Oral hearings took place on November 27, 1991. The Advocate General delivered his opinion on January 21, 1992.

JUDGMENT

(1) By an application lodged at the Court Registry on 31 October 1989 the Commission of the European Communities brought an action under Article 169 of the EEC Treaty for a declaration that, by failing to implement in its domestic legislation and to apply correctly Council Directive 80/778/EEC of 15 July 1980 relat-

---

[1] Summary by the author.

[2] [1980] O.J. L229/11.

[3] See **Article 18**: "1. Member States shall bring into force the laws, regulations and administrative provisions necessary to comply with this Directive and its Annexes within two years following its notification . . . "
Article 19: "the Member States shall take the necessary measures to ensure that the quality of water intended for human consumption complies with this Directive within five years of its notification."

[4] Report for the Hearing, no. 11, last para. As regards the political background to this see for instance Oral Question H-51/92 (Ms Pollack) discussed in the European Parliament, Annex to the O.J. 3-423, p. 269, debates of October 28, 1992.

ing to the quality of water intended for human consumption (Official Journal 1980 L 229, p. 11, hereinafter referred to as "the directive"), the United Kingdom has failed to fulfil its obligations under the EEC Treaty.

(2) Article 18(1) of the directive requires the Member States to bring into force the laws, regulations and administrative provisions necessary to comply with the directive and its annexes within two years following its notification and to inform the Commission forthwith. In addition, Article 19 requires the Member States to take the necessary measures to ensure that the quality of water intended for human consumption complies with the directive within five years of its notification. In the case of the United Kingdom, those periods expired on 18 July 1982 and 18 July 1985 respectively.

(3) The Commission's complaints are, first, that the United Kingdom failed to implement within the prescribed periods all or part of the provisions of the directive (depending on the regions of the United Kingdom concerned) and, secondly, that it failed to comply in certain supply zones with the maximum admissible concentration for nitrates and lead laid down by the directive.

(4) Reference is made to the Report for the Hearing for a fuller account of the facts of the case, the procedure and the pleas in law and arguments of the parties, which are mentioned or discussed hereinafter only in so far as is necessary for the reasoning of the Court.

Admissibility

(5) The United Kingdom claims that, in both the letter of formal notice and the reasoned opinion, the complaint concerning the non-implementation of the directive related solely to private water supplies. It adds that in its judgment in Case C–42/89 *Commission* v *Belgium* [1990] ECR I-2821, which also concerned this directive, the Court held that the directive did not apply to private water supplies. Consequently, the complaint concerning the non-implementation of the directive must be considered inadmissible in its entirety.

(6) It should be noted, however, that in the letter of formal notice and in the reasoned opinion the Commission made a general complaint concerning the non-implementation of the directive and that private water supplies were mentioned only by way of example. In support of its complaint the Commission pointed out that the administrative circulars which, according to the United Kingdom Government, had been issued for the purpose of implementing the directive did not impose legal requirements, particularly as regards private suppliers, and that this constituted sufficient evidence that the directive had not been implemented in domestic law.

(7) In its application the Commission did not enlarge the scope of the alleged infringement but, on the contrary, limited the general complaint made in the pre-litigation phase to certain areas in which the directive was said not to have been implemented.

(8) The United Kingdom's objection must therefore be rejected.

Substance

The non-implementation of the directive

(9) The Commission claims that the United Kingdom failed, first, to implement the provisions of the directive concerning water used in the food industry in the regulations applicable to England and Wales and, secondly, to adopt measures for the implementation of any of the provisions of the directive in Scotland and Northern Ireland. Whilst acknowledging that the Water Supply Regulations 1990 constitute "satisfactory formal implementation" of the directive in Scotland, the Commission adheres to its complaint in its entirety in respect of that part of the United Kingdom.

(10) The defendant argues that the water used for food production comes, in virtually all cases, from the same source as water used for domestic purposes, and that the latter conforms to the requirements of the directive.

(11) In that regard suffice it to note that, as the defendant itself acknowledges, some water used for food production comes from sources other than domestic water.

(12) The defendant argues further that, as far as Scotland is concerned, the competent Member of the Commission of the European Communities stated, in a letter of 13 April 1989, that the adoption of appropriate regulations under the Water Act 1973 would lead to the withdrawal of the application with respect to the implementation of the directive in Scotland. Since those regulations were adopted, the Commission is said to have failed in its duty of cooperation under Article 5 of the Treaty by pursuing this complaint.

(13) That argument cannot be upheld. Without its being necessary to assess the legal significance of the letter, it is to be noted that its author confined himself to the possibility that the application might be withdrawn in the event of the United Kingdom legislation constituting not merely formal, but complete, implementation of all the provisions of the directive. No undertaking was therefore given by the Commission.

(14) The defendant claims finally that, as far as Northern Ireland is concerned, difficulties relating to the organization of the public authorities in that part of the United Kingdom explain the delay in the implementation of the directive.

(15) However, as the Court has consistently held, a Member State may not plead provisions, practices or circumstances in its internal legal system in order to justify a failure to comply with obligations or time-limits imposed by directives (see *inter alia* the judgment in Case 279/83 *Commission v Italy* [1984] ECR 3403).

(16) It follows that the Commission's complaint is well founded.

Nitrate levels

(17) The Commission claims that water supplied in 28 supply zones in England does not conform to the maximum admissible concentration (hereinafter referred to as "MAC") of 50 mg/l for nitrates and that the excessive levels are not justified by the derogations provided for in Article 9 of the directive.

(18) The United Kingdom Government argues, first, that the directive does not impose an obligation to achieve a result but merely requires Member States to take all practicable steps to comply with the standards laid down. The United Kingdom claims to have done so in this case. It adds that the failure to achieve the objective is due to extraneous factors relating in particular to techniques used in agriculture.

(19) It argues further that the Commission's view that a State is in breach of the directive where the MAC is not observed, even if the State has taken all practicable steps to secure compliance, would mean that the directive would be infringed wherever a MAC was exceeded after 18 July 1985 even though the excessive level went unnoticed when the inspections required by the directive were carried out. The State would therefore be in breach of the directive even before it was afforded the opportunity of verifying whether there was a breach and of remedying the situation.

(20) That argument cannot be upheld.

(21) It follows from Article 7(6) of the directive that the Member States must take the steps necessary to ensure that water intended for human consumption at least meets the requirements specified in Annex I.

(22) That result had to be achieved within a period of five years from notification of the directive (Article 19), that period being longer than that allowed for implementation of the directive, namely two years from notification (Article 18), in order to enable Member States to satisfy the abovementioned requirements.

(23) As the Court stated in its judgment in Case 228/87 *Pretura Unificata di Torino* v *X* [1988] ECR 5099 (paragraph 10), the only derogations from the obligation on Member States to ensure that water intended for human consumption conforms to the requirements of the directive are those provided for in Articles 9, 10 and 20. The first of those provisions permits derogations to take account of situations arising from the nature and structure of the ground in the area from which the supply in question comes, as well as situations arising from exceptional meteorological conditions; the second authorizes derogations in the event of emergencies; and, finally, the third provision permits Member States, in exceptional cases and for geographically defined population groups, to submit a special request to the Commission in order to obtain a longer period for compliance with Annex I.

(24) The directive therefore requires Member States to ensure that certain results are achieved and, except within the limits of the derogations laid down, they may not rely on special circumstances in order to justify a failure to discharge that obligation.

(25) It follows that the defendant's claim that it took all practicable steps to secure compliance cannot justify, except within the limits of the derogations expressly laid down, its failure to comply with the requirement to ensure that water intended for human consumption at least meets the requirements of Annex I of the directive.

(26) Finally, the United Kingdom Government claims that it granted derogations under Article 9 of the directive for the zones in which the MAC specified for

nitrates was exceeded and that it notified those derogations to the Commission on 9 October 1985. The Commission did not express any view concerning those derogations until it issued the letter of formal notice on 11 August 1987, in which it stated that, where the MAC for nitrates had been exceeded, Article 9 could not be used as a basis for the derogations so notified. The United Kingdom Government considers that in those circumstances the Commission, instead of proceeding with its complaint, should have automatically granted the United Kingdom an extension of the time-limit notwithstanding the expiry of the period within which a request under Article 20 must be submitted.

(27) As the Court held in its judgment in *Commission* v *Belgium*, mentioned above (paragraph 23), a request under Article 20 of the directive for a longer period for complying with Annex I must be made within the period laid down in Article 19 for implementation of the directive. Notification of the derogations in accordance with Article 9 of the directive occurred after 18 July 1985, that is to say after that period had expired. Consequently, it is unnecessary to rule on the request made by the United Kingdom Government.

(28) The second complaint is therefore also well founded.

Lead levels

(29) The Commission considers that compliance with the MAC for lead (parameter 51) has not been secured in Scotland in 17 supply zones serving a population of approximately 52 000 inhabitants. According to the applicant, the directive must be interpreted as meaning that, in the case of water distributed through lead pipes, the samples taken after flushing, that is to say from running water, must comply with the MAC of 50 μg/l laid down for parameter 51, whereas direct samples must not exceed 100 μg/l frequently or to an appreciable extent. According to the table produced by the United Kingdom Government as an annex to its defence, of 204 samples taken after flushing, nine had a lead content of between 51 and 100 μg/l and four exceeded 100 μg/l. From the figures available at the time when the application was lodged it appears that, out of 151 samples, four had a lead content of between 51 and 100 μg/l and two exceeded 100 μg/l; the situation has therefore worsened since the application was lodged.

(30) According to the comments concerning parameter 51:

"Where lead pipes are present, the lead content should not exceed 50 μg/l in a sample taken after flushing. If the sample is taken either directly or after flushing and the lead content either frequently or to an appreciable extent exceeds 100 μg/l, suitable measures must be taken to reduce the exposure to lead on the part of the consumer."

(31) As the United Kingdom Government has correctly pointed out, those comments would be superfluous if they were to be interpreted in the manner suggested by the Commission. The obligation to comply with the MAC of 50 μg/l in the case of running water is already apparent from the values specified for parameter 51.

(32) The comments relating to that parameter must therefore be interpreted as referring to the values to be observed in the case of lead pipes, for which

special rules have been laid down. In such a case the 50 μg/l value is for guidance only, and suitable measures are required only where samples are taken directly or after flushing and the lead content exceeds 100 μg/l frequently or to an appreciable extent.

(33) By virtue of Article 7(5) of the directive, which provides that account is to be taken of the comments for the purpose of interpreting the values shown in Annex I, it is those special rules which apply in the case of lead piping.

(34) The United Kingdom Government claims that, contrary to the Commission's assertion, the rules are observed in the 17 zones in question. It refers in that regard to the results of the samples taken in accordance with a procedure agreed between the Commission and the United Kingdom; according to those results, which appear in the abovementioned table, 4% of the samples had a lead content exceeding 50 μg/l and 2% a lead content exceeding 100 μg/l.

(35) The Commission replies that those sampling results do not establish compliance with the parameter in question. In its view, the United Kingdom would need to indicate the number of flushed samples taken per household supplied by lead pipes, the proportion of those samples which did not conform to the 100 μg/l limit and the extent to which that limit was exceeded in each case. Only on the basis of such data could the United Kingdom validly claim that the lead content did not exceed 100 μg/l frequently or to an appreciable extent.

(36) That argument cannot be upheld. As the United Kingdom Government has asserted without being challenged, the samples in question were taken in accordance with Annex II to the directive, and in any event the Commission has not shown that, if the samples had been taken according to the method which it indicates, they would have shown that the 100 μg/l limit was exceeded frequently or to an appreciable extent.

(37) This complaint must therefore be rejected.

(38) In the light of all the foregoing considerations, it must be held that, by failing, first, to implement Council Directive 80/778/EEC of 15 July 1980 in the regulations applicable in Scotland and Northern Ireland and, as regards water used in the food industry, also in England and Wales and, secondly, to ensure that the quality of water supplied in 28 supply zones in England conforms to the requirements of the directive concerning nitrates, the United Kingdom has failed to fulfil its obligations under the EEC Treaty.

Costs

(39) Under Article 69(2) of the Rules of Procedure the unsuccessful party is to pay the costs if they have been asked for in the successful party's pleading. Since the United Kingdom has for the most part failed in its submissions, it must be ordered to pay the costs.

On those grounds,

THE COURT

hereby:

(1) Declares that, by failing, first, to implement in the regulations applicable in Scotland and Northern Ireland and, as regards water used in the food industry, also in England and Wales Council Directive 80/778/EEC of 15 July 1980 relating to the quality of water intended for human consumption and, secondly, to ensure that the quality of water supplied in 28 supply zones in England conforms to the requirements of the directive concerning nitrates, the United Kingdom has failed to fulfil its obligations under the EEC Treaty;

(2) Dismisses the remainder of the application;

(3) Orders the United Kingdom to pay the costs.

COMMENTARY

(1) This judgment is the first environmental case which the Court of Justice decided against the United Kingdom and already this fact makes the reading of the Report for the Hearing, the opinion of the Advocate General and the judgment itself worthwhile and interesting. Indeed, the facts of the case were, throughout the procedure, undisputed; only the legal interpretation of these facts were at issue. And yet it took overall more than 62 months between the letter of formal notice and the decision by the Court. The procedure before the Court itself took more than three years, a delay which is not simply to be explained by the general workload of the Court, but partly also by continued "discussions between Ministers and officials of the United Kingdom and the Commission."[5]

Readers of the Report for the Hearing will appreciate to what extent the United Kingdom referred to judgments of the Court in other cases, general principles of interpretation and other tools that are probably widely used in common law. In contrast, the judgment of the Court concentrates on the text of the Directive.

(2) The Court started by examining the objection of the United Kingdom that the Commission had, in its application to the Court, enlarged its complaint against the United Kingdom compared with that originally contained in the letter of formal notice. The Court did not follow this reasoning, but declared

---

[5] See n. 4 above.

rather soberly that the Commission's application was a limitation of the original complaint made during the pre-litigation phase rather than an extension. This part of the judgment is in full coherence with the Advocate General's opinion, who examined the scope of the dispute in great detail.[6]

The judgment did not comment on the theoretical question of how the scope of a dispute is identified and whether the letter of formal notice or the reasoned opinion or both must be examined for this purpose. This aspect was examined in detail by the Advocate General[7] who summarised the four different approaches adopted by the Court so far:

(1) The letter of formal notice is intended to define the subject-matter of the dispute; the subsequent reasoned opinion may set out in detail the complaints which had already been made more generally in the letter of formal notice;[8]

(2) The subject-matter of a dispute is determined solely by the letter of formal notice;[9]

(3) The subject-matter of a dispute is determined by the reasoned opinion;[10]

(4) The pre-litigation procedure as a whole determines the subject matter of a dispute.[11]

The Advocate General's conclusion from this jurisdiction is that:

"it is necessary to form a synthesis combining a purely formal approach focusing on what facts and conclusions are expressly mentioned with an analysis which is based on the meaning and purpose of the pre-litigation procedure and looks at whether the defendant Member State had the opportunity to comment on specific complaints or was unable to do so owing to the time at which the events took place or to an element of surprise in the Commission's arguments. The approach which lays emphasis on the

---

[6] See Advocate General's opinion, paras. 24 to 39.

[7] See Advocate General's opinion, paras. 11 to 23; the following references are taken from that opinion.

[8] Case 274/83, *Commission* v. *Italy:* [1985] E.C.R. 1107, [1987] 1 C.M.L.R. 345; Case 74/82, *Commission* v. *Ireland:* [1984] E.C.R. 317.

[9] Case 31/69, *Commission* v. *Italy:* [1970] E.C.R. 25, [1970] C.M.L.R. 175; Case 211/81, *Commission* v. *Denmark:* [1982] E.C.R. 4547, [1984] 1 C.M.L.R. 278; Case 51/83, *Commission* v. *Italy:* [1984] E.C.R. 2793 [1986], 2 C.M.L.R. 274; Case 229/87, *Commission* v. *Greece:* [1988] E.C.R. 6347, [1990] 1 C.M.L.R. 741.

[10] Case 166/82, *Commission* v. *Italy:* [1984] E.C.R. 459, [1985] 2 C.M.L.R. 615; Case C–217/88, *Commission* v. *Germany:* [1990] I E.C.R. 2879 [1993] 1 C.M.L.R. 18; Case C–347/88, *Commission* v. *Italy:* [1990] I E.C.R. 4747.

[11] Case 124/81, *Commission* v. *United Kingdom:* [1983] E.C.R. 203, [1983] 2 C.M.L.R. 1; Case 166/82, cited above; Case 325/82, *Commission* v. *Germany:* [1984] E.C.R. 777, [1985] 2 C.M.L.R. 719; Case 309/84, *Commission* v. *Italy:* [1986] E.C.R. 605, [1987] 2 C.M.L.R. 657; Case 298/86, *Commission* v. *Belgium:* [1988] E.C.R. 4343.

procedural guarantees provided by the pre-litigation phase can modify the results produced by a purely formal examination."[12]

(3) This conclusion is convincing. It should be added that the letter of formal notice cannot play a decisive role in determining the subject-matter of a dispute. Indeed, Article 169 of the EEC Treaty[13] does not require a letter of formal notice to be sent but merely requests that before a reasoned opinion is issued, a Member State has a possibility to comment on the complaints made by the Commission.[14] Article 169 is thus a due process provision which aims at avoiding surprise-reasoned opinions and surprise applications.

It should be noted that at least in environmental cases, even the letter of formal notice is preceded by a letter which allows the Member State to comment on the Commission's complaints.[15]

(4) Next, the Court addressed the questions of whether Directive 80/778 was completely and properly transposed into national law by the United Kingdom. The United Kingdom had taken the necessary legislative steps to transpose the Directive into national law in 1989, *i.e.* seven years after the transposal date fixed by Article 18 of the Directive,[16] and even then rules for Northern Ireland and for the food industry were lacking. Again, the Court's reasoning is almost laconic in its rejection of the United Kingdom's arguments.

(5) The third point addressed by the Court was the—uncontroversial—excessive levels of nitrate in 28 water supply zones of the United Kingdom. In that context, the United Kingdom first argued that Directive 80/778 does not impose an obligation to achieve a result, but merely requires Member States to take all practicable steps to comply with the Directive's standards. This argument is of course not restricted to nitrates, but goes far beyond that question and even far beyond this specific directive. Indeed, the problem raises the general question of the nature and extent of the Member States' obligations following the adoption of a directive by the Council.

The judgment refers to Article 7(6) of the Directive[17] and confirms that Member States must achieve a result and not only make reasonable efforts.

---

[12] Advocate General's opinion, para. 23.
[13] "If the Commission considers, that a Member State has failed to fulfil an obligation under this Treaty, it shall deliver a reasoned opinion on the matter after giving the State concerned the opportunity to submit its observations. If the State concerned does not comply with the opinion within the period laid down by the Commission, the latter may bring the matter before the Court of Justice."
[14] The Commission could use, *e.g.* meetings with a Member State to confront that State with its findings and ask for observations. In practice, however, the letter of formal notice is the rule.
[15] See Commission, Eighth Annual Report to the European Parliament on Monitoring Application of Community law (1990): [1991] O.J. C338/1, Annex C, 8.
[16] See n. 3 above.
[17] **Article 7(6)**: "Member States shall take the steps necessary to ensure that water intended for human consumption at least meets the requirements specified in Annex 1."

This interpretation is confirmed by Article 19,[18] a provision which would not make sense if only "best efforts" were to be made.

(6) The United Kingdom's argument, furthermore, fundamentally misunderstands the meaning of a directive, which, according to Article 189 of the EEC Treaty, is binding upon Member States as to the results to be achieved.[19] Thus, it would need a specific rule in a Directive in order to make part of a directive "non-binding" so that best efforts suffice in order to comply with it. Nothing in Directive 80/778 indicates that compliance with its standards would not be compulsory, despite the long arguments developed by the United Kingdom.[20]

The much discussed question of subsidiarity also comes into this discussion. Indeed, Member States rightly argue—and Article 130r(4) expressly confirms this for the environmental sector—that it is up to them to implement and enforce environmental measures which have been decided at Community level.[21] Therefore, the Commission, or indeed other Member States, cannot intervene with Member States and ask them to invest this or that amount of money, to close this or that installation or to build a water treatment work, to reduce the use of this or that pesticide or not to have recourse to this or that type of agricultural practice. All these and other aspects—on monitoring, inspecting, measuring, publishing and thousand others—are in the hands of Member States.

(7) Because, as a legal instrument, a directive is *binding* as to its results, it follows as a consequence that a Member State has to reach a specific result and that the Member State is responsible where this result has not been reached. Requesting only the best practicable means to be taken turns a directive into a non-binding recommendation. This is all the more true where one talks of "practicable" measures, since this notion includes economic, social, political and other considerations. Indeed, every Member State could—and in environmental matters would—argue that there was not enough money available to take this or that measure, that public opinion or the industry or farmers were against it, or that the national Parliament had objected, etc.

(8) An important factor in this context is the question of the burden of proof. If one looks into the United Kingdom's reasoning in the present case, one is confronted with four kinds of measures which have, according to the United King-

---

[18] See n. 3 above.

[19] **Article 189(3)**: "A directive shall be binding, as to the result to be achieved, upon each Member State to which it is addressed, but shall leave to the national authorities the choice of form and methods."

[20] See Report for the Hearing, section IV 2(b).

[21] **Article 130r(4)**: ". . . Without prejudice to certain measures of a Community nature, the Member States shall finance and implement the other measures."

dom authorities, been taken in order to combat the nitrate problem.[22] Under the general rules on the burden of proof it would be up to the Commission to prove that these measures were not "enough"—an impossible task, since the Commission has no local or regional administration,[23] or inspectors,[24] or any administrative unit to examine and assess the practicability of measures taken by Member States at local or regional level in order to reach compliance with the requirements of a Community directive.

The only correct interpretation of the obligations which flow out of a directive is therefore that of the Court: a result must be achieved, nothing less. Taking practicable or reasonable steps in order to comply with a directive is not enough.

(9) Next, the Court addressed the question whether the United Kingdom could grant an authorisation to exceed the nitrate levels of Directive 80/778 or whether it could obtain such an authorisation from the Commission. The Court found that no authorisations to exceed the nitrate levels was possible.[25]

Directive 80/778 allows the maximum admissible concentrations laid down in the directive to be exceeded in three cases spelt out in Article 9,[26] Article 10[27] and Article 20.[28]

(10) As regards Article 9, the United Kingdom itself had recognised, in its correspondence with the Commission, that excessive level of nitrates in drinking water were not due to the "nature and structure of the ground in the area from which the supply in question emanates."

Indeed, the presence of nitrates in surface and underground water and

---

[22] See Report for the Hearing, section IV 2(b) at the end. Those measures were (a) the bringing into service of denitrification plans (it is not clear how many); (b) the collection of information; (c) research; (d) the legal possibility to designate "nitrate sensitive areas".

[23] This is different for instance in the U.S. where the Environment Protection Agency (EPA) has also staff at local and regional level in order to monitor and enforce compliance with federal rules. However, the EPA has a staff of some 15,000 people, whereas the Commission's environmental staff is some 220 officials and about the same number of persons under temporary contract.

[24] The Commission disposes of inspectors in areas such as competition, veterinary questions, fishery, nuclear safety, but not in the field of the environment.

[25] Paras. 26 and 27.

[26] **Article 9(1)**: "Member States may make provisions for derogations from this Directive in order to take account of:
   (a) situations arising from the nature and structure of the ground in the area from which the supply in question emanates . . . ;
   (b) situations arising from exceptional meteorological conditions . . . "

[27] **Article 10**: "In the event of emergencies, the competent national authorities may, for a limited period of time . . . allow the maximum admissible concentration shown in Annex I to be exceeded . . . "

[28] **Article 20**: "Member States may, in exceptional cases and for geographically defined population group, submit a special request to the Commission for a longer period for complying with Annex I.
This request, for which grounds must be duly put forward, shall set out the difficulties experienced and must propose an action programme with an appropriate timetable to be undertaken for the improvement of the quality of water intended for human consumption . . . "

subsequently in drinking water was due to human agricultural activity. Since derogations under Article 9 are permanent and are taken unilaterally by a Member State, such derogations only apply, where a form of natural situation, a form of "force majeure" (Act of God) exists.[29] This is not the case where agricultural activity leads to water contamination, even where the soil is particularly permeable and lets the nitrate sieve through very easily.

The Court did not address this question since the United Kingdom had admitted that Article 9 was inapplicable.

(11) The United Kingdom had, however, notified derogations for the nitrate levels to the Commission under Article 9 and asked the Court to decide that it could benefit from Article 20, the second provision which allowed the levels of the Directive not to be respected. The Court did not decide in favour of this request and observed the rules which it had already interpreted in Case C–42/89:[30] any request under Article 20 should have been made before the time-period of Article 19 had elapsed, that is before July 18, 1985.

However, the United Kingdom's "request"—be it repeated that it was not a request under Article 20, but a notification under Article 9—had only been made on October 9, 1985. The Court found this delay sufficient to declare Article 20 inapplicable.

Before such a ruling is considered too formalistic, it should be noted that, where a request is made under Article 20, the following conditions must be fulfilled:[31]

(1) it must be an exceptional case;
(2) the request must be made for geographically defined population groups;
(3) the grounds for asking for a longer delay must be put forward;
(4) the difficulties to respect the period under Article 19 must be set out;
(5) an action programme and an appropriate timetable to respect the parameters of the Directive must be submitted.

(12) Nothing in the report for the hearing or in the judgment indicates that the United Kingdom had complied with a single one of these five requirements. All the arguments in law which were put forward by the United Kingdom in order to justify the interpretation of the notification under Article 9 as a request under Article 20 are defensive arguments rather than arguments relating to the substance. The Court could not have reached another conclusion if it had examined the substance of Article 20: the United Kingdom had no legal right

---

[29] See also Dir. 75/440 concerning the quality required of surface water intended for the abstraction of drinking water in the Member States: [1975] O.J. L194/26, **Article 8(d)**: "Natural enrichment means the process whereby, without human intervention, a given body of water receives from the soil certain substances contained therein."

[30] Case C–42/89, *Commission* v. *Belgium*: [1990] I E.C.R. 2821; see also p. 237 above.

[31] See Art. 20, n. 28 above.

under the Directive not to respect the directive's requirements as regards nitrates.

(13) The last question which the Court had to examine concerned the levels of lead in drinking water. The factual side was largely undisputed: out of 151 samples taken in Scottish water supply zones, four had a lead content of between 51 and 100 μg per litre and two exceeded 100 μg per litre. The dispute was on the method of sampling. The Court followed the interpretation of the United Kingdom and rejected, to this extent, the Commission's application.

(14) The first observation to be made is that the comments on the lead parameter in the Directive[32] are a model of imprecise drafting. The Court's interpretation of what these comments mean[33] is one out of several, though with this judgment it will become the only one which is applied. What is worrying is the fact that lead is very toxic and one would have wished an interpretation which tries to ensure the protection of health to a greater extent. Indeed it is hard to understand why the protection of human health requires a parameter of 50 μg per litre in normal cases, but that such a level can be doubled in cases where lead pipes are present; and that even then improvement measures are required only where 100 μg per litre are frequently or to an appreciable extent exceeded. The risk to human health is the same, whether lead pipes are present or not. The Court *de facto* blames the bad drafting of the Directive and thus indirectly underlines the need to amend it.

(15) As regards the sampling itself the Court is rather strict with the Commission[34] it would be up to the Commission to demonstrate that the 100 μg per litre would have been exceeded frequently or to one appreciable extent, had the United Kingdom measured according to the method which the Commission had favoured. Since the Commission has neither inspectors nor agents in Scotland—how can it find out whether a Member State is taking samples in the correct way? How can it, more generally, check that Member States comply with the requirements of a Directive? Directive 80/778 does not even provide for a report by Member States to the Commission on the state of drinking water's quality at national level.[35] Thus, the conclusion to be drawn from the Court's reasoning on the lead parameter is that where the sampling methods or the sampling frequency or the respect of the Directive's parameters are disputed, the Commission will normally not be able to win a case in Court against a Member State.

(16) Directive 80/778 is not fully respected in any Member State. The United

---

[32] See para. 30 of the judgment.
[33] Para. 32.
[34] Para. 36.
[35] It is true that Dir. 91/692: [1991] O.J. L377/48 has amended Dir. 80/778; Member States will, in future, have to report on the quality of their drinking water. The first report on the situation within the Community is to be published in 1997.

Kingdom introduced rules in 1989 which transposed the requirements of the Directive into national law. However, where drinking water did not comply with the legal requirements, water suppliers were allowed to submit "undertakings" whereby they would clean up the water within a specific time-span. The United Kingdom Government then accepted these undertakings, without doing anything further to enforce compliance. Whether this practice is compatible with Directive 80/778 is more than doubtful.

Other Member States found other ways not to fully comply with the requirements of the Directive; one elegant way was not to measure the water quality or not to publish or otherwise communicate the results. Nitrates and pesticides are the two parameters which are most frequently exceeded; both parameters are heavily influenced by agricultural practice and the use of chemicals. Thus, there is a considerable pressure on the Commission to modify Directive 80/778 and to introduce less stringent parameters. The decision-making body for any such amendment is the Council. How the debate evolves remains to be seen. The European Court has—and this is the nature of its jurisdiction—almost no influence on this decision which is political by nature.

Waste

16. THE NOTION OF WASTE

**Judgment of the Court (First Chamber) of March 28, 1990
in Joined Cases C–206/88 and C–207/88**

Preliminary ruling in criminal proceedings pending before the Pretura di Asti
against G. Vessoso and G. Zanetti

[1990] I E.C.R. 1461

FACTS AND PROCEDURE[1]

Mr. Vessoso and Mr. Zanetti are hauliers. They collect, transport and store products for other people, which the Italian public authorities qualify as urban or special waste. An Italian decree makes it a criminal offence to collect, transport or store wastes without prior authorisation.[2] Charges were brought against Mr. Vessoso and Mr. Zanetti before an Italian court. The defendants argued in their defence that they were not collecting, transporting and storing waste, since the various materials were capable of economic reutilisation. The national court found that the Italian decree intended to transpose into Italian law Directives 75/442 on waste[3] and 78/319 on toxic and dangerous waste.[4] On December 18, 1987 it submitted a question for a preliminary ruling to the European Court, asking whether the notion of "waste" in the two directives also covered objects which are capable of economic reutilisation.[5]

The question was registered with the Court on July 28, 1988. The Commission and the Italian Government submitted written observations. On October 4, 1989 the case was assigned to the Court's First Chamber. Oral hearings took place on November 21, 1989. The Advocate General delivered his opinion on December 13, 1989.

JUDGMENT

(1) By two orders dated 18 December 1987, which were received at the Court on 28 July 1988, the Pretura di Asti referred to the Court for a preliminary ruling under Article 177 of the EEC Treaty a question on the interpretation of Article 1 of Council Directive 75/442/EEC of 15 July 1975 on waste (Official Journal 1975, L 194, p. 39) and Article 1 of Council Directive 78/319/EEC of 20 March 1978 on toxic and dangerous waste (Official Journal 1978, L 84, p. 43).

(2) That question arose in the context of two criminal prosecutions brought against

---

[1] Summary by the author.
[2] Decree of September 10, 1982: [1982] 343 G.U.R.I. 9071.
[3] [1975] O.J. L194/47.
[4] [1978] O.J. L874/43.
[5] The Italian cases were criminal proceedings. It is doubtful whether the interpretations of Community law which the Court of Justice is asked to give under Art. 177, is really capable of influencing the interpretation of Italian penal law—according to the principle "*nullum crimen sine lege*", the question whether this is an offence under Italian law has to be examined under Italian law; see Advocate General Jacobs: [1990] I E.C.R. 1471, paras. 24 and 25.

a number of haulage contractors who are charged with transporting substances on behalf of third parties without obtaining prior authorization, thereby infringing Decree No 915 of the President of the Italian Republic of 10 September 1982 (GURI (Italian Official Gazette) No 343, 15.12.1982, p. 9071), hereinafter referred to as 'the Presidential Decree'. That decree, which was adopted for the purpose of transposing the two abovementioned directives into national law, lays down penalties under criminal law for persons who transport or dispose of waste on behalf of third parties without obtaining the authorization of the competent Italian regional authority.

(3) In their defence, the defendants maintained that the substances transported did not constitute waste within the meaning of the Presidential Decree, Article 2 of which defines waste as including 'any substance or object produced by human activity or natural processes which is, or is intended to be, abandoned'; they claimed that in this case the substances transported were capable of economic reutilization and were not therefore abandoned or intended to be abandoned. In their view, since the activity to which the charges related did not fall within the scope of the Presidential Decree, the criminal penalties laid down therein were not applicable.

(4) The Pretura considered that, since the aim of the Presidential Decree was to transpose the two abovementioned directives into national law, it was bound to interpret the definition given in Article 2 of the Presidential Decree in a manner compatible with Article 1 of each directive, in which it is provided that waste is to be understood as 'any substance or object which the holder disposes of or is required to dispose of pursuant to the provisions of national law in force'.

(5) The Pretura therefore stayed the proceedings in both cases and sought a preliminary ruling from the Court on whether

'Article 1 of Council Directive 75/442/EEC of 15 July 1975 on waste and Article 1 of Council Directive 78/319/EEC of 20 March 1978 on toxic and dangerous waste must be interpreted as meaning that the legal concept of waste must also cover things which the holder has disposed of which are capable of economic reutilization and whether the said articles must be interpreted as meaning that the term "waste" presupposes the establishment of *animus dereliquendi* on the part of the holder of the substance or object'.

(6) Reference is made to the Report for the Hearing for a fuller account of the facts of the case in the main proceedings, the applicable legislation and the written observations submitted to the Court, which are mentioned or discussed hereinafter only in so far as is necessary for the reasoning of the Court.

(7) The first part of the Pretura's question seeks to ascertain whether the concept of waste within the meaning of Article 1 of both Council Directive 75/442 and Council Directive 78/319 is to be understood as excluding substances and objects which are capable of economic reutilization.

(8) The fourth recital in the preamble to Directive 75/442 and the fifth recital in the preamble to Directive 78/319 both stress the importance of encouraging the recovery of waste and the use of recovered materials in order to conserve natural resources. Furthermore, the second indent of Article 1(b) of Directive 75/442 and the second indent of Article 1(c) of Directive 78/319 provide that waste dis-

posal is to be understood as including the transformation operations necessary for the recovery, reuse or recycling of waste. Finally, Article 3(1) of Directive 75/442 and Article 4 of Directive 78/319 require Member States to take appropriate steps to encourage the prevention, recycling and processing of waste, the extraction of raw materials and possibly energy therefrom and any other process for the reuse of waste. It is clear from those various provisions that a substance of which its holder disposes may constitute waste within the meaning of Directives 75/442 and 78/319 even when it is capable of economic reutilization.

(9) The answer to the first part of the question must therefore be that the concept of waste within the meaning of Article 1 of Council Directive 75/442 and Article 1 of Council Directive 78/319 is not to be understood as excluding substances and objects which are capable of economic reutilization.

(10) The second part of the Pretura's question seeks to ascertain whether the concept of waste, within the meaning of Article 1 of both Council Directives 75/442 and 78/319, presumes that a holder disposing of a substance or an object intends to exclude all economic reutilization of the substance or object by others.

(11) Article 1 of each of those directives refers generally to any substance or object of which the holder disposes, and draws no distinction according to the intentions of the holder disposing thereof. Moreover, those provisions specify that waste also includes substances or objects which the holder 'is required to dispose of pursuant to the provisions of national law in force'. A holder may be required by a provision of national law to dispose of something without necessarily intending to exclude all economic reutilization thereof by others.

(12) The essential aim of Directives 75/442 and 78/319, set out in their preambles in the third and fourth recitals respectively, namely the protection of human health and the safeguarding of the environment, would be jeopardized if the application of those directives were dependent on whether or not the holder intended to exclude all economic reutilization by others of the substances or objects of which he disposes.

(13) The answer to the second part of the question must therefore be that the concept of waste, within the meaning of Article 1 of Council Directive 75/442 and Article 1 of Council Directive 78/319, does not presume that the holder disposing of a substance or an object intends to exclude all economic reutilization of the substance or object by others.

Costs

(14) The costs incurred by the Italian Government and the Commission of the European Communities, which have submitted observations to the Court, are not recoverable. Since these proceedings are, in so far as the parties to the main proceedings are concerned, in the nature of a step in the proceedings pending before the national court, the decision on costs is a matter for that court.

On those grounds,

THE COURT (FIRST CHAMBER),

in answer to the questions referred to it by the Pretura di Asti, by orders of 18 December 1987, hereby rules:

The concept of waste, within the meaning of Article 1 of Council Directive 75/442/EEC and Article 1 of Council Directive 78/319/EEC, is not to be understood as excluding substances and objects which are capable of economic reutilization. The concept does not presume that the holder disposing of a substance or an object intends to exclude all economic reutilization of the substance or object by others.

COMMENTARY

(1) This judgment is one of the many that the Court has given on the problems of waste. Indeed, the list of environmental judgments[6] contains no less than 25 judgments on waste between 1980 and mid-1993. At least six further cases are at present pending before the Court, which illustrates the relevance of the issue in the present discussions on the environment in Western Europe.

The Court had to address the very basic question of what is "waste", though it did not have to give an overall definition for it. The case which the national judge had to decide was rather simple: in Italy, an authorisation is needed for the transport of waste. When the police stopped an undertaking which transported waste without such an authorisation, they defended themselves with the argument that they did not transport "waste" but recyclable material for which an authorisation is not needed.

(2) The European Court of Justice was asked by the national court whether Directives 75/442 on waste[7] and 78/319 on toxic and dangerous waste[8] also covered waste which can be recycled. The Court examined the recitals[9] and different provisions[10] of these two Directives and came to the conclusion that

---

[6] See the Appendix 1 on p. 437.

[7] See n. 3 above.

[8] See n. 4 above.

[9] Dir. 75/442, **recital 4**: "Whereas the recovery of waste and the use of recovered materials should be encouraged in order to conserve natural resources."

Dir. 78/319, **recital 5**: "Whereas the prevention, recycling and recovering of toxic and dangerous waste and the use of recovered materials should be encouraged in order to conserve natural sources."

[10] Dir. 75/442, **Article 1**: "For the purposes of this Directive ... (b) 'disposal' means: ... —the transformation operations necessary for its re-use, recovery or recycling."

Article 3(1): "Member States shall take appropriate steps to encourage the prevention, recycling and processing of waste, the extraction of raw materials and possibly of energy therefore and any other process for the re-use of waste."

Dir. 78/319, **Article 1**: "For the purpose of this Directive ... (c) 'disposal' means. ... —the transformation operations necessary for its recovery, re-use or recycling."

Article 4: "Member States shall take appropriate steps to encourage as a matter of priority, the prevention of toxic and dangerous waste, its processing and recycling, the extraction of raw materials and possibly of energy therefrom and any other process for the re-use of such waste."

substances and objects which can be recycled are included in the notion of waste in both Directives.[11]

(3) The Court then examined whether the notion of waste presumed that an undertaking must have the intention to exclude all economic reutilisation of the substance or object by others. Relying on the wording of Article 1 of each of the two Directives, the Court found no reference to a necessity for such an intention of the holder of substances or objects.[12] The Court then considered the "essential aim" of the two Directives as expressed in their recitals[13] and noted that the holder's intention could not be a decisive point for differentiation.[14]

(4) In another judgment given the same day, the Court ruled that national legislation:

"which defines waste as excluding substances and objects which are capable of economic reutilization is not compatible with Council Directives 75/442/EEC and 78/319/EEC",[15]

thus confirming its judgment in Cases C–206/88 and C–207/88. Furthermore, in the judgment in Case of C–2/90 given on July 9, 1992, the Court ruled that under Article 30 of the EEC Treaty[16] a differentiation between waste which is capable of economic reutilisation and waste which is not, was not feasible.[17]

(5) What then is the notion of "waste" under Community law? The Treaty does not mention, let alone contain a definition of waste; the Maastricht Treaty on European Union which still has to be ratified by Member States in order to come into effect, mentions in its amended Article 130s(2) that "waste management" measures may be be adopted by majority decisions.[18]

---

[11] Para. 9.

[12] Dir. 75/442, **Article 1(a)**: " 'Waste' means any substance or object which the holders dispose of or is required to dispose of pursuant to the provisions of national law in force."
Dir. 78/319, Art. 1 is identical with that provision.

[13] Dir. 75/442: [1975] O.J. L194/47, **recital 3**: "Whereas the essential objectives of all provisions relating to waste disposal must be the protection of human health and the environment against harmful effects caused by the collections, transport, treatment, storage and tipping of waste."
Dir. 78/319, [1978] O.J. L84/43, **recital 4**: "Whereas the essential objective of all provisions relating to the disposal of toxic or dangerous waste must be the protection of human health and the safeguarding of the environment against harmful effects caused by the collection of toxic and dangerous waste as well as its carriage, treatment, storage and tipping."

[14] Paras. 13 and 14.

[15] Case C–359/88, *Criminal proceedings against E. Zanetti and others* [1990] I E.C.R. 1509.

[16] **Article 30**: "Quantitative restrictions on imports and all measures having equivalent effect shall, without prejudice to the following provisions, be prohibited between Member States."

[17] Case C–2/90, *Commission v. Belgium* [1992] I E.C.R. 4431, [1993] 1 C.M.L.R. 365 see p. 71 above.

[18] Maastricht Treaty: [1992] O.J. C191/1, Art. 130s. The mention of "waste management" in Art. 130s(2) does not prejudge the question whether the Commission measures for waste management still have to be based on Art. 100a or Art. 130s, since Art. 130s(2) states that its rules apply.

Directives 75/442 and 78/319 both have the same definition of waste.[19]

"For the purposes of this Directive (a) 'waste' means any substance or object which the holder disposes of or is required to dispose of pursuant to the provisions of national law in force."

Directive 84/631 on the transboundary shipment of waste indirectly refers to those definitions.[20] This Directive sets up a system of prior informed consent for transboundary shipments of hazardous waste: before a transport may take place, the holder of the waste shall notify the competent authorities of the Member State concerned of its intention. The Member State of destination has to acknowledge receipt of the notification.[21]

(6) Article 17 of Directive 84/631 contains a so-called "recycling loophole":[22] waste from non-ferrous metals which is intended for reuse, regeneration or recycling is exempted from the provisions of Directive 84/631, provided that some conditions are fulfilled.[23]

(7) Directive 75/442 was amended by Directive 91/156[24] where waste is now defined as follows:

"For the purpose of this Directive 'waste' shall mean any substance or object in the categories set out in Annex I which the holder discards or intends or is requested to discard. The Commission will draw up, not later than April 1993, a list of wastes belonging to the categories listed in Annex I. This list will be periodically reviewed and, if necessary, revised . . . "[25]

---

[19] See n. 13 above.

[20] [1984] O.J. L326/31.

[21] *Ibid.* Arts. 3 and 4. The Directive also contains rules on export to third countries, inserted in particular by Dir. 86/279: [1986] O.J. L181/13.

[22] A. Schmidt, "Transboundary movements of waste under EC law: the emerging regulatory framework," (1992) *Journal of Environmental Law* pp. 61 and 78.

[23] **Article 17**: "Waste (including in particular pesticide waste, scrap, sledge, ash and dust) from non-ferrous metals which is intended for re-use, regeneration or recycling on the basis of a contractual agreement regarding such operations shall be exempt from the provision of this Directive provided that the following conditions are fulfilled:
  (a) the holder must make a declaration on a uniform document, the contents of which is set out in Annex III, and which must accompany the shipment, to the effect that these materials are intended for the operations in question, and must forward a copy of this document to the competent authorities of the Member State referred to in Article 4(2)(a) or (b);
  (b) the consignee must declare in the same document, which he shall forward to the competent authorities of the Member State referred to in (a) not later than 15 days from receipt of the materials that these operations will actually be carried out"

[24] [1991] O.J. L78/32.

[25] Dir. 91/156, Art. 1(1). It is very unusual for Community Directives not to mention the substances and objects, to which it applies. How can Member States transpose such a Directive into their national law?

Annex I lists 16 "categories of waste", some of rather vague[26] nature. Of particular interest, as far as a definition of waste is concerned, is Q16 which reads:

"Q16: Any materials, substances or products which are not contained in the above categories."

This notion includes literally any substance or object. Since Directive 91/156 came into effect on April 1, 1993,[27] and by the same day, the list of waste mentioned in Article 1(a) had to be set up, I come to the conclusion that "waste" in the meaning of Directive 91/156 is any material, substance or product or object which is discarded or which must be or is intended to be discarded. The so-called "definition" of Article 1 of Directive 91/156 has no distinctive character as regards wastes and goods, in particular since the intention of the holder is decisive. If this is correct, then "waste" is no more than a name given to substances and objects.

Directive 78/319 on toxic and dangerous waste will be repealed, as of December 31, 1993 by Directive 91/689 on hazardous waste.[28] As regards the definition of waste, Directive 91/689 refers to Directive 75/442.[29]

(8) Thus it may be concluded from the wording of Directive 75/442 as amended by Directive 91/159, from Directive 91/689 and from the interpretation given to Article 30 by the Court of Justice in Cases C–2/90 and by Cases C–206/88 and C–207/88[30] that the notion of waste does not differentiate whether waste is reusable, recyclable or actually reused or recycled.

(9) This conclusion does not prevent the Community—or the national—legislator from setting different standards for waste which is recyclable or reusable or which is actually recycled or reused. Similarly, such differentiation is possible for example with chemicals, where differentiations for use are also made. The specific problem with waste lies in its economic value which is sometimes negative,[31] *i.e.* the holder of waste pays in order to get rid of it. Things become more complex when only parts of waste may be recyclable or reusable—for example some kilograms of metal out of a waste bulk of several tonnes—since it is doubtful whether the whole waste bulk should then be considered recyclable or reusable. Furthermore, it is difficult for a legislator to

---

[26] *Ibid.* Annex I; see for instance Q1: "Production or consumption residues not otherwise specified below"; Q3: "Products whose date for appropriate use has expired"; Q8: "Residues of industrial process (*e.g.* slags, still bottoms, etc.)"; Q12: "adulterated materials (*e.g.* oils contaminated with PCBs, etc.)"; Q13: "Any materials, substances or products whose use has been banned by law"; Q14: "Products for which the holder has no further use (*e.g.* agricultural, household, office, commercial and shop discards, etc.)".

[27] *Ibid.* Art. 2.

[28] [1991] O.J. L377/20.

[29] *Ibid.* **Article 1(3)**: "The definition of 'waste' and of the other terms used in this Directive shall be those in Directive 75/442/EEC."

[30] Paras. 9 and 13.

[31] See Case C–2/90, *Commission* v. *Belgium* [1992] I E.C.R. 4431, [1993] 1 C.M.L.R. 365, discussed on pp. 71–87 above.

differentiate according to whether a holder or a buyer of waste "intends" to recycle or reuse it, since intentions may change.

(10) Directive 91/156 very markedly differentiates between waste which is recycled or reused—the Directive uses the word "recovery"—and waste which is to be disposed of.[32] While, for instance, for waste which is to be disposed of, a network of disposal installations shall be established which "must enable waste to be disposed of in one of the nearest appropriate installations,"[33] no such objective exists for waste recovery installations. Thus, the intention of Directive 91/156 was certainly to introduce the "proximity principle" into Community legislation, which is formulated in a communication from the Commission to the Council[34] in the following terms:

"as far as possible waste is disposed of in the nearest suitable centres, making use of the most appropriate technologies to guarantee a high level of production for the environment and public health."[35]

Such a restriction does not apply to installations for recycling and reuse[36] and neither the Court's decision in the present Cases nor the decision in Case C–2/90 seem to differentiate in the handling of waste. Indeed, the present decision interprets Directives 75/442 and 78/319, but does not refer to rules in Community legislation which introduces such a differentiation.

(11) More doubts exist as regards the decision in Case C–2/90 since this decision concludes from the wording of Article 130, paragraph 2:

"Action by the Community relating to the environment shall be based on the principles that environmental damage should as a priority be rectified at source"

that there is a rule of law which requires waste to be disposed of according to the proximity principle.[37]

The judgment made no distinction between recovery and disposal operations which was not really required.[38] The judgment may be read in a way that it left undecided the possibilities for Community directives to provide a completely free circulation of wastes for reuse and recycling and to apply the proximity principle only to the disposal of waste. However, Directive 75/442 does not contain any reference to a clause providing for the free circulation of

---

[32] Arts. 4, 5 and 7.
[33] Art. 5(2).
[34] Commission, "A Community Strategy for waste management," SEC(89)934 final of September 18, 1989.
[35] *Ibid.* p. 23.
[36] Arts. 8, 10 and 11.
[37] *Ibid.* p. 23.
[38] See the discussion on p. 71 above.

waste, a point which the Court has expressely raised in Case C–2/90.[39] The amendment by Directive 91/156 does not change this situation. Unless such a "free circulation clause"[40] is being introduced into Directive 91/156, Member States or regions will not be prevented from applying the proximity principle to waste recovery operations as well.

(12) Until now the factual distinction has been described; the question has not yet been addressed whether it is environmentally sound to differentiate between waste intended for further use and waste which is to be disposed of.

"It is true that recovering recoverable waste is ecologically[41] sensible. But it seems that the Commission, believing in the advantages of the internal market and in what Greenpeace calls the "myth of recycling" has not taken due regard of the fact that waste for further use is, in principle, just as detrimental to the environment as non-recyclable waste and that its transport is just as risky. Finally, the dual standard encourages abuse. Thus, by opening the recycling loophole, the Commission weakens the entire control system".[42]

(13) This criticism will not be discussed in detail, since it would require a full study of waste streams and their evolution in Western Europe. However, two points need to be underlined from the legal point of view. The first is that Directive 91/156 and 91/689 hardly contain any concrete measures for the prevention of waste generation and the minimisation of waste.[43] Secondly, Member States are expressly required to "take appropriate measures to encourage ... the use of waste as a source of energy."[44]

While the incineration of waste on land or at sea is a "disposal operation"[45], the use of waste as a fuel or other means to generate energy is considered a "recovery operation" under Directive 91/156.[46] This orientation is likely to produce increased incineration of waste all over the Community. The Community is about to adopt the necessary legislation on waste incineration installations[47] but the draft Directive does not make it an obligation to burn that waste only in such incineration installations.

(14) Thus, it appears that a Community-wide system of waste management which takes care of the environment is taking shape only very slowly. The dif-

---

[39] The normal "free circulation" clause reads as follows: "Member States may not, on grounds relating to this directive, prohibit, restrict or impede the placing on the market of substances which comply with the requirements of this Directive and the Annexes hereto"; example from Directive 67/548: [1967] O.J. L196/1.

[40] See n. 39 above.

[41] As well as "economically" probably.

[42] A. Schmidt, *op. cit.* p. 79.

[43] See Dir. 91/156 and Dir. 91/689, cited above.

[44] Dir. 91/156, Art. 3(1)(*b*) (ii).

[45] Dir. 91/156, Annex II A, points D10 and D11.

[46] Annex II B, point R9.

[47] See Dir. 89/369: [1989] O.J. L163/32 and Dir. 89/429: [1989] O.J. L203/50 on municipal waste incineration.

ferent Court decisions play a major role in forming a Community waste policy and ensuring that this policy is, made and implemented within the legal framework of the Treaty. The Court's decision in Cases C–206/88 and C–207/88, by deciding unambiguously on the notion of waste, has contributed its part to the establishment of such a Community-wide system.

17. INFORMATION IN THE WASTE SECTOR

Judgment of the Court of June 13, 1990
in Case C–162/89

E.C. Commission v. *Belgium*

[1990] I E.C.R. 2391

FACTS AND PROCEDURE[1]

Directives 75/439 on the disposal of waste oils,[2] 75/442 on waste,[3] 76/403 on the disposal of polychlorinated biphenyls and polychlorinated terphenyls,[4] and 78/319 on toxic and dangerous waste[5] each provide that every three years Member States shall send a report to the Commission on the implementation of the individual directive.[6]

Since the Commission had not received any report from Belgium, it sent, on February 18, 1987 a letter of formal notice to the Belgian authorities. No answer was received. On July 4, 1988, the Commission sent a reasoned opinion. With its answer on January 16, 1989, Belgium sent a report on the implementation of the four Directives, but only as regards the Walloon region.

The Commission applied to the Court. The application was registered on May 8, 1989. During the written procedure before the Court, Belgium submitted four reports for the Flemish region. Oral hearings took place on May 16, 1990 and the Commission declared itself satisfied as regards the Walloon

---

[1] Summary by the author.

[2] [1975] O.J. L194/23.

[3] [1975] O.J. L194/47.

[4] [1976] O.J. L108/41.

[5] [1978] O.J. L84/43.

[6] Dir. 75/439, **Article 18**: "Every three years, Member States shall draw up a situation report on the disposal of waste oils in their respective countries and shall send it to the Commission."

Dir. 75/442, **Article 12**: "Every three years, Member States shall draw up a situation report on waste disposal in their respective countries and shall forward it to the Commission. To this effect, the installations or undertakings referred to in Articles 8 and 10 must supply the competent authority referred to in Article 5 with the particulars on the disposal of waste. The Commission shall circulate this report to the other Member States. The Commission shall report every three years to the Council and to the European Parliament on the application of this Directive."

Dir. 76/403, **Article 10**: "Every three years, each Member State shall draw up for the Commission a situation report, within the framework of the report referred to in Article 12 of Directive 75/442/EEC, on the disposal of PCB in their territory. To this effect, the installations, establishments or undertakings referred to in Article 6 must supply the competent authorities referred to in that same Article with particulars of the disposal of the PCBs. The Commission shall circulate this report to the other Member States. The Commission shall report every three years to the Council and to the European Parliament on the applications of this Directive."

Dir. 78/319, **Article 16**: "1. Every three years, and for the first time three years following the notification of this Directive, Member States shall draw up a situation report on the disposal of toxic and dangerous waste in their respective countries and shall forward it to the Commission. The Commission shall circulate this report to the other Member States. 2. The Commission shall report every three years to the Council and to the European Parliament on the application of this Directive."

and the Flemish region. The Advocate General delivered his opinion on May 16, 1990.

ARRÊT

(1) Par requête déposée au greffe de la Cour le 8 mai 1989, la Commission des Communautés européennes a introduit, en vertu de l'article 169 du traité CEE, un recours visant à faire constater que, en ne transmettant pas à la Commission, dans les délais prescrits, les rapports visés à l'article 18 de la directive 75/439/CEE du Conseil, du 16 juin 1975, concernant l'élimination des huiles usagées (JO L 194, p. 23), modifiée par la directive 87/101/CEE du Conseil, du 22 décembre 1986 (JO L 42, p. 43), à l'article 12 de la directive 75/442/CEE du Conseil, du 15 juillet 1975, relative aux déchets (JO L 194, p. 39), à l'article 10 de la directive 76/403/CEE du Conseil, du 6 avril 1976, concernant l'élimination des polychlorobiphényles et polychloroterphényles (JO L 108, p. 41) et à l'article 16 de la directive 78/319/CEE du Conseil, du 20 mars 1978, relative aux déchets toxiques et dangereux (JO L 84, p. 43), en ce qui concerne la région flamande et celle de Bruxelles-Capitale, le royaume de Belgique a manqué aux obligations qui lui incombent en vertu du traité CEE.

(2) Aux termes de l'article 18 de la directive 75/439, précitée, "(tous) les trois ans, les Etats membres établissent un rapport sur l'état de l'élimination des huiles usagées dans leur pays et le transmettent à la Commission".

(3) Aux termes de l'article 12, première phrase de la directive 75/442, précitée, "(tous) les trois ans, les Etats membres établissent un rapport sur la situation concernant l'élimination des déchets dans leur pays et le transmettent à la Commission. (. . .)".

(4) Aux termes de l'article 10, première phrase, de la directive 76/403, précitée, "(tous) les trois ans, les Etats membres font rapport à la Commission, dans le cadre du rapport visé à l'article 12 de la directive 75/442/CEE, sur la situation concernant l'élimination des PCB sur leur territoire. (. . .)".

(5) Aux termes de l'article 16, paragraphe 1, de la directive 78/319, précitée, "(tous) les trois ans, et pour la première fois trois ans après la notification de la présente directive, les Etats membres établissent un rapport sur la situation concernant l'élimination des déchets toxiques et dangereux dans leur pays respectif et le transmettent à la Commission, qui le communique aux autres Etats membres".

(6) Ayant constaté que le Royaume de Belgique n'avait transmis aucun rapport prévu par les directives précitées, la Commission a, par lettre du 18 février 1987, mis le Royaume de Belgique en demeure de présenter ses observations sur le manquement reproché, conformément à l'article 169, premier alinéa, du traité. Le gouvernement de Belgique n'ayant pas répondu, la Commission a émis, le 4 juillet 1988, l'avis motivé. Aprés avoir reçu, le 16 janvier 1989, des autorités belges les premiers rapports concernant la région wallonne seulement, la Commission a introduit le présent recours.

(7) En annexe au mémoire en défense, le gouvernement belge a déposé devant la Cour les quatre rapports prévus par les directives précitées, qui concernent la région flamande. A l'audience, le représentant de la Commission s'est désisté formellement de la partie des conclusions de la Commission relative à cette région.

(8) Pour un plus ample exposé des faits du litige, du déroulement de la procédure et des moyens et arguments des parties, il est renvoyé au rapport d'audience. Ces éléments du dossier ne sont repris ci-dessous que dans la mesure nécessaire au raisonnement de la Cour.

(9) Le Royaume de Belgique ne conteste pas le manquement qui lui est reproché par la Commission en ce qui concerne la région de Bruxelles-Capitale. Il explique qu'un projet de loi visant à la mise en oeuvre des directives précitées a été déposé au Conseil d'Etat, qui a émis son avis le 29 mai 1989, et que le Conseil régional se prononcera prochainement sur ce projet.

(10) A cet égard, il suffit de constater qu'il est de jurisprudence constante qu'un Etat membre ne saurait exciper de dispositions, pratiques ou situations de son ordre interne pour justifier le non-respect des obligations résultant du droit communautaire (voir en dernier lieu l'arrêt du 5 avril 1990, Commission/Belgique, 6/89, non encore publié au Recueil).

(11) Par conséquent, il y a lieu de constater qu'en ne transmettant pas à la Commission, dans les délais prescrits, les rapports nécessaires en ce qui concerne la région de Bruxelles-Capitale, pour se conformer aux dispositions de l'article 18 de la directive 75/439, de l'article 12 de la diective 75/442, de l'article 10 de la directive 76/403, et de l'article 16 de la directive 78/319, le Royaume de Belgique a manqué aux obligations qui lui incombent en vertu du traité.

Sur les dépens

(12) Aux termes de l'article 69, paragraphe 2, du règlement de procédure, toute partie qui succombe est condamnée aux dépens. Le Royaume de Belgique ayant succombé en ses moyens, il y a lieu de la condamner aux dépens.

Par ces motifs,

LA COUR

déclare et arrête:

1. En ne transmettant pas à la Commission, dans les délais prescrits, les rapports nécessaires, en ce qui concerne la région de Bruxelles-Capitale, pour se conformer aux dispositions de l'article 18 de la directive 75/439/CEE du Conseil, du 16 juin 1975, concernant l'élimination des huiles usagées, modifiée par la directive 87/101/CEE du Conseil, du 22 décembre 1986, de l'article 12 de la directive 75/442/CEE du Conseil, du 15 juillet 1975, relative aux déchets, de l'article 10 de la directive 76/403/CEE du Conseil, du 6 avril 1976, concernant l'élimination des polychlorobiphényles et polychloroterphényles, et de l'article 16 de la directive

78/319/CEE du Conseil, du 20 mars 1978, relative aux déchets toxiques et dangereux, le Royaume de Belgique a manqué aux obligations qui lui incombent en vertu du traité CEE.

2. Le Royaume de Belgique est condamné aux dépens.

JUDGMENT*

(1) By application lodged at the Court Registry on the 8 May 1989, the Commission of the European Communities brought an action under Article 169 of the EEC Treaty for a declaration that by not forwarding to the Commission in the prescribed periods the reports referred to in Article 18 of Council Directive 75/439/EEC of 16 June 1975 on the disposal of waste oils (OJ L194/23) as amended by Council Directive 87/101/EEC of 22 December 1986 (OJ L42/43), in Article 12 of Council Directive 75/442/EEC of 15 July 1975 on waste (OJ L194/39), in Article 10 of Council Directive 76/403/EEC of 6 April 1976 on the disposal of polychlorinated biphenyls and polychlorinated terphenyls (OJ L108/41) and in Article 16 of Council Directive 78/319/EEC of 20 March 1978 on toxic and dangerous waste (OJ L84/43), regarding the Flemish region and Brussels-region, the Kingdom of Belgium has failed to fulfil its obligations arising under the EEC Treaty.

(2) Under Article 18 [Art.16] of Directive 75/439 referred to above, "Every three years, Member States shall draw up a situation report on the disposal of waste oil in their respective countries and shall send it to the Commission".

(3) Under Article 12, first sentence, of Directive 75/442 referred to above, "Every three years, Member States shall draw up a situation report on waste disposal in their respective countries and shall forward it to the Commission. (. . .)".

(4) Under Article 10, first sentence, of Directive 76/403 referred to above, "Every three years, each Member State shall draw up for the Commission a situation report, within the framework of the report referred to in Article 12 of Directive 75/442/EEC, on the disposal of PCB in their territory. (. . .)".

(5) Under the first paragraph of Article 16 of Directive 78/319 referred to above, "Every three years, and for the first time three years following the notification of this Directive, Member States shall draw up a situation report on the disposal of toxic and dangerous waste in their respective countries and shall forward it to the Commission. The Commission shall circulate this report to the other Member States".

(6) Having taken note of the fact that the Kingdom of Belgium had not forwarded any of the reports called for by the abovementioned Directives, the Commission gave formal notice to the Kingdom of Belgium by a letter dated 18 February 1987 to submit its observations on the alleged non-compliance, as provided in the first paragraph of Article 169 of the Treaty.
Since there was no response from the Belgian government, the Commission issued a reasoned opinion on 4 July 1989.

---

* Publisher's translation. Publisher's comments in square brackets.

After receiving from the Belgian authorities, on 16 January 1989, the first reports on the French speaking region only, the Commission brought this action.

(7) In the annex to its submissions in defence, the Belgian government forwarded to the Court the four reports required in the abovementioned Directives regarding the Flemish region. At the hearing the agent for the Commission formally discontinued the part of the action concerning this region.

(8) Reference is made to the Report for the Hearing for a fuller account of the facts of the case, the course of the procedure and the submissions and arguments of the parties, which are mentioned or discussed hereinafter only insofar as is necessary for the reasoning of the Court.

(9) The Kingdom of Belgium did not deny non-compliance regarding Brussels-capital. It explained that a bill for the implementation of the above Directives was submitted to the *Conseil d'Etat* which delivered its opinion on 29 May 1989 and that the *Conseil Régional* was to deliver its opinion shortly.

(10) In this respect it suffices to note that according to an established body of case-law a Member State may not rely on national provisions, practices or circumstances of its internal legal order to justify non-compliance with its obligations under Community law (see the latest judgment of 5 April 1990 in case 6/89, *Commission* v. *Belgium*, not yet reported).

(11) It must therefore be held that, by failing to forward to the Commission in the periods laid down the reports needed, in relation to the capital region, Brussels, in order to comply with Article 18 [16] of Directive 75/439, Article 12 of Directive 75/442, Article 10 of Directive 76/403 and Article 16 of Directive 78/319, the Kingdom of Belgium has failed to fulfil its obligations under the Treaty.

Costs

(12) Under 69(2) of the Rules of Procedure, the unsuccessful party is to be ordered to pay the costs. Since the Kingdom of Belgium has failed in its submissions, it must be ordered to bear the costs.

On those grounds,

THE COURT

hereby:

(1) Declares that, by failing to forward to the Commission within the periods laid down the reports needed, in relation to the capital region, Brussels, in order to comply with Article 18 of Council Directive 75/439/EEC of 16 June 1975 on the disposal of waste oils as amended by Council Directive 87/101/EEC of 22 December 1986, Article 12 of Council Directive 75/442/EEC of 15 July 1975 on waste, Article 10 of Council Directive 76/403/EEC of 6 April 1976 on the disposal of polychlorinated biphenyls and polychlorinated terphenyls and of Article 16 of Council Directive 78/319/EEC of 20 March 1978 on toxic and dangerous

waste, the Kingdom of Belgium has failed to fulfil its obligations under the EEC Treaty.

(2) Orders the Kingdom of Belgium to pay the costs.

COMMENTARY

(1) The judgment is reproduced here in French as there is no official English version of it. The version published in the collection of the Court's judgments only reproduces the gist of the decision, not the reasoning. For law students who use this book in English, it might be quite useful to understand that French language—and through this vehicle also French legal thinking—plays an important role in Community law and also in the way the Court approaches and construes it.

(2) The facts of this case are simple. The Commission took four directives in the waste sector, for which Belgium had not sent the implementation reports, and started legal action under Article 169 of the EEC Treaty. During the proceedings, reports for two of the three Belgium regions where sent to the Commission. The Court then pronounced judgment on the failure to transmit reports for the Brussels region. In its reasoning, the Court argued that a Member State may not invoke reasons of its internal distribution of functions to justify non-compliance with Community law.

(3) On several occasions in this book attention is drawn to the importance of waste aspects within the general context of the Community's environmental policy.[7] Questions of waste are at the crosspoint of environmental and internal market considerations. The conception and implementation of an integrated waste policy within the framework of the Community requires a longterm effort to work out Community-wide solutions that are acceptable for the EEC on the one hand, for Member States, regions and local authorities on the other hand.

Such an integrated Community strategy cannot be conceived and put into practice without the greatest possible transparency. Indeed, local concern and resistance against work disposal facilities, based on the NIMBY-principle—**N**ot **I**n **M**y **B**ackyard—can only be overcome by a maximum of open, democratic discussion and decision making.

(4) Statistical data on waste, its provenance, composition and disposal are even now, 1993, rather poor, as far as the Community is concerned.[8] This is

---

[7] See pp. 71 *et seq.*
[8] See Commission, "The State of the Environment in the European Community", overview, COM(92)23 final, vol. III of March 27, 1992 pp. 36 *et seq.* and—within this document—EUROSTAT, Environmental Statistics (1991) pp. 117 *et seq.*

partly due to the fact that Community-wide definitions of "waste", "dangerous waste" and other basic notions have no formal general acceptance or general entry into the statistics, despite the existence of Directives 75/442 and 78/319.[9]

Against this background, it becomes clear, what a potentially important role those reports could have played, which Member States were obliged to draw up under the different waste directives. They could have contributed to co-ordinate and integrate national waste policies, all the more since Member States and the EEC had set up a Waste Management Committee.[10]

(5) In practice, however, matters have not worked out that way. Member States did not send the work reports and the Commission did not press too hard for them: in fact, the present case was the first case against a Member State for not sending reports, and the proceedings were started only in 1987. In 1989, the Commission made a report on the application by Member States of three of the four Directives mentioned in case C–162/89.[11] In this report the Commission stated that it had not received the three-year reports on the application of the directives by most Member States. Since then, the situation has hardly improved, partly because amendments to the Directives were dis-cussed at Community level.[12]

(6) However, the absence of Member States' reports on the application of directives is not limited to these four waste directives. In the waste sector Directive 84/631 on the transfrontier shipment of waste[13] requires Member States to send a report on the application of the Directive every two years since 1987;[14] until 1992, the Commission did not received one single report. Directive 85/339 on containers of liquids for human consumption[15] requests Member States to send a report every four years starting in 1987. Directive 86/278 on the use of sewage sludge in agriculture[16] requests a report to be sent to the Commission in 1991 and then every four years.

(7) Outside the waste sector, numerous environmental directives contain pro-visions which provide that Member States shall draw up reports on the appli-

---

[9] See for more details pp. 269–278.

[10] Commission decision of April 21, 1976: [1976] O.J. L115/73.

[11] Commission, "Report on the implementation by Member States of the Community Waste Directives 75/442, 75/439 and 78/319." SEC(89)1455 final of September 27, 1989.

[12] Dir. 75/439 was substantially amended by Dir. 87/101: [1987] O.J. L42/43; Dir. 75/442 was sub-stantially amended by Dir. 91/156: [1991] O.J. L78/32; Dir. 78/319 was substantially amended by Dir. 91/689: [1991] O.J. L337/20; see further proposal for an amendment of Dir. 76/403: [1988] O.J. L319/57.

[13] Dir. 84/631 on the supervision and control within the European Community of the transfrontier shipment of hazardous waste: [1984] O.J. L326/31.

[14] Dir. 84/631, Art. 13.

[15] Art. 6 of Dir. 85/339 on containers of liquids for human consumption: [1985] O.J. L176/18.

[16] Art. 17 of Dir. 86/278 on the protection of the environment, and in particular of the soil, when sewage sludge is used in agriculture: [1986] O.J. L181/6.

cation of the directive at national level.[17] Generally, with the exception of Directive 76/160 on the quality of bathing waters,[18] where reports came in quite regularly,[19] the number of reports which the Commission received, was extremely low. "It is the exception rather than the rule for the Commission to receive the reports provided for in many Directives."[20] As a consequence, the Commission drew up very few situation reports on the application of Community directives in the Member States. This situation, in turn, reduced the ability of the European Parliament and Member States to control the application of Community environmental law within the Community.

(8) In view of this situation the Commission decided not to pursue its policy to open proceedings under Article 169 against those Member States which had not sent their situation reports. Instead, it presented a proposal for a Council directive harmonising and rationalising the Member States' reports on the application of environmental directives. Such reports were, in future, to be drawn up every three years sector by sector—water, air, waste, etc.—in accordance with a questionnaire prepared by the Commission. The Council adopted this Directive end 1991.[21] As a result, the first Community "water" report will be drawn up in 1997 on the basis of data collected between 1993 and 1995; a report on air pollution directives will be drawn up in 1998 on the basis of data collected between 1994 and 1996, etc.

(9) For the waste sector, the first report under Directive 91/692 will be produced in 1999; in view of the impact which waste has and will have on the achievement of the Internal Market by the beginning of 1993, this appears to be much too late. The absence of reliable data, and of transparency, coupled with emotional reactions from the population, might seriously hamper an integrated waste management policy at Community level and lead to "re-nationalising" this sector.

---

[17] In the water sector, Dir. 76/160 on bathing water: [1976] O.J. L31/1: Dir. 78/659 on fishwater: [1978] O.J. L222/1; Dir. 79/923 on shellfish water: [1979] O.J. L281/47; Dir. 78/176 on waste from the titanium dioxide industry: [1978] O.J. L54/19; and Dir. 91/271 on urban waste water treatment: [1991] O.J. L135/40 provide for reports. In the air sector, Dir. 80/779 on limit values for SO_2 and suspended particulates: [1980] O.J. L229/30; Dir. 82/884 on a limit value for lead: [1982] O.J. L378/15; Dir. 85/203 on limit values for nitrogen dioxide: [1985] O.J. L87/1 require regular reports to be drawn up. In the nature sector, Dir. 79/409: [1979] O.J. L103/1 requests a situation report every three years.

[18] Dir. 76/160 above.

[19] See Commission, "Quality of Bathing Water"the latest report 1992 EUR 5031. (Brussels-Luxembourg, 1993).

[20] Commission, Ninth report on monitoring the application of Community law: [1992] O.J. C250/163.

[21] Dir. 91/692: [1991] O.J. L377/48.

18. NATIONAL MANAGEMENT OF WASTE

**Judgment of the Court of March 17, 1993
in Case C–155/91**

E.C. Commission, supported by the European Parliament v. *E.C. Council,
supported by Spain*

Not yet reported

FACTS AND PROCEDURE[1]

Council Directive 91/156 was adopted on March 18, 1991.[2] It amended Directive 75/442 on waste.[3] The Council based Directive 91/156 on Article 130s, though the Commissions' proposal had been based on Article 100a.

The Commission considered Article 130s to be the wrong legal basis and applied to the Court. Its application was registered on June 11, 1991. Spain intervened on the side of the Council, and the European Parliament on the side of the Commission.

Oral proceedings took place on November 25, 1992. The Advocate General delivered his opinion on December 1, 1992.

JUDGMENT[*]

(1) By application lodged with the Court Registry on 11 June 1991, the Commission of the European Communities brought an action pursuant to Article 173 EEC, for the annulment of EEC Directive 91/156 of 18 March 1991, amending EEC Directive 75/442 on waste (OJ 1972 L78/32).

(2) Directive 75/442 set up a Community system for the disposal of waste. Drawing from experience in the implementation of this Directive by the Member States, the Commission issued a draft proposal for the above 91/156 Directive, based on Article 100a. The Council for its part adopted a joint position that based the future Directive on Article 130s EEC. Consulted by the Council under Article 130s, the European Parliament considered the Commission's legal basis justified but, depsite the Parliament's objections, the Council based the Directive on Article 130s.

(3) In support of its action, the Commission only invokes the incorrect legal basis for the Directive. The Parliament, intervening in the action, further requests the annulment of Article 18 of the Directive.

(4) Reference is made to the Report for the Hearing for a fuller account of the facts of the case, the course of the procedure, and the submissions and arguments of the parties, which are mentioned or discussed hereinafter only insofar as they are necessary to the reasoning of the Court.

---

[1] Summary by the author.

[2] Dir. 91/156 amending Dir. 75/442 on waste: [1991] O.J. L78/32 (dated March 26, 1991).

[3] Dir. 75/442 on waste: [1975] O.J. L194/47.

[*] Publisher's translation.

Legal basis

(5) The Commission, supported by the Parliament, submitted in substance that the object of the Directive was both the protection of the environment and the setting up and operating of the internal market. Hence, the Directive should have been adopted solely on the basis of Article 100a EEC, like the Directive on waste in the titanium dioxide industry, which was in dispute in the judgment of 11 June 1991, *Commission v. Council* (Case C–300/89, [1991] E.C.R. 2867, hereinafter the "titanium dioxide judgment").

(6) The Council contended however that Article 130s EEC was the correct legal basis for Directive 91/156, the aim and contents of which are mainly concerned with the protection of health and the environment.

(7) As the Court has consistently held, in the Community's institutional framework, the choice of the legal basis of an act must be determined by objective factors which can be judicially reviewed. These factors include, *inter alia*, the aim and content of the act (see latest judgment of 7 July 1992, *Parliament v. Council*, Case C–295/90 [1992] I E.C.R. 4193 [1992] 3 C.M.L.R. 281, point 13).

(8) As for the aim of Directive 91/156, Recitals (4), (6), (7) and (9) underline that, in order to achieve a high degree of environmental protection, Member States must take the appropriate steps to limit the production of waste, to encourage recycling and reuse with a view to extracting secondary raw material, and that they must be able to ensure the disposal of waste by their own means as well as limiting its movement.

(9) As for its contents, it should be noted that the Directive makes it an obligation for Member States to encourage the prevention or reduction of waste production, to ensure the recovery of waste or its disposal without endangering human health or the environment, and to prohibit the abandonment, dumping or uncontrolled disposal of waste (Articles 3 and 4). Under the Directive, Member States are obliged to establish an integrated and adequate network of disposal installations which would enable the Community as a whole as well as Member States taken individually to become self-sufficient in waste disposal and to enable them to dispose of the waste in one of the nearest appropriate installations (Article 5). In order to attain these objectives, Member States should draw up management plans and may prevent the movements of waste which are not in accordance with these plans (Article 7). Lastly, the Directive states that Member States must make provision for a system of permits, registration and control for undertakings and disposal installations (Articles 9–14) and reasserts, in the field of waste disposal, the "polluter pays" principle enunicated in Article 130r, paragraph 2 EEC (Article 15).

(10) The above considerations show that, from its aim and content, the object of the Directive is to ensure the management of waste, be it of industrial or domestic origin, with a view to complying with the requirements of environmental protection.

(11) However, the Commission further observed that the Directive implements the principle of free movement of waste destined for reuse and submits waste to be disposed of to conditions complying with the rules of the internal market.

(12) It is true that waste, whether recyclable or not, must be considered as goods the

movement of which, under Article 30 EEC, should not be hindered (judgment of the Court of Justice of 9 July 1992 in Case C–2/90, *Commission v. Belgium,* [1992] I E.C.R. 4431, [1993] 1 C.M.L.R. 357, point 28).

(13) However, the Court stated that mandatory requirements relating to the protection of the environment may be regarded as justifying exceptions to the rules on free movement of goods. Against this background, the Court acknowledged that the principle whereby environmental damage should be rectified at source—as laid down in Article 130r(2) EEC for action by the Community in the field of environment—implies that it is for each region, commune or other local authority to take the appropriate measures to ensure reception, processing treatment and disposal of its own waste. Consequently waste should be disposed of as close as possible to the place where it was produced in order to keep transport to a minimum (judgment in Case C–2/90 above, point 34).

(14) The object of the Directive is precisely to implement these guidelines. Article 5 in particular embodies the principle of proximity of the place where the waste is to be disposed of in relation to the place where it is produced in order to ensure, insofar as possible, that each Member State is responsible for the disposal of its own waste. Furthermore, Article 7 of the Directive permits Member States to prohibit the movement of waste, whether it is to be reused or disposed of, which does not comply with their management plans.

(15) Under these conditions, the Directive cannot be regarded as aiming to implement the free movement of waste, as admitted by the Commission at the hearing.

(16) The Commission also argues that the Directive leads to an approximation of national laws insofar as it contains in Article 1 a single definition for waste and related activities. In this context, the Commission refers to Recital 5 of the Directive which states that discrepancy between the laws of Members States relating to the disposal and reuse of waste may affect the quality of the environment and the proper functioning of the internal market.

(17) Lastly, the Commission invokes the fact that the Directive contributes likewise to the harmonisation of the conditions of competition at both the stage of industrial production and that of disposal of waste. In this respect, the Commission points out that, to some extent, the Directive puts an end to the advantages enjoyed by some industries in Member States regarding production costs as a result of rules on the processing of waste which were not so strict as in other Member States. Article 4 for instance, which provides for reuse and disposal of waste without "risk to water, air, soil and plants and animals", would be precise enough to ensure, if adequately transposed in Member States, that the burden on economic operators would from then on be largely comparable in all Member States.

(18) It has to be admitted that some provisions in the Directive, and in particular the definitions in Article 1, have an impact on the functioning of the internal market.

(19) However, and despite the Commission's allegations to the contrary, the sole fact that the establishment or the functioning of the internal market is concerned is not sufficient for Article 100a EEC to apply. Indeed, as the Court has consistently held, the legal basis of Article 100a is not justified where harmonisation of the

conditions of the market within the Community are only ancillary to the act to be adopted (judgment of 4 October 1992 in Case C–70/88, *Parliament v. Council,* [1991] I E.C.R. 4529 [1992] 1 C.M.L.R. 91, point 17).

(20) This is the case in the present situation. Harmonisation, as provided for by Article 1 of the Directive, seeks principally, with a view to protecting the environment, to ensure efficient management of waste in the Community, whatever its origin, and its effects on the conditions of competition and on the flow of trade are only ancillary. For this reason, the Directive must be distinguished from Directive 89/428 which was the subject of the aforementioned "titanium dioxyde case" and whose aim is to approximate national laws on the conditions of production in a given industrial sector for the purpose of eliminating distortions of competition in this particular sector.

(21) It follows from these considerations that the Directive at issue was correctly based on the sole Article 130s EEC. The grounds of incorrect legal basis must therefore be dismissed.

Article 18 of the Directive

(22) The Parliament seeks the annulment of Article 18 of Directive 91/156 laying down the rules of procedure of the regulation committee, on the grounds that these rules are not in accordance with the EEC Treaty.

(23) Under Article 37(3) of the Statute of the Court, the submissions for an action in intervention cannot have any object other than supporting the submissions of one of the parties.

(24) It must be observed that the Commission's submissions seek the annulment of Directive 91/156 whereas the Parliament's submissions seek the annulment of Article 18 of the Directive on grounds which are completely extraneous to those invoked by the Commission. Consequently, the latter cannot be regarded as having the same object as those of the Commission and must therefore be dismissed as inadmissible.

(25) It follows from the foregoing considerations that the action must be dismissed.

Costs

(26) Under Article 69(2) of the Rules of Procedure, the unsuccessful party is to be ordered to pay the costs. Since the Commission has failed in its submissions, it must be ordered to pay the costs. Pursuant to Article 69(4) of the same Rules, the Kingdom of Spain and the European Parliament will bear their own costs.

On those grounds,

THE COURT

hereby:

(1) Dismisses the action.

(2) Orders the Commission to pay the costs. The Kingdom of Spain and the European Parliament shall bear their own costs.

COMMENTARY

(1) The present judgment seems to bring to some sort of end to the discussion about the legal basis of Community measures for waste. Whether this is indeed the case, however, only the future can tell. Also, it is as yet unclear to what extent the general relationship between Articles 130s and other provisions of the Treaty, in particular Article 100a, will be influenced by the judgment.

(2) The Commission's action against the Council was based on Article 173 of the EEC Treaty.[4] This article provides that an application must be filed within two months and expressly specifies when this time-limit begins to run. Since Directive 91/156 was adopted on March 18, 1991 and published in the *Official Journal* of March 26, 1991,[5] the registration of the application on June 11, 1991 occurred after the two-month delay had elapsed.

However, the Court's rules of procedure provide in Article 81 that where a measure is published in the *Official Journal of the European Communities*, time-limits for application to the Court only begin to run 15 days after such publication. Furthermore, Article 81(2) and Annex II of the rules of procedure allow two supplementary days for calculating the procedural time-limits where the parties normally are resident in Belgium. These extended time-limits were introduced, because it cannot be expected that the *Official Journal* is available all over the Community on the day of its publication, and the day which is printed on the *Official Journal* might not necessarily be the date when it is actually available.[6] In order to avoid disputes on such questions the above-mentioned general provision of 15 plus two days in the Court's rules of procedure, seem fully justified, though this might lead, as in the present case, to applications which are registered more than two months after the measure was adopted.

In the present case, the application was made within two months and 17

---

[4] **Article 173** EEC: "The Court of Justice shall review the legality of acts of the Council and the Commission other than recommendations or opinions. Its shall for this purpose have jurisdiction in actions brought by a Member State, the Council or the Commission on grounds of lack of competence, infringement on an essential procedural requirement, infringement of this Treaty or of any rule of law relating to its application, or misuse of powers.

. . .

The proceedings provided for in this Article shall be instituted within two months of the publication of the measure, or of its notification to the plaintiff, or, in the absence thereof, of the day on which it came to the knowledge of the latter, as the case may be."

[5] See n. 2 above.

[6] For instance, in Case C–337/88, *Societá Agricola*: [1990] I E.C.R. 1, [1991] 1 C.M.L.R. 872, the difference between the date on the number of the O.J. and its actual availability was 22 days.

days after the publication of Directive 91/156 in the *Official Journal*. Since no party had raised the issue of time-limits, the Court rightly did not discuss this point in its judgment.

(3) Neither did the Court discuss an aspect of the decision-making process which is linked to the choice of the legal basis. Indeed, the decision-making process is different under Articles 100a and 130s. Article 100a provides for a co-operation procedure between the Council and the European Parliament, whereas Article 130s only provides for the consultation of the Parliament.[7] The question is thus who decides which procedure is to be followed.

In practice, when the Council wants to change the legal basis of a Commission proposal, such as in the present case, it consults informally with the European Parliament a second time. This consultation does not take place under the co-operation procedure of Article 149 of the EEC Treaty but without a specific legal basis; it takes the form of a "right to be heard" which is given to the European Parliament.

The problem lies in the point that the initiative for Community legislation lies exclusively with the Commission; and it would be normal that it is the Commission which determines the way in which its proposals are to be handled, by choosing this or that legal basis.[8] Where the Commission bases a proposal on Article 100a, the European Parliament has, in my view, a "constitutional right" which flows out of the Treaty, to be seized with the proposal in the form of the co-operation procedure, and this right cannot be reduced by the Council. Indeed, the second deliberation by the Parliament within the co-operation procedure is not the same as a second consultation procedure: where, for instance, within the framework of the co-operation procedure, the European Parliament rejects a common position by the Council, the Council can only decide unanimously.[9] Where the European Parliament is only consulted a second time on an informal basis, the Council may also decide by majority decision.[10]

I therefore believe that the European Parliament is entitled to a co-operation procedure, whenever the Commission bases a proposal on an article of the EEC Treaty which provides for such a procedure. Should the Commission base its proposal on an article which does not provide for a co-operation procedure and the Council wishes to change the legal basis and choose an article which does provide for a co-operation procedure, the Council will have to use the procedure under Article 149. This follows from the

---

[7] For details of the co-operation procedure, see Art. 149 EEC.
[8] See L. Krämer, *EEC Treaty and Environmental Protection* (London, 1990) para. 3.03 on pp. 32–33.
[9] See Art. 149 (2)(*b*) EEC.
[10] It is no argument that the Council could decide, under Art. 130s, only with unanimity anyway: indeed, Art. 130s(2) does allow majority decisions; and also one might easily imagine a case where the Commission submits a proposal under Art. 100a and the Council wishes to recur to Art. 43, a provision which provides for majority decisions, after consultation with the European Parliament.

general principle which the Court has developed in particular in Case C–300/89,[11] that the co-operation procedure is more democratic than the consultation procedure: in other terms, because of its institutional role, the European Parliament is entitled to have the "most favourable procedure" applied where changes occur in the legal basis.

As stated, the Court did not approach these questions. They might, however, one day become relevant, in particular after the Maastricht Treaty on European Union is in force.

(4) The judgment of the Court is short; it consists of 26 paragraphs. It first mentions the facts and the procedural questions (paragraphs 1 to 4), then examines, in the context of the discussion of the appropriate legal basis of Directive 91/156, the objective and content of Directive 91/156 (paragraphs 5 to 10), discusses the question of free circulation of wastes (11 to 15), the approximation of legislation and harmonisation of competitive conditions (16 to 21) and finishes on the third-party-intervention from the European Parliament (22 to 25) and the costs (26).

(5) As regards the legal basis, the Court starts by repeating earlier statements that the choice of a legal basis of a legislative act must be made according to objective criteria and in particular the objective and the content of the legislative act.[12] Little is to be said on the legal analysis of the Court as to the objective and content of Directive 91/156.[13]

However, at a later stage,[14] the Court stated that the principal objective of Directive is efficient waste management with the view to protect the environment and the Court came to this conclusion relying on Article 1 of Directive 91/156[15]—without further reasoning.

When commenting on the Court's decision in Case C–300/89, I already pointed out that the notion of "principal objective" is a rather subjective one.[16] Indeed, both the Council and the Commission argued in that case that the legal basis of a legislative act should be determined by its principal objective—but both had come to opposite conclusions as to the principal objective of the directive which was in dispute in that case. Therefore, it was of no surprise that, in case C–300/89, the Court did not consider the principal objective of a legislative act to be decisive. It is all the more astonishing that the Court stated in the present case, with regard to Case C–300/89, that the harmonisation of competitive conditions was the principal objective of Directive 89/428.[17]

---

[11] Case C–300/89, *Commission* v. *Council* [1991] I E.C.R. 2867, see also p. 21.
[12] Para. 7.
[13] Paras. 8 and 9.
[14] Para. 20.
[15] Dir. 91/156 (see n. 2 above) Art. 1; It should be noted, though, that Art. 1 of Dir. 91/156 covers the whole of the new articles for Dir. 75/442
[16] See p. 27 above.
[17] Para. 20.

(6) My main objection to the recourse to the "principal objective"-approach
and/or, in this case, to Article 1 of Directive 91/156 is that the wording of the
legislative act becomes so decisive for the choice of the legal basis. It is
always possible to draft a directive or a specific article in one way or the other
and examples of bad, inconsistent or contradictory drafting can be found in
quite a number of environmental directives. What is more important is that the
drafting is done by the Council. The Council may thus, by drafting the first
article of a directive in a specific way, decide on the principal objective of that
directive. In my understanding, however, it is the EEC Treaty, which prede-
termines the choice of the legal basis, not the Council's drafting.

(7) By having recourse to the argument of the "principal objective", the Court
opened gates which might lead to yet unclear consequences. Such a method
of construction would have an important impact on the interpretation of environmental Directives. Directive 88/76 for instance, which limits air emissions
from motor vehicles and practically requires the use of catalytic converters in
cars,[18] certainly aims at the reduction of air pollution, thus the protection of the
environment. Arguments of free circulation of goods, approximation of legis-
lations or harmonisation of competitive conditions hardly appear in the text of
Directive 88/76, and yet the Council based that Directive on Article 100a. If the
Court's reasoning is right, then the principal objective of Directive 88/76
would be the approximation of legislation or the free circulation of goods or
the harmonisation of conditions of competition, though these objectives are
hardly mentioned. And the objective which is almost exclusively mentioned,[19]
the protection of the environment, is only the ancillary objective, which therefore does not come into consideration for the choice of the legal basis.

Similarly, Directive 91/173[20] considerably restricts the use of pentachlorophenol, a substance "dangerous to man and the environment and in particular
to the aquatic environment." That Directive deals with no other product and
exclusively aims at reaching a reduction in the use of the substance, and yet,
the Directive is based on Article 100a, not on 130s, as if the protection of the
environment—would one follow the Court's arguments—was an ancillary
objective.[21]

(8) In my opinion, both Directives 88/76 and 91/173 were correctly based on
Article 100a. However, such an approach seems incompatible with the doctrine of "principal" and "ancillary" objective. Product standards which are set
by the Council are "inherently" designed to be applicable in the whole inter-

---

[18] Dir. 88/76 relating to measures to be taken against air pollution by gases from the engines of
motor vehicles: [1988] O.J. L36/18.

[19] See the Recitals of Dir. 88/76 (n. 18 above).

[20] Dir. 91/173 amending for the ninth time Dir. 76/769 relating to restrictions on the marketing and
use of certain dangerous substances and preparations: [1991] O.J. L85/34.

[21] Apart from a standard recital which one finds in almost all directives on the free circulation of
goods, which refers to the completion of the internal market by the end of 1992 and what an
internal market is, the other four considerants just deal with environmental questions.

nal market, to the extent to which they fix uniform standards. The Council may insert into the Recitals and into the different articles of such a directive whatever it wishes: it cannot escape the provisions on the internal market as contained in Article 100a which are enshrined in the Treaty and therefore not available to the Council at will. It is for this reason—the need for uniform standards in an internal market where national borders are no longer economic borders—that even a ban on a product for environmental purposes is a rule to be adopted under Article 100a and not under Article 130s. In other terms, one cannot have both a Single Market without internal frontiers and at the same time standards set at Community level for products on this market which are different from one region to the other.

A further argument against the theory of "principal" and "ancillary" objective is the rather discretionary character of such distinction. Member States which vote in Council might have very different motives, ranking, in the case of a ban on a product, from prohibiting imports, protecting the environment, protecting a specific sector of industry, promoting the use of another product, influencing competition, reacting on an accident at national level, etc.[22]

(9) In the past, these arguments against the doctrine of "principal" and "ancillary" objectives have prevailed in the drafting of product-related legislation; and the Court did not seem to put this into question. It even repeated that wastes are products under Article 30 of the EEC Treaty.[23] However, it declared that wastes are not to come under the classical doctrine, since the protection of the environment justifies exemptions from the general product rules.[24] Here, the Court referred to its judgment in Case C-2/90[25] in which it declared that the mere quantity of waste may constitute a risk for the environment which requires measures to be taken by local, regional or national authorities. However, the judgment in Case C-2/90 concerned a situation where Community legislation did not exist, whereas in the present case the the interpretation of a specific Community measure is in question, which sets Community-wide rules. It is one thing to declare that the Community must be progressively integrated and that, until this is fully achieved Member States may take the measures to protect the environment. This follows from the general principle enshrined in the Treaty that the environment must not remain unprotected and that the Community cannot, where it has not set protection rules itself, prevent Member States from doing so. But it is quite another thing to declare the same principle to be applicable in situations where Community-wide rules apply.

The Court's argument in case C-2/90—repeated in the present case—that wastes present, by their pure quantity, a threat to the environment so that

---

[22] See also L. Krämer, *op. cit*, paras. 3.29 and 3.30.
[23] Para. 12.
[24] Para. 13.
[25] Case C-2/90, *Commission* v. *Belgium*: [1992] I E.C.R. 4431, [1993] 1 C.M.L.R. 365; see p. 71 above.

exemptions from the general rules on free circulation are justified, raises further doubts. Indeed, for instance, large quantities of chemicals may also have adverse environmental effect: thus one could conceive local, regional or national measures with regard to chemicals. A high number of trucks may cause considerable environmental impairment, so that measures are necessary. Those illustrations may show that the situation of wastes is not that much different from other substances or products.

This is also shown by the fact that the Council adopted Directive 91/157, which aims "to approximate the laws of the Member States in the recovery and controlled disposal of batteries and accumulators"[26] on the basis of Article 100a. In this case, waste standards were set for the whole Community.

The Advocate General tried to justify this possible inconsistency—that general waste directives should be based on Article 130s, whereas Directive 91/157 was based on Article 100a—with the argument that Directive 91/157 concerned specific waste products, whereas Directive 91/156 concerned wastes in general.[27] I fail to see this point as regards waste. Why should general rules for waste, including batteries, be based on Article 130s and more detailed provisions, which only deal with batteries, on Article 100a? The Court did not try to explain the different legal basis for Directives 91/156 and 91/157.

(10) To sum up: the Court allowed the Council to set rules for waste which do not create uniformity within the boundaries of the EEC, such as the self-sufficiency of individual Member States as regards waste disposal.[28] It declared that because of these rules, the principal objective (as determined by the Council) and the content of Directive 91/156 are the protection of the environment which justifies Article 130s as the legal basis, allowing thereby implicitly each Member State to introduce or maintain more stringent environmental provisions.[29]

My own position is that the Treaty is not available to the Council, which may not, therefore, set whatever rule it deems appropriate. In particular, the principle of national self-sufficiency is incompatible with the principle of a uniform market contained in Article 100a. Thus, the Council was not free to adopt, at Community level, such a rule, but was bound by Article 100a to set up uniform standards for waste disposal. Considerations of "principal objective" of a legal act are not decisive.

(11) One should, however, understand that these considerations do not affect the conclusion that, for the foreseeable future, the Court has authorised Mem-

---

[26] Dir. 91/157 on batteries and accumulators containing certain dangerous substances: [1991] O.J. L78/38. The quotation is taken from Art. 1.

[27] See Advocate General's opinion, para. 10.

[28] See **Article 5(1)** of Dir. 75/442 in the form amended by Directive 91/156: " . . . The network (of disposal installations) must enable the Community as a whole to become self-sufficient in waste disposal and the Member States to move towards that aim individually . . . "

[29] See Art. 130t EEC.

ber States to have a national waste policy which aims at self-sufficiency and has encouraged them as members of the Council, to set rules at Community level only on the basis of the lowest common denominator.[30] It is a well-known fact that Germany, in particular, pursued for a couple of years a policy of national disposal of waste, which finally led the Commission to bring a case against Germany before the European Court.[31] The present judgment is also likely to influence the decision on the legal basis of Directive 91/689 on dangerous waste,[32] which the Commission equally had submitted to the Court, In the medium or long term, the Court's approach will, in my assessment, not be able to stand. Indeed, much more emphasis is placed in recent waste legislation at national or at Community level on preventing the generation of waste, on waste recovery and waste recycling. This shows the growing economic importance of waste and which is also due to the fact that waste disposal is such a risk for the environment. The German Government, in a legislative proposal submitted in spring 1993 to the German parliament, even goes as far as to abandon the notion of "waste" and instead refers to "production residues" (Produktionsrückstände). If this tendency continues—and I have little doubt that it will—then waste will become again what in law it has always been: a movable good. Presumably nobody will question, at that future stage, that if the European Union with an internal market still exists and functions—future Community (Union) rules on product residues will have to be uniform and thus be based on Article 100a of the EEC Treaty.

(12) The present judgment tried to pacify the institutional controversy between the Commission and the Council—or should one say between the Community and the Member States?—on the origin of waste management rules and whether they should be taken primarily at national or at Community level. The general answer is clear: priority is given to national action. This favours Member States with an active environmental policy on waste. Whether it favours the Western European environment will depend on the political determination of all 12 Member States to conceive and implement an active waste management policy. Past Community waste directives have only had limited success in producing such a waste management policy within the Community. It is to be hoped that the emphasis which this judgment lays upon national action will lead to better environmental protection all over the Community and will not only make (environmentally) strong Member States stronger. At Community level, law and policy are intricately intertwined and the present Court's decision on the legal basis of Directive 91/156 is a confirmation of that rule.

---

[30] The lowest common denominator is inherently enshrined in directives based on Art. 130s, because each Member State which argues for more protection at Community level will be referred back to Art. 130t EEC which allows it to introduce more stringent protection measures at national level.

[31] See Case C–422/92, *Commission* v. *Germany.* [1993] O.J. C35/6.

[32] Dir. 91/689 on dangerous waste: [1991] O.J. L377/20.

Chemicals

19. MAJOR-ACCIDENT HAZARDS

**Judgment of the Court of May 20, 1992
in Case C–190/90**

E.C. Commission v. *The Netherlands*

[1992] I E.C.R. 3265

FACTS AND PROCEDURE[1]

Council Directive 82/501 on the major-accident hazards of certain industrial activities was adopted in 1982.[2] Member States had to comply with its requirements by January 8, 1984. The Commission, not being satisfied that the Dutch legislation was entirely compatible with the Directive, sent letters of formal notice on November 27, 1985 and December 4, 1986, in which it argued that seven Articles of the Directive were not at all or not completely transposed into Dutch law.[3]

The Netherlands answered by letter of September 14, 1988. On September 20, 1988 the Commission sent a Reasoned Opinion, which the Dutch government answered by letter of December 1988.

Since the Commission was still not satisfied with the implementation measures taken by the Dutch authorities, it applied to the Court on June 14, 1990. Written proceedings took place, during which the parties exchanged arguments. Oral hearings were held on February 5, 1992. At these hearings, the Commission withdrew parts of its claims; the Dutch government acknowledged that Articles 8(1) and 10 of the Directive had not been transposed into Dutch law.[4]

The Advocate General gave his opinion on February 5, 1992.

JUDGMENT*

(1) By application received by the Court Registry on 14 June 1990, the Commission of the European Communities brought an action under Article 169 of the EEC Treaty for a declaration that, by not adopting all the laws, regulations and administrative provisions necessary for complying with Council Directive 82/501/EEC on the major-accident hazards of certain industrial activities (Official Journal L230, p. 1, hereinafter called "the Directive"), particularly Articles 3, 4, 5(1)(b), (c) and (3), as well as Articles 8(1) and 10(1) and (2), the Kingdom of the Netherlands has failed to fulfil its obligations under the EEC Treaty.

(2) The Directive concerns the prevention of major accidents which could be caused by certain industrial activities and the limitation of their consequences for man and the environment.

---

[1] Summary by the author.
[2] [1982] O.J. L230/1.
[3] See for details the report for the hearing, paras. 9 to 14.
[4] See Court of Justice, number 10, last para.
* Publisher's translation.

(3) Article 3 of the Directive provides that:

'Member States shall adopt the provisions necessary to ensure that, in the case of any of the industrial activities specified in Article 1, the manufacturer is obliged to take all the measures necessary to prevent major accidents and to limit their consequences for man and the environment.'

(4) Under Article 4 of the Directive,

'Member States shall take the measures necessary to ensure that all manufacturers are required to prove to the competent authority at any time for the purposes of the controls referred to in Article 7(2), that they have identified existing major-accident hazards, adopted the appropriate safety measures, and provided the persons working on the site with information, training and equipment in order to ensure their safety.'

(5) Under Article 5(1) of the Directive, the Member States must introduce the necessary measures to require manufacturers to notify the competent authorities of, *inter alia*, the following:

(a) . . .

(b) information relating to the installations, that is to say:— . . .
—the maximum number of persons working on the site of the establishment and particularly of those persons exposed to the hazard,
— . . .

(c) information relating to possible major-accident situations, that is to say:
— . . .
— . . .
—the names of the person and his deputies or the qualified body responsible for safety and authorized to set the emergency plans in motion and to alert the competent authorities specified in Article 7.

Article 5(3) of the Directive provides that:

'The notification specified in paragraph 1 shall be updated periodically to take account of new technical knowledge relative to safety and of developments in knowledge concerning the assessment of hazards.'

(6) Article 8(1) of the Directive is worded as follows:

'Member States shall ensure that information on safety measures and on the correct behaviour to adopt in the case of an accident is supplied in an appropriate manner, and without their having to request it, to persons liable to be affected by a major accident originating in a notified industrial activity within the meaning of Article 5.'

(7) Article 10 of the Directive provides as follows:

1. Member States shall take the necessary measures to ensure that, as soon as a major accident occurs, the manufacturer shall be required:

(a) to inform the competent authorities specified in Article 7 immediately;
(b) to provide them with the following information as soon as it becomes available:
  —the circumstances of the accident,
  —the dangerous substances involved within the meaning of Article 1(2)(d),
  —the data available for assessing the effects of the accident on man and the environment,
  —the emergency measures taken;
(c) to inform them of the steps envisaged:
  —to alleviate the medium and long-term effects of the accident,
  —to prevent any recurrence of such an accident.

2. The Member States shall require the competent authorities:
(a) to ensure that any emergency and medium and long-term measures which may prove necessary are taken;
(b) to collect, where possible, the information necessary for a full analysis of the major accident and possibly to make recommendations.

(8) In the oral procedure the Commission withdrew the complaints relating to the failure to incorporate the second indent of Article 5(1)(b), Article 5(3) and Article 10(2) of the Directive into national law. Therefore the complaints concerning Articles 3, 4, the third indent of Article 5(1)(c), Article 8(1) and 10(1) of the Directive are maintained.

(9) The Kingdom of the Netherlands contends that the obligations laid down by its national legislation correspond to the terms of the Directive. Thus the following provisions are said to correspond to Article 3 of the Directive:

—Articles 2 and 17(1) of the 1952 Law on obnoxious, unhealthy or dangerous establishments (the "Hinderwet", published in the Stb 1981, 410),

—the Law of 26 November 1970 on atmospheric pollution (the "Wet inzake de luchtverontreiniging", published in the Stb 1970, p. 580),

—the Order of 23 May 1972 implementing Article 19(1) of the abovementioned Law (published in the Stb 1972, p. 294),

—Articles 1, 12 and 13 of the 1985 Law on fire brigades (the "Brandweerwet", published in the Stb 1985, p. 87) and the Order on fire brigades in enterprises (the "Besluit bedrijfs brandweren", published in the Stb 1990, p. 80),

—Article 2 of the Law on environmentally dangerous substances (the "Wet milieugevaarlijke stoffen", published in the Stb 1985, p. 639).

The following provisions are said to correspond to Article 4 of the Directive:

— Articles 2(1), 5, 30 *et seq.* of the Hinderwet,

— Article 2 of the 1953 Order on obnoxious, unhealthy or dangerous establishments, as amended in 1988 (the "Hinderbesluit", published in the Stb 1988, p. 433).

The following are said to correspond to the third indent of Article 5(1)(c) of the Directive:

— Articles 14 and 26 of the Hinderwet,

— Articles 2(1) and 4(1)(a) of the Royal Decree of 15 September 1988 concerning major accident hazards (the "Besluit inzake risico's van zware ongevallen", published in the Stb 1988, p. 432).

The Dutch Government admits that only Articles 8(1) and 10(1) have not been incorporated in Dutch law.

(10) Reference is made to the Report for the Hearing for a fuller account of the facts of the case, the course of the procedure and the parties's submissions and arguments, which are mentioned or discussed hereinafter only in so far as is necessary for the reasoning of the Court.

Article 3 of the Directive

(11) Article 2 of the Hinderwet lays down a general prohibition on setting up or operating establishments likely to create a danger, hazard or inconvenience outside the establishment, and on extending or altering such establishments or changing the working methods used therein, without special authorisation. The manager of the establishment has a duty to give notice of any alteration in the establishment and in working methods to the authority which has power to authorise such alterations and also to the inspector and head of the district, the authorities of the province and the local authority where the whole or part of the establishment is situated. Under Article 17(1) of the Hinderwet, an authorisation is accompanied by directions necessary for preventing or limiting the dangers, hazards or inconveniences likely to arise outside the establishment. These directions may include an obligation to arrange for means of preventing or limiting specified dangers, hazards or inconveniences, an obligation to take measures in accordance with a stated method to determine whether the establishment creates or is likely to create a danger, hazard or inconvenience outside, or again an obligation to notify the results of the measures taken to the administrative authorities designated for that purpose.

(12) The Wet inzake de luchtverontreiniging also provides for a number of measures for the prevention and reduction of atmospheric pollution caused by the types of establishment referred to by the Order of 23 May 1972 implementing Article 19(1) of the said Law. Pursuant to Article 42 of the Law, if, as a result of an emergency in an establishment, the air is polluted or threatened with pollution to such an extent that it creates a significant risk to health, or causes intolerable inconvenience or serious damage, adequate measures must be taken immediately to put an end to the situation. The mayor of the local authority where the establishment is situated must be informed immediately of the emergency and the measures taken. These obligations must be carried out by the director of the establishment and the personnel responsible for safety.

(13) Articles 1, 12 and 13 of the Brandweerwet, in conjunction with the Besluit bedrijfs brandweren, create an obligation for local authorities to set up a fire brigade and impose a similar obligation on the directors or managers of

establishments likely to create a special risk for public safety. The establishment's internal firefighting service must meet the requirements concerning the number of personnel and equipment laid down by the local authorities. The director or manager of an establishment must ensure that the firefighting service follows the instructions given for that purpose by the person legally responsible for the actual management of measures against fires and other internal hazards.

(14) Article 2 of the Wet milieugevaarlijke stoffen provides that any person who by way of business produces a substance or preparation, makes it available to a third party, imports it or uses it in the Netherlands and who knows, or ought reasonably to have suspected, that these activities create a danger to humans and the environment is required to take all the measures which he may reasonably be expected to take to keep the danger to the minimum possible.

(15) The Commission observes that the obligation laid down by Article 3 of the Directive, which requires Member States to ensure that manufacturers are obliged to take all the measures necessary to prevent major accidents and to limit their consequences for man and the environment, has been disregarded. The Commission considers that this general obligation ought to have been fulfilled by a rule which is binding on the competent national authorities. However, Article 17 of the Hinderwet is said to give the Dutch authorities a discretionary power with regard to the grant of authorisations to the industrial establishments in question and with regard to specifying the accompanying directions and as to whether they are optional or mandatory.

(16) According to the Dutch Government, the first sentence of Article 17(1) of the Hinderwet obliges the competent authorities to grant authorisations and accompany them with the necessary directions to prevent and limit the dangers, hazards or inconveniences likely to arise outside the establishment. The fact that the list of specific measures mentioned in the second sentence of that paragraph is given by way of example does not mean that the rule set out in the first sentence is not mandatory. Furthermore, the first sentence applies to "dangers, hazards or inconveniences" and therefore, it is said, has a wider ambit than Article 3 of the Directive, which is confined to "major accidents". The Dutch Government adds that the prevention or limitation of major-accident hazards by compulsory individual authorisations, accompanied by directions adapted to the nature and specific situation of the establishment, are more effective than a general rule which in any case has to be amplified for every instance. Finally, the Dutch Government observes that the Wet inzake de luchtverontreiniging, the Brandweerwet, the Besluit bedrijfs brandweren and the Wet milieugevaarlijke stoffen contribute to implementing Article 3 of the Directive.

(17) It should be observed that, in accordance with settled case law (cf. the judgment of 30 May 1991, *E.C. Commission* v. *Federal Republic of Germany*, Case C–59/89, not yet published in E.C.R., para. 18), the incorporation of a directive into national law does not necessarily require the formal repetition of its rules word for word in an express, specific statutory provision and may, depending on its content, be satisfied in a general legal context, provided that the latter effectively ensures full application of the directive in a way which is sufficiently clear and precise so that, if the directive aims to create rights for individuals, they will be able to ascertain the full extent of their rights and to rely on them before the national courts, if necessary.

(18) In this connection it should be borne in mind that the objective of Directive 82/501 consists in the adoption of the measures necessary to prevent major accidents caused by certain industrial activities and to limit their consequences. Pursuant to Article 1 of the Directive, the activity covered is any operation carried out in an industrial installation referred to in Annex I involving, or possibly involving, one or more dangerous substances and capable of presenting major accident hazards, and also transport carried out within the establishment for internal reasons and the storage associated with this operation within the establishment (Article 1(2)(a), first indent). It follows that the ambit of this obligation is very wide and that its implementation involves the existence or enactment of a number of provisions covering all these activities and ensuring that each manufacturer is required to take measures suited to the type of industrial activity in question, in order to avoid major accidents and to avoid the consequences for man and the environment.

(19) It must be said that, like the Directive, all the national legislation to which the Dutch Government refers has the objective of the adoption of specific, effective measures for preventing major accidents and any consequences they may have outside the establishment.

(20) Firstly, the Hinderwet sets up a system of prior, compulsory authorisation accompanied by the necessary directions to prevent or limit any danger, hazard or inconvenience.

(21) Secondly, the authorisation which must be granted to industrial establishments likely to cause atmospheric pollution is, under the Wet inzake de luchtverontreiniging, also accompanied by specific directions, depending on the activity in question.

(22) Finally, Article 2 of the Wet milieugevaarlijke stoffen requires any person carrying out operations likely to create a danger to man and the environment to take measures to limit such danger, and thus meets the requirements of Article 3 of the Directive.

(23) It follows from what has been said that the implementation of Article 3 of the Directive is ensured by the specific mandatory national measures which fulfil the obligations of the Kingdom of the Netherlands under Article 189 of the EEC Treaty.

Article 4 of the Directive

(24) Pursuant to Article 5 of the Hinderwet, an application for authorisation to open, operate, extend or alter an establishment must be submitted together with a large number of particulars which are set out in Article 2 of the Hinderbesluit and relate to the safety measures taken to identify and prevent major-accident hazards. Articles 30 *et seq.* of the Hinderwet provides that the officials responsible for checking the application of the Law shall have access to the documents and the premises of the establishment if this is reasonably necessary for performing their task, in which they must be given assistance by the manufacturer and his employees.

(25) The Commission considers that, under Article 4 of the Directive, manufacturers

have a continuing, general obligation to prove at any time that they have identified the major-accident hazards existing by reason of technical developments or changes in production. According to the Commission, the fact that a manufacturer has to submit a report on external safety with the application for authorisation does not fulfil this obligation. Moreover, the Commission takes the view that Articles 30 *et seq.* of the Hinderwet does not conform with Article 4 of the Directive because the former sections concern only controls relating to the information contained in the application for authorisation and to the accompanying directions.

(26) The Dutch Government contends that Article 4 of the Directive does not entail an obligation for manufacturers to prove at any time that they have taken the measures necessary for preventing major accidents. It considers that the Commission's assertion on this point renders Article 6 of the Directive devoid of purpose. It adds, however, that in any case Articles 30 *et seq.* of the Hinderwet creates an obligation for continuous information on the particulars furnished in support of an application for authorisation and on the directions contained in it and therefore that Dutch law conforms to Article 4 of the Directive.

(27) It should be observed that Article 4 of the Directive creates an obligation for manufacturers to prove to the competent authority at any time that they have identified existing major-accident hazards and have adopted the measures laid down by that provision, and that this obligation is reproduced in the Dutch legislation.

(28) Under Articles 30 *et seq.* of the Hinderwet, the national officials responsible for applying that Act may at any time, firstly, require a manufacturer to provide information concerning the particulars furnished in support of the application for authorisation, the directions accompanying it, and the books and other documents relating to the establishment and, secondly, carry out inspections on the site accompanied, if necessary, by other persons, and take samples or inspect property if this is reasonably necessary for performing their task of control. The task of control which entails an obligation for the manufacturer to co-operate and provide the information required amounts, so far as he is concerned, to an obligation of constant information.

(29) It should also be observed that, pursuant to Article 6 of the Directive, the Member States must take appropriate measures to ensure that the manufacturer, *inter alia*, revises the measures specified in particular in Article 4 of the Directive in the event of modification of an industrial activity which could have significant consequences as regards major-accident hazards. Therefore one of the objectives of Article 6 is to impose on the Member State an obligation to compel the manufacturer to identify major-accident hazards arising from changes and to modify accordingly measures concerning information, training and the equipment of persons working on the site in order to ensure its safety.

(30) Likewise Article 5(3) of the Directive provides for the updating of the notification specified in paragraph 1 of the same Article to take account of new technical knowledge relative to safety and of developments in knowledge concerning the assessment of hazards.

(31) In so far as the Commission does not complain of failure in respect of the updating obligations provided for by Article 5(3) and 6 of the Directive, it must be

deemed to admit that the Dutch measures conform to the objectives of these two provisions and, consequently, also to admit implicitly that the measures conform to the objectives of Article 4 of the Directive, as compliance with the obligations laid down by Article 5(3) and 6 of the Directive necessarily presupposes compliance with those of Articles 4 and 5(1) of the same Directive.

Article 5(1)(c), third indent, of the Directive

(32) Articles 14 and 26 of the Hinderwet provide that an authorisation to carry on an industrial activity is valid for the applicant and his legal successors, and that the competent authority for granting authorisation may alter or withdraw the directions accompanying it. Pursuant to Articles 2(1) and 4(1)(a) of the Besluit risico's van zware ongevallen, any person who controls an establishment where a dangerous substance is kept must every 5 years send the competent authority a report on external safety, containing a general description of the establishment, the substances therein and their properties.

(33) In the Commission's opinion, these provisions permit identification of the person legally responsible for safety, but not the competent body or individual on the spot from whom the authorities may seek assistance in the event of an accident.

(34) According to the Dutch Government, the general context of the Hinderwet, particularly Articles 14 and 26, and Article 1(1)(a) of the Besluit inzake risico's van zware ongevallen, permit identification of the holder of an authorisation who has the task of securing compliance with all statutory obligations, including those relating to the external safety of the establishment. The holder of the authorisation is said to be responsible for safety, to have a certain decision-making power in this respect and therefore he corresponds to the person or qualified body within the meaning of Article 5(1)(c), third indent, of the Directive. Therefore, it is said, the Dutch legislation conforms to that provision.

(35) On this point it should be observed that the notification provided for by Article 5(1)(c), third indent, of the Directive must contain the names of the person or the qualified body authorized to set the emergency plans in motion and to alert the competent authorities. This presupposes *de facto* power to put into effect the safety measures necessary in the event of an accident. It follows that the said provision refers not only to the person with legal responsibility for safety, including the external safety of the establishment, but also the person with the task of achieving such safety in practice.

(36) It must be said that the provisions cited by the Dutch Government do not permit identification of the person responsible for setting emergency plans in motion and alerting the authorities in the event of a major accident.

(37) Consequently the Commission's complaint regarding the implementation of Article 5(1)(c), third indent, of the Directive must be allowed.

Articles 8(1) and 10(1) of the Directive

(38) The Dutch Government, while pointing out that legislative initiatives are under way for implementing Articles 8(1) and 10(1) of the Directive, does not deny that these provisions have not been incorporated into Dutch law.

(39) In this connection it is sufficient to observe that, at the date of expiry of the period allowed in the reasoned opinion, no measure necessary for ensuring the application of these provisions had been taken.

(40) It follows that the Commission's action is justified with regard to Articles 8(1) and 10(1) of the Directive.

(41) In view of the whole of the foregoing, it must be found that, by not adopting within the prescribed periods all the laws, regulations and administrative provisions necessary for complying with Article 5(1)(c), third indent, Article 8(1) and Article 10(1) of Council Directive 82/501/EEC on the major-accident hazards of certain industrial activities, the Kingdom of the Netherlands has failed to fulfil its obligations under the EEC Treaty.

Costs

(42) Under Article 69(2) of the Rules of Procedure, the unsuccessful party is to be ordered to pay the costs if they are applied for in the successful party's pleadings.

(43) As the Kingdom of the Netherlands is only partly unsuccessful and the Commission has partly withdrawn its action, each party should be ordered to pay its own costs.

On those grounds,

THE COURT

hereby:

1. Declares that, by not adopting within the prescribed periods all the laws, regulations and administrative provisions necessary for complying with Article 5(1)(c), third indent, Article 8(1) and Article 10(1) of Council Directive 82/501/ EEC on the major-accident hazards of certain industrial activities, the Kingdom of the Netherlands has failed to fulfil its obligations under the EEC Treaty.

2. Dismisses the action in other respects.

3. Orders each party to pay its own costs.

COMMENTARY

(1) This judgment, the only one on Directive 82/501 to this day, followed proceedings which took, between the first letter of formal notice and the judgment, six and a half years, though it was concerned purely with legal questions. This is mainly due to the difficulties in finding out what the relevant Dutch legislative provisions were. The report for the hearing lists 15 pieces of

legislation, the first of which dates from 1934 and concerns worker protection, environmental protection, and measures to combat accidents and their consequences.[5] It might not be easy for the operator of an industrial installation to know precisely his rights and obligations as regards accident prevention, not to mention workers inside the installation or the persons living next to such an installation.

The Advocate General, not the Court itself, made some observations on the usefulness of bringing such a case to the Court, stating more or less clearly that this might be a waste of resources.[6] He rightly pointed out that the issue of the case depended largely on the degree of precision which the Court asked for as regards the transposition of a directive into national law. To that extent the Advocate General pointed out that the Commission, in its pleadings, had referred to the Court's case law which requested a detailed and precise transposition of directives, whereas the Dutch government had referred to case law which referred to the general legal framework that existed in a Member State.[7]

(2) The Court tackled the different provisions one by one. As regards Article 3 of the Directive,[8] the Court first described the content of Dutch law, then the opinions of either party, followed by an interpretation of the general objective of Directive 82/501—not of its Article 3 only![9]—and concluded that altogether the Dutch legislation complied with the objectives of the Directive. This conclusion is supported by three short references to provisions in the Dutch legislation.[10]

The Commission pointed out that Article 3 contained a specific, autonomous obligation on the manufacturer permanently to take measures in order to prevent accidents and limit their consequences both for human beings and the environment. The summary assessment by the Court of the Dutch legislation hardly goes into this matter: the references to the Dutch Hinderwet[11] and the Wet inzake de luchtverontreiniging[12] only concern the authorisation to start an industrial activity and thus do not deal with the necessity to take preventive measures during the operation of the installation. The Wet milieugevaarlijke stoffen[13] corresponds, so the Court stated in a very short remark, to the requirements of Article 3. However, the Advocate General expressly stated his conviction that this rule does not ensure that the manufacturer continuously takes preventive measures.[14] Thus, the Court's reluctance to explain why its

---

[5] See the Report for the Hearing, para. 8.
[6] Advocate General Gulmann, opinion in Case C–190/90, n. 5, last para.
[7] *Ibid.* and notes 5 and 6.
[8] The text of this provision is reproduced in the judgment, para. 3.
[9] See para. 18.
[10] See paras. 20 to 22.
[11] Para. 20.
[12] Para. 21.
[13] Para. 22.
[14] See Advocate General (n. 6 above), para. 12.

conclusion was reached, might be regretted. It is however clear that the practical differences between the diverging interpretations are relatively small. Indeed, much if not all will depend on the question of how the Dutch authorities actually enforce Article 2 of the Dutch Wet milieugevaarlijke stoffen: if they seriously control manufacturers and installations as regards (environmental) accident prevention measures, the objectives of the Directive will be reached; if they fail to do so, the objectives will not be reached. But then, another wording of the Dutch legislation would probably not ensure better compliance either.

(3) As regards Article 4 of the Directive[15] similar considerations were made by the Court. The Court described the Dutch legislation, summed up the arguments of the parties and then gave its arguments. These arguments surprise a bit: indeed, the Court discussed the Dutch legislation which entitles the administration to check at any moment whether the legal dispositions are actually complied with inside an installation.

This possibility for the administration implies, according to the Court, an obligation on the manufacturer to co-operate and to give the requested information. Thus, there is an obligation for the manufacturer to inform the administration at any time of preventive measures which have been taken.[16] The "passive" obligation to answer questions and give information that was asked for is seen as fulfilling the Directive's objective to make the manufacturer become active and provide information.

Again, it seems doubtful whether all manufacturers will read such an obligation into the text of the Dutch Hinderwet,[17] in other words, whether they will know sufficiently well their obligations flowing out of Article 4 of the Directive.

The Dutch legislation only referred to safety measures taken at the beginning of the operation of the installation and included in the request for an authorisation. Subsequent safety measures were not included. However, Directive 82/501 dealt with subsequent changes in Article 6, a provision which the Commission had finally[18] not raised before the Court. Thus the Court stated that the Commission had to be considered as having accepted the compliance of Dutch legislation with the provision of the Directive in this regard.[19]

(4) This passage in the Court's judgment raises the more general problem of who has or who should have standing in environmental matters. If we suppose for a second that the Commission's agent was wrong in not tackling the question of subsequent safety measures before the Court: should this be to the

---

[15] The text of this provision is reproduced in the judgment, para. 4.

[16] The wording of Article 4 seems, in that context, rather obvious.

[17] The content of the Dutch Hinderwet is described in the Advocate General's conclusions, para 16.

[18] In the proceedings under Article 169 the Commission had, prior to its application to the Court, raised these questions, but at the end of the day decided not to submit them to the Court's judgment, see the conclusions of the Advocate General, para. 20 and note 12.

[19] Para. 31.

detriment of safety standards for human beings and the environment? Or, more generally, who can bring an action to a court in the name of the environment? Who may sue in cases of a destruction of flora or fauna habitats, in cases where a species is exterminated, where trees are cut, where groundwater is polluted, where the coastal waters are contaminated, where the air is polluted etc?

The traditional legal systems in all 12 Member States mainly allow court actions where attributed items of property are affected. The owner of a tree which was cut might bring an action, but not a person who is just interested in the urban environment remaining green. An action in the name of the trees,[20] in the name of the environment generally or—even broader—court actions in the public interest are almost impossible in all Member States, though it is true to say that, especially in matters of nature protection some Member States have given a right of action to environmental organisations.

These problems with the traditional legal systems also exist when one turns to the question of what can be asked for in a court action. Lawyers have not been able to put a price on the environment: the disappearance of a species, the destruction of the ozone layer, the pollution of surface or ground- or marine water, the climate change or the gradual death of forests are not, at present, defined in financial terms. This becomes even more obvious in cases involving Community law: where the Commission is of the opinion that a chemical company has failed to take the necessary safety measures under Directive 82/501 and that this has resulted in an accident,[21] it may bring an action before the European Court against the responsible Member State. The Court may then declare that a Member State has failed to fulfil its obligation under the EEC Treaty.[22] Where the Commission finds that the same company has infringed the Community rules on competition, it may impose fines or pecuniary sanctions on that company.[23]

The Court, as is usual, did not touch upon all these questions, but remained within the classical procedural concepts that the Commission had not raised problems of Article 6 of Directive 82/501 and was therefore to be treated as if it had thus accepted the compatibility of Dutch law with Directive 82/501.[24] Under the present rules of procedure of the Court, no other solution could possibly have been achieved.

(5) The third point that was examined by the Court was whether Dutch law

---

[20] See in this regard, *e.g.* Ch. Stone, *Should Trees Have Standing?* (Los Altos/California, 1974).

[21] Until 1988, there were 34 major accidents reported under the Directive, see Commission, Report on the application in the Member States of Directive 82/501 of June 24, 1982 on the major-accident hazards of certain industrial activities, COM(88)261 final of May 18, 1988, Annex II.

[22] See **Article 171** EEC: "If the Court of Justice finds that a Member State has failed to fulfil an obligation under this Treaty, the State shall be required to take the necessary measures to comply with the judgment of the Court of Justice."

[23] See in particular Reg. 17: [1962] O.J. 13/204, Arts. 15 to 17.

[24] This provision is reproduced in para. 5 of the judgment.

had fully complied with Article 5(1)c, third indent, of Directive 82/501. The dispute focused on the question whether the name of the person, who is actually responsible for taking the factual steps in order to ensure the safety on-site and off-site was to be given to the public authorities, or whether that of the person who is legally responsible was enough.[25] The Court, in conformity with the opinion of the Advocate General, concluded that manufacturers had to give the name of the person who is actually responsible for the safety inside and outside the installation. The wording of the third indent indeed shows that it must be the name of the person who is naturally capable "to set the emergency plans in motion and to alert the competent authorities." This responsibility goes beyond that of the manufacturer himself.

This part of the judgment may have a considerable impact on industrial companies. Indeed, it is of great importance in a major accident to know precisely who is responsible for safety measures in a specific installation in order to determine civil and criminal responsibilities, to check whether the safety measures were appropriate and whether the internal organisational structure of the company was adequate. In particular in the case of companies which have a number of different industrial installations, it is important for the competent authorities to have available, at any moment, the name of the person responsible in order to ask him to take safety measures for instance, or to set an emergency plan in motion.

Companies, on the other hand, must have an interest to protect their staff and not to reveal the individual responsibilities inside the company. However, since in the question of major-accident hazards, there is a considerable amount of general interest in seeing the safety measures properly controlled and applied, this private interest has, in my opinion, rightly been set aside by Directive 82/501 and by the Court.

(6) The Court further stated that the Netherlands had not properly transposed Articles 8 and 10(1) of the Directive; this failure was recognised by the Dutch government so that the Court did not go into any further detail.

From the point of view of the environment, it might be significant that both articles 8 and 10(1) which introduce new obligations in order to protect human beings and the environment, were not transposed into Dutch law. Indeed, many of the other provisions of the Directive concern aspects which were, in several Member States, covered by legislation on workers' protection. The protection of the general public and of the environment is not really part of traditional labour law, and a detailed analysis of national law—which the Court had no reason to undertake in the present case—might show to what extent major-accident hazards are linked in their legal concept to accidents affecting man rather than the environment.

(7) Looking at the judgment in general, one might wonder whether the Advo-

---

[25] See also the detailed conclusions of the Advocate General, on this question, paras. 26 to 30.

cate General's observation on the waste of human resources is correct. In that respect it should be pointed out that the Netherlands has adopted four of its 15 relevant pieces of legislation during the time where the Commission had opened formal proceedings under Article 169.[26] And that three provisions of the Directive had not or not correctly been transposed into Dutch law 10 years after the adoption of the Directive, by a Member State which is—rightly— considered to be an environmentally progressive Member State.

Directive 82/501 was adopted in 1982 after a number of serious industrial accidents inside and outside the Community and in particular an accident at Seveso (Italy) in 1978. It was amended in 1987;[27] in 1988, following an accident in Basel (Switzerland) in 1986, when the storage of certain chemicals was included into the Directive.[28] The Commission has announced, for 1993, a proposal for a fundamental revision of the Directive.[29]

The Directive is generally seen as an important instrument for the prevention of accidents. Its structure and details have led to several third countries imitating it in their effort to prevent accidents rather than, via a system of sophisticated liability rules, trying to mitigate the negative consequences of accidents.

---

[26] See the enumeration in the report for the hearing, para. 8.
[27] Dir. 87/216: [1987] O.J. L85/36.
[28] Dir. 88/610: [1988] O.J. L336/14.
[29] See Commission (n. 21 above), para. 3.3 (p. 51).

20. A COMMUNITY-WIDE MARKET FOR CHEMICALS

**Judgment of the Court of October 14, 1987
in Case 278/85**

E.C. Commission v. *Denmark*

[1987] E.C.R. 4069

FACTS AND PROCEDURE[1]

Directive 67/548 provides for rules on the classification, packaging and labelling of dangerous substances.[2] The sixth amendment of this Directive, made by Directive 79/831 introduced, amongst others, a system of notification to public authorities before a new substance is marketed.[3]

The Commission was of the opinion that several provisions of the Danish legislation, which implemented Directive 79/831, were not in conformity with the requirements of that Directive. Therefore it sent, on January 28, 1984, a letter of formal notice to the Danish Government, which answered on April 30, 1984. The Commission was not entirely satisfied with the answer and on December 28, 1984, sent a reasoned opinion, to which the Danish Government replied on April 23, 1985.

The Commission applied to the Court; its application was registered on September 11, 1985. Oral hearings took place on February 11, 1987. The Advocate General presented his opinion on April 7, 1987.

JUDGMENT

(1) By an application lodged at the Court Registry on 11 September 1985, the Commission of the European Communities brought an action under Article 169 of the EEC Treaty for a declaration that by not adopting all the laws, regulations and administrative provisions necessary to comply with Council Directive 79/831/EEC of 18 September 1979 amending for the sixth time Directive 67/548/EEC on the approximation of the laws, regulations and administrative provisions relating to the classification, packaging and labelling of dangerous substances (Official Journal 1979, L 259, p. 10), the Kingdom of Denmark had failed to fulfil its obligations under the EEC Treaty.

(2) The Commission considers that certain provisions of the Danish legislation adopted to implement Directive 79/831/EEC, in particular provisions of Law No 212 of 23 May 1979 on chemical substances and products (hereinafter referred to as 'the Law') and of Decree No 409 of the Ministry of the Environment of 17 September 1980 on the notification of chemical substances (hereinafter referred to as 'the Decree'), do not adequately transpose the directive into national law.

(3) Reference is made to the Report for the Hearing for a fuller account of the facts

---

[1] Summary by the author.
[2] Dir. 67/548: [1967] O.J. L196/1.
[3] Dir. 79/831: [1979] O.J. L259/10.

of the case, the course of the procedure and the submissions and arguments of the parties, which are mentioned or discussed hereinafter only in so far as is necessary for the reasoning of the Court.

(4) Before the individual complaints made by the Commission with regard to the Danish legislation are examined, it is appropriate to describe the scheme of Directive 67/548/EEC, as amended by Directive 79/831/EEC (hereinafter referred to as 'the Directive').

The scheme of the Directive

(5) Directive 79/831/EEC amends for the sixth time Directive 67/548/EEC, which laid down the basic rules on the classification, packaging and labelling of dangerous substances and preparations.

(6) Directive 79/831/EEC introduced certain amendments to that scheme in the form, in particular, of reinforced controls in order—as is stated in the first recital of the preamble to the Directive—to protect man and the environment against potential risks which could arise from the placing on the market of new substances.

(7) The Directive contains, first of all, rules governing the placing on the Community market of new substances and, secondly, rules governing old dangerous substances, that is to say substances which were placed on the market prior to 18 September 1981, the date on which the amendments introduced by Directive 79/831/EEC entered into force, and which were previously governed by the preceding provisions.

(8) As regards new substances, Article 6 of the Directive requires any manufacturer or importer into the Community, at the latest 45 days before a substance is placed on the market, to submit to the competent national authority appointed by the Member State in accordance with Article 7 of the Directive a notification including a technical dossier supplying the information necessary for evaluating the foreseeable risks and the information and results of scientific studies and the methods used, a declaration concerning the unfavourable effects of the substance in terms of the various uses envisaged, the proposed classification and labelling of the substance and proposals for any recommended precautions relating to the safe use of the substance. Under Article 13(2) of the Directive, all substances so notified are to be included on a list kept by the Commission. In addition, all notification dossiers and information received by the Member States are to be forwarded by the Commission to the other Member States. Provision is also made for direct consultation between the competent authorities of the Member States and the Commission. Paragraphs (2) and (3) of Article 6 provide for simplified procedures for the notification of substances which have already been notified. Lastly, Article 6(4) lays down an obligation to provide information about substances already notified in the event of changes in the quantities placed on the market, new knowledge of the effects of the substance, new uses or any change in the properties of the substance.

(9) As regards old substances, that is to say those already placed on the market before 18 September 1981, the Directive lays down different rules. Article 13(1) requires the Commission to draw up an inventory of such substances, on the

basis in particular of information provided by the Member States. Article 1(4) provides that the obligation to notify does not apply to old substances until six months after the publication of the inventory and, six months after publication of the inventory, to substances which appear in that inventory. Furthermore, the second subparagraph of Article 5(2) provides that substances included in the list or already on the market before 18 September 1981 must be packaged and labelled in accordance with the rules of the Directive.

(10) In addition, there are provisions in the Directive which apply to both old and new substances. In particular, Article 22 provides that the Member States may not prohibit, restrict or impede the placing on the market of any substances which comply with the Directive, whether old or new, on grounds relating to notification, classification, packaging or labelling.

(11) Article 23 also applies to all substances covered by the Directive. It provides that where a substance, although satisfying the requirements of the Directive, constitutes a hazard for man or the environment, a Member State may provisionally prohibit the sale of that substance or subject it to special conditions in its territory; however, the Member State concerned must immediately inform the Commission and the other Member States of such action and, after consulting the Member States within six weeks, the Commission must give its view without delay and take the appropriate measures.

(12) It is clear from that description of the scheme of the Directive that the Community legislature has laid down an exhaustive set of rules governing the notification, classification, packaging and labelling of substances, both old and new, and that it has not left the Member States any scope to introduce other measures in their national legislation.

The individual complaints

Article 11(2) of the national law

(13) Article 11(2) of the law provides as follows:

'A chemical substance shall be regarded as new if it has not been placed on the market or imported into Denmark as a chemical substance or constituent of a chemical product before 1 October 1980.'

(14) The Commission complains that, in adopting that provision, the Danish Government departed from the Directive by fixing a date prior to 18 September 1981 and by thus imposing an obligation to notify even substances placed on the market before 18 September 1981 and exempting only substances placed on the market before 1 October 1980.

(15) The Danish Government acknowledges that the obligation to notify imposed by the national provision is wider than that provided for in the Directive, but denies that the provision is contrary to the Directive. It maintains that the Directive is not meant to regulate 'old substances', that is to say substances which were placed on the market before 18 September 1981; such substances therefore continue to be subject to national rules.

(16) It should be noted in the first place, that Directive 79/831/EEC is designed to attain two objectives: the protection of the population and the environment and the elimination of obstacles to trade in dangerous substances in the Community. Although it is true that in its preamble Directive 79/831/EEC refers only to the first objective, it should not be overlooked that the second objective is mentioned in the preamble to Directive 67/548/EEC, to which Directive 79/831/EEC merely introduced amendments, intended in particular to reinforce the controls provided for; the second objective is also referred to in Article 22 of the Directive.

(17) Secondly, it must be pointed out that the date provided for in the Directive, 18 September 1981, was meant to be the date from which both objectives, in particular the measures concerning the obligation to notify new substances, were to take effect. It follows that in the Directive the Community legislature has laid down exhaustive rules on this point and that it has not left the Member States any scope to introduce earlier or later dates in their rules adopted to implement the Directive.

(18) It follows from the foregoing that the Danish Government's argument cannot be upheld and that the Commission's complaint is well founded.

Article 11(3) of the national law

(19) Article 11(3) of the national law provides as follows:

'The provisions applicable to new chemical substances also apply to any chemical substance sold or imported into Denmark before 1 October 1980, where it is marketed or imported after that date for an essentially different use or in substantially larger quantities.'

(20) The Commission complains that in that provision the Danish Government requires fresh notification for substances already on the market, even though the Directive does not provide for such a possibility, and therefore the Member States cannot require notification of such substances.

(21) The Danish Government does not deny that the national legislation is drafted differently but maintains that the provision at issue is consistent with the general objective of the Directive, which is to protect man and the environment. The national provision has the same preventive purpose as the Directive. The protection of workers and of the population referred to in the sixth amendment to the original directive would be illusory if there was no fresh notification of substances sold in substantially larger quantities or used for essentially different purposes.

(22) As was stated when the first complaint was examined, the protection of man and the environment is only one of the objectives of the Directive; the other objective is to eliminate obstacles to trade in the substances in question within the Community. Consequently, the rules of the Directive relating to notification are not meant to be rules providing a minimum degree of protection which leave the Member States free to widen the obligations provided for therein, but are intended to be exhaustive.

(23) It follows that old substances may not be treated like new substances for the

purposes of notification and that this complaint of the Commission is also well founded.

Article 17 of the Law and Article 9(3) of the Decree

(24) Article 17 of the Danish Law provides as follows:

'The Minister may adopt provisions under which notification in another Member State of the European Communities may, on certain conditions, be regarded as notification in Denmark.'

(25) Pursuant to that enabling provision, the Minister of the Environment provided in Article 9(1) and (2) of the Decree that new substances imported into Denmark which have already been notified in another Member State are exempt from the obligation to notify. Article 9(3), however, provides as follows:

'As regards the chemical substances referred to in paragraphs (1) and (2) of this article, any importer into Denmark shall, however, be required to inform the National Agency for the Protection of the Environment prior to importation into Denmark of the substance concerned and to declare that that substance has been notified in another Member State of the Community in accordance with the provisions of paragraphs (1) and (2) of this article.'

(26) It appears from the explanations contained in the reply that the Commission complains that, in Article 9(3) adopted pursuant to Article 17 of the Law, the Danish Government requires importers to inform the competent Danish authority before they import into Denmark a substance already notified in another Member State. According to the Commission, that requirement is contrary to the Directive.

(27) The Danish Government contends that paragraphs (1) and (2) of Article 9 of the Decree exempt from fresh 'notification' in Denmark substances already notified in another Member State. Although Article 9(3) imposes an obligation to 'inform' the authorities, that obligation is compatible with the Directive and is intended to enable the competent authority to fulfil its obligation, laid down in Article 5 of the Directive, to check whether the pre-conditions for placing substances on the market have been satisfied.

(28) It must be stated that the mere requirement to 'inform' the authorities about imported substances is not in itself contrary to the Directive in view, in particular, of Article 5, which requires the Member States to take all the measures necessary to ensure that when substances are placed on the market the requirements regarding notification, packaging and labelling are observed.

(29) However, the obligation to inform the authorities laid down in Article 9(3) of the Decree is a pre-condition for importation and non-compliance results in the imposition of a penalty, provided for in Article 22(1) of the Decree. Furthermore, the required notice must be given to the same national authority, namely the National Agency for the Protection of the Environment, that is authorized to receive notification of substances placed on the market. Under those circumstances, such a requirement is liable to cause uncertainty among traders and to

create obstacles to intra-Community trade in the substances concerned, contrary to the provisions of the Directive.

(30) In that regard, reference should be made to Article 22 of the Directive, cited above, and to Article 10, whose purpose is precisely to establish a system for forwarding to the other Member States information received by the Commission following notifications communicated to it by the national authorities. Elsewhere in the Directive, provision is also made for the exchange of information between the Member States and the Commission in order to avoid the risks presented by dangerous substances without, however, creating unjustified obstacles to intra-Community trade.

(31) Consequently, the Commission's complaint is well founded.

Article 18 of the Decree

(32) Article 18 of the Decree provides as follows:

'*Derogation*

(1) In individual cases, the National Agency for the Protection of the Environment may grant a derogation from the provisions of Chapter II and of Article 12(1) of this Decree.
(2) The National Agency for the Protection of the Environment may also, in individual cases, grant a derogation from the provisions of Chapter III of this Decree.'

(33) In the reply, the Commission indicated that its action was directed against this provision, whereas in its original application it simply referred, in the section concerned with the Law, to 'Article 18'. Article 18 of the Law provides as follows:

'The Minister may adopt provisions relating to the analysis and notification of certain categories of chemical substances which do not need to be notified under Article 12(1), including provisions indicating the information which must be supplied at the time of such notification.'

(34) The Danish Government objects to such a change in the subject-matter of the action and also points out that, even in the reasoned opinion, the Commission did not state precisely the provision to which it objected but merely referred to 'Article 18' of the Danish legislation.

(35) It must be observed that both in the arguments and in the relevant conclusions of its application the Commission referred only to Article 18 of the Danish Law as a provision granting the Minister a discretionary power to grant exemptions not provided for by the Directive.

(36) However, in its reply, the Commission stated, in the light of explanations contained in the defence of the Danish Government, that it was 'changing' its complaint so as to direct it against Article 18 of the Decree.

(37) It is established case-law of the Court that a party may not change the subject-

matter of the dispute in the course of the proceedings. It follows that the substance of the application must be examined only with regard to the conclusions contained in the application originating the proceedings.

(38) It follows that the 'changed' complaint is not admissible and, consequently, that the complaint must be rejected.

Article 6 of the Decree

(39) Article 6 of Decree No 409/80 provides that:

'The new chemical substances listed below shall not be subject to the notification required in Article 5 of this Decree:

(1) Substances marketed or imported in quantities of less than one tonne per annum per manufacturer or importer ... '

(40) The Commission claims that because this provision grants exemption from notification both to the manufacturer and to the importer, it is contrary to the fourth indent of Article 8(1) of the Directive, which grants such exemption to the manufacturer alone. The widening of the exemption to include importers could give rise to abuse and undermine the possibilities of control afforded by the normal notification procedure.

(41) The Danish Government argues that the widening of the exemption to include importers is in line with the Council's wish to see importers and manufacturers treated in the same way in law, as is clear from a declaration made by the Council when the Directive was adopted. Furthermore, it does not consider that Article 6 of the Decree may give rise to any abuse.

(42) It should be borne in mind that one of the fundamental elements of the Directive is the obligation to notify, imposed on any manufacturer or importer in the Community of the substances in question, in order to control the effects on man and the environment, as is stated in the third recital of the preamble to the Directive. For that purpose, Articles 6 and 7 of the Directive lay down detailed rules regarding the notification procedure. According to those provisions, any new substance covered by the Directive must, as a general rule, be notified to the competent authorities before it is placed on the market by the manufacturer or importer.

(43) Exceptions to that rule are provided for in Article 8(1) of the Directive and are justified by the fact that, because the substances concerned are placed on the market in limited quantities or for scientific or research purposes, they may be controlled and the risks are limited. For that reason, the fourth indent of Article 8(1) exempts from the obligation to notify 'substances placed on the market in quantities of less than one tonne per year per manufacturer ... '. According to Article 2(1)(e) of the Directive, importation is deemed to be placing on the market for the purposes of the Directive.

(44) Considered in the light of the abovementioned provisions of the Directive, Article 6 of the Decree constitutes a widening of the exception provided for by

the Directive which was not intended by the Community legislature. Article 6 may be interpreted as meaning that the same manufacturer may place on the market, through different importers, quantities of substances of less than one tonne several times a year. This does not accord with the aim of the Directive of ensuring that the placing of new substances on the market without notification is restricted to small quantities and occurs only for precisely defined purposes, whilst it also renders the control of such substances ineffective.

(45) Consequently, the Commission's complaint is well founded.

(46) It follows from all the foregoing considerations that by not adopting all the laws, regulations and administrative provisions necessary to comply with Council Directive 79/831/EEC of 18 September 1979 amending for the sixth time Directive 67/548/EEC on the approximation of the laws, regulations and administrative provisions relating to the classification, packaging and labelling of dangerous substances, the Kingdom of Denmark has failed to fulfil its obligations under the Treaty.

Costs

(47) Under Article 69(2) of the Rules of Procedure, the unsuccessful party is to be ordered to pay the costs. Since the Danish Government has essentially failed in its submissions, it must be ordered to bear the costs.

On those grounds

THE COURT

hereby:

(1) Declares that by not adopting all the laws, regulations and administrative provisions necessary to comply with Council Directive 79/831/EEC of 18 September 1979 amending for the sixth time Directive 67/548/EEC on the approximation of the laws, regulations and administrative provisions relating to the classification, packaging and labelling of dangerous substances, the Kingdom of Denmark has failed to fulfil its obligations under the Treaty;

(2) Orders the Kingdom of Denmark to bear the costs.

COMMENTARY

(1) This judgment draws a line between national and Community competence in an area where the EEC has enacted legislation. Chemical substances in "products" or "goods"—in the terminology of the EEC Treaty—play an important economic role. At the same time it is obvious that chemicals, in the larger

sense, are one of the main causes of the present threat to the environment and in particular to flora and fauna.

The Court's judgment discussed Directive 67/548 on the classification, packaging and labelling of chemical substances.[4] This Directive was first adopted in 1967 long before the Community started its environmental policy. It is therefore not astonishing to find that Directive 67/548, in its recitals, did not even mention the environment; rather, this Directive concentrated on the aspects of health and safety of persons on the one hand, on the free circulation of chemical substances on the other hand. Environmental considerations were, in a significant amount, first introduced into Directive 67/548 when amended for the sixth time by Directive 79/831, adopted in 1979.[5] This change in emphasis is best illustrated by the different recitals; Directive 67/548 stipulates:

"Whereas any rules concerning the placing on the market of dangerous substances and preparations must aim at protecting the public, and in particular the workers using such substances and preparations;

Whereas the differences between the national provisions of the six member States on the classification, packaging and labelling of dangerous substances and preparations hinder trade ... and hence affect the establishment and functioning of the common market;

Whereas it is therefore necessary to remove such hindrances; whereas this entails approximating the laws, regulations and administrative provisions on classification, packaging and labelling; ... "[6]

(2) In contrast to that, Directive 79/831 states:

"Whereas to protect man and the environment against potential risks which could rise from the placing on the market of new substances, it is necessary to lay down appropriate measures and in particular to reinforce the recommendations provided in Council Directive 67/548 ... ;

Whereas it is necessary for these reasons to amend Directive 67/548 ... ;

Whereas in order to control the effects on man and the environment it is advisable that any new substance placed on the market be subjected to a prior study by the manufacturer or importer and a notification to the competent authorities conveying mandatorily certain informations ... "[7]

It appears thus, that the amendment of 1979 changed the emphasis of Directive 67/548 by introducing research, notification and information "prior" to the marketing of a substance. This emphasis is in line with the principle of

---

[4] See n. 2 above.
[5] See n. 3 above.
[6] Recitals 1 to 3.
[7] Recitals 1 to 3.

preventive action in environmental policy, which was introduced into the EEC Treaty in 1987.[8]

(3) Before the Court examined point by point the differences between Directive 67/548—as amended by Directive 79/831—and Danish law, it first developed its understanding of the general philosophy of the Directive.[9] The Court analysed the different provisions of the Directive on new chemical substances[10] and those dealing with existing chemical substances. Some provisions apply both to old and new substances. The Court concluded on the basis of this analysis that the Directive sets up a system of total harmonisation for old and for new chemical substances and has not left to Member States the possibility to introduce other, for instance more stringent measures at national level.[11]

This reasoning is convincing. Indeed, it would be difficult to imagine any other solution within the framework of an internal market, where national frontiers no longer may constitute economic frontiers. A specific problem arising from Article 100a(4) of the EEC Treaty[12] will be discussed below.

Having established the general philosophy of Directive 67/548, the Court turned to the individual points, which the Commission had raised.

(a) Definition of a new chemical substance

(4) Directive 67/548, as amended by Directive 79/831, introduces a notification system prior to the marketing of substances placed on the market after September 18, 1981.[13] All substances placed on the market before that date are thus "existing" substances for which an inventory was to be drawn up;[14] substances which were placed on the market after September 18, 1981 were "new" substances.

The date of September 18, 1981 came from the two-year delay of the entry into effect of Directive 79/831[15] which introduced the notification system.

The Danish law was adopted on May 23, 1979, shortly before Directive 79/831. It is not quite clear why Denmark did not wait until the formal adoption of

---

[8] **Article 130r(2)** EEC: "Actions by the Community relating to the environment shall be based on the principles that preventive actions should be taken . . . "

[9] Paras. 5 to 8.

[10] The notions of "new" and "existing" substances are not defined. It follows from Arts. 5(3) and 13 that a substance which was on the market within the Community on September 18, 1981 is an existing substance. If the substance is marketed inside the Community after September 18, 1981, it is a "new" substance.

[11] Para. 12.

[12] See the text of Art. 100a(4) p. 449 below.

[13] Dir. 67/548 in the version of Dir. 79/831, **Article 6**: "1 . . . any manufacturer or importer into the Community of a substance within the meaning of this directive shall be required to submit to the competent authority . . . a notification . . . "

[14] Dir. 67/548, **Article 13**: "1. The Commission shall, on the basis in particular of information provided by the Member States, draw up an inventory of substances on the Community market by 18 September 1981."

[15] Dir. 79/831, **Article 5**: "Not later than 18 September 1981 the Member States shall implement the laws . . . necessary to comply."

Directive 79/831, since most of the essential elements had been elaborated at Community level by May 1979. Maybe, the Danish Parliament wanted to confirm its independence.[16] As it stood, the Danish legislation fixed the "borderline" date between new and existing substances on October 1, 1980. Thus under Danish law, substances which were marketed between October 1, 1980 and September 18, 1981 were "new" substances whereas under Community legislation, they were "existing" substances.

The Court first reiterated the double purpose of Directive 67/548,[17] namely the protection of the environment and the elimination of barriers to trade. It then referred to its earlier remarks and repeated that the Directive provides for total harmonisation. This logically excluded the possibility for Denmark to set another "borderline" date than September 18, 1981.

(b) Existing substances marketed in different quantities or for different use

(5) This problem is linked to the previous one. Indeed, Danish legislation considered an "existing" substance to be a "new" substance—and thus subject to notification prior to marketing—when it was marketed in increased quantities or for a significantly different use.

There is no such rule in Directive 67/548, and the Court argued again that a system of total harmonisation could not allow Member States to introduce more stringent provisions; the necessity to eliminate barriers to trade requires uniform rules. Therefore, the provisions of Directive 67/548 must be seen as exhaustive provisions.

(c) The obligation to inform Danish authorities of any import into Denmark.

(6) Danish law imposed an obligation to inform the Danish authorities whenever dangerous substances were imported into Denmark. Directive 67/548 in the version of Directive 79/831 does not require any such information.

The Court argued in three ways.[18] It first pointed out that there is a criminal sanction in Danish law in any case where the information has not been given. Since the information is a condition for importing substances into Denmark this is a requirement which goes, *de facto*, beyond prior information and becomes a supplementary legal obligation. This argument was strengthened by the second argument of the Court which was taken from the fact that any

---

[16] Rehbinder-Stewart, *Environmental Protection Policy* (Berlin-New York, 1985) report on p. 342 of a similar attitude of the German Government and Parliament when Dir. 79/831 was transposed into national law: "During the debate in 1980 on the west German toxic substances bill, the government sought to claim political credit for several provisions in a proposed regulation on chemicals without making it clear that it was just incorporating the sixth amendment of the EC Directive on toxic substances into national law. Opponents of the bill called for stiffer control, which in some respects were clearly inconsistent with the Directive . . . "

[17] Para. 16.

[18] Paras. 29 and 30.

such information had to be given to the Danish administration which also received the notification. The two arguments together turn the "information" into a "notification". This was the reproach of the Commission,[19] though the Court did not expressly take it up. The Court argued instead that "uncertainty" was created among the economic agents and that the requirement constituted a barrier to trade.

The third argument of the Court was that there is already a system of information set up by Articles 10 and 22 of Directive 67/548[20] which, according to the implicit reasoning, is sufficient to ensure adequate information for the Danish authorities.

(7) There is one point in this reasoning where doubts arise. The Court argued[21] that information as such given to the Danish authorities is not contrary to the principles of Directive 67/548 since Article 5 provides that:

"The Member States shall take all the measures necessary to ensure that ... substances cannot be placed on the market on their own or in preparations unless the substances have been:

— notified to the competent authorities of one of the Member States in accordance with this Directive;
— packaged and labelled in accordance with ... "

However, Article 5(2) of Directive 67/548 provides:

"The measures referred to in the second indent of paragraph 1 shall apply until the substance is listed in Annex I or until a decision not to list it has been taken."

This provision indicates that "all measures necessary" referred to in Article 5(1) only apply as long as there is no Community decision which declares the chemical substance as "dangerous"—and lists it in Annex 1 to Directive 67/548—or as not dangerous. A general obligation to inform the Danish authorities of *all* substances marketed in Denmark thus goes too far, even if such an obligation is not accompanied by a criminal sanction.

---

[19] See para. 26.
[20] Dir. 67/548, in the version of Dir. 79/831, **Article 10**: "On receipt of the copy of notification ... the Commission shall forward:—the notification dossier or the summary thereof to the other Member States,—any other relevant information it has collected pursuant to this Directive to all Member States." **Article 22** does not contain any information system: "Member States may not, on grounds relating to notification, classification, packaging or labelling within the meaning of this Directive, prohibit, restrict or impede the placing on the market of substances which comply with the requirements of this Directive and the annexes thereto."
[21] Para. 28.

(8) Apart from that, one should be aware of the practical impact of even this "limited" obligation of information. The inventory of existing chemicals which were on the Community market on September 18, 1981, and which the Commission had to draw up under Article 13 of Directive 67/548 (in the version of Directive 79/831) has since been published.[22] It contains more than 100,000 substances. Out of these, some 2,500 have, in the meantime, been included in Annex 1 to Directive 67/548. There might be some one thousand more, which have not been listed because they are not considered "dangerous", though such decisions are not published. In practical terms, therefore, the import of more than 90,000 substances would be subject to prior information to the Danish authorities if one completely follows the Court's decision.

The well-known "Dassonville" formula of the Court,[23] which interprets the notion of technical barriers to trade, qualifies as such a measure having an effect equivalent to quantitative restrictions "all trading rules enacted by Member States which are capable of hindering, directly or indirectly, actually or potentially, intra-Community trade."

In my opinion, the obligation to provide even the mere information of the marketing of chemical substances in Denmark constitutes a barrier to trade, all the more since it is not clear what measures Danish authorities could take when they are informed of the thousands of economic transactions which are likely to take place every day.

(d) Derogation powers for Danish authorities[24]

(9) This complaint by the Commission was rejected by the Court since the Commission had not expressely clarified whether it had tackled article 18 of the Danish legislation or article 18 of the Danish Decree 409/80 of September 17, 1980. The Court's decision is certainly justified since the Commission had not been sufficiently clear and precise.[25]

In substance, it seems that both Danish provisions are inconsistent with Directive 67/548. Indeed, the system for chemical substances established by the Directive is a system of total harmonisation. It is based on the mutual confidence of Member States' administrative authorities that the measures fixed by the Directive are complied with everywhere, and on the assurance given to producers and Community importers that the conditions for notification, packaging and labelling are the same everywhere in the Community. In my opinion, this excludes the possibility for any national authority to grant derogations from the provisions of Directive 67/548, as article 18 of the Danish

---

[22] European Inventory of Existing Commercial Chemical Substances (EINECS), [1990] O.J. C146A/1.

[23] Case 8/74, *Dassonville*: [1974] E.C.R. 837, [1974] 2 C.M.L.R. 436, para. 5.

[24] Paras. 32 to 38.

[25] See also Case C–43/90, *Commission* v. *Germany*: [1992] I E.C.R. 1909, where the Court declared the Commission's application inadmissible, since the application was not sufficiently clear and precise. This case also concerned Dir. 67/548.

decree permits, or to put new conditions for the marketing of chemical substances, as article 18 of the Danish Decree allows.

(e) Marketing by an importer[26]

(10) Directive 67/548 exempts some chemical substances from notification requirements. As regards small quantities of chemical substances, Article 8(1) provides:

> "The substances listed below, shall be considered as having been notified within the meaning of this Directive when the following conditions are fulfilled: ... substances placed on the market in quantities of less than one tonne per year per manufacturer ... "

Denmark had legislated in a way which exempted substances which were marketed in quantities of less than one tonne per year per manufacturer *or importer*. Thus, a producer from a third country could market, within the Community, 12 tonnes of a chemical substance, without having to notify it, provided he used 12 different importers in the 12 Member States. The Court rightly rejected the Danish interpretation as being capable of leading to different results than envisaged by Directive 67/548.

The Court did not accept the Danish argument which invoked a statement in the Council's minutes, without further discussing it. This point was discussed in more detail in Case 429/85, which concerned the same interpretation of Article 8 of Directive 67/548.[27] The Italian Government also invoked the statement in the Council's minutes. The answer of the Court was plain and unambiguous:

> "The Italian Government ... maintains that the exemption was extended to importers following a declaration by the Council enacted in the minutes of the meeting at which the Directive was approved, which refers to the manufacturer or importer in order to avoid any discrimination between them. It must be observed in this regard that an interpretation based on a declaration by the Council cannot give rise to an interpretation different from that resulting from the actual wording of the fourth indent of Article 8(1) of the Directive."[28]

(11) It is clear that Member States' or Council's statements in the minutes of the Council, whether they have been published or not, cannot contribute to an interpretation of a text of Community legislation. However, it is also clear, that the political weight of such a statement may be considerable, for instance

---

[26] Paras. 39 to 45.
[27] Case 429/85, *Commission* v. *Italy.* [1988] E.C.R. 843, [1989] 3 C.M.L.R. 423.
[28] *Ibid.* paras. 8 and 9.

when the Commission considers starting infringement proceedings under Article 169 of the EEC Treaty.[29]

Since the Commission's decisions were almost all upheld, the Court stated the non-compliance of Danish legislation with the requirements of Directive 67/548 without listing individually the different complaints and without rejecting the Commission's complaints as regards the derogation powers. Denmark was also asked to pay all the costs.[30]

(12) There is one uncertainty which remains, as regards the effect of the Court's decision. As mentioned, the core of the Court's argument is that Directive 67/548 establishes a system of total harmonisation from which Member States may not derogate. In 1987, the EEC Treaty was amended and Article 100a was introduced which provided, for measures intended to achieve the internal market and necessitating adopting decisions:

"If, after adoption of a harmonisation measure by the Council acting by a qualified majority, a Member State deems it necessary to apply national provisions on grounds of major needs referred to in Article 36, or relating to protection of the environment or the working environment, it shall notify the Commission of these provisions. The Commission shall confirm the provisions involved after having verified that they are not a means of arbitrary discrimination or a disguised restriction on trade between Member States."

(13) In 1992, Directive 67/548 was amended by Council Directive 92/32,[31] which was based on Article 100a EEC Treaty and which replaced all the provisions of Directive 67/548. Supposing that Directive 92/32 was adopted by majority decisions,[32] two questions are of legal interest:

(1) Would Denmark or any other Member State now be allowed to introduce provisions which diverge from the system set up by Directive 67/548 in its version of Directive 92/32? As an example one might think of a system of prior authorisation instead of notification, or a different "borderline" date between "existing" and "new" substances.

---

[29] Another famous statement in the Council's minutes in environmental matters concerns Directive 75/440. The question in dispute was whether the Directive also applied to surface water, which, before being used for the production of drinking water, is filtered through the soil. Germany, which produces some 8 per cent. of its drinking water by way of filtering surface water through the soil, uses a statement in the Council's minutes in order not to apply Directive 75/440. See P. Kromarek, "Vergleichende Untersuchung über die Umsetzung der EG-Richtlinien Abfall und Wasser", *Umweltbundesamt*, Texte 9/87 p. 26.

[30] According to Art. 69(1) of the Court's Rules of Procedure, the losing party shall pay the costs of procedure. Under Art. 69(3) the Court may ask both parties to bear their own costs, if each party has partially lost. In the present case, the Court did not recur to Art. 69(3), obviously because the Commission's application was almost actively upheld.

[31] Dir. 92/32: [1992] O.J. L154/1.

[32] It is not possible from the published version of a directive to find out whether it was adopted by majority decision or unanimously. It is submitted that this should be made clear in the decision adopting the directive.

(2) Would the result be different, if the new directive was not an amendment of a directive which existed prior to 1987? As an example one might think of Directive 90/220 which is based on Article 100a and introduces a Community-wide notification system prior to the deliberate release of genetically modified organisms.[33]

(14) As regards the first question, the problem lies in the word "apply" in Article 100a.[34] There is some discussion among legal experts whether this means that Member States only may (continue to) apply legislation which existed already at the moment of adoption of the Community measures or whether they are also entitled to introduce new legislation. In our question the problem is slightly more complicated, because the original Directive 67/548 was adopted at a time, when Article 100a(4) did not yet exist.

This legal problem was ardently discussed when the Community considered the introduction of standards for cars requiring cars to be equipped with catalytic converters. Directive 70/720 had—at least for trade within the Community—set up a system of total harmonisation of technical standards.[35] After the amendment of the EEC Treaty by the Single European Act 1986, some Member States claimed the right, based on Article 100a(4), to introduce unilaterally technical or fiscal[36] standards which required cars to be equipped with catalytic converters.

Eventually, the EEC did reach an agreement on the introduction of standards for catalytic converters at Community level, and also fixed rules on fiscal incentives for promoting the equipment of new or used cars with such converters.[37] Therefore, no case under Article 100a(4) with regard to cars has appeared until now, though the new directives are all based on Article 100a.

(15) The final arbiter of the interpretation of Article 100a(4) will be the Court of Justice. Article 100a pursues a double objective: create uniform standards in order to achieve the internal market and ensure a high level of environmental[38] protection. In this understanding, Article 100a(4) has the function to prevent that, in a case of majority decision, a Member State has to lower its existing degree of environmental protection. If it were also possible to introduce new environmental legislation at national level, even after the adoption

---

[33] Dir. 90/220 on the deliberate release into the environment of genetically modified organisms: [1990] O.J. L117/15.

[34] See, by way of context, Art. 130t (n. 39 below) and Art. 118a(3) EEC, which both give the possibility to maintain or introduce more stringent protective measures.

[35] Dir. 70/220 on the approximation of the laws of the Member States relating to measures to be taken against air pollution by gases from positive-ignition engines of motor vehicles: [1970] O.J. L76/1.

[36] Fiscal measures which are introduced in order to ensure or facilitate compliance with a technical standard, are considered by some authors as technical barriers to trade. The Court of Justice has not yet finally decided on this question.

[37] See Directives amending Dir. 70/220: Dir. 88/76: [1988] O.J. L36/1; Dir. 88/436: [1988] O.J. L214/1; Dir. 89/458: [1989] O.J. L226/1; Dir. 89/491: [1989] O.J. L238/43; Dir. 91/441: [1991] O.J. L242/1.

[38] Art. 100a also aims at ensuring a high level of protection in the area of health, safety and consumer protection, see Art. 100a(3).

of common Community standards, then the first objective—the achievement of the internal market—could never be reached.

In my opinion, therefore, both questions have to be answered in the negative: Member States are not allowed to introduce new legislation which gives better protection to the environment where a directive was based on Article 100a. Article 100a is not worded in the same way as Article 130t of the EEC Treaty[39] and pursues a different purpose. Article 130t aims at the protection of the environment only, while Article 100a(4) aims at the protection of the environment and the completion of the Internal Market.

---

[39] **Article 130t** EEC: "The protective measures adopted in common pursuant to Article 130s shall not prevent any Member State from maintaining or introducing more stringent protective measures compatible with this Treaty."

21. NATIONAL RESTRICTIONS AND COMMUNITY MEASURES

**Judgment of the Court (Third Chamber) of November 7, 1989
in Case 125/88**

Preliminary ruling in the criminal proceedings pending before the
Gerechtshof, The Hague, against H. F. M. Nijman

[1989] E.C.R. 3533, [1991] 1 C.M.L.R. 92

FACTS AND PROCEDURE[1]

Mr. Nijman marketed a product called "Improsol" in the Netherlands, for use in the construction of buildings, which is intended to be injected into wooden cladding. This product was imported into the Netherlands from Sweden, possibly via other Member States. Mr. Nijman did not have a Dutch authorisation to market the product.

The Dutch authorities started criminal proceedings against him. During these proceedings, the Regional Court of Appeal of The Hague asked the European Court of Justice to give a preliminary ruling on the Community law aspects of the case.

The request was registered with the European Court on April 15, 1988. During the proceedings, written observations were submitted by Mr. Nijman, by the Governments of the Netherlands, Germany, Belgium and the United Kingdom and the E.C. Commission.

By decision of February 23, 1989 the Court assigned the case to the Third Chamber. Oral hearings took place on May 23, 1989, but it is not known who submitted oral arguments. The Advocate General delivered his opinion on June 13, 1989.

JUDGMENT

(1) By judgment of 29 January 1988, which was received at the Court Registry on 25 April 1988, the Gerechtshof, The Hague, referred to the Court for a preliminary ruling under Article 177 of the EEC Treaty two questions on the interpretation of Council Directive 79/117/EEC of 21 December 1978 prohibiting the placing on the market and use of plant-protection products containing certain active substances (Official Journal 1979, L 33, p. 36), Articles 30 and 36 of the Treaty and the Community provisions on commercial policy.

(2) The questions were raised in criminal proceedings brought against H. F. M. Nijman for infringement of the Bestrijdingsmiddelenwet (Law on plant-protection products) 1962. Article 2 of that law prohibits the sale, placing in stock or store, or use of any plant-protection product not shown to be authorized by it.

(3) Before the national court, Mr Nijman contends that the product 'Improsol', which is imported exclusively or mainly from Sweden, cannot be regarded as a plant-

---
[1] Summary by the author.

protection product within the meaning of the Bestrijdingsmiddelenwet 1962. The Gerechtshof considers that, in order to determine whether a substance or mixture of specific substances constitutes a plant-protection product within the meaning of the abovementioned law, it is necessary to take account of Directive 79/117/EEC. It has therefore stayed the proceedings and referred the following questions to the Court for a preliminary ruling:

'In the present state of Community law, and in particular in the light of Council Directive 79/117/EEC, prohibiting the placing on the market and use of plant-protection products containing certain active substances,

(1) Is a national court bound to interpret and apply the relevant provisions laid down in a national law containing rules on the marketing and use of plant-protection products (such as the Bestrijdingsmiddelenwet 1962), which must be regarded as implementing *inter alia* the aforesaid Directive 79/117/EEC, in such a way that the content and purpose of those rules fully correspond to those defined in the directive, notwithstanding a potentially different definition?

(2) What factors and circumstances would a national court take into account in deciding whether and to what extent a national law such as that referred to in Question 1 above, which prohibits the sale, placing in stock or storage or the use of a plant-protection product which is not shown to be permitted by that law and imposes a penalty in criminal law for failure to comply,

(a) constitutes an obstacle to trade which directly affects the establishment and functioning of the common market, as referred to in the directive,

(b) correctly and fully implements Directive 79/117/EEC, as required by Article 189 of the EEC Treaty, and

(c) is compatible or incompatible with other relevant rules of Community law, in particular with Article 30 of the EEC Treaty and any directly applicable Community rules on commercial policy, laid down in the framework of Part 3, Title II, Chapter 3, of the EEC Treaty?'

(4) Reference is made to the Report for the Hearing for a fuller account of the facts of the case, the relevant Community provisions, the course of the procedure and the submissions and arguments of the parties, which are mentioned or discussed hereinafter only in so far as is necessary for the reasoning of the Court.

The first question

(5) Having regard to the facts of the case, the first question must be understood as seeking to determine to what extent the national court must take account of Directive 79/117/EEC in interpreting a national law governing the marketing and use of plant-protection products.

(6) As the Court held in its judgment of 10 April 1984 in Case 14/83 *Von Colson and*

Kamann v *Land Nordrhein-Westfalen* [1984] ECR 1891, the Member States' obligation arising from a directive to achieve the result envisaged by the directive and their duty under Article 5 of the Treaty to take all appropriate measures, whether general or particular, to ensure the fulfillment of that obligation, is binding on all the authorities of Member States, including, for matters within their jurisdiction, the courts. It follows that national courts, in applying their national law, are required to interpret it in the light of the wording and the purpose of the directive in order to achieve the result referred to in the third paragraph of Article 189 of the Treaty.

(7) However, the prohibition imposed by Directive 79/117/EEC of marketing and using plant-protection products containing certain active substances applies only, by virtue of Article 3 thereof, to the substances listed in the annex. Directive 79/117/EEC does not therefore pursue complete harmonization of national rules concerning the marketing and use of plant-protection products.

(8) It must therefore be stated, in reply to the first question, that the court of a Member State is not bound to interpret national rules on the marketing and use of plant-protection products in the light of the wording and purpose of Directive 79/117/EEC for the purpose of applying that directive to products not containing any of the active substances listed in the annex to the directive.

The second question

(9) By its second question, the national court seeks to determine whether national legislation which, supported by penalties in criminal law, prohibits the sale, placing in stock or store or use of any plant-protection product which is not authorized by the Bestrijdingsmiddelenwet 1962, is compatible with Directive 79/117/EEC, Articles 30 and 36 of the Treaty and the Community provisions on commercial policy.

(10) As far as the compatibility of the national legislation with Directive 79/117/EEC is concerned, it is apparent from the answer to the first question that Directive 79/117/EEC covers only plant-protection products containing active substances listed in the annex to the directive. In the present case, the national court has established that the product 'Improsol' does not contain substances listed in the annex to the directive. The question of the compatibility of the national legislation with the directive does not therefore arise. Accordingly, it is unnecessary to reply to the first part of the second question.

(11) As to whether the national legislation meets the requirements of Articles 30 to 36 of the Treaty, it must first be borne in mind that those provisions apply without distinction to products originating in the Community and to those admitted into free circulation in any of the Member States, whatever the real origin of such products. It is therefore subject to those reservations that Articles 30 to 36 of the Treaty apply to the product 'Improsol'.

(12) In the present case, the prohibition, enforced by penalties in criminal law, of selling, storing or using any plant-protection product not authorized by a national law is capable of affecting imports from other Member States where the same product is admitted wholly or in part and thus of constituting a barrier to intra-Community trade. Such rules therefore constitute a measure having an effect equivalent to a quantitative restriction.

(13) However, it is undisputed that plant-protection products present significant risks to the health of humans and animals and to the environment, as the Court has held in relation to pesticides (see the judgments of 19 September 1984 in Case 94/83 *Albert Heijn BV* [1984] ECR 3263, paragraph 13, and of 13 March 1986 in Case 54/85 *Ministére public* v *Xavier Mirepoix* [1986] ECR 1067, paragraph 13). Those risks are also recognized in the fourth recital in the preamble to Directive 79/117/EEC, according to which 'the effects of these plant-protection products may not be wholly favourable for plant production . . . since, in the main, they are toxic substances or preparations having dangerous effects'.

(14) It is therefore for the Member States, pursuant to Article 36 of the Treaty and in the absence of full harmonization in this matter, to decide at what level they wish to set the protection of the life and health of humans, whilst at the same time taking account of the requirements laid down in the Treaty, in particular in the last sentence of Article 36, regarding the free movement of goods.

(15) It must therefore be stated in reply to the second part of the second question that, in an area which has not been fully harmonized at the Community level, Articles 30 and 36 do not preclude national legislation prohibiting the sale, placing in stock or storage or the use of a plant-protection product not authorized by such legislation and imposing a penalty in criminal law for failure to comply.

(16) Finally, as regards the compatibility of a law such as the Bestrijdingsmiddelenwet 1962 with the Community provisions on commercial policy, it must be stated that, according to the national court's findings, the product 'Improsol' is imported exclusively or mainly from Sweden. As the Commission observed, the question must therefore be understood as relating to the relevant provisions of the free-trade agreement between the European Economic Community and the Kingdom of Sweden (Official Journal, English Special Edition 1972 (31.12.1972), p. 99).

(17) Article 13(1) of that agreement provides that no new quantitative restriction on imports or measures having equivalent effect may be introduced in trade between the Community and Sweden. Article 13(2) abolishes quantitative restrictions on imports as from 1 January 1973 and any measures having an effect equivalent to quantitative restrictions on imports as from 1 January 1975 at the latest.

(18) According to Article 20, the agreement is not to preclude prohibitions or restrictions on imports, exports or goods in transit justified on grounds of, in particular, the protection of life and health of humans, animals or plants. However, such prohibitions or restrictions must not constitute a means of arbitrary discrimination or a disguised restriction on trade between the contracting parties.

(19) It must therefore be stated, in reply to the third part of the second question, that Articles 13(1) and 20 of the free-trade agreement between the European Economic Community and the Kingdom of Sweden do not preclude national legislation prohibiting the sale, placing in stock or store or the use of a plant-protection product not authorized by such legislation and imposing a penalty in criminal law for failure to comply.

Costs

(20) The costs incurred by the Governments of the Kingdom of the Netherlands, the Federal Republic of Germany, the Kingdom of Belgium and the United Kingdom and by the Commission of the European Communities, which submitted observations to the Court, are not recoverable. As these proceedings are, in so far as the parties to the main proceedings are concerned, a step in the action before the national court, the decision on costs is a matter for that court.

On those grounds,

THE COURT (THIRD CHAMBER),

in reply to the questions submitted to it by the Gerechtshof, The Hague, by judgment of 29 January 1988, hereby rules:

(1) The court of a Member State is not bound to interpret national rules on the marketing and use of plant-protection products in the light of the wording and purpose of Directive 79/117/EEC for the purpose of applying that directive to products not containing any of the active substances listed in the annex to the directive.

(2) In an area which has not been fully harmonized at Community level, Articles 30 and 36 do not preclude national legislation prohibiting the sale, placing in stock or store or the use of a plant-protection product not authorized by such legislation and imposing a penalty in criminal law for failure to comply.

(3) Articles 13(1) and 20 of the free-trade agreement between the European Economic Community and the Kingdom of Sweden do not preclude national legislation prohibiting the sale, placing in stock or store or the use of a plant-protection product not authorized by such legislation and imposing a penalty in criminal law for failure to comply.

COMMENTARY

(1) This judgment is one of several where the Court has, to date, pronounced on the question of national restrictions or bans of chemicals.[2] Though the word "environment" appears only once and in a marginal place in the Court's judgment,[3] it is obvious that the indication of what a Member State, in the area of chemicals, may or may not do under Community law has an enormous bearing on the environment. The different problems are not yet solved and it will be interesting to see the evolution after January 1, 1993 when the internal mar-

---

[2] See Case 272/80, *Biologische Produkten* [1981] E.C.R. 3277, [1982] 2 C.M.L.R. 497; Case 94/83, *Heijn* [1984] E.C.R. 3263; Case 54/85, *Mirepoix* [1986] E.C.R. 1067, [1992] 1 C.M.L.R. 83.

[3] See **paragraph 13**: "It is undisputed that plant-protection products present significant risks to the health of humans and animals and to the environment."

ket is achieved. The Court was asked by the Dutch Court on the interrelationship of Directive 79/117[4] with a Dutch Act from 1962. The Dutch Court did not ask whether the requirement of a Dutch authorisation to market "Improsol" was compatible with Community law. Presumably the Dutch Court was of the opinion that this was the case. However, doubts might rise at least insofar as "Improsol" had already received an authorisation in another Member State; on this issue the present case says nothing.

(2) The Court had already decided this question in Case 272/80.[5] Because of the importance of that decision for the environment, it will be described here in short.

A Dutch company wanted to import and market a plant protection product. This product had been authorised in France. It requested a Dutch authorisation in 1967. Dutch authorities asked for tests to be made the cost of which were estimated by the company to be 150,000 to 200,000 HFL, whereas the expected annual turnover was estimated to be 10,000 HFL. In 1975, the authorisation was still not granted. The company sold the product in the Netherlands without authorisation. The European Court was asked whether the Dutch provisions requiring an authorisation despite the existence of the French authorisation was compatible with Articles 30 and 36.

(3) The Court decided that in the absence of harmonised Community rules it was:

"for the Member States to decide what degree of protection of the health and life of humans they intended to assure and in particular how strict the checks to be carried out were to be."[6]

However, it introduced a provision in order to avoid abuses and thus stated:

"It follows from Article 30 in conjunction with Article 36 of the Treaty that a Member State is not prohibited from requiring plant protection products to be subject to prior approval, even if those products have already been approved in another Member State. The authorities of the importing State are however not entitled to require unnecessary technical or chemical analyses or laboratory tests when the same analysis or tests have already been carried out in another Member State and their results are available to those authorities or may at their request be placed at their disposal."

The Court did not expressly take up an environmental argument from the Advocate General which gives further justifications for national authorisation:

---

[4] Dir. 79/117 prohibiting the placing on the market and use of plant-protection products containing certain active substances: [1979] O.J. L33/36; last amendment by Dir. 91/188: [1991] O.J. L92/42.

[5] Case 272/80, see n.2 above.

[6] *Ibid.* para. 413.

"The condition in which a product is used, and thus the risks involved in such use, are necessarily different from one Member State to another. Thus, the Danish Government has pointed out that the minimum period of time to be observed between the last treatment with pesticide and the harvest varies according to the rate of growth of the plant varieties so treated as well as according to the rate of decomposition of the pesticide used which in its turn, is affected, amongst other things, by the ambient temperature."[7]

(4) As stated, in the present Case 125/88, the question of authorisation was not considered. The Court examined whether Directive 79/117 which prohibits the placing on the market and use of plant-protecting products containing certain active substances[8] was applicable. The answer to that question was easy, since already the title of Directive 79/117 makes it clear, that it does not ensure complete harmonisation of plant-protecting products but only refers to certain substances; these substances are listed in the Annex to that Directive. Member States are thus entitled to prohibit or restrict the use of other pesticides than those mentioned in Directive 79/117. And since the substances contained in "Improsol" were not listed in Directive 79/117, the Dutch legislation was free to set national rules on this pesticide as considered appropriate.

(5) The Court then addressed the question of the compatibility of the national measure with Articles 30 and 36. The Court's reasoning was as follows:

(a) Plant-protection products present significant risks to the health of humans and animals and to the environment;
(b) There is not yet full harmonisation of plant-protection products;
(c) Under Article 36 it is thus up to Member States to decide at what level they wish to set the protection of the life and health of humans, taking account of the requirements of the free movement of goods.

(6) As regards the risks of pesticides for humans and the environment—point (a)—the Court referred to previous judgments: in Case 94/83,[9] the Court had to judge on the question whether a Dutch prohibition to market apples which were treated with the pesticide Vinchlorol was compatible with Community law. The Court had found that there was no Community legislation in force and that in particular Directive 76/895 on the fixing of maximum levels for pesticide residues in and on fruit and vegetables[10] did not constitute a total harmonisation of pesticide residues, and did not regulate Vinchlorol either. Thus Articles 30 and 36 of the EEC Treaty applied.

---

[7] *Ibid.* para. IV(a) (p. 3302).
[8] Dir. 79/117, see n.4 above.
[9] 94/83, see n.2 above.
[10] Dir. 76/895, last amendment by Dir. 89/186: [1986] O.J. L221/37; Dir. 86/363 on the fixing of maximum levels for pesticide residues in and on foodstuffs of animal origin: [1986] O.J. L221/43; Dir. 90/642 on the fixing of maximum levels for pesticide residues in and on certain products of plant origin, including fruit and vegetables: [1990] O.J. L350/71.

The Court had found that pesticides present significant risks to the health of humans and animals and to the environment. Therefore national measures to limit pesticide residues are justified by virtue of Article 36. Such limitations may be different from one Member State to the other, according to climatic conditions, eating habits of the population and the general health conditions. Member States may even set different limits for the same pesticide residues on different food.[11]

(7) In Case 54/85,[12] the Court had to decide on a French prohibition to use the pesticide Malecanic acid for agricultural use. The Court found that there was no Community legislation on that pesticide. Therefore the French prohibition was to be decided according to Articles 30 and 36 of the EEC Treaty. The Court referred to its decision in Case 94/83[13] and repeated its general statement that pesticides present significant risks to humans and the environment. It further stated that the quantity of pesticides which the consumer takes in every day with his food, is not foreseeable and can not be controlled; therefore, strict measures to limit the risks for consumers are justified. This had led the Court to reach the conclusion, that national measures which prohibit the marketing of products treated with Malecanic acid, are justified under Article 36 of the EEC Treaty.[14]

(8) When the Court gave its judgment in Case 125/88, the statement that there was no full harmonisation of plant-protection products was certainly correct, in particular since Directive 79/117 concerned only certain pesticides.[15] Since then, Council adopted Directive 91/414 concerning the placing of plant-protection products on the market.[16] This Directive entered into force in July 1993. It is based on Article 43 of the EEC Treaty[17] and provides for rules on the Community-wide system for placing plant-protection products on the market. The active ingredients which come under this Directive are to be listed in an Annex I to it. Until now, this Annex has not been adopted.

(9) Directive 91/414 provides rules for the Community-wide marketing of pesticides. In this, it will have considerable implications on Member States' competence to restrict or prohibit certain pesticides. This might be illustrated by the fact that some 40 pesticides are at present prohibited in Germany, about twice as many as at Community level. One of the pesticides prohibited in Ger-

---

[11] Case 94/83, (n.2 above) paras. 13 to 16.
[12] See n.2 above.
[13] 94/83, see n.2 above.
[14] Case 54/85, (n.2 above), paras. 13 to 15.
[15] Dir. 79/117, see n.4 above.
[16] [1991] O.J. L230/1.
[17] Article 43 EEC: "The Council shall, on a proposal from the Commission and after consulting the European Parliament, acting unanimously during the first two stages and by a qualified majority hereafter, make regulations, issue directives or take decisions, without prejudice to any recommendations it may also make . . . "

many is Atrazine, a pesticide which easily migrates through the soil into the groundwater and in a number of Member States is found back in drinking water, in concentrations above the maximum admitted level.[19] Provided that the active ingredients of Atrazine will be listed in Directive 91/414, it is not clear if a national ban of Atrazine could be maintained. Indeed, Article 100a, paragraph 4[20] which allows national environmental measures to be upheld despite differing Community provisions, is not directly applicable, since Directive 91/414 is not based on Article 100a but on Article 43. It might be possible though, to develop a general rule which makes the philosophy underlying Article 100a paragraph 4 and 130t[21] also applicable to those provisions based on Article 43 which aim at the Community-wide regulation of agricultural practices. Such a legal interpretation would forward the view that the environment must not remain unprotected and that environmental requirements are a component of other Community policies.[22] Where agricultural measures aim at a Community-wide system they must take into consideration the environmental necessities.

(10) It becomes obvious that this reasoning is very close to the question whether Community legislation may be incompatible with the requirements of the EEC Treaty on the protection of the environment; such an interpretation could open other possibilities to the taking into consideration of environmental protection. It might be remembered, that the Court, in Case C–2/90[23] decided that it followed from Article 130r, paragraph 2—"environmental damage should as a priority be rectified at source"—that there was a legal rule according to which waste should be eliminated at the nearest possible installation. Thus, any Community legislation on waste elimination which does not take into consideration this principle would be incompatible with Article 130r, paragraph 2. In the same way one might argue that any Community legislation which does not take the necessary steps to prevent Atrazine from entering surface and groundwater and finally drinking water could be considered to be against the principle of Article 130r, paragraph 2 that "preventive action should be taken." The space available here does not permit the development of these sketchy ideas.

---

[19] Dir. 80/778 relating to the quality of water intended for human consumption: [1980] O.J. L229/1 fixes the maximum admitted concentration per pesticide at 0.1 microgrammes per litre; see also p. 246 above.

[20] **Article 100a**, paragraph 4 EEC: "If after the adoption of a harmonisation measure by the Council acting by a qualified majority, a Member State deems it necessary to apply national provisions on grounds of major needs referred to in Article 36 or relating to protection of the environment or the working environment, it shall notify the Commission of these provisions . . . "

[21] **Article 130t** EEC: "The productive measures adopted in common to Article 130s shall not prevent any Member State from maintaining or introducing more stringent protective measures compatible with this Treaty."

[22] **Article 130r** EEC, paragraph 2, 2nd sentence: "Environmental protection requirements shall be a component of the Community's other policies."

[23] C–2/90, *Commission* v. *Belgium* [1992] I E.C.R. 4431, [1993] 1 C.M.L.R. 365; see p. 71 above.

(11) Going back to Case 125/88 it has to be realised that the pesticide "Improsol" was intended for use in buildings. Thus, Directive 91/414[24] on plant-protection products does not seem to apply. The Commission is at present preparing a directive on pesticides used elsewhere than in agriculture, for instance in gardens, for wood preservation etc. Any such directive would be based on Article 100a and the problems of national bans would reappear. In fact, there is already one case where Article 100a has become relevant in this area: in 1988 Germany prohibited the use of Pentachlorophenol, a wood preservation product.[25] The Community later adopted a directive which restricted the use of that product, but did not contain a total prohibition.[26] Germany notified, under Article 100a, its national legislation. In 1992, the Commission accepted this total ban so that Pentachlorophenol will remain prohibited in Germany. In the meantime, France has brought an action before the Court contesting the Commission's decisions.

(12) This legal discussion has, until now, left unanswered the question of how such local, regional or national bans will be controlled in practice. Indeed border controls having been abolished since January 1, 1993, it will be more and more difficult not to have uniform bans and prohibitions all over the Community. If one presumes that Mr. Nijman was in good faith when he marketed the product, one has to accept that the number of such cases might increase in the future.

As regards the fact that "Improsol" was imported from Sweden, the decision was rather short. It analysed the free trade agreement between the EEC and Sweden and found in Article 20 of that agreement a provision which is almost word for word identical to Article 36[27] and which led the Court to the conclusion that national measures which prohibit the marketing of pesticides on grounds of protection of humans or animals do not contradict that agreement, to the extent that such measures are justified under Article 36.

(13) In spring 1992, the Commission submitted to the Council a proposal for a decision to create a European Economic Area between the EEC and Austria, Finland, Iceland, Liechtenstein, Norway, Sweden and Switzerland.[28] This European Economic Area (EEA) aims at the abolition of economic frontiers between the EEC and the States mentioned, to create a greater internal market. This decision, based on Article 238 of the EEC Treaty[29] is mainly intended to prevent difficulties in economic relations between the EEC and those coun-

---

[24] Dir. 91/414, see n.16 above.
[25] See L. Krämer, _Focus on EEC Environmental Law_ (London, 1992), p. 47.
[26] Dir. 91/173: [1991] O.J. L85/34.
[27] Para. 18.
[28] Commission, Proposal for a Council decision, SEC(92)814 final of April 28, 1992. Switzerland decided in the meantime by way of a referendum not to ratify the EEA Agreement.
[29] **Article 238** EEC: "The Community may conclude with a third state, a union of States or an international organization agreements, establishing an association involving rights and obligations, common action and special procedures. These agreements shall be concluded by the Council, acting unanimously after consulting the European Parliament . . . "

tries which might follow from the achievement of the internal market. Article 13 contains a provision which reads as follows:[30]

> "The provisions of Articles 11 and 12 shall not preclude prohibitions or restrictions on imports, exports or goods in transit justified on grounds of public morality, public policy or public security; the protection of health and life of humans, animals or plants, the protection of national treasures possessing artistic, historic or archaeological value; or the protection of industrial and commercial property. Such prohibitions or restrictions shall not, however, constitute a means of arbitrary discrimination or a disguised restriction on trade between Member States."

Article 11 takes over Article 30 of the EEC Treaty, Article 12 the provisions of Article 34(1) of the EEC Treaty.

(14) The environment is not expressly mentioned in Article 13 nor in Article 11. This legal drafting undoubtedly refers to the jurisprudence of the Court which had developed the principles of environmental protection under Articles 30 and 36 without mentioning it.[31]

Before the EEA Agreement was signed the Court gave two opinions on the draft agreement[32] under Article 228(1) of the EEC Treaty,[33] which had influenced the content of the Agreement. Since environmental aspects are not directly affected by these opinions, they will not be discussed here.

(15) Chemical substances and preparations other than pesticides are the subject matter of different rules. As regards their access to the market and their free circulation, two specific Community directives have been adopted.[34]

As regards the restriction on their use, the Council adopted, in 1976, Directive 76/769, on the approximation of the laws, regulations and administrative provisions of the Member States relating to restrictions on the marketing and use of certain dangerous substances and preparations.[35] As the title already indicates, Directive 76/769 does not constitute a total harmonisation of such restrictions. Rather, it stipulates in Article 2 "that the dangerous substances and preparations listed in the Annex may only be placed on the market or used subject to the conditions specified therein." The Annex to the Directive

---

[30] Non-official translation by the author.

[31] See in particular pp. 80 *et seq.* and 94 *et seq.* above.

[32] Court of Justice Opinion 1/91 of December 14, 1991: [1992] O.J. C110/1 and Opinion 1/92 of April 10, 1992: [1992] O.J. C136/1.

[33] **Article 228(A1)** EEC: "The Council, the Commission or a Member State may obtain beforehand the opinion of the Court of Justice as to whether an agreement envisaged is compatible with the provisions of this Treaty . . . "

[34] (a) Dir. 67/548 on the classification, packaging and labelling of dangerous substances: [1967] O.J. L196/1; 7th amendment by Dir. 92/32: [1992] O.J. L154/1; the Directive was adapted 16 times to technical progress, last by Dir. 92/37 (Commission): [1992] O.J. L154/30.
(b) Dir. 88/379 on the classification, packaging and labelling of dangerous preparations: [1988] O.J. L187/14; last amendment by Dir. 92/32.

[35] [1976] O.J. L262/201.

is regularly updated. Till mid-1992 the following substances were included in the Annex:

1. PCB, PCT and preparations with a PCB or PCT content higher than 0.005 per cent. by weight
2. Chloro-1-ethylene
3. Liquid substances or preparations which are dangerous under Directive 67/548[36]
4. Tris phosphate
5. Benzene
6. Asbestos fibres
7. Trisphosphinoxide
8. Polybrominated biphenyls
9. Soap bark powder
   Powder of the roots of Helleborus vividis and Helleborus niger
   Powder of the roots of Veratrum album and nigrum
   Benzidine
   O-nitrobenzoldehyde
   Wood powder
10. Ammonium sulphide
11. Volatile esters of bromoacetic acids
12. Naphtylamine
13. Benzidine
14. 4-nitrobiphenyl
15. 4-aminobiphenyl
16. Lead carbons
17. Lead sulphates
18. Mercury compounds
19. Arsenic compounds
20. Organostannic compounds
21. DBB
22. Pentachlorophenol
23. Cadmium and its compounds
24. Monomethyl-tetrachlorodiphenyl methane
25. Monomethyl-dichlorodiphenyl methane
26. Monomethyl-dibromodiphenyl methane

(16) The insertion of a new substance into the Annex takes a long time, since each time the procedure for the adoption of a directive has to be followed. For the first 12 amendments the time-span between the submission of the Commission's proposal to the Council and the adoption of the amendment varied between 3[37] and 42[38] months with an average of slightly over 15 months.

---

[36] See n. 34 above.
[37] Dir. 79/663: [1979] O.J. L197/37 inserting nos. 3 and 4 above into the Annex.
[38] Dir. 83/478: [1983] O.J. L263/33 inserting rules on asbestos into the Annex.

The Council did not agree to establish an accelerated procedure for inserting substances into the Annex. However, it did agree that a substance which is already included in the Annex may be the subject of amendments under a simplified procedure.[39] Apart from this procedure, the principle remains that Member States may prohibit or restrict the use of a substance or a preparation. They are obliged to follow the procedural rules of Directive 83/189,[40] *i.e.* normally to inform the Commission beforehand of their intention, and to respect the standstill delays which Directive 83/189 imposes.

---

[39] Dir. 89/678: [1989] O.J. L398/24 introducing a new **Article 2a** which reads: "Amendments required to adapt the Annexes to technical progress, with regard to the substances and preparations already covered by the Directive, shall be adopted in accordance with the procedure laid down in Article 21 of Directive 67/548/EEC, as last amended by Directive 88/490 EEC."
[40] Dir. 83/189 laying down a procedure for the provision of information in the field of technical standards and regulation: [1983] O.J. L109/8.

Air

22. A RIGHT TO CLEAN AIR?

Judgment of the Court of May 30, 1991
in Case C–361/88

E.C. Commission v. *Germany*

[1991] I E.C.R. 2567

FACTS AND PROCEDURE[1]

Directive 80/779 of July 15, 1980 fixes limit values and guide values for sulphur dioxide and black smoke.[2] Member States had to transpose its requirements into national law within two years of its notification, thus before July 18, 1982.

The Commission was of the opinion that Germany had not entirely complied with the Directive's requirements. It therefore addressed, on May 6, 1986, a letter of formal notice to the German government, raising in total five complaints.[3] Germany answered by letter of September 4, 1986. Since its answer did not satisfy the Commission, the Commission sent, on November 12, 1987, a reasoned opinion, repeating the five complaints. Germany answered on May 19, 1988.

The Commission applied to the Court on December 13, 1988, but only as regards the first complaint.[4] Written arguments were exchanged between the parties. Oral hearings took place on December 6, 1990. The Advocate General delivered his opinion on February 6, 1991.

JUDGMENT

(1) By application lodged at the Court Registry on 13 December 1988, the Commission of the European Communities brought an action under Article 169 of the EEC Treaty for a declaration that, by not adopting all the laws, regulations and administrative provisions necessary to ensure the complete transposition into national law of Council Directive 80/779/EEC of 15 July 1980 on air quality limit values and guide values for sulphur dioxide and suspended particulates (Official Journal 1980 No L 229, p. 30), the Federal Republic of Germany has failed to fulfil its obligations under the EEC Treaty.

(2) That directive is intended, on the one hand, to eliminate or prevent unequal conditions of competition capable of arising from the existence of discrepancies between the various national laws concerning the presence of sulphur dioxide and suspended particulates which can be tolerated in the air and, on the other

---

[1] Summary by the author.

[2] Dir. 80/779 on air quality limit values and guide values for sulphur dioxide and suspended particulates: [1980] O.J. L229/30.

[3] See for the subject matter of the complaints the report for the hearing.

[4] On a request of the Court, the Commission had stated that at the moment the application to the Court had been made, the remaining complaints did not constitute serious infringements of the Directive's provisions anymore, see the report for the hearing.

hand, to protect human health and the quality of the environment. For those purposes it prescribes the approximation of national laws.

(3) Article 2 of that directive provides that the limit values, that is the concentrations of sulphur dioxide and of suspended particulates "which, in order to protect human health in particular, must not be exceeded throughout the territory of the Member States during specified periods and under the conditions laid down in the following Articles", are those fixed in Annex I to the directive.

(4) Article 3(1) provides that, without prejudice to certain exceptions specified in paragraph (2), the Member States are to take appropriate measures to ensure that as from 1 April 1983 the concentrations of sulphur dioxide and suspended particulates in the air are not greater than the limit values given in Annex I.

(5) Article 10(2), however, authorizes the Member States, on a temporary basis and provided they use certain sampling and analysis methods, to use limit values other than those in Annex I, namely those defined in Annex IV.

(6) Under Article 15(1) the Member States were required to bring into force the laws, regulations and administrative provisions necessary in order to comply with the directive within 24 months of its notification. Since the directive was notified to the Federal Republic of Germany on 18 July 1980, it should therefore have been transposed into German law by no later than 18 July 1982.

(7) The Commission accuses the Federal Republic of Germany of not fulfilling the obligation, arising from Article 2(1) of the directive, to adopt a mandatory rule, accompanied by effective sanctions, with a view to expressly prohibiting, throughout the national territory, the exceeding of the limit values fixed in Annex I to the directive. It also charges the Federal Republic of Germany with not taking the appropriate measures to ensure that the limit values are actually observed, as required by Article 3(1) of the directive.

(8) The Federal Republic of Germany replies that the protection sought by the directive is in line with that resulting from the Federal Law of 15 March 1974 on protection against the harmful effects of air pollution, noise, vibrations and other types of nuisance on the environment (BGBl., I, p. 721, hereinafter referred to as the "Law on protection against pollution"), and also from the measures implementing it. It adds that the concrete results which it has achieved regarding pollution by sulphur dioxide and suspended particulates amply satisfy the requirements of the directive.

(9) Reference is made to the Report for the Hearing for a fuller account of the facts of the case, the procedure and the pleas in law and arguments of the parties, which are mentioned or discussed hereinafter only in so far as is necessary for the reasoning of the Court.

The absence of a general mandatory rule

(10) Paragraph 3 of the Law on protection against pollution defines effects harmful to the environment as being "nuisances which, because of their magnitude or their duration, are likely to give rise to dangers, substantial disadvantages or sub-

stantial nuisances for the environment or the neighbourhood". However, that law does not specify the threshold beyond which those nuisances must be regarded as harmful to the environment. Under Paragraph 48 it is for the Federal Government, after hearing the sectors concerned and receiving the consent of the Bundesrat, must adopt "the general administrative provisions necessary in order to implement" the law.

(11) On the basis of Paragraph 48, the Federal Government adopted, in 1974, the first general administrative provision to implement the Law on protection against pollution (hereinafter referred to as the "technical circular 'air' "). That circular was amended on various occasions, in particular on 27 February 1986 (GMBl., p. 95). It is common ground that paragraph 2.5.1 of that circular fixes, for sulphur dioxide and suspended particulates, nuisance values which correspond to those appearing in Annex IV to the directive.

(12) The Commission takes the view, however, that that circular is not mandatory in nature. It further considers that the scope of its application is more limited than that of the directive.

(13) The Commission considers that, under the German legal system, administrative circulars are not generally recognized as rules of law. The Basic Law, and in particular Article 80(1) thereof, make the adoption of regulations by the administration subject to certain conditions, in particular regarding procedure, which are not satisfied in the present case. Furthermore, it is admitted, both in case-law and in academic legal writing, that administrative circulars need not necessarily be observed when an atypical situation arises, that is to say a situation which the author of the administrative provisions could not, or did not wish to, resolve by reason of the fact that he had to settle the problem in a general way. Moreover, the provisions of the circular do not apply to sources of pollution other than the industrial plant referred to therein.

(14) The Federal Republic of Germany contends that the technical circular "air" is not an ordinary administrative provision. First, it was adopted according to a special procedure, calling for the co-operation of representatives from science, interested parties, the economic sectors affected, transport services and the higher administrative authorities of the Länder, and was submitted for the approval of the Bundesrat. Moreover, since its purpose is to give detailed content to a rule having binding force, it, like that rule, is binding in nature. In that respect it leaves no discretion to the administration. National case-law confirms this. Finally, the general concept "effect harmful to the environment" contained in the Law on protection against pollution was put into concrete form by the limit values laid down in the circular and, accordingly, those limit values apply to all cases where sulphur dioxide and suspended particulates are present in the atmosphere.

(15) It should be borne in mind in that respect that, according to the case-law of the Court (see, in particular, the judgment in Case C–131/88 *Commission* v *Germany* [1991] ECR I-825), the transposition of a directive into domestic law does not necessarily require that its provisions be incorporated formally and verbatim in express, specific legislation; a general legal context may, depending on the content of the directive, be adequate for the purpose, provided that it does indeed guarantee the full application of the directive in a sufficiently clear and precise manner so that, where the directive is intended to create rights for

individuals, the persons concerned can ascertain the full extent of their rights and, where appropriate, rely on them before the national courts.

(16) In that respect, it should be pointed out that the obligation imposed on the Member States to prescribe limit values not to be exceeded within specified periods and in specified circumstances, laid down in Article 2 of the directive, is imposed "in order to protect human health in particular". It implies, therefore, that whenever the exceeding of the limit values could endanger human health, the persons concerned must be in a position to rely on mandatory rules in order to be able to assert their rights. Furthermore, the fixing of limit values in a provision whose binding nature is undeniable is also necessary in order that all those whose activities are liable to give rise to nuisances may ascertain precisely the obligations to which they are subject.

(17) It should first be observed, however, that the limit values prescribed by the directive are to be found only in the technical circular "air" and that the latter has only a limited area of application.

(18) Contrary to the contentions of the Federal Republic of Germany, that circular does not apply to all plant. Paragraph 1 confines the scope of its application to plant for which a licence is required, within the meaning, in particular, of Paragraph 4 of the Law on protection against pollution, that is to say, to plant which, because of its specific nature or of the use to which it is put, is liable to give rise to effects particularly harmful to the environment, or to cause danger, substantial damage or particular disadvantage to the community or the neighbourhood. The same paragraph imposes obligations on the administrative authorities only, essentially, when applications for a licence to construct, operate or alter such plant are examined, or when obligations are subsequently imposed on that plant, or, again, in the case of an inquiry into the nature and the magnitude of the discharges from that plant, or into the nuisances emanating from the area in which it is operated.

(19) The area of application of the circular is therefore the immediate neighbourhood of well-defined buildings or plant, while the directive has a wider scope of application, which concerns the entire territory of the Member States. As the Commission rightly points out, the nuisances created by sulphur dioxide and suspended particulates may originate elsewhere than in the plant subject to a requirement of authorization, for example in a high density of road traffic, private heating systems or pollution from another State. The general nature of the directive cannot be satisfied by a transposition confined to certain sources of the exceeding of the limit values which it lays down and to certain measures to be adopted by the administrative authorities.

(20) Nor, secondly, is the concern to enable individuals to assert their rights satisfied in the sphere of application of the circular itself, namely plant for which a licence is required. The Federal Republic of Germany and the Commission differ on the question of the extent to which, in German academic legal writing and case-law, technical circulars are recognized as being binding in nature. The Commission was able to refer to judicial decisions denying the binding nature of such circulars, in particular in the sphere of tax law. The Federal Republic of Germany, for its part, referred to a line of decisions recognizing that binding nature in the field of nuclear energy. It must be stated that, in the particular case of the technical circular "air", the Federal Republic of Germany has

not pointed to any national judicial decision explicitly recognizing that that circular, apart from being binding on the administration, has direct effect vis-á-vis third parties. It cannot be claimed, therefore, that individuals are in a position to know with certainty the full extent of their rights in order to rely on them, where appropriate, before the national courts or that those whose activities are liable to give rise to nuisances are adequately informed of the extent of their obligations.

(21) It follows from the foregoing considerations that it is not established that Article 2(1) of the directive has been implemented with unquestionable binding force, or with the specificity, precision and clarity required by the case-law of the Court in order to satisfy the requirement of legal certainty.

The absence of appropriate measures for securing observance of the limit values.

(22) The Commission charges the Federal Republic of Germany with having failed to adopt the appropriate measures for ensuring that the limit values prescribed by the directive are actually observed, as required by Article 3 of the directive. It points out first of all that there are no "anti-smog" regulations in the Länder of Bremen and Schleswig-Holstein. It goes on to stress that the plans for the protection of the air which the Länder must draw up and implement, under Paragraphs 44 to 47 of the Law on protection against pollution, when air pollution is likely to produce effects harmful to the environment, do not make it possible to ensure that the limit values fixed in the directive are actually observed. The reason for this is, it claims, firstly that those measures are not valid for all areas, but only for certain zones specified by the regulations of the Länder. In the second place, the administrative authorities have a discretion with regard to the decision to implement those plans for the protection of the air. In the third place, it does not follow from any provision that those plans must ensure that the limit values of the directive are observed.

(23) The Federal Republic of Germany contends that the limit values prescribed by the directive have not in fact been exceeded since 1983. It states that the "anti-smog" regulations are envisaged only in the zones where atmospheric pollution is likely to appear. It adds that it would be pure formalism to impose preventive measures in the areas where there is no risk that the limit values prescribed by the directive will be exceeded. It maintains further that the administrative authorities have no margin of discretion with regard to the decision to implement the plans for the protection of the air when specific dangers became clearly apparent. Finally, it states that, since 1 September 1990, those plans must observe the limit values of the directive.

(24) It must first be pointed out that the fact that a practice is in conformity with the requirements of a directive in the matter of protection may not constitute a reason for not transposing that directive into national law by provisions capable of creating a situation which is sufficiently precise, clear and transparent to enable individuals to ascertain their rights and obligations. As the Court held in its judgment in Case C–339/87 *Commission* v *Netherlands* [1990] ECR I-851, paragraph 25, in order to secure the full implementation of directives in law and not only in fact, Member States must establish a specific legal framework in the area in question.

(25) It follows from the foregoing that the argument of the Federal Republic of Germany, according to which no case contrary to the directive has been reported in practice, cannot be upheld.

(26) It is necessary, therefore, to consider whether the provisions referred to by the Federal Republic of Germany guarantee a correct implementation of the directive.

(27) Under Paragraph 44 of the Law on protection against pollution the competent authorities under the law applicable in the Länder must continuously determine the nature and magnitude of certain atmospheric pollutions capable of creating effects harmful to the environment in certain particularly exposed zones. According to Paragraph 47, in the version in force when the action was brought, if those determinations indicate that the atmospheric pollutions are creating effects harmful to the environment or if such effects are to be expected in the whole of the exposed zone or in a part thereof, those competent authorities must draw up a plan for the protection of the air for that zone.

(28) Article 3(1) of the directive requires the Member States to take appropriate measures so that the concentrations of sulphur dioxide and of suspended particulates in the air are not higher than the limit values.

(29) In that respect, it must be pointed out that the competent authorities of the Länder have to implement plans for the protection of the air only when they find the existence of effects which are harmful to the environment. As stated above, the Law on protection against pollution does not specify the threshold beyond which effects on the environment may be found to be harmful. The technical circular "air" imposes obligations on the administrative authorities only in the event of well-defined acts and in respect of specified plant. There are, therefore, no general and mandatory rules under which the administrative authorities are required to adopt measures in all the cases where the limit values of the directive are likely to be exceeded.

(30) It follows that Article 3 of the directive has not been transposed into the national legal system in such a way as to cover all the cases capable of arising and that the national rules do not have the binding nature necessary in order to satisfy the requirement of legal certainty.

(31) The fact that, after the action was brought, the German legislation was amended cannot alter that assessment. The Court has consistently held that the subject-matter of an action brought under Article 169 of the Treaty is the Commission's reasoned opinion and that, even when the default has been remedied after the time-limit prescribed by the second paragraph of that article has expired, there is still an interest in pursuing the action in order to establish the basis of liability which a Member State may incur as a result of its default towards other Member States, the Community or private parties.

(32) In the light of all the foregoing considerations, it must be declared that, by not adopting within the prescribed period all the measures necessary in order to comply with Council Directive 80/779/EEC of 15 July 1980 on air quality limit values and guide values for sulphur dioxide and suspended particulates, the Federal Republic of Germany has failed to fulfil its obligations under the EEC Treaty.

Costs

(33) Under Article 69(2) of the Rules of Procedure the unsuccessful party is to be ordered to pay the costs. Since the Federal Republic of Germany has failed in its submissions it must be ordered to pay the costs.

On those grounds,

THE COURT

hereby:

1. Declares that, by not adopting within the prescribed period all the measures necessary in order to comply with Council Directive 80/779/EEC of 15 July 1980 on air quality limit values and guide values for sulphur dioxide and suspended particulates, the Federal Republic of Germany has failed to fulfil its obligations under the EEC Treaty;

2. Orders the Federal Republic of Germany to pay the costs.

COMMENTARY

(1) This judgment is one of the few, which deals with questions of air pollution. Indeed, the list of judgments in Appendix 1 of this book classifies the judgments by environmental subject item; groupings are as follows [as at June 30, 1993]:

(a) water pollution (20)
(b) air pollution (7)
(c) waste (26)
(d) chemicals (10)
(e) nature protection (14)[5]
(f) others (4)

The judgment again deals with the legal questions of transposition of an environmental directive into national law rather than with questions of actual air pollution. Since the Commission has no environmental inspectors, no laboratories and no other means of measuring the actual concentration of pollutants in the air, this is not surprising: it will only be in exceptional circumstances that the Commission will have sufficiently strong evidence for a case on actual air pollution to stand in the European Court.

(2) The main question of substance which the Court had to address was the

---

[5] It is obvious that this counting is somehow arbitrary.

question of the meaning of the Directive's limit values and whether German rules adequately complied with the Community requirements.

Directive 80/779 fixes limit values for sulphur dioxide (SO_2) and black smoke, "which must not be exceeded throughout the territory of the Member States."[6] Limit values are thus of a binding nature, in contrast to the guide values which only constitute the objective, which Member States should try to achieve. These limit values are expressed in concentrations—for instance 200 milligram per cubic meter air—which were measured and determined according to methods and procedures laid down in the annexes to the Directive.[7]

The Court submitted that these limit values have been imposed "in order to protect human health in particular."[8] It therefore concluded that exceeding the limit value could in the opinion of the EEC legislator, negatively affect human health. This lead the Court to the conclusion that the system set up by the Directive implies that persons must be able to defend their rights, whenever the exceeding of the limit values could put their health at risk.

(3) In another part of the judgment, the Court expressly mentioned that individuals have acquired legal rights under Directive 80/779, which they must be capable of defending in courts;[9] the context excludes that the Court was thinking of industrial polluters.[10] Thus the reasoning of the Court can only be understood in the following way: the limit values fixed by Directive 80/779 aim at protecting human health, and thus individuals. This implies that where the limit values are not respected, individuals must be capable of defending their rights in (national) courts. In order to be able to do that the transposing measure taken by a Member State must be clear and precise and give individuals full information on their rights.

The Court argued in the same way as regards industrial and other polluters. They, too, must know exactly what their rights and obligations are, in order to be capable of defending their rights, for instance against an administration which is imposing too strict conditions, or too lose conditions on a competitor.

(4) The Court has not addressed the question of what would happen if national law did not give a right of action to individuals who wanted to oppose, for instance, an authorisation for an industrial installation, or who wanted the administration to impose restrictions on excessive air pollution. It is doubtful what the consequences would be. One possibility would be to consider that where the legislation of a Member State does not give a right to individuals to address courts, the "right" which individuals have received under Directive 80/779 cannot be enforced in courts.

---

[6] Art. 2(1).
[7] See Art. 10 and Annexes I to V of Dir. 80/779.
[8] Para. 16 of the judgment.
[9] *Ibid.*
[10] Otherwise, the last phrase of para. 16 would not have been necessary.

(5) I am of the opinion that the solution must be found elsewhere. Indeed, according to the Court, the Directive is granting a specific right to individuals, *i.e.* to see the limit values not exceeded. Where there is a risk that by virtue of an administrative authorisation there is such an excess of the limit values, the individual must be able to prevent the authorisation from being granted or to have it repealed once it has been granted. And where there is an excess of the limit values without a specific authorisation being granted, the individual has the right to request that the administration take appropriate steps in order to respect the limit values, for instance by taking measures to reduce traffic. Only in this way can the "right" which individuals have received by virtue of the Directive, be made operational.

(6) In substance, thus, there is a "right to a clean environment" which the Court has granted to individuals in the present case. It remains to be seen whether a case will be brought before a national court, where this matter will be tested; the Court could then be seized under Article 177 of the EEC Treaty[11] and asked to clarify and specify its considerations as to the content and meaning of the "right" of individuals under Directive 80/779.

(7) Having stated that the Directive gives rights to and contains obligations on private persons, the Court's conclusion is in line with numerous other judgments: where a Directive contains rights and obligations for individuals it must be transposed into national law by clear and precise provisions which enable these individuals to exactly know the content of their rights and obligations.[12] This normally excludes the adoption of administrative circulars in order to transpose a directive. Administrative circulars—which exist in a great variety of forms in different Member States—have in common that they are binding upon the administration, but do not create rights and obligations for private persons.

(8) The Court examined whether the German "Technische Anleitung Luft" (TA Luft—technical instruction air) which is a circular, should exceptionally be considered as a real piece of legislation, as the German government had argued.[13] The Court rejected this argument, because the "TA Luft" was not recognised, in German courts, as being of a binding nature—at least the Ger-

---

[11] **Article 177**: "The Court of Justice shall have jurisdiction to give preliminary ruling concerning:
... (b) the validity and interpretation of acts of the institutions of the Community ...
Where such a question is raised before any court or tribunal of a Member State, that court or tribunal may, if it considers that a decision on the question is necessary to enable it to give judgment, request the Court of Justice to give a ruling thereon.
Where any such question is raised in a case pending before a court or tribunal of a Member State, against whose decisions there is no judicial remedy under national law, that court or tribunal shall bring the matter before the Court of Justice."

[12] See in particular Case C–131/88, *Commission* v. *Germany:* [1991] E.C.R., discussed at p. 109 above; Case 29/84, *Commission* v. *Germany:* [1985] E.C.R. 1661, [1986] 3 C.M.L.R. 579; Case 363/85, *Commission* v. *Italy:* [1987] E.C.R. 1733; Case 116/86, *Commission* v. *Italy:* [1988] E.C.R. 1323.

[13] See para. 20.

man Government had not produced any jurisprudence in the air sector which recognised that the TA Luft was binding upon third persons.[14] Since normally a circular does not have a binding nature, the burden of proof of the contrary was on the German government.

(9) Another argument, which would have been sufficient on its own was examined by the Court. In fact, the system chosen by the TA Luft to tackle air pollution had only a limited area of application: it refers to air pollution in the environment of specific installations which the Court expressly enumerates.[15] But it does not have a general field of application covering the entire German territory. In regions, where no installations that come under TA Luft exist, the requirements of that circular would not apply.

(10) Furthermore, the TA Luft provides that the limit values for SO_2 may be exceeded because of dense traffic, or because of energy use in private households or because there is pollution coming from another Member State or a third country.[16] Unlike the TA Luft, the Directive does not address the question of the source of pollution, but requires instead that the concentrations of sulphur dioxide and black smoke are not exceeded over the entire territory of a Member State. This argument on its own was enough to state that Germany had not taken all the measures necessary to comply with the requirements of the Directive.

(11) Finally, the Court went on to examine whether Germany had taken the measures requested by Article 3(1) of Directive 80/779.[17] The Court found the German legislation too vague and imprecise, because it did not precisely indicate the moment at which the German authorities have to interfere to prevent the limit-values from being exceeded. German law requires measures to be taken only upon the occurrence of "dangerous effects," without stipulating that this occurrence of "dangerous effects" means that the limit values of the Directive have been exceeded.[18]

(12) If one looks at the judgment in general, it is probably correct to say that the reasoning applied to circulars and their non-binding nature for individuals is in conformity with a number of previous judgments. Also the Court's statement that practical compliance with the Directive is not enough but that Member States have to adopt specific legislation to transpose a directive which creates rights and obligations for individuals, is not new, but conforms to previous judgements.

---

[14] *Ibid.*
[15] Para. 18.
[16] See para. 19.
[17] **Article 3** "(1): "Member States shall take appropriate measures to ensure that as from 1 April 1983 the concentrations of sulphur dioxide and suspended particulates in the atmosphere are not greater than the limit values given in Annex I ... "
[18] Para. 29.

(13) What is new is the application of these general principles to the TA Luft. Indeed, reading previous judgments was not enough to convince the legal advisors of the German authorities of the necessity to adopt specific legally binding rules instead of the TA Luft.[19]

Also new is the requirement of legal certainty and precision which is now applied to air pollution limit values. The judgment must be understood as requesting the national legislator to regulate in such a way that enables individuals to find the limit value fixed by the Directive, in their national statute books. It is surprising that the Court has been so precise and outspoken on such a question—but it is true that it was the first time that the Court had to consider the interpretation of a limit value.

(14) The most important part of the judgment is, however, the reference to the "rights" of individuals. Limit values, maximum admissible concentrations[20] and other limitations of emissions are fixed, normally, in order to protect humans and the environment. Where such limitations are not respected, individual rights are affected; this even applies, such as in the present case, where the limit value is general and does not refer to individual exposure. The individual right gives—this is my conclusion—a right to defend it in Court against possible breaches. We can only hope that more clarity will be brought to those questions of the individual's right to a clean environment.

(15) On the same day the Court gave another judgment against Germany, in a case about air pollution with almost identical arguments.[21] At the end of 1991, the Court gave three decisions against France which had transposed three air pollution directives into national law by way of circulars.[22] Again, the reasoning was quite similar to the reasoning in the present case. Hopefully circulars will gradually disappear from environmental law-making.

(16) As regards the problem of law-making and standard-setting, one should be aware that the German concept is founded on a well-conceived idea: the legislation fixes general objectives—the best available technology is to be used, deleterious effects to be avoided, the state of the art must be practised, etc.; the details, and thus what these terms mean in practice, are either laid down in administrative circulars or fixed, on a case-by-case basis, in the individual permits. Such concepts are in use in a number of Member States and in a number of sectors (water, air, waste). They allow a great amount of flexibility

---

[19] See in particular Case 208/85, *Commission* v. *Germany:* [1987] E.C.R. 4035, where the Court had not accepted technical circulars in the area of dangerous substances; see also the comment by U. Everling, a former German judge at the European Court: "It is difficult to understand that it (Germany) nevertheless used uncertain procedures and even accepted to litigate in court in a case with a foreseeable result." U. Everling, "Umweltschutz durch Gemeinschaftsrecht in der Rechtsprechung des EUGH," p.29 (p.35) in: P. Behrens—H. J. Koch (ed.) *Umweltschutz in der Europaschen Gemeinschaft* (Baden-Baden, 1991) (translation by the author).

[20] Such concentrations are to be found in Dir. 80/778 on drinking water: [1980] O.J. L229/11.

[21] Case 59/89, *Commission* v. *Germany,* not yet reported.

[22] Cases C–14/90, C–64/90, C–134/90, *Commission* v. *France,* not yet reported.

for the administration, which may negotiate standards with industry, set up provisional rules, agree standards limited in time, etc. This approach, however, poses the problem that the power of standard-setting is largely shifted over to the administration. And the general public, including its elected representatives, often does not know what standards are really applied, negotiated, bargained or agreed. From the point of view of the environment, a system of general rules with delegation of power to the administration is quite acceptable, to the extent that and as long as the administration really tries to protect the environment. From the democratic point of view the "power" is shifted away from Parliaments to administrations. "Power tends to corrupt", says an English proverb: thus the problem of controlling the administration is posed. In my opinion this can, in environmental matters, only be done by public opinion, its watchdogs and the media on the one side, and environmental organisations on the other side.

These considerations concern law-making rather than judicial control and they will not be elaborated upon here. However, it will be interesting to see how the two different concepts will develop in a European Community which aspires to uniform rules within the internal market but has so many different legal cultures. There are signs which seem to indicate that general clauses will be preferred, since they guarantee political success; but it is not certain that the environment profits from such an approach.

Part 4

Procedural Aspects

23. ARTICLE 169: NON-CONFORMITY OR PARTIAL CONFORMITY OF
NATIONAL MEASURES

**Judgment of the Court of December 13, 1990
in Case C–70/89**

E.C. Commission v. *Italy*

[1990] I E.C.R. 4817

FACTS AND PROCEDURE[1]

Council Directive 76/464 on pollution caused by certain dangerous substances discharged into the aquatic environment[2] draws up a list of substances characterised by their toxicity, persistence and bioaccumulation. Article 6 of Directive 76/464 provides that the Council was to set limit values and quality objectives for those substances[3] which included cadmium and its compounds.[4] Council Directive 83/513[5] lays down such limit values and quality objectives for cadmium. Member States had to transpose Directive 83/513 into national law within two years.

Italy informed the Commission in October 1985 that Italian legislation of 1976 and 1979[6] contained the necessary provisions to comply with Directive 83/513. The Commission was of the opinion that the Italian legislation did not constitute an adequate transposition. On September 2, 1987, the Commission sent a letter of formal notice and on September 12, 1988, a reasoned opinion. No reply was received.

In its application registered to the Court on March 7, 1989, the Commission raised seven specific points where it was of the opinion that Italian legislation was not in compliance with Directive 83/513.[7] The Italian Government did not answer in substance and did not question the application.

Oral hearings took place on November 21, 1990; the Advocate General delivered his opinion the same day.

JUDGMENT

(1) By application lodged at the Court Registry on 7 March 1989, the Commission of the European Communities brought an action under Article 169 of the EEC Treaty for a declaration that, by not adopting within the prescribed time-limit all

---

[1] Summary by the author.
[2] [1976] O.J. L129/23.
[3] *Ibid.* **Article 6**: "The Council, acting on a proposal from the Commission, shall lay down the limit values which the emission standards must not exceed for the various dangerous substances included in the families and groups of substances within list I . . . The Council, acting on a proposal from the Commission, shall lay down quality objectives for the substances within list I . . . "
[4] *Ibid.*, Annex, List I, no. 6.
[5] Dir. 83/513 on limit values and quality objectives for cadmium discharges: [1983] O.J. L291/1.
[6] See for details of the legislation, para. 4, p. 378 below.
[7] See for details the Report for the Hearing, p. 4818.

the legislative and administrative provisions needed to transpose Council Directive 83/513/EEC of 26 September 1983 on limit values and quality objectives for cadmium discharges (Official Journal 1983 L 291, p. 1), the Italian Republic had failed to fulfil its obligations under the EEC Treaty.

(2) In Directive 76/464/EEC of 4 May 1976 on pollution caused by certain dangerous substances discharged into the aquatic environment of the Community (Official Journal 1976 L 129, p. 23), the Council set out a list of substances characterized by their toxicity, persistence and bioaccumulation, one of which was cadmium. Article 6 of the directive provides that the Council is to adopt limit values and quality objectives for those substances.

(3) Directive 83/513 (hereinafter referred to as 'the directive') lays down those values and objectives for cadmium. The period for its implementation expired on 28 September 1985.

(4) In order to fulfil their obligation to provide information under Article 6(1) of the directive, the Italian authorities informed the Commission on 28 October 1985 that the rules laid down by the directive were already contained in various legislative instruments, namely Law No 319 of 10 May 1976 on protection of water against pollution (*Gazzetta ufficiale della Republica italiana*) (GURI No 141 of 29.5.1976), amending Law No 650 of 24 December 1979 (GURI No 352 of 29.12.1979), the circular of 29 December 1976 from the Interministerial Committee and the decision of that committee of 4 February 1977 (supplemento ordinario alla GURI, No 69 of 21.2.1977).

(5) Considering that those instruments did not constitute an adequate transposition of the directive, the Commission initiated the procedure for a declaration of failure by a Member State to fulfil its obligations under the Treaty.

(6) Reference is made to the Report for the Hearing for a fuller account of the facts of the case, the course of the procedure and the submissions and arguments of the parties, which are mentioned or discussed hereinafter only in so far as is necessary for the reasoning of the Court.

(7) The Commission states that the Italian legislation fails to comply with the directive on the following seven points.

(8) First, the Italian legislation does not lay down limit values expressed in grammes of cadmium discharged per kilogram of cadmium treated, whereas Annex I to the directive requires such values to be laid down.

(9) Secondly, the Italian legislation required certain existing industrial establishments to observe those limit values no later than 1 March 1989, whereas Annex I to the directive required them to observe those values no later than 1 January 1986.

(10) Thirdly, the Italian legislation provides that the limit values are to be measured upstream of the point where the waste is discharged into the surrounding environment, whereas Article 3(2) of the directive requires measurement to be carried out at the point of discharge of the waste waters, that is to say where they leave the industrial establishment or treatment plant.

(11) Fourthly, the Italian legislation lays down no procedure for monitoring the quan-

tities of cadmium treated, whereas Annex I, point 4, of the directive requires such a procedure to be established.

(12) Fifthly, the Italian legislation makes no provision for prior authorization for discharges, whereas a system of authorization is required by Article 3(3) and (4) of the directive.

(13) Sixthly, the methods of analysis provided for in the Italian legislation to determine the presence of cadmium in waste waters do not conform to those prescribed by Article 3(5) and Annex III, point 1, of the directive.

(14) Finally, since, under the Italian system, authorization for discharge is granted automatically, the provincial laboratories responsible for monitoring discharges cannot carry out the supervisory duty required of the authorities of the Member States by Article 4 of the directive.

(15) In its defence, the Italian Republic did not dispute that the Commissions's submissions were well founded.

(16) It must therefore be declared that, by not adopting within the prescribed time-limit all the legislative and administrative provisions needed to transpose Council Directive 83/513 of 26 September 1983 on limit values and quality objectives for cadmium discharges fully and correctly into its national law, the Italian Republic has failed to fulfil its obligations under the EEC Treaty.

Costs

(17) Under Article 69(2) of the Rules of Procedure, the unsuccessful party is to be ordered to pay the costs. Since the Italian Republic has failed in its submissions, it must be ordered to pay the costs.

On those grounds,

THE COURT

hereby:

(1) Declares that, by not adopting within the prescribed time-limit all the legislative and administrative provisions needed to transpose Council Directive 83/513/ EEC of 26 September 1983 on limit values and quality objectives for cadmium discharges fully and correctly into its national law, the Italian Republic has failed to fulfil its obligations under the EEC Treaty;

(2) Orders the Italian Republic to pay the costs.

COMMENTARY

(1) This judgment is presented here in order to demonstrate how the Community institutions[8] monitor Community environmental legislation. Article 130r, paragraph 4 provides that as a rule, Member States shall implement the measures which are decided at Community level.[9] Article 155 requests the Commission to act as guardian of EEC law:

> "In order to ensure the proper functioning and development of the common market, the Commission shall:—ensure that the provisions of this Treaty and the measures taken by the institutions pursuant thereto are applied . . . "

The only possibility of action, which the Treaty provides for cases where Community rules are not applied, is Article 169 which reads:

> "If the Commission considers that a Member State has failed to fulfil an obligation under this Treaty, it shall deliver a reasoned opinion on the matter after giving the State concerned the opportunity to submit its observations.
>   If the State concerned does not comply with the opinion within the period laid down by the Commission, the latter may bring this matter before the Court of Justice."

(2) Thus there are three steps in the procedure, a letter of formal notice, a reasoned opinion and the referral to the Court of Justice. Each stage requires a specific and formal decision by the Commission.
    In monitoring the application of Community law, three aspects are checked:

(a) whether Member States have adopted and notified the national measures to implement the directives;
(b) whether the national measures incorporate the obligation deriving from Community law fully and correctly;
(c) whether the national implementing measures are correctly applied in practice.

As regards the failure to adopt or to notify national implementation measures it should be noted that there is a specific provision in each directive requiring the Member State to transpose the obligations flowing out of the Directive within a specific time-span into national law and to inform the Commission thereof.

---

[8] For details of the procedure, see in particular Commission, Eighth Annual Report on Commission monitoring of the application of Community law (1990): [1991] O.J. C338/1; Annex C to this report, pp. 204 *et seq.* gives a detailed description of monitoring of environmental directives.

[9] **Article 130r** EEC, paragraph 4, phrase 2: "Without prejudice to certain measures of a Community nature, the Member States shall finance and implement the other measures."

(3) The complete absence of implementation measures is rather exceptional; therefore, Court decisions which state that a Member State has not adopted any measure to transpose an environmental directive into national law, are rather exceptional.[10] Furthermore, the borderline between absence of implementation measures and incomplete or incorrect implementation measures—the second aspect of checking—is not very precise, as is well illustrated by the present Case C–70/89: Italy did inform the Commission of some water legislation which provided, *inter alia*, for authorisation procedures and other measures. Thus, it was not possible for the Court to state that Italy had not implemented at all Directive 85/513. However, Italy had not adopted any specific measure as regards limit values for cadmium discharges, monitoring measures and so on.

(4) Member States raise a number of arguments before the Court in order to justify absence of implementation measures or delays in transposing directives into national law. The Court of Justice has, for instance, rejected the following arguments:[11]

(a) national practice already conforms with Community requirements, so that the diverging legal situation is irrelevant;[12]

(b) a directive has direct effect in Member States so there is no need to adopt specific implementation measures;[13]

(c) the time allowed for implementation is too short;[14]

(d) implementation was impossible in view of the end of the legislative [parliamentary] period;[15]

(e) constitutional difficulties prevented implementation;[16]

(f) implementation measures had to be adopted by regions, Länder or provinces;[17]

(g) other Member States did not implement in time either;[18]

(h) implementation was delayed, since an amendment to the directive was expected.[19]

---

[10] See, *e.g.* Case 92/79, *Commission* v. *Italy*: [1980] E.C.R. 1115, [1981] 1 C.M.L.R. 331; Cases 30–34/81, *Commission* v. *Italy*: [1981] E.C.R. 3379; Case C–252/89, *Commission* v. *Luxembourg*: [1988] E.C.R. 2243.

[11] This enumeration largely follows R. Wägenbaur, "European Community's prospects for enforcement of directives," pp.173 *et seq.* in Ministry of Housing, Physical Planning and Environment (VROM)—United States Environmental Protection Agency (ed), *Proceedings of the International Enforcement Workshop 8–10 May, 1990, Utrecht.* (Utrecht, 1990).

[12] Case 29/84, *Commission* v. *Germany*: [1985] E.C.R., 1661 [1986] 3 C.M.L.R. 579; Case 102/79, *Commission* v. *Belgium*: [1980] E.C.R. 1473, [1981] 1 C.M.L.R. 282.

[13] Case 301/81, *Commission* v. *Belgium*: [1983] E.C.R. 467, [1984] 2 C.M.L.R. 430.

[14] Case 52/75, [1976] E.C.R. 277, [1976] 2 C.M.L.R. 320.

[15] Case 91/79, *Commission* v. *Italy*: [1980] E.C.R. 1099, [1981] 1 C.M.L.R. 331.

[16] Case 102/79, (n.12 above).

[17] Case C–33/90, *Commission* v. *Italy*, [1992] 2 C.M.L.R. 353; see also p. 387 below.

[18] Case C–38/89, *Blanguernon*: [1990] I E.C.R. 83, [1990] 2 C.M.L.R. 340.

[19] Case C–310/89, *Commission* v. *Netherlands*: [1991] I E.C.R. 1381.

In the present case, the argument by the Italian government that it had sought legislative authorisation from Parliament to enable it to take the necessary measures[20] seemed so weak to the Court of Justice that the Court did not even discuss it.

(5) The comparison between Community environmental law and national environmental law may seem relatively easy. However, such a comparison is often complicated. Indeed, Member States sometimes transpose the requirements of a directive by several national measures, which can be spread in time; legislation which is prior to the directive, is amended later; or they adopt measures with a different hierarchical value—an act of Parliament is completed by regulations and circulars; or measures are spread geographically— regions, Länder or provinces adopt measures in complement or instead of nation-wide measures. The interdependency of several national laws within a given legal system may give rise to intricate legal considerations and one is entitled to wonder whether a Community environmental directive is indeed fully and correctly implemented.[21]

"The Commission has systematically asked the Member States to send it synoptic tables clearly showing which national norm incorporates a Community provision into national law. So far, such information is the exception."[22]

(6) In the present case, the Commission had examined in detail the failures of Italian legislation and raised seven points where it found inconsistencies. Since Italy did not dispute the legal analysis, the Court did not examine the details of each point of inconsistency. In cases where a Member State does object to the legal analysis of the Commission, the Court examines in detail the meaning of the Community legislation at stake.[23]

The seven points will not be discussed here; however, attention is drawn to the environmental discussion of aspects such as an automatic authorisation or the measuring of concentrations upstream at the point of discharge: legal solutions such as these make a mockery of environmental protection. Mid 1993, Italy had still not complied with the requirements of Directive 83/513, so that the Commission had initiated fresh proceedings.[24]

(7) In 1988, the Council adopted a resolution which invited the Commission to develop specific measures for a Community action programme to combat

---

[20] See the Report for the Hearing, p. 4819.

[21] See, *e.g.* Case C–190/90, *Commission* v. *Netherlands* [1991] I E.C.R. 3265, where the Court discusses the transposition of Directive 82/501 on the prevention of accidents into Dutch law. See p. 307 above.

[22] Commission, Eighth Annual Report (n.8 above) No. 92.

[23] See, *e.g.* Case 262/85, *Commission* v. *Italy*. [1987] E.C.R. 3073; see also p. 185 above; Case 291/ 84, *Commission* v. *Netherlands*. [1987] E.C.R. 3483.

[24] See Commission, Ninth Report on Commission monitoring of the application of Community law 1991: [1992] O.J. C250/1.

environmental pollution by cadmium.[25] Subsequent to that, in June 1991, the Council adopted Directive 91/338[26] amending for the 10th time Directive 76/769 regarding the restrictions on the marketing and use of certain dangerous substances and preparations.[27] This Directive limits the use of cadmium in and on products and came into effect at the end of 1992.

---

[25] [1988] O.J. C30/1.
[26] [1991] O.J. L186/59.
[27] [1976] O.J. L262/201.

24. ARTICLE 169: UNSATISFACTORY ENFORCEMENT OF COMMUNITY ENVIRONMENTAL LAW

Judgment of the Court of December 13, 1991
in Case C–33/90

E.C. Commission v. *Italy*

[1991] I E.C.R. 5987, [1992] 2 C.M.L.R. 353

FACTS AND PROCEDURE[1]

In 1987, the Italian Member of the European Parliament Ms Squarcialupi put a written question to the Commission in which she denounced the problems of disposal of wastes in the region of Campania (Italy). She indicated amongst other things that Campania produced annually some 1,620,000 tonnes of waste, while it only had uncontrolled and non-authorised waste disposal facilities. Furthermore, Campania was on the point of accepting 500,000 tonnes of waste from the United States which were to be incinerated; however, Campania had no waste incineration facility.[2]

On June 29, 1987 the Commission sent a letter to the Italian authorities[3] asking how many tonnes of wastes according to Directive 75/442[4] and how many tonnes of dangerous wastes according to Directive 78/319[5] were generated annually in Campania, what measures had been taken in Campania to prevent abusive abandonment and uncontrolled disposal, asking for further details about the agreement between Campania or Italy and the United States, and enquiring on the respect of Directive 84/631 as regards the transport of dangerous waste.[6]

This letter remained unanswered. On June 20, 1988 the Commission sent a letter of formal notice, arguing that Italy had not answered its letter of June 29, 1987 and that in Articles 5 and 6 of Directive 75/442[7] and 6 and 12 of Directive 78/319[8] has not been complied with as regards Campania. Not having

---

[1] Summary by the author.

[2] QE 426/87 (V. Squarcialupi) [1987] J.O. L295/29.

[3] See Report for the Hearing: [1991] I E.C.R. 5987.

[4] [1975] O.J. L194/47.

[5] Dir. 78/319 on toxic and dangerous waste: [1978] O.J. L84/43.

[6] Dir. 84/631 on the supervision and control within the European Community of the transfrontier shipment of hazardous waste: [1984] O.J. L326/31.

[7] **Article 5**: "Member States shall establish or designate the competent authority or authorities to be responsible, in a given zone, for the planning, organisation, authorisation and supervision of waste disposal operations."

Article 6: "The competent authority or authorities referred to in Article 5 shall be required to draw up as soon as possible one or several plans relating to, in particular:
— the type and quality of waste to be disposed of,
— general technical requirements,
— suitable disposal sites,
— any special arrangements for particular wastes . . . "

[8] **Article 6**: "Member States shall designate or establish the competent authority or authorities to be responsible, in a given area, for the planning, organisation, authorisation, and supervision of operations for the disposal of toxic and dangerous waste."

Article 12: "The competent authorities shall draw up and keep up to date plans for the disposal of toxic and dangerous waste. The plans shall cover in particular:
— the type and quantity of waste to be disposed of;

received an answer, the Commission sent a reasoned opinion on May 23, 1989. Since Italy did not answer to the reasoned opinion, the Commission applied to the Court on January 31, 1990.

The Court put several questions to Italy and to the Commission.[9] Oral hearings took place on October 9, 1991. The Advocate General delivered his opinion on November 5, 1991.

JUDGMENT

(1) By an application received by the Court Registry on 31 January 1990 the E.C. Commission brought an action under Article 169 EEC for a declaration that the Italian Republic had failed to fulfil certain obligations arising from Council Directive 75/442 on waste ('the Waste Disposal Directive'), Council Directive 78/319 on toxic and dangerous waste ('the Toxic and Dangerous Waste Disposal Directive') and Article 5 EEC.

(2) By means of the abovementioned directives the Council prescribed the harmonisation of national law concerning the disposal of certain types of waste. As their preambles show, these directives have two aims. Firstly, they are intended to remove obstacles to trade in the Community and the inequality in competition conditions arising from differences in national laws concerning waste. Secondly, they aim to protect human health and safeguard the environment against the harmful effects caused by the disposal of certain types of waste.

(3) To secure the attainment of these aims, the directives require the member-State to adopt certain measures.

(4) Firstly, they must set up or designate 'the competent authorities to be responsible, in a given zone, for the planning, organisation, authorisation and supervision of waste disposal operations'. This obligation is set out in Article 5 of the Waste Disposal Directive and Article 6 of the Toxic and Dangerous Waste Disposal Directive.

(5) Secondly, these competent authorities must draw up plans or programmes for the disposal of waste, with particular reference to the types and quantities of waste in question, disposal methods and suitable sites for tips. These obligations arise from Article 6 of the Waste Disposal Directive and Article 12(1) of the Toxic and Dangerous Waste Disposal Directive.

—the methods of disposal;
—specialized treatment centres where necessary;
—suitable disposal sites.
The competent authorities of the Member States may include other specific aspects, in particular the estimated cost of the disposal operation. 2. The competent authorities shall make public the plans referred to in paragraph 1. The Member States shall forward these plans to the Commission. 3. The Commission, together with the Member States, shall arrange for regular comparisons of the plans in order to ensure that implementation of this Directive is sufficiently coordinated."
[9] See Report for the Hearing.

(6) In addition, to enable the Commission to verify whether the Member States have duly fulfilled their obligations, they must forward these programmes to the Commission, as well as three-yearly reports on the disposal of toxic and dangerous waste. These information obligations arise from Articles 12(2) and 16 of the Toxic and Dangerous Waste Disposal Directive.

(7) On receiving information concerning certain problems created by the disposal of waste in the region of Campania (Italy), the Commission, by letter of 29 June 1987 expressly referring to the abovementioned directives, requested the Italian Government to submit its observations on the situation. In particular the Commission asked for information on the production of waste in Campania, the measures taken by the region to dispose of it, and the existence of an agreement with the United States concerning the importation of waste.

(8) As the Italian Government failed to reply to this request, the Commission sent it a letter of formal notice on 20 June 1988.

(9) In this letter the Commission stated that, by not replying to its request for information, Italy had failed to fulfil its obligations under Article 5(1) EEC. It added that, by omitting to secure the implementation of the abovementioned directives in Campania, this Member State has also failed to fulfil its obligations under Articles 5 and 6 of the Waste Disposal Directive and Articles 6 and 12 of the Toxic and Dangerous Waste Disposal Directive.

(10) As there was no answer to this formal notice, the Commission issued a reasoned opinion on 23 May 1989. The Italian Government did not reply to this either.

(11) Taking the view that the latter had not met its obligations, the Commission decided to bring the present action.

(12) In the framework of the written procedure, however, the Commission stated, in reply to a question by the Court, that it would withdraw its submissions concerning the violation of Article 5 of the Waste Disposal Directive and Article 6 of the Toxic and Dangerous Waste Disposal Directive. The Commission considered that Italy had, by means of section 6 of Decree of the President of the Republic 915 at 10 September 1982 ('the Decree') designated the regions as competent authorities to be responsible for drawing up the plans and programmes laid down by those Articles. The Commission added that the failure to fulfil Article 12(2) of the Toxic and Dangerous Waste Disposal Directive, i.e. the obligation to forward programmes, had already been established in Case C–48/89, *E.C. Commission* v. *Italy* and that it was unnecessary for the Court to give a further ruling on this subject.

(13) Reference is made to the Report for the Hearing for a fuller account of the facts of the case, the course of the procedure and the submissions and arguments of the parties, which are mentioned or discussed hereinafter only in so far as is necessary for the reasoning of the Court.

Procedure

(14) The first objection raised by the Italian Government is that the Commission's complaints in the formal notice, which merely refers to the failure to reply to the

letter of 29 June 1987, are not identical to the allegations in the framework of the present action concerning the failure to fulfil obligations under the Treaty.

(15) This objection cannot be upheld. It is sufficient to observe that the formal notice and the reasoned opinion both refer, like the application, not only to the violation of Article 5 EEC but also to the violation of Articles 5 and 6 of the Waste Disposal Directive and Articles 6 and 12 of the Toxic and Dangerous Waste Disposal Directive. Therefore Italy was aware from the beginning of the preliminary administrative stage that the Commission's criticism related not only to the absence of a reply to its letter, but also to the implementation of the directives themselves. Consequently the Member State was in a position to justify its point of view in good time or, as the case may be, to fulfil its obligations.

Violation of Article 5(1) EEC

(16) The Commission considers that the Italian Government's failure to reply to the letter of 29 June 1987 is a violation of Article 5(1) EEC.

(17) Italy replies that it had no obligation to furnish the Commission with the information requested. According to the defendant, in the framework of the above-mentioned directives the Member States have no obligations of information other than those laid down by Article 12 of the Waste Disposal Directive and Articles 12(21) and 16 of the Toxic and Dangerous Waste Disposal Directive. However, the information requested by the Commission is said to be outside the ambit of those provisions.

(18) On this point it should be observed that, as the Court held in Case 272/86, *E.C. Commission* v. *Greece* the Member States are required by Article 5 EEC to facilitate the achievement of the Commission's task consisting in particular, pursuant to Article 155 EEC, in ensuring that the measures taken by the institutions pursuant to the Treaty are applied. In order for the said task to be performed, it is essential that the Commission be fully informed of the measures taken by the member-States to apply those provisions.

(19) However, during the enquiries made by the Commission before the procedure which resulted in the present action, the Italian Government abstained from providing information concerning the production, processing and importation of waste in the region of Campania and concerning the measures taken at the regional or local level in that region, although the latter had been designated, pursuant to the Italian legislation, as the competent authority to be responsible for implementing the abovementioned directives. Because the request for information concerned the disposal of waste covered by the Waste Disposal Directive and the Toxic and Dangerous Waste Disposal Directive, that request, and the competent authority responsible for waste disposal operations, were within the ambit of supervision by the Commission.

(20) The Italian Government's failure to comply, thus preventing the Commission from obtaining knowledge of the true situation in Campania, must be regarded as a refusal to co-operate with that institution. It should be added that, in failing to supply the information, Italy was in any case required, by virtue of the duty of loyal co-operation arising from Article 5(1) EEC, to explain its attitude.

(21) It must therefore be found that, by failing to reply to the Commission's questions

in the letter of 29 June 1987, Italy has failed to fulfil its obligations under Article 5(1) EEC.

Violation of Article 5 of the Waste Disposal Directive and Article 12(1) of the Toxic and Dangerous Waste Disposal Directive

(22) The Commission contend that, as the region of Campania has not drawn up the plans provided for by Article 6 of the Waste Disposal Directive or prepared and kept up to date the programmes provided for by Article 12(1) of the Toxic and Dangerous Waste Disposal Directive, Italy has failed to fulfil its obligations arising from those provisions.

(23) The Italian Government denies that it has failed in this respect. It contends that it has incorporated the two directives into national law by means of the above-mentioned decree. Consequently, in the event of any violation by the regional authorities of the national measures implementing the directives, sanctions could be sought to be imposed only in the framework of national law.

(24) This argument cannot be accepted. The fact that a Member State has entrusted to its regions the responsibility for implementing directives can have no effect on the application of Article 169. It is clear from settled case law that a Member State cannot plead circumstances existing in its internal legal system to justify failure to meet obligations and time limits arising from Community directives. Although each Member State is free to distribute legislative powers as it wishes in the internal respect, for the purposes of Article 169 it nevertheless remains responsible to the Community for fulfilling obligations under Community law.

(25) In the present case the directives lay down, firstly, an obligation for the Member States to designate authorities to be responsible for implementing them and, secondly, specific obligations on the part of those authorities such as the preparation and updating of plans or programmes. Therefore the fact that a Member State, after designating such authorities, refrains from taking the necessary measures to ensure that they fulfil their obligations amounts to a failure by the Member State to fulfil its own obligations within the meaning of Article 169 EEC.

(26) In this connection it should be observed that, in spite of an express request by the Court, Italy has not furnished proof that the region of Campania had drawn up plans within the meaning of Article 6 of the Waste Disposal Directive and programmes within the meaning of Article 12(1) of the Toxic and Dangerous Waste Disposal Directive before the time limit imposed in the reasoned opinion expired. Nor has it explained what concrete measures it had taken within that period to ensure that such plans or programmes were actually drawn up in Campania.

(27) It must therefore be found that, as the region of Campania failed to drawn up plans concerning the types and quantities of waste to be disposed of, the general technical requirements, suitable sites for disposal and all the special provisions concerning particular types of waste, and also failed to draw up and keep up to date programmes for the disposal of toxic and dangerous waste, Italy has failed to fulfil its obligations under Article 6 of Council Directive 75/442 on waste and Article 12(1) of Council Directive 78/319 on toxic and dangerous waste.

Costs

(28) Pursuant to Article 69(2) of the Rules of Procedure, the unsuccessful party is to be ordered to pay the costs. As Italy has failed in its submissions, it must be ordered to pay the costs.

On those grounds,

THE COURT

hereby rules:

1. By failing in reply to the questions put by the Commission in its letter of 29 June 1987 the Italian Republic has failed to fulfil its obligations pursuant to the first paragraph of Article 5 EEC.

2. Since the Region of Campania has not drawn up plans relating in particular to the types and quantities of waste to be disposed of, general technical provisions, appropriate sites for the disposal and all the special provisions relating to particular waste or drawn up or maintained plans for the disposal of toxic and dangerous waste, the Italian Republic has failed to fulfil its obligations pursuant to Article 6 of Council Directive 75/442 on waste and Article 12(1) of Council Directive 78/319 on toxic and dangerous waste.

3. The Italian Republic is ordered to pay the costs.

COMMENTARY

(1) The judgment concerns the actual application of Community environmental law within a Member State. Indeed, Italy had taken the necessary legal steps to comply with the requirements of both Directives 75/442[10] and 78/319[11] by adopting the Presidential decree 915 of December 15, 1982[12] which was not in dispute in the present case. However, it is obvious from Article 189 of the EEC Treaty that Member States are not only obliged to take the necessary legislative measures in order to transpose a Community directive into national law but are also obliged to ensure a certain result. Indeed, Article 189 reads:

" . . . A directive shall be binding, as to the result to be achieved, upon each Member State to which it is addressed, but shall leave to the national authorities the choice of form and methods . . . "

Thus, whether Italy decided to have one national waste plan or many

---

[10] [1975] O.J. L194/47.
[11] [1978] O.J. L84/43.
[12] Decree No. 915 of October 10, 1982 [1982] 343 G.U.R.I. 9071.

regional waste plans, is irrelevant from the point of view of Community law, as long as the different waste plans conform to the requirements of Directives 75/442 and 78/319 and as long as they cover the whole Italian territory. The existence and the monitoring of such plans, however, were part of the obligations under Community law. And this obligation went beyond the mere adoption of legislation.

(2) A considerable number of Community environmental directives oblige Member States to set up clean-up plans or programmes or, as in Directives 75/442 and 78/319, monitoring plans. In the water area, one should mention Directive 75/440 on the quality of surface water[13] Directive 76/464 on discharges of dangerous substances into the aquatic environment,[14] Directive 78/659 on the quality of fish water,[15] Directive 79/923 on the quality of shellfish water.[16] As regards air pollution, several directives are worth noting: Directive 80/779 on limit values for sulphur dioxide and black smoke provides for clean-up plans in polluted zones,[17] Directive 82/884 on a limit value for lead[18] and Directive 85/203 on limit values for nitrogen dioxide.[19] Directive 88/609 on emissions from large combustion plants provides for a clean-up plan,[20] while Directive 84/360 on air emissions from industrial installations provides for policies and strategies in order to adopt existing installations to best available technologies.[21]

In the waste sector, apart from Directives 75/442 and 78/319, Directive 85/339 on liquid beverage containers[22] and Directive 91/271 on urban waste water treatment[23] provide for clean-up programmes.

In its Ninth Annual Report on monitoring of the application of Community law 1991[24] the Commission stated, as regards environmental law that the implementation situation "is at its least satisfactory in cases where Community legislation lays down obligations to plan ahead, since few Member States do so satisfactorily."[25]

(3) It is rather typical that the present case, which concerns questions of the

---

[13] Art. 4 of Dir. 75/440 on the quality required of surface water intended for the abstraction of drinking water in the Member States: [1975] O.J. L194/26.

[14] Art. 7 of Dir. 76/464 on pollution caused by dangerous substances discharged into the aquatic environment of the Community: [1976] O.J. L129/23.

[15] Art. 5 of Dir. 78/659 on the quality of fresh water needing the protection or improvement in order to support fish life: [1978] O.J. L222/1.

[16] Art. 5 of Dir. 79/923 on the quality required for shellfish waters: [1979] O.J. L281/47.

[17] Art. 3(2) of Dir. 80/779 on air quality limit values and guide values for sulphur dioxide and suspended particulates: [1980] O.J. L229/30.

[18] Art. 3(2) of Dir. 82/884 on a limit value for lead in the air: [1982] O.J. L378/15.

[19] Art. 3(2) of Dir. 85/203 on air quality standards for nitrogen dioxide: [1985] O.J. L87/1.

[20] Art. 3 of Dir. 88/609 on the limitations of emissions of certain pollutants into the air from large combustions plants: [1988] O.J. L336/1.

[21] Art. 13 of Dir. 84/360 on the combating of air pollution from industrial plants: [1984] O.J. L188/20.

[22] Art. 3 of Dir. 85/339 [1985] O.J. L176/18.

[23] Art. 17 of Dir. 91/271 [1991] O.J. L135/40.

[24] [1992] O.J. C250/1.

[25] *Ibid.* p. 150

practical application of Community environmental law, was initiated by a Member of the European Parliament. In its Eighth Annual Report on monitoring of the application of Community law, the Commission acknowledged the fact that most of its information on practical implementation of environmental directives came from complaints, written or oral questions, members of the European Parliament and petitions.[26] In the complaint form which the Commission published, it made the commitment to look into the merits of each complaint.[27] The same commitment was taken by the President of the Commission towards the European Parliament as regards written or oral questions.[28]

(4) Complaints and cases where the Commission believes in a "presumed infringement" of Community law have increased considerably over the last years as the following list indicates:[29]

	Complaints	Presumed infringements
1982	10	–
1983	8	–
1984	9	2
1985	37	10
1986	165	32
1987	150	38
1988	216	33
1989	465	60
1990	480	42
1991	353	113
1992	515	121

It should be noted, however, that under Article 169 the Commission alone is empowered to start proceedings. A complainant or a member of the European Parliament cannot enforce such a decision, nor can they apply to the Court under Article 173 of the EEC Treaty,[30] on grounds that the Commission has wrongly failed to start proceedings under Article 169.[31]

(5) The present case illustrates quite well the practical difficulty for the Commission in obtaining information on practical implementation. Written requests from 1987, 1988 and 1989 remained unanswered. Not even during the

---

[26] [1991] O.J. C338/1, Annex C (p. 204), nos. 32 *et seq.* and nos. 93 *et seq.*

[27] [1989] O.J. C26/8.

[28] Commission, Third Report on monitoring of the application of Community law 1985: [1986] O.J. C220/1 (p. 4, no. 9) and Fourth Report on monitoring of the application of Community law 1986: [1987] O.J. C338/1 (p. 4, no. 12).

[29] Commission, Eigth Report (n. 26 above) p. 226. Parliamentary questions figure in column "cases detected by Commission".

[30] **Article 173** EEC: " . . . Any neutral or legal person may . . . institute proceedings against a decision addressed to that person or against a decision which, although in the form of a regulation or a decision addressed to another person, is of direct and individual concern to the former."

[31] Case 48/65, *Lütticke*: [1966] E.C.R. 28; Case 247/87, *Star Fruit* [1989] E.C.R. 291; Case C–87/89, *Société nationale*: [1990] I E.C.R. 1981.

Court proceedings did Italy answer the questions posed in the letter of 1987; thus, four and a half years have not helped gathering information on the more than dubious contact about waste imports from the United States to Campania.

(6) As regards the Italian argument that the Commission had no right to put questions which were not directly covered by Directives 75/442 and 78/319, the Court restated that the Commission does have rights which flow out of Article 5 of the EEC Treaty. This provision requires Member States "to facilitate the achievement of the Community's tasks." Since the Commission has, under Article 155, the obligation to "ensure that the provisions of this Treaty and the measures taken by the institutions pursuant thereto are applied" the Commission must be entitled, so the Court stated, to ask for information on the application of measures. The Court was relatively stiff when reproaching Italy for having neglected to co-operate loyally with the Commission and not even explaining its attitude.[32]

(7) The Court was equally severe about the Italian argument that the application of the Commission should be rejected because it was up to the region of Campania to draw up plans for the disposal of waste. The region of Campania is not a Member State of the EEC, but Italy is. In the eyes of Community law, Italy is responsible for the absence of implementation measures in the region of Campania. It is certainly true that, in principle, it is up to the Commission to prove that Community law is not respected. However, in the present case, the Commission had specified in detail that it had not received any plans from Italy, despite its express request. In such a case the Court asked Italy to present its plans and concluded, in the absence of a satisfactory Italian reply, that no such plans existed. Nothing has to be added to that.

(8) The environmental questions remain:

(1) What has the region of Campania done since 1977, date of entry into force of Directive 75/442, to comply with its requirements?
(2) How is waste and dangerous waste disposed of in Campania?
(3) Has there been import of wastes from the United States into Campania? What has happened to that waste?

In April 1992, the Court also gave a judgment against Greece regarding waste disposal in Crete[33] in a case started on the basis of a complaint by a Greek citizen. The facts of the case (according to the Greek defence, the realisation of the programme in Crete had met too many objections from local population and was thus not carried out) demonstrate the difficulties which Greece, too, has with waste disposal. It may be suggested as a conclusion that questions of waste management are likely to be a major environmental topic

---

[32] Para. 20.
[33] Case C–45/91, *Commission* v. *Greece*: [1992] I E.C.R. 2509.

within the Community, until the end of this century and beyond. The present case, together with Case C–45/91 against Greece, provides good arguments for the present author's thesis that the main problem of Community environmental law is not the making of rules but rather their application. Principles and objectives exist, in the EEC Treaty and in secondary legislation. Directives are produced, standards are set and legal requirements are finalised, but as long as their full application throughout the Community is not ensured, all this remains "Greenspeak".

25. ARTICLE 186: INTERIM MEASURES TO PROTECT THE ENVIRONMENT

**Order of the President of the Court of August 16, 1989
in Case 57/89R**

E.C. Commission v. *Germany*

[1989] E.C.R. 2849

FACTS AND PROCEDURE[1]

On the basis of a complaint, the Commission was informed in 1985 that Germany intended to undertake construction work within a special protection area for birds, in the Leybucht, which lies in the Wattenmeer in East Friesland, north of Emden. The Commission investigated the case and sent, on July 7, 1987, a letter of formal notice under Article 169 to the German Government. Having received no answer, the Commission issued a reasoned opinion on July 4, 1988. Germany answered on September 6, 1988. On February 28, 1989 the Commission applied to the European Court. On July 14, 1989, it applied for interim measures to suspend dike construction work.

The German Government answered in writing; oral hearings took place on August 9, 1989, where the Commission and the German Government presented their arguments.

ORDER

(1) By an application lodged at the Court Registry on 28 February 1989, the Commission of the European Communities brought an action under Article 169 of the EEC Treaty for a declaration that by planning or undertaking construction work which damages the habitat of protected birds in special protection areas, contrary to Article 4 of Council Directive 79/409 of 2 April 1979 on the conservation of wild birds (Official Journal 1979, L 103, p. 1, hereinafter referred to as 'the directive'), the Federal Republic of Germany has failed to fulfil its obligations under the EEC Treaty.

(2) By a separate application lodged at the Court Registry on 14 July 1989, the Commission sought the adoption of interim measures under Article 186 of the EEC Treaty and Article 83 of the Rules of Procedure and requested the Court to order the Federal Republic of Germany to take the necessary measures to suspend dike construction work in the area of the Leybucht and in particular to refrain temporarily from starting work on stage IV of the construction programme until the Court has given its decision on the main application.

(3) The Leybucht is a bay in the Wattenmeer in East Friesland, to the north of Emden, and is approximately five kilometres in diameter. It has long been a nesting, feeding and staging area for various species of both sedentary and migratory birds and is in particular an important breeding area for the avocet.

---

[1] Summary by the author. For the facts regarding Case C–57/89, see also Chapter 13 above. The present case and comments lays emphasis on the procedural aspects.

(4) The Leybucht was placed under special protection on 21 December 1985 by legislation of Lower Saxony establishing the 'Niedersächsisches Wattenmeer' national park. The area covered by this park is shown on the maps appended to the legislation. On 6 September 1988 the German Government informed the Commission under Article 4(3) of the directive that it had classified the Leybucht as a special protection area.

(5) The disputed construction work resulted from the introduction by the Bezirksregierung Weser-Ems, the competent regional authority, of a coastal defence project which included development of the Leybucht. That project was approved on 25 September 1985 after planning proceedings which had, *inter alia*, given all interested parties the opportunity to submit comments and raise objections. The project provides for the construction, to the west of the Leybucht, of a reservoir enclosed by a dike with locks leading to the sea and a ship canal from the small fishing port of Greetsiel to these locks; to the south-east, the project provides for the reinforcement, heightening and extension of the existing dike and the construction of a drainage channel behind the new dike; and to the north-east, the closure of part of the bay by a new dike, along with some sluices and drainage work. Work on the first stage, which covers the construction of the reservoir, started at the beginning of 1986.

(6) The Commission claims that the construction work in question contravenes Article 4(4) of the directive, since it will result in a sizeable reduction in the ecologically useful area and a fall in the population density of certain birds referred to in Annex 1 to the directive, in particular the avocet, the white-fronted goose and two species of tern. That work, the Commission claims, thus has a significant effect on the protection of birds within the meaning of Article 4(4).

(7) According to the Commission, the general structure of the directive, in particular the gradation of protective measures of a general nature (Article 3(1)) and those of a specific nature (Article 4(1)), makes it clear that Member States must comply with specific obligations in regions which they themselves have designated as special protection areas in order to ensure active protection for species of birds which are particularly endangered, listed in Annex 1 to the directive. In accordance with the first sentence of Article 4(4) of the directive, any active interference with these protection areas which is motivated by economic or tourist interests and is likely to disturb the habitat of the birds must be prohibited.

(8) The German Government stresses that the measures envisaged are designed to ensure the safety of the dike; there is no tourist project or any other economic project in the Leybucht area. The violent storms of 1953, 1962 and 1976 demonstrated that the existing dikes were no longer thick and high enough to ensure protection for the land and its inhabitants. Since the level of storm tides has risen considerably over the last few decades, it was vital to heighten and strengthen the dikes so that they might be capable of protecting the population against the worst storm tides. The German Government accepts as undeniable that the dike works may disturb the birds. However, completion of the work will bring an end to regular dredging of the navigable channels, which will be beneficial from the ecological point of view.

(9) The German Government disputes the interpretation of Article 4 of the directive put forward by the Commission, and takes the view that measures required to

protect the coastline take priority over the protection of birds, even in protection areas within the meaning of Article 4(1) of the directive. An interpretation which allows interference only in so far as it is designed to protect the habitat of birds would, it is claimed, be incompatible not only with the letter and intention of the directive, but also with higher principles of Community law. The defence of birds, the German Government submits, can never take precedence over the protection of human lives.

(10) The parties presented oral argument on 9 August 1989. During the hearing of the application for interim measures, the Commission stated that, in view of the progress in construction of the dike as far as kilometre 10.7, its application seeking suspension of work in the Leybucht would confine itself to the south-east and north-east sections, more specifically those east of kilometre 10.7 along the new dike, work on which is planned to start in 1990.

(11) The Commission submits that the urgency of interim measures is dictated, as the Court has consistently held, by the risk that serious and irreparable damage might be caused if it were necessary to wait for the Court to reach a decision in the main application. In the present case, there is reason to fear that the rapid progress of work, in particular the completion of stage IV, could result in the disappearance of the habitat of bird species which are specially protected and that the birds could be systematically driven out of the protection area by disturbances directly attributable to the work. Completion of stage IV would itself affect almost 10% of the breeding pairs which have settled in the Leybucht. A subsequent decision by the Court stating that the defendant ought not to have adopted the measures in question could not put right the disturbance and damage caused.

(12) The Commission states that the sole disadvantage of a temporary suspension of the work would be to delay completion of the project; it would not have any appreciable financial repercussions. Even if the Court were to adopt interim measures but reject the Commission's main application, the damage incurred by the defendant would amount only to a delay in completion of the project of approximately 18 months.

(13) The German Government disputes the urgency of the measures sought and points out that at present almost two-thirds of the total dike construction work has been completed. With regard to the section of the dike up to kilometre 10.7, construction has been substantially completed. On the next section of work, from kilometre 10.7 to kilometre 13, work is due to commence at the start of 1990. The result of the essential heightening and strengthening of the dike will be that the dike base will be extended out to sea by approximately 40 to 50 metres. According to the German Government, extension of the dike on the landward side is not possible since the available space is restricted by a main road running behind the dike and the drainage channel, for technical drainage reasons, must flow between the main road and the dike. Work on the section from kilometre 13 to kilometre 15 is not due to start before the beginning of 1991. The line of the dike in this section will run approximately 2 000 metres away from the present line in order to form a rounded shape.

(14) The German Government accepts that it is not impossible, from a purely technical point of view, to suspend the work at kilometre 10.7, subject, however, to a number of rather costly temporary adjustments. However, the disadvantage of

such a solution lies not only in the financial consequences of cessation of work and interference with the performance of contracts concluded with construction companies, but also in the delay in the completion of the coastal defence structures, which could lead to the loss of human life in the event of storm tides.

(15) The Court is empowered under Article 186 of the EEC Treaty to prescribe any necessary interim measures in cases before it. For a measure of this type to be ordered, applications for the adoption of interim measures must, in accordance with Article 83(2) of the Rules of Procedure, state the circumstances giving rise to urgency and the factual and legal grounds establishing a prima-facie case for the interim measures applied for.

(16) The main problem which this application for interim measures presents is that of urgency. The project for the works in the Leybucht was drawn up in September 1985; work started in 1986; the construction of the reservoir to the west of the Leybucht, which extends a few kilometres into the sea, is almost complete. German nature and environmental protection groups pointed out to the Commission as early as September 1984 the potential threat to the bird population in the area. It was not until August 1987, roughly two years after the contested project had been adopted, that the Commission, by way of a letter of formal notice, set in motion the procedure outlined in Article 169 of the EEC Treaty; the reasoned opinion was delivered in July 1988. The application for interim measures dates from July 1989, although the main application was lodged on 28 February 1989.

(17) This chronology of events shows that the Commission submitted its application after the regional government's project was well under way, through conclusion of the necessary contracts and the start of construction work. It did not apply for interim measures until a large part of the work had already been completed. In effect, the Commission is requesting the Court to stop work which has already been partially completed.

(18) In those circumstances, the application for interim measures can only be allowed if it is precisely the next stage in the construction work, that is to say the stage due to be carried out in 1990, which will cause serious harm to the protection of birds in the Leybucht. There is nothing in the file relating to the case or in the arguments presented before the Court to show that that is in fact true. Three different factors must be considered in this regard.

(19) In the first place, it is necessary to remember that the work scheduled for 1990 involves the heightening, extension and reinforcement of an existing sea dike. This work is not designed to reduce the area of the bay, as in the case of the work already completed and that scheduled for 1991, but only to extend the base of the dike by between 40 and 50 metres into the sea. Information provided by the German Government concerning the breeding grounds of avocets—the only species for which data were supplied to the Court—shows that, in general, the distance separating these areas from the work scheduled for 1990 is no less than that which separates them from the other work under the 1985 project.

(20) Secondly, statistics drawn up by the Lower Saxony authorities show that there has been a steady fall since 1984 in the number of avocets breeding in the Leybucht, with a slight tendency to stabilization since 1987, and that the most signifi-

cant fall occurred before the disputed work began. Consequently, there are no grounds for the view that the start of work on stage IV will have the effect of driving the avocet away from its traditional breeding areas in the Leybucht.

(21) Finally, the Commission has been unable to substantiate the fears expressed in its application concerning the development, in the short term, of mass tourism likely to disturb the birds. It is agreed that one of the specific objectives of the 1985 project was to reduce considerably the scope for pleasure-boat sailing in the Leybucht. With regard to the dry land, the Commission merely mentioned rumours to the effect that large car parks were to be constructed close to Greet-siel, rumours, moreover, which the German Government says are unfounded.

(22) It follows from the foregoing considerations that the facts which the Court has at its disposal do not enable it to conclude that the construction work scheduled for 1990 is characterized, in comparison with other work envisaged under the 1985 project and particularly in comparison with work already completed in the western area of the Leybucht, by the significant effect which it would have on the conservation of birds protected under Annex 1 to the directive. The Commission has thus failed to establish that there is an urgent need to interrupt the work already started.

(23) The application for interim measures must therefore be rejected.

On those grounds,

T. KOOPMANS, PRESIDENT OF CHAMBER,

replacing the President of the Court in accordance with Article 85, second paragraph, and Article 11 of the Rules of Procedure,

ruling on an application for interim measures,

hereby orders:

(1) The application for interim measures is rejected.

(2) Costs are reserved.

COMMENTARY

(1) This order is, to date, the only case where the Commission has applied for interim measures in an environmental case. It should be remembered that procedures which the Commission starts under Article 169 of the EEC Treaty against a Member State, do not have suspensory effect. Even "actions brought before the Court of Justice shall not have suspensory effect."[2] Article 186 pro-

---

[2] Art. 185, first sentence.

vides: "The Court of Justice may in any cases before it prescribe any necessary interim measures." This provision makes it abundantly clear, that no
interim measures can be taken, neither by the Commission nor by the Court,
in cases which are not yet before the Court.

Article 83 of the Court's Rules of Procedure provides that an interim
measure of the Court requires an express application by one of the parties to
a pending case.[3] The applicant must justify the urgency of the requested
measure and indicate why the interim measures are necessary.[4]

(2) When the Commission applies for an interim measure, it does not have to
show a specific interest in the matter. Indeed, under Article 155 of the EEC
Treaty,[5] the Commission is guardian of the Treaty. Since it follows from Article
86(3) and (4) of the Court's Rules of Procedure that interim measures only aim
at maintaining the status quo until the Court's decision in the main case,[6] the
interest of the Commission to bring the case follows from its general interest to
see Community law respected and not breached by *faits accomplis*. Thus,
although the Court may, in procedures under Article 169, only state "that a
Member State has failed to fulfil an obligation" under the Treaty,[7] the interim
measures may go further, by temporarily suspending a national measure.

(3) In the present case, the Court examined, by way of priority, the question
whether there really was an argument for the suspension of the works. Its
reasoning was as follows: the application for interim measures was only made
when a large part of the work was already completed: the remaining part,
which was to be constructed in 1990, would not affect the birds' habitat. Statistics did not prove that birds would be driven away from their breeding
areas, and there would not be, in 1990, development of mass tourism likely to
disturb the birds.[8]

(4) This order seems convincing in its reasoning. As regards the chronology of
events the only problem was how the Commission could have known that
work had started in 1986. When the Commission received the complaint in
1985—the Order indicates 1984—work could not yet have started since the
project was only approved in September 1985.[9] There is no element in the file

---

[3] Art. 83 of the Court's Rules of Procedure.
[4] *Ibid.*
[5] **Article 155** EEC: "In order to ensure the proper functioning and development of the common
market, the Commission shall:
  —ensure that the provisions of this Treaty and the measures taken by the institutions pursuant thereto are applied;
  —exercise the powers conferred on it by the Council for the implementation of the rules
laid down by the latter."
[6] Art. 86 of the Court's Rules of Procedure.
[7] Art. 171 EEC.
[8] Paras 16 to 22.
[9] Para. 16.

which allows the affirmation that the Commission was informed of the beginning of the work considerably earlier than July 1989, when it applied to the Court.

When considering this, account must be taken of the fact that the Commission has no inspectors or other means of finding out whether and what kind of work is going on in Member States. Construction works with a potentially adverse impact on the environment take place all over the Community, from Corsica to Greece and Copenhagen to the Algarve. Complainants are under no obligation to inform the Commission. The limited staff available to the Commission does not allow it to follow the evolution of facts which lead to a complaint in every case.[10]

(5) The Commission's agent in the interim case went personally to the Leybucht in order to find out about the progress of the work.[11] Such visits are certainly useful and helpful. Until now, Member States have always accepted such visits—with one exception[12]—and Germany agreed to the agent's visit. The right to such visits, even without an agreement by the Member State, follows from Articles 5 and 235 of the EEC Treaty, though it is obvious that the Commission must have all interest to act in concertation with Member States. Besides, it should be borne in mind that visits by a lawyer who is obliged to assess ecological situations, remain of limited efficiency. Under structural funds operations and even, in order to monitor the spending of Community funds for environmental purposes,[13] officials from the Commission often visit habitats at threat, installations or regions, without any problems having occurred.

(6) Procedures in environmental cases under Article 169 take a long time. The Commission has identified a number of causes for these delays,[14] but there is limited hope that things will change for the better. It is therefore not surprising

---

[10] Commission, Eigth Annual Report on Commission Monitoring of the application of Community law: [1991] O.J. C338/1 (Annex C, para. 94).

[11] G. Winter, "Der Säbelschnäbler als Teil fürs Ganze," *Natur und Recht* (1992) p.21, no. 6.

[12] See House of Courts, Select Committee on the European Communities, Fourth Environmental Action Programme, London 1987, No. 36:

"in the last two years, officers of DG XI have begun to make visits to monitor the practical implementation of Community directives. So far, only three visits have been made, two in connection with the Birds Directive, and one regarding the Bathing Water Directive. These visits were intended as 'fact-finding' exercises, and followed local complaints that the Directives were being breached. One of these fact-finding visits took place in the United Kingdom, at Duich Moss on Islay, where a breach of the 'Birds' Directive was alleged by the Royal Society for the Protection of Birds, who claimed that the drainage of Duich Moss was affecting bird habitats. Mr. Krämer was the official of DG XI who made this inspection. The visit was made with the sole intention of establishing the facts of the case, which could be used to form a legal assessment in due course ... "

[13] See in particular Regs. 1872/84: [1984] O.J. L176/1; Reg. 2242/87: [1987] O.J. L207/8.

[14] Commission, (n. 10 above) paras. 90 *et seq.*: lack of staff, high number of complaints and procedures, problems with transposition of environmental directives in national law, enforcement infrastructure in Member States, etc.

that current political reflections, inspired by the "subsidiarity principle,"[15] suggest that it could be better to let Member States themselves ensure implementation and enforcement of environmental legislation. This political discussion is still ongoing.

(7) The other arguments of the Court rejecting the urgency of the interim measure are factual. It is obvious that the Commission is not able to demonstrate the evolution of species in the habitat area with the help of statistics. To that extent, all factual statements made by the German Government can hardly be contradicted. There is no Community office which could provide data of this kind.

In 1990, the Community set up an Environmental Agency[16] to collect, process and distribute data on the environment. However the regulation setting up the Agency will only enter into force once the Member States have agreed on the location of the Agency, which has not yet taken place.

The order only discusses the avocet breeding grounds with the argument that this was "the only species for which data were supplied to the Court."[17] The Commission had mentioned several birds in its application "in particular the avocet, the white-fronted goose and two species of tern."[18] As Germany only presented figures for the avocet, the discussion was limited to that species.

(8) It is interesting to note that the Order mentions on three occasions, that there is no urgency for an interim measure with regard to the work to be carried out in 1990.[19] It must be understood that the Order implicitly presupposed that the Court's decision in the main case would be given during 1990, *i.e.* before the work scheduled for 1991 would be carried out. In fact, the judgment in Case C–57/89 was given on February 28, 1991.[20]

(9) It has already been mentioned that the Commission spends some part of its budget to finance environmental investments.[21] Considerable amounts of money are made available to Member States under the structural funds.[22] The

---

[15] **Article 130r(4)** EEC: "The Commission shall take action relating to the environment to the extent to which the objectives referred to in paragraph 1 can be attained better at Community level than at the level of the individual Member States. Without prejudice to certain measures of a Community nature, the Member States shall finance and implement the other measures."
The word "subsidiarity" does not appear here. And it seems that the first phrase refers to actions at Community level rather than to implementation and the Commission's monitoring under Article 155 EEC Treaty. The discussion on subsidiarity is more a political discussion on the future of European Union after the signing of the Maastricht Treaty.

[16] Reg. 1210/90 on the establishment of the European Environment Agency and the European Environment Information and Observation Network: [1990] O.J. L120/1.

[17] Para. 19.

[18] Para. 6.

[19] Paras. 18, 19 and 22.

[20] See p. 220 above.

[21] See above.

[22] Between 1988 and 1993, the overall amount was some 60 billion ECU.

basic regulation for these structural funds[23] provides that measures which are financed or co-financed by Community funds must comply with environmental law and policy.[24] Thus, where a project is financed or co-financed by the Community, but does not comply with environmental law or policy requirements, the Commission has the ability to suspend payments—which, in substance, is often equivalent to the suspension of the project. On some occasions, the Commission has made use of this ability.[25] The political pressure on the Commission is, in such cases, extraordinarily high and, until now, no case has arisen where the Commission did not agree, in the end, to (co)finance the project.

---

[23] Reg. 2052/88 on the tasks of the Structural Funds and their effectives: [1988] O.J. L185/9.

[24] *Ibid.* **Article 7**: "Measures financed by the structural funds or receiving assistance from the European Investment Bank or from another existing financial instrument shall be in keeping with the provisions of the Treaties, with the instruments adopted pursuant thereto and with Community policies, including those concerning environmental protection."

[25] Commission (n. 10 above) Chap. 11 F: "In several cases, the Commission has withheld finance from projects where an assessment of the impact on the environment has not been carried out as required."

26. ARTICLE 177: NATIONAL COURTS AND ENVIRONMENTAL PROTECTION

**Judgment of the Court (Fifth Chamber) of June 11, 1987
in Case 14/86**

Preliminary ruling in the criminal proceedings Pretore di Salò against
Persons unknown

[1987] E.C.R. 2545, [1989] 1 C.M.L.R. 71

FACTS AND PROCEDURE[1]

In 1984 an "ecological association of fishermen for the safeguard of the river Chiese" in Italy brought an action before the Pretore of Salò in the province of Brescia with regard to the high fish mortality of the river. The association argued that this was mainly due to strong and sudden variations in the quantity of water; these changes came from numerous dams which have been built along the river for irrigation and hydro-electrical purposes. On application by the association, the Pretore investigated the case and found that the river was particularly capable of supporting salmonids, that high quantities of river water were taken for irrigation purposes or production of electrical energy, and that dangerous substances from industrial and urban activities were discharged into the river. He opened criminal proceedings against persons unknown and had some doubts whether Italian water legislation was compatible with Directive 78/659.[2] Therefore, he suspended the proceedings and put two questions for a preliminary ruling to the Court of Justice:

1. Is the existing system of rules established by the Italian Republic for the protection of waters from pollution consistent with the principles and quality objectives laid down in Directive 78/659/EEC of 18 July 1978 on the quality of fresh waters needing protection or improvement in order to support fish life?
2. Do the quality objectives, as laid down in the Directive, presuppose the comprehensive management of water resources—that is to say a system regulating the discharge and the volume of water—and, consequently, the need for rules which apply to water basins or watercourses and are capable of assuring a constant flow with a view to preserve the minimum volume of water which is essential for the development of fish species?

His request was registered by the Court of Justice on January 21, 1986. The Italian Government and the E.C. Commission submitted written arguments. On October 3, 1986, the case was referred to the Fifth Chamber. Oral hearings

---

[1] Summary by the author.
[2] Dir. 78/659 on the quality of fresh waters needing protection or improvement in order to support fish life: [1978] O.J. L222/1. This Directive states in **Article 1(4)**: "For the purposes of this Directive:—salmonid waters shall mean waters which support or become capable of supporting fish belonging to species such as salmon (salmo salar), trout (Salmo trutta), grayling (thymallus thymallus) and whitefish (coregonus), . . . "

took place on November 25, 1986. The Advocate General delivered his opinion on March 17, 1987.

JUDGMENT

(1) By order of 13 January 1986, which was received at the Court on 21 January 1986, the Pretore di Salò referred to the Court for a preliminary ruling under Article 177 of the EEC Treaty a question on the interpretation of Council Directive 78/659 of 18 July 1978 on the quality of fresh waters needing protection or improvement in order to support fish life (Official Journal L 222, p. 1).

(2) Those questions were raised in criminal proceedings against persons unknown concerning certain offences contrary to a number of legislative provisions relating to the protection of waters.

(3) The proceedings were initiated following a report submitted by an anglers' association as a result of the death of many fish in the River Chiese, due essentially to the many dams placed in the river for hydro-electric and irrigation purposes, which were said to cause significant and sudden changes in the water level. Other anglers' associations had already submitted reports on the same matters and on the discharge of noxious substances into the same river, but it had been decided that no action was to be taken on those reports.

(4) In the context of the preparatory inquiry in the aforementioned criminal proceedings, the Pretore di Salò considered it necessary to refer the following questions to the Court of Justice:

'(1) Is the existing system of rules established by the Italian Republic for the protection of waters from pollution consistent with the principles and quality objectives laid down in Directive 78/659/EEC of 18 July 1978 on the quality of fresh waters needing protection or improvement in order to support fish life?

(2) Do the quality objectives, as laid down in the directive, presuppose the comprehensive management of water resources—that is to say a system of regulating the discharge and the volume of water—and, consequently, the need for rules which apply to water basins or watercourses and are capable of ensuring a constant flow with a view to preserving the minimum volume of water which is essential for the development of fish species?'

(5) Reference is made to the Report for the Hearing for the facts of the case, the course of the procedure and the observations submitted by the Italian Government and by the Commission, which are mentioned or discussed hereinafter only in so far as is necessary for the reasoning of the Court.

(6) Without expressly arguing that the Court does not have jurisdiction to reply to the questions referred to it, the Italian Government draws the Court's attention to the nature of the functions performed in this case by the Pretore, which are

both those of a public prosecutor and those of an examining magistrate. The Pretore carries out preliminary investigations in his capacity as public prosecutor and, where these disclose no grounds for continuing the proceedings, makes an order accordingly in the place of an examining magistrate. That order is not a judicial act because it cannot acquire the force of *res judicata* or create an irreversible procedural situation and because no reasons need be given for it, whereas Article 111 of the Italian Constitution imposes an obligation to state reasons in the case of judicial acts.

(7) It must be observed that the Pretori are judges who, in proceedings such as those in which the questions referred to the Court in this case were raised, combine the functions of a public prosecutor and an examining magistrate. The Court has jurisdiction to reply to a request for a preliminary ruling if that request emanates from a court or tribunal which has acted in the general framework of its task of judging, independently and in accordance with the law, cases coming within the jurisdiction conferred on it by law, even though certain functions of that court or tribunal in the proceedings which gave rise to the reference for a preliminary ruling are not, strictly speaking, of a judicial nature.

(8) At the hearing, the Italian Government also maintained that, having regard to the present stage of the proceedings, at which the facts have not been sufficiently established and those who may be responsible have not yet been identified, a reference for a preliminary ruling is premature.

(9) The Commission considers that the reference for a preliminary ruling is inadmissible because in criminal proceedings against persons unknown it is possible that a decision may never be given on the substance of the case. All that is required for that to be the case is for those responsible never to be identified. At the hearing, the Commission also relied on another argument in support of the proposition that the Court does not have jurisdiction: if, after the Court's decision, the persons responsible were identified, they would be prevented from defending before the Court the interpretation of Community law most in conformity with their interests. That would constitute a violation of the right to a fair hearing.

(10) It must be pointed out first that, as the Court decided in its judgment of 10 March 1981 (Joined Cases 36 and 71/80 *Irish Creamery Milk Suppliers' Association* v *Ireland* [1981] ECR 735), if the interpretation of Community law is to be of use to the national court, it is essential to define the legal context in which the interpretation requested should be placed. In that perspective, it might be convenient in certain circumstances for the facts of the case to be established and for questions of purely national law to be settled at the time when the reference is made to the Court of Justice so as to enable the latter to take cognizance of all the matters of fact and law which may be relevant to the interpretation of Community law which it is called upon to give.

(11) However, as the Court has already held (see the same judgment and, most recently, the judgment of 20 July 1984 in Case 72/83 *Campus Oil* v *Minister for Industry and Energy* [1984] ECR 2727), those considerations do not in any way restrict the discretion of the national court, which alone has a direct knowledge of the facts of the case and of the arguments of the parties, which will have to take responsibility for giving judgment in the case and which is therefore in the best position to appreciate at what stage of the proceedings it requires a pre-

liminary ruling from the Court of Justice. The decision at what stage in proceedings a question should be referred to the Court of Justice for a preliminary ruling is therefore dictated by considerations of procedural economy and efficiency to be weighed only by the national court and not by the Court of Justice.

(12) It should also be pointed out that the Court has consistently held that the fact that judgments delivered on the basis of references for a preliminary ruling are binding on the national courts does not preclude the national court to which such a judgment is addressed from making a further reference to the Court of Justice if it considers it necessary in order to give judgment in the main proceedings. Such a reference may be justified when the national court encounters difficulties in understanding or applying the judgment, when it refers a fresh question of law to the Court, or again when it submits new considerations which might lead the Court to give a different answer to a question submitted earlier (see, most recently, the order of 5 March 1986 in Case 69/85 *Wünsche* v *Federal Republic of Germany* [1986] ECR 947).

(13) It follows that where the accused are identified after the reference for a preliminary ruling and if one of the abovementioned conditions arises, the national court may once again refer a question to the Court of Justice and thereby ensure that due respect is given to the right to a fair hearing.

(14) In those circumstances, the objections raised by the Commission and the Italian Government concerning the jurisdiction of the Court must be rejected.

First question

(15) As the Court has consistently held, it may not, in proceedings under Article 177 of the EEC Treaty, rule on the conformity of national measures with Community law (see, most recently, the judgment of 9 October 1984 in Joined Cases 91 and 127/83 *Heineken Brouwerijen* v *Inspecteurs der Vennootschapsbelasting* [1984] ECR 3435).

(16) The Court may, however, extract from the wording of the questions formulated by the national court, and having regard to the facts stated by the latter, those elements which concern the interpretation of Community law for the purpose of enabling that court to resolve the legal problems before it. In this case, however, in view of the generality of the question and the absence of any specific elements which would make it possible to identify the doubts entertained by the national court, it is not possible for the Court to reply to the question referred to it.

Second question

(17) According to the national court's order for reference, the Community rules are relevant to the questions of criminal law raised before it 'in view of the fact that such rules constitute an essential basis for the criteria to be applied in the investigation, in view of their decisive importance for the purpose of the requirements laid down by the rules of criminal law in force and in view of the undeniable possibilities which may emerge from the directive of broadening the sphere of the protection afforded by the criminal law.'

(18) The national court is therefore essentially seeking to ascertain whether Directive 78/659 may, of itself and independently of the internal law of a Member State, have the effect of determining or aggravating the liability in criminal law of persons who act in contravention of the provisions of that directive.

(19) In that regard, the Court has already held in its judgment of 26 February 1986 in Case 152/84 *Marshall* v *Southampton and South-West Hampshire Area Health Authority (Teaching)* [1986] ECR 723 at p. 737 that 'a directive may not of itself impose obligations on an individual and that a provision of a directive may not be relied upon as such against such a person'. A directive which has not been transposed into the internal legal order of a Member State may not therefore give rise to obligations on individuals either in regard to other individuals or, *a fortiori*, in regard to the State itself.

(20) Consequently, the reply to the second question must be that Council Directive 78/659 of 18 July 1978 cannot, of itself and independently of a national law adopted by a Member State for its implementation, have the effect of determining or aggravating the liability in criminal law of persons who act in contravention of the provisions of that directive.

Costs

(21) The costs incurred by the Italian Government and by the Commission of the European Communities, which have submitted observations to the Court, are not recoverable. As these proceedings are, in so far as the parties to the main proceedings are concerned, in the nature of a step in the proceedings pending before the national court, the decision as to costs is a matter for that court.

On those grounds,

THE COURT (FIFTH CHAMBER),

in answer to the questions referred to it by the Pretore di Salò by order of 13 January 1986, hereby rules:

Council Directive 78/659 of 18 July 1978 (Official Journal L 222, p. 1) cannot, of itself and independently of a national law adopted by a Member State for its implementation, have the effect of determining or aggravating the liability in criminal law of persons who act in contravention of the provisions of that directive.

COMMENTARY

(1) This judgment was given under Article 177 of the EEC Treaty which reads as follows:

"The Court of Justice shall have jurisdiction to give preliminary rulings concerning:

(a) the interpretation of this Treaty;
(b) the validity and interpretation of acts of the institutions of the Community;
(c) the interpretation of the statutes of bodies established by an act of the Council, where those statutes so provide.

Where such a question is raised before any Court or tribunal of a Member State, that Court or tribunal may, if it considers that a decision on the question is necessary to enable it to give judgment, request the Court of Justice to give a ruling thereon.

Where any such question is raised in a case pending before a court or a tribunal of a Member State, against whose decisions there is no judicial remedy under national law, that court or tribunal shall bring the matter before the Court of Justice."

In 1986, the Court received 91 requests for a preliminary ruling, 144 in 1987, 179 in 1988, 139 in 1989, 141 in 1990, and 153 in 1991.[3] Only an extremely small number of cases were concerned with environmental matters.

(2) If one takes environmental matters as such, decisions by the Court of Justice under Article 177 might account for about one quarter of all cases decided by the Court of Justice.[4]

Very generally, they might be divided into two categories: the first group is concerned with cases pending before national Courts where a person is accused of not having respected a rule which aims—rightly or wrongly—at protecting the environment; in defence this person invokes Community provisions, arguing that these supersede national provisions. To this group belong, almost exclusively, criminal law cases, for instance Case 125/88, where the compatibility of a national provision prohibiting the use of a pesticide was in question[5] and joined Cases C–206 and 207/88, where it was doubtful whether national waste law complied with some waste directives;[6] Case C–169/89, where the national law of marketing of specific bird species was in dispute;[7] Case 380/87, where a local law on non-biodegradable plastic bags was contested;[8] Case 240/83, where a national provision on waste disposal

---

[3] Figures from the annual reports on Commission monitoring of the application of Community law; Fourth Report (1986), [1987] O.J. C338/33; Fifth Report (1987), [1988] O.J. C310/43; Sixth Report (1988), [1989] O.J. C330/53; Seventh Report (1989), [1990] O.J. C232/54; Eighth Report (1990), [1991] O.J. C338/77; Ninth Report (1991), [1992] O.J. C250/1.

[4] All depends on the question of what is, statistically, an environmental case. To give only one example: Case 302/86, *Commission* v. *Denmark*, is normally attributed to "internal market" cases. Kromarek, "Grands Arrêts Communautaires", *Jurisclasseurs–Environnement*, Fascicule 1110 (Paris, 1992) lists 73 judgments, out of which 19 are given under Article 177. The Commission stated in Written Question 3090/91 (J. Stewart-Clark), [1992] O.J. C209/34 that it could not give reliable figures on environmental cases brought to the Court, because of terminological and statistical difficulties.

[5] 125/88, *Nijman*: [1989] E.C.R. 3533, [1991] 1 C.M.L.R. 92 see p.343 above.

[6] C–206 & 207/88, *Zanetti*: [1990] I E.C.R. 1461; see p.269 above.

[7] C–169/89, *Van den Berg*: [1990] I E.C.R. 2143; see p.149 above.

[8] 380/87, *Enichem*: [1989] E.C.R. 2491, [1991] 1 C.M.L.R. 313; see p.131 above.

was challenged,[9] or Cases 372 to 374/85, where it was doubtful whether certain waste disposal activities were covered by Community waste legislation.[10]

(3) The second group is much smaller. It considers Community environmental provisions as a means of protecting the environment and/or submits questions to the European Court in order to find out whether Community law does provide appropriate protection. Examples for this group are Case 228/87, where the national court had doubts whether Directive 80/778 on drinking water allowed a specific derogation which the national law had introduced;[11] Case C–236/92, where the national court wished to know whether Directive 75/442 on waste[12] conferred rights onto individual persons;[13] or the present Case 14/86 where the national judge wanted to know what consequences flowed out of the Community provisions. More generally, all cases where a national Court asks whether a Community environmental directive has direct effect[14] or what its useful effect[15] is, fall into this second group.

The surprising thing is that until now only Italian judges or courts have submitted questions for a preliminary ruling to the Court of Justice which come into the second group of cases.

Case C–236/92[16] is the very first case where a question was submitted to the Court whether individual persons had been conferred any rights under environmental law directives. Such questions are more frequently submitted by national courts in social[17] or tax cases,[18] areas where individual interests are directly concerned. Community environmental law which deals with problems of "general interest"[19] has been much less frequently the object of attention by national courts, which is reflected in the absence of questions for preliminary rulings.

(4) This raises the general problem of the position of the individual in environmental law. A constitutional right of the individual to a healthy environment is not really recognised by Member States' constitutions—nor by the EEC Treaty.

---

[9] 240/83, *ADBHU* [1985] E.C.R. 531; see p.5 above.

[10] 372–374/85, *Traen* [1987] E.C.R. 2141, [1988] 3 C.M.L.R. 511.

[11] 228/87, *Pretore di Torino* [1988] E.C.R. 5099, [1990] 1 C.M.L.R. 716.

[12] [1975] O.J. L194/47.

[13] C–236/92, *Difesa della Cava* [1992] O.J. C177/13; the case is pending before the Court.

[14] See below at point 4. The Court described the "direct-effect doctrine" by "wherever the provisions of a directive appear, as far as their subject-matter is concerned, to be unconditional and sufficiently precise, those provisions may, in the absence of implementing measures adopted within the prescribed period, be relied upon", Case 152/84, *Marshall* [1986] E.C.R. 723, [1986] 1 C.M.L.R. 688.

[15] See below at point 4.

[16] See n. 13 above.

[17] Mainly as regards the question of equal rights between men and women.

[18] Case 8/81, *Becker* [1982] E.C.R. 53, [1982] 1 C.M.L.R. 499.

[19] Case 240/83, (n. 9 above) para. 15; repeated in Case 302/86, *Commission* v. *Denmark* [1988] E.C.R. 4607, [1989] 1 C.M.L.R. 619 (see p.91 above) and C–2/90, *Commission* v. *Belgium* [1992] I E.C.R. 4431, [1993] 1 C.M.L.R. 365. (see p. 71 above).

Four national constitutions expressly mention environmental protection, the constitution of the Netherlands,[20] Greece,[21] Spain[22] and Portugal.[23] Access to the national Courts in environmental matters is subject to the national rules of procedure. The national courts apply national environmental law. According to the "direct effect" doctrine and the "effet utile" doctrine developed in Community law, they are, however, obliged to apply Community environmental law in certain cases.

The direct effect doctrine was developed by the Court of Justice. It means in short that where a provision of Community law is clear, precise and unconditional and leaves to the Member States no discretion as to its applications, public authorities of the Member States, including courts and tribunals, must apply this provision in favour of individual persons, even where the Member State has not transposed it into national law or where such transposition has been incorrect or incomplete. In the case of discrepancy with existing national rules, the courts and administrative bodies must set aside these national rules and apply Community law.[24]

The "useful-effect" doctrine, less clearly developed by the Court, requires national authorities and courts to take all necessary steps in order to ensure that the intended effect of Community law is really achieved. To that extent, national law must be interpreted in a way which allows the effect of Community law to be reached.[25]

(5) Where a national court is of the opinion that the effect of Community law influences the outcome of a case before it, it may ask the European Court for a preliminary ruling under Article 177, and in certain cases is obliged to do so.[26] Of course Article 177 presupposes that the national court does know Community (environmental) law. This is the reason why it is important for solicitors, legal consultants, courts and other members of the legal profession—as well as environmentally interested persons—to develop their interest and knowledge of EEC environmental law.[27]

Individuals cannot apply directly to the European Court in environmental matters, since Articles 173 and 175 allow such an action only where a Com-

---

[20] Dutch Constitution of 1982, Art. 21.

[21] Greek Constitution of 1975, Art. 24.

[22] Spanish Constitution of 1978, Art. 45.

[23] Portuguese Constitution of 1975, Art. 66.

[24] Case 41/74, *Van Duyn*: [1974] E.C.R. 1337, [1975] 1 C.M.L.R. 1; Case 8/81, *Becker* (n. 18 above); Case 103/84, *Costanzo*: [1988] E.C.R. 339, [1987] 2 C.M.L.R. 825.

[25] The Court's case law is less precise as regards this doctrine. Directive 78/659 might however be a good illustration. In its judgment in Case 322/86, *Commission* v. *Italy*: [1988] E.C.R. 3995 the Court ruled that, in order to give full effect to that directive, Member States had to designate fish waters all over their territory, not only in one region; the directive itself does not contain any indications as to geographical or numerical designations.

[26] See wording of Art. 177, pp.415–416 above.

[27] The Commission expressly stressed its effort to promote the knowledge of Community law among solicitors, magistrates and other, see Commission Sixth Report, (n. 3 above), p.7; Eighth Report (*ibid.* p.7.)

munity measure is of concern to an individual.[28] However directives and regulations are addressed to Member States and/or are of general nature.

The Commission has set up a complaints procedure which also affects individual, and which is described elsewhere in this book,[29] since complaints could lead to proceedings under Article 169 and not under Article 177.

(6) In the present case, the Court had some difficulties in deciding whether it considered the Pretore di Salò to be a "Court" in the meaning of Article 177.[30] This problem will not be discussed here, since it has little bearing on environmental questions. The Court of Justice also had difficulties in understanding the questions which the Pretore had put forward.

The Court frequently has to find out the true meaning of a question which is put under Article 177. As the wording of this Article indicates, the Court's jurisdiction is restricted to the interpretation of Community law. However, national courts sometimes either ask for the compatibility of national law with Community law—a question not to be decided by the Court of Justice, but by the national court[31]—or put other questions than on the interpretation of EEC law. The Court of Justice then often "adapts" such questions, stating that a question "must be understood as"[32], or that it "raises in substance"[33] or a similar formula. The formula used by the Court in paragraph 16 of the present judgment, that it may give the elements of interpretation to the national judge, is rather common.

(7) In contrast, it is extremely rare for the Court, as in the present case, not to answer a question. The Commission and the Advocate General both thought that it was impossible to answer the first question.[34] Indeed, it seems difficult to understand the doubts which the Pretore had and which he wanted to see dissipated by an answer from the Court, all the more so as he referred to the Italian system of water protection legislation in general.

A possible reformulation of the Pretore's first question could have been: "What are the principles and objectives of Directive 78/659 which the national legislator must transpose into national law?" The Court could then have been obliged to interpret in detail the content of Directive 78/659, as the Court has done with other directives, though admittedly in proceedings under Article

---

[28] **Article 173** EEC: " . . . Any national or legal person may . . . institute proceedings against a decision addressed to that person or against a decision which, although in the form of a regulation or a decision addressed to another person, is of direct and individual concern to the former . . . "

Article 175 EEC: " . . . Any national or legal person may . . . complain to the Court of Justice that an institution of the Community has failed to address to that person any act other than a recommendation or an opinion."

[29] See p.394 above.

[30] Paras. 6 to 14.

[31] See however the commentary to Case 240/83 on pp.5 *et seq.* above, n. 20, where a case is reported where the Court did interpret national law.

[32] Case 125/88, (n. 5 above).

[33] Case C–169/89, [1990] I E.C.R. 2143, para. 6; see also para. 18 of the present Case 14/86.

[34] Report for the hearing, [1987] E.C.R. 2545, 2547; Opinion of the Advocate General, point 9.

169 of the EEC Treaty.[35] However, since the case was historically practically the first case under Article 177 which belonged to the second of the two groups mentioned above[36] and since both the Commission and the Advocate General had advised on the impossibility of answering that question, the Court's answer seems understandable.

(8) The second question seems, in my opinion, clear and unambiguous. It is difficult to see why the Court tries to interpret what the question "in substance" means.[37] The question whether the Pretore is allowed to use the interpretation given to Community law by the Court of Justice in Italian criminal proceedings is a question of Italian (criminal) law, but has nothing to do with the interpretation of Community law—and had not been asked by the Pretore. It was, again, the Advocate General who led the Court to this line of interpretation of the second question, though the Advocate General himself did answer the question which was put by the Pretore.[38] Thus the Court should have answered the question as it was put forward.

Together with the Commission's submission[39] and the Advocate General's opinion,[40] I am of the opinion that Directive 78/659 obliges Member States to assure that designated waters[41] have enough water to allow fish to survive. Indeed, such designated waters constitute habitats for fish and Member States are obliged to assure that fish can survive in the designated habitats. Thus there is an obligation for Member States not to reduce the stream of rivers which are designated, to an extent that there is no water at all or so little water that fish life is impossible.

The Court's unrequested answer is certainly also correct: it is difficult to see how criminal liability of a person can be established under Italian law where the relevant Directive 78/659 had not even yet been transposed into the Italian legal order.

(9) The Court did not raise a problem which demonstrates the theoretical value of Directive 78/659 but its practical limits to protect or even improve the environment. Indeed, Article 1(1) of the Directive provides:

"This Directive concerns the quality of fish waters and applies to those waters designated by the Member States as needing protection or improvement in order to support fish life."

Thus, the requirements of Directive 78/659 as regards the quality of fish waters

---

[35] See, *e.g.* Case C–70/89, *Commission* v. *Italy*: [1990] I E.C.R. 4817; Case 291/84, *Commission* v. *Netherlands*: [1987] E.C.R. 3483, [1989] 1 C.M.L.R. 479.
[36] See p.417 above.
[37] Paras. 17 and 18.
[38] See the proposal for the answer to be given by the Court, formulated by the Advocate General, [1987] E.C.R. 2545, 2553 [1989] 1 C.M.L.R. 71, 74.
[39] Report for the hearing, [1987] E.C.R. 2545, 2547.
[40] Opinion of the Advocate General, para. 10.
[41] Under Dir. 78/659 Member States have to designate waters to which the Directive applies.

only applies to those waters which have been designated by Member States. The Directive does not contain criteria for the designation of fish waters. A number of Member States has either not designated waters or has designated only such waters which already complied with the requirements of the Directive. The practical effect of the Directive is thus rather limited.[42]

A decision by the Court of Justice in 1988 in Case 322/86, *Commission* v. *Italy*[43] opened a path to improve the effect of Directive 78/659. In that decision the Court ruled that Directive 78/659 obliged Member States to designate fish water all over their territory, not only in one region. As the Commission pointed out in 1992, fresh proceedings had started against Italy because it had not yet complied with the Court's judgment[44]. In other terms, Italy had still not designated fish water all over its territory under Directive 78/659.

It is therefore more than likely that the attempts by the Pretore di Salò to use Community environmental provisions in order to protect the river Chiese, will not be successful.

---

[42] See for instance N. Haigh (ed): *Comparative Report: Water and Waste in Four Countries. A Study of the Implementation of the EEC Directives in France, Germany, Netherlands and United Kingdom* (London, 1986) p. 29: "The Directive has not yet had any effect in improving water quality." This situation does not seem to have changed in the meantime.

[43] 322/86, (n. 25 above).

[44] Commission, Ninth Report [1992] O.J. C250/1 p. 156.

27. ARTICLE 171: FRESH PROCEEDINGS AND SANCTIONS IN
COMMUNITY LAW

**Judgment of the Court of February 6, 1992
in Case C–75/91**

E.C. Commission v. *The Netherlands*

[1992] I E.C.R. 549

FACTS AND PROCEDURE[1]

On October 13, 1987 the Court gave a judgment in Case 236/85 against the Netherlands which stated that:

"by not adopting within the prescribed period all the laws, regulations and administrative provisions needed to comply with Council Directive 79/409/ EEC of 2 April 1979 on the conservation of wild birds, the Kingdom of the Netherlands has failed to fulfill its obligations under the EEC Treaty."[2]

The Court found that out of the five complaints which the Commission had submitted to its judgment, four had to be upheld.[3] On April 24, 1989, the Commission sent a letter of formal notice to the Dutch Government, since it had not been notified of the measures adopted by the Dutch Government in order to comply with the Court's judgment. The Dutch answer indicated that draft legislation was in preparation. On February 27, 1990 the Commission issued a reasoned opinion. In its answer of May 2, 1990, the Dutch Government indicated that very soon a bill would be sent to Parliament.

The Commission applied to the Court on February 22, 1991. On August 15, 1991, the Dutch Government presented draft legislation to the second Chamber of Parliament.

Oral hearings before the Court took place on January 16, 1992. The Advocate General gave his opinion on the same day.

---

[1] Summary by the author.

[2] 236/85, *Commission* v. *Netherlands.* [1987] E.C.R. 3989.

[3] The Court stated:

    (a) Article 10 of the Dutch Vogelwet does not make the grants of permits conditional upon the absence of any other satisfactory solution

    (b) The list of birds in Article 9 and 10 of the Dutch Vogelbesluit which lists the birds that are not protected as far as capture for caging or hunting are concerned, is not identical with the list of birds of Article 6(2) and (3) and Annex III of Directive 79/409; furthermore, Articles 15, 15bis and 16 of the Dutch Vogelwet which allows permits to be issued for trade in protected dead and stuffed birds, are not in conformity with Article 9(1) of Directive 79/409

    (c) Articles 17 to 20 are not in conformity with Article 9 of the Directive

    (d) Article 14 of the Vogelbesluit was not in conformity with Directive 79/409 when the Commission sent a reasoned opinion.

JUDGMENT*

(1) By application lodged with the Court Registry on 22 February 1991, the Commission brought an action pursuant to Article 169 EEC for a declaration that, by failing to comply with the judgment of the Court of 13 October 1987 in Case 236/85 *Commission v. Netherlands*, the Kingdom of the Netherlands has failed to fulfil its obligations under Article 171 EEC.

(2) In this judgment, the Court declared that, by not adopting in the prescribed time-limits the laws, regulations and administrative provisions needed to comply with Council Directive 79/409/EEC of 2 April 1979 on the conservation of wild birds, the Kingdom of the Netherlands has failed to fulfil its obligations under the EEC Treaty.

(3) As no measure of transposition of the Directive was taken following the judgment, the Commission sent the Netherlands Government a letter of formal notice on 24 April 1989, urging it to comply with its obligations. The Commission found the Netherlands Government's reply insufficient and sent a reasoned opinion on 27 February 1990.

(4) In its reply to the opinion, the Netherlands Government announced in a letter dated 2 May 1990 that two draft laws amending the *Jachtwet* (Law on Hunting) and the *Vogelwet* (Law on Birds) were in the process of being submitted to the Parliament. Having received no further information allowing it to conclude that the said Bills had been submitted to the Parliament, the Commission then initiated the present action.

(5) Reference is made to the Report for the Hearing for the background to the dispute, the course of the procedure and the submissions and arguments of the parties, which are mentioned or referred to hereinafter only insofar as they are necessary to the reasoning of the Court.

(6) The Netherlands Government admits that it has not yet taken the measures that will ensure compliance with the Court's judgment and justifies this fact by the demands of the national legislative procedure which affects the time required to amend the abovementioned laws.

(7) It must be observed that, even though Article 171 EEC does not impose specific time-limits to comply with a judgment, it is in the interest of a direct and uniform application of Community Law that measures be taken immediately and come into effect without undue delay (see judgment of 30 January 1992 in Case C–328/90, *Commission v. Hellenic Republic*, paragraph 6, not yet published in the European Court Reports).

(8) It must therefore be stated that by failing to take the measures necessary to comply wih the judgment of the Court of Justice of 13 October 1987, the Kingdom of the Netherlands has failed to fulfil its obligations under Article 171 EEC.

---

* Publisher's translation.

Costs

(9) Under Article 69(2) of the Rules of Procedure, an unsuccessful party is to be ordered to pay the costs. Since the Kingdom of the Netherlands has failed in its submissions, it must be ordered to pay the costs.

On those grounds

THE COURT

hereby:

(1) Declares that by failing to adopt the measures necessary to comply with the judgment of the Court of Justice of 13 October 1987, the Kingdom of the Netherlands has failed to fulfil its obligations under Article 171 EEC.

(2) Orders the Kingdom of the Netherlands to pay the costs.

COMMENTARY

(1) This judgment is one of the few, where the Court of Justice declared that a Member State had breached its obligations under Article 171 of the EEC Treaty and it also happens to be an environmental case. Article 171 reads as follows:

"If the Court finds that a Member State has failed to fulfil an obligation under this Treaty, the State shall be required to take the necessary measures to comply with the judgment of the Court of Justice."

Thus, a decision under Article 171 is practically the second "condemnation" of a Member State concerning specific behaviour. It is obvious that this second judgment only states the Netherlands' failure to fulfil its obligations under the Treaty, a statement which the first judgment had already made. However, the new reproach is that the Netherlands have also not respected the judgment of the Court and thus, if this phrase be permitted, added "insult to injury": the second judgment does contain some element of a contempt of court-decision; this is the underlying reason why a judgment stating a breach of Article 171 is considered to be even more serious than a decision under Article 169.

(2) This is also the reason why the Maastricht Treaty on European Union[4] provides for a new Article 171(2) of the EEC Treaty, which reads as follows:

"If the Commission considers that the Member State concerned has not

---

[4] [1992] O.J. C191/1.

taken such measures it shall, after giving that State the opportunity to submit its observations, issue a reasoned opinion specifying the points on which the Member State concerned has not complied with the judgment of the Court of Justice. If the Member State concerned fails to take the necessary measures to comply with the Court's judgment within the time-limit laid down by the Commission, the latter may bring the case before the Court of Justice. In doing so it shall specify the amount of the lump sum or penalty payment to be paid by the Member State concerned which it considers appropriate in the circumstances. If the Court of Justice finds that the Member State concerned has not complied with its judgment it may impose a lump sum or a penalty payment on it . . . "

(3) As the Court indicated in its judgment, Article 171 does not prescribe a specific time within which a Member State has to take the measures in order to comply with a judgment of the Court.[5] However, the measures must be started immediately and lead to a result as soon as possible. This interpretation corresponds to a consistent line of decisions of the Court.[6] It is justified in particular by the consideration that the obligation to take specific measures had not been created by the first judgment, but by the relevant provision of Community law; in the present case, Directive 79/409 on the conservation of wild birds had been adopted on April 2, 1979[7] and had requested Member States to take the necessary measures within two years.[8] Dutch law was therefore not in compliance with Community law for more than 10 years, when the Court gave its judgment in the present case.

(4) The Dutch defence, which raised the time-limits and complications of national legislative procedure,[9] was not really a defence. Indeed the Dutch Government was not able to explain why it had not started the legislative procedure earlier than in summer 1991; it knew its difficult position and therefore did not even ask for the application of the Commission to be rejected.[10]

(5) There is another environmental case in which the Court pronounced judgment under Article 171 of the EEC Treaty, namely Joined Cases 227 to 230/85.[11] There the Court found that Belgium had not taken the necessary measures to comply with the judgments in Cases 68/81,[12] 69/81,[13] 70/81,[14]

---

[5] Para. 7.
[6] See, *e.g.*, Case 131/84, *Commission* v. *Italy*: [1985] E.C.R. 3531, [1986] 3 C.M.L.R. 693; Case 160/85, *Commission* v. *Italy*: [1986] E.C.R. 3245; Cases 227–230/85, *Commission* v. *Belgium*: [1988] E.C.R. 1, [1989] 2 C.M.L.R. 797.
[7] [1979] O.J. C191/1.
[8] Art. 18 of the Directive.
[9] Paras. 4 and 6.
[10] Report for the hearing.
[11] 227–230/85, *Commission* v. *Belgium*: [1988] E.C.R. 1, [1989] 2 C.M.L.R. 797.
[12] 68/81, *Commission* v. *Belgium*: [1982] E.C.R. 153.
[13] 69/81, *Commission* v. *Belgium*: [1982] E.C.R. 163.
[14] 70/81, *Commission* v. *Belgium*: [1982] E.C.R. 169.

71/81[15] and, in substance, that Belgium had not transposed Directives 78/176,[16] 75/442,[17] 75/439[18] and 76/403[19] into Belgian law. Belgium defended itself essentially by arguing that the constitutional reform, which had led to the transfer of almost all environmental competence to the Belgian regions, had made it impossible to comply with the judgments of the Court.[20]

The Court did not accept this argument. Its reasoning was that each Member State was free to organise its internal structure as it deemed appropriate, and to transfer the competence to implement a Community directive to regional or even local authorities. However, this did not relieve it from the obligation under Community law to assure full and complete implementation and enforcement of a directive within its territory.[21] As regards the interpretation of Article 171, the Court's reasoning was almost word for word the same as in the present case.

(6) In its judgment in Cases 227 to 230/85, the Court did not take the legal point which the Advocate General in that case had raised very cautiously, calling it a "delicate" question.[22] Indeed, during the oral hearings of the cases, the Belgian Government again had indicated that under Belgian constitutional law, the central Government has no possibility whatsoever to compel the Regions to implement Community environmental legislation and cannot either take implementation measures in their place, for instance in cases where there is a continued delay from their side.[23]

The Advocate General mentioned Article 5(2) of the EEC Treaty, which obliges Member States to "abstain from any measure which could jeopardise the attainment of the objectives of this Treaty" and reminded the Court that this provision also applied to constitutional measures. He thus implicitly raised the question whether the Belgian constitutional measures, which gave legislative power for transposing Community law to the regions without giving the central state, which is Member State of the EEC, the power to compel them, were not themselves compatible with Community law and in particular with Article 5 of the EEC Treaty.[24]

This question was not discussed further. The Court did not take it up and the Commission has never taken any action against Belgium on that point.

(7) The problem of complying with judgments of the Court is closely linked to the general problem of complying with Community environmental provisions. Since 1984, the Commission has published an annual report on "Commission

---

[15] 71/81, *Commission* v. *Belgium*: [1982] E.C.R. 175.
[16] Dir. 78/176 on waste from the titanium dioxide industry: [1978] O.J. L54/19.
[17] Dir. 75/442 on waste: [1975] O.J. L194/39.
[18] Dir. 75/439 on the disposal of waste oils: [1975] O.J. L194/23.
[19] Dir. 76/403 on the disposal of PCBs and PCTs: [1976] O.J. L108/41.
[20] Cases 227–230/85, (n. 11 above), para. 6.
[21] *Ibid.* paras. 9 and 10.
[22] Advocate General Mancini, para. 2.
[23] Para. 8.
[24] Advocate General Mancini.

monitoring of the application of Community law."[25] These reports contain information on judgments of the Court of Justice, "not complied with" and give, for environmental cases, the following information:

Second Report 1984[26]

(1) Cases 68 to 71, Belgium: fresh infringement proceedings

Third Report 1985[27]

(1) Cases 68 to 71/81, Belgium: fresh infringement proceedings
(2) Case 173/83, France: fresh infringement proceedings

Fourth Report 1986[28]

(1) Cases 68 to 71/81, Belgium: fresh infringement proceedings
(2) Case 173/83, France: fresh infringement proceedings; new French decree of 1985 still not conform with Community law.

Fifth Report 1987[29]

(1) Cases 68 to 71, Belgium: on January 14, 1988 the Court has pronounced a second judgment (Cases 227 to 230/85)
(2) Case 173/83, France: fresh infringement proceedings (A 103/86). French authorities have indicated that they are prepared to amend the decree

Sixth Report 1988[30]

(1) Case 1/86, Belgium: fresh infringement proceedings (A 291/88). The decree of September 17, 1987 is not satisfactory
(2) Case 412/85, Germany: fresh infringement proceedings (148/89)
(3) Case 239/85, Belgium: fresh infringement proceedings
(4) Case 247/85, Belgium: fresh infringement proceedings
(5) Case 278/85, Denmark: fresh infringement proceedings
(6) Case 262/85, Italy: fresh infringement proceedings (A 49/89)
(7) Case 291/84, Netherlands: fresh infringement proceedings (A 532/88)
(8) Case 236/85, Netherlands: fresh infringement proceedings (A 60/89)

---

[25] Commission reports on Commission monitoring of the application of Community law; First Report 1983, COM(84)181 final of April 11, 1984; Second Report 1984, COM(85)149 final of May 13, 1985; Third Report 1985: [1986] O.J. C220/1; Fourth Report 1986: [1986] O.J. C338/1; Fifth Report 1987: [1988] O.J. C310/1; Sixth Report 1988: [1989] O.J. C330/1; Eighth Report 1990: [1991] O.J. C338/1; Ninth Report 1991: [1992] O.J. C250/1.

[26] pp.29 *et seq.*
[27] pp.24 *et seq.*
[28] pp.26 *et seq.*
[29] pp.34 *et seq.*
[30] pp.44 *et seq.*

Seventh Report 1989[31]

(1) Case 239/85, Belgium: fresh infringement proceedings
(2) Case 322/86, Italy: fresh infringement proceedings
(3) Case 236/85, Netherlands: fresh infringement proceedings. On July 5, 1989 the Commission decided to issue a reasoned opinion
(4) Case 412/85, Germany: fresh infringement proceedings. On July 5, 1989, the Commission decided to issue a reasoned opinion
(5) Case 1/86, Belgium: fresh infringement proceedings (A 291/88)
(6) Case 247/85, Belgium: fresh infringement proceedings
(7) Case 262/85, Italy: fresh infringement proceedings. On July 5, 1989, the Commission decided to issue a reasoned opinion
(8) Case 291/84, Netherlands: fresh infringement proceedings. On July 5, 1989, the Commission decided to issue a reasoned opinion (A 532/88)

Eighth Report 1990[32]

(1) Case 239/85, Belgium: fresh infringement proceedings. On December 5, 1990 the Commission decided to issue a reasoned opinion (A 212/90)
(2) Case 1/86, Belgium: fresh infringement proceedings. On July 11, 1990 the Commission decided to apply to the Court (A 291/88)
(3) Case 162/89, Belgium: a letter of warning of action under Article 171 has been sent.
(4) Case 322/86, Italy: fresh infringement proceedings. On December 5, 1990 the Commission decided to send a reasoned opinion
(5) Case 291/84, Netherlands: fresh infringement proceedings The Commission is studying the reply which it received to its reasoned opinion
(6) Case 236/85, Netherlands: fresh infringement proceedings. On July 11, 1990 the Commission decided to refer the matter to the Court
(7) Case 412/85, Germany: fresh infringement proceedings. On December 5, 1990 the Commission decided to refer the matter to the Court
(8) Case 288/88, Germany: Article 171 proceedings are being initiated
(9) Case 247/85, Belgium: fresh infringement proceedings. On December 5, 1990 the Commission decided to send a reasoned opinion
(10) Case 42/89, Belgium: a letter giving notice of action under Article 171 has been sent to the Belgian authorities
(11) Case 252/85, France: the letter giving formal notice was transmitted on July 11, 1990 (Article 171)
(12) Case 262/85, Italy: a reasoned opinion was sent to Italy on August 28, 1990
(13) Case 48/89, Italy: a letter giving notice of action under Article 171 has been sent to the Italian authorities

---

[31] pp.44 *et seq.*
[32] pp.63 *et seq.*

(14) Case 339/87, Netherlands: a letter giving notice of action under Article 171 was sent on January 13, 1991

Ninth Report 1991[33]

(1) Case 412/85, Germany: on December 5, 1990 the Commission decided to refer the matter to the Court
(2) Case 288/85, Germany: Article 171 proceedings are being initiated
(3) Case 131/88, Germany: a letter warning of action under Article 171 was sent on July 23, 1991
(4) Case 361/88, Germany: a letter of warning of action under Article 171 was sent on November 7, 1991
(5) Case 59/89, Germany: a letter warning of action under Article 171 is being sent
(6) Case 59/89, Germany: a letter warning of action under Article 171 is being sent
(7) Case 239/85, Belgium: on December 5, 1990 the Commission decided to send a reasoned opinion
(8) Case 1/86, Belgium: case pending before the Court (C–174/91)
(9) Case 247/85, Belgium: on December 5, 1990 the Commission decided to send a reasoned opinion
(10) Case 42/89, Belgium: a letter giving formal notice was sent to the Belgian authorities on December 2, 1991
(11) Case 290/89, Belgium: a warning letter of action under Article 171 was sent on September 4, 1991
(12) Case 252/85, France: fresh infringement proceedings
(13) Case 262/85, Italy: on June 26, 1991 the Commission decided to refer the matter to the Court
(14) Case 322/86, Italy: fresh infringement proceedings (A 90/203)
(15) Case 70/89, Italy: on September 25, 1991 a letter warning of action under Article 171 was sent
(16) Case 157/89, Italy: on November 7, 1991 a letter warning of action under Article 171 was sent
(17) Case 334/89, Italy: on November 7, 1991 a letter warning of action under Article 171 was sent
(18) Case 360/87, Italy: on November 25, 1991 a letter giving notice of action under Article 171 was sent
(19) Case 291/84, Netherlands: fresh infringement proceedings (A 88/532)
(20) Case 236/85, Netherlands: case pending before the Court. (C–75/91)
(21) Case 339/87, Netherlands: a letter giving formal notice under Article 171 was sent on June 26, 1991.

(8) The considerable increase in the number of cases, where action under Article 171 has been taken—the phenomenon is not limited to environmental

---

[33] pp.38 *et seq.* see also Annex C, pp.150 *et seq.*

cases—has undoubtedly contributed to the above-mentioned amendment brought to Article 171 by the Maastricht Treaty. The success of this amendment remains to be seen. The reasons which are given by the Member States for not complying with a judgment are essentially the same as the reasons given for not complying with the requirements of a directive. In this reference can be made to the chapters on Article 169-procedures.[34]

The Commission does not start a second procedure under Article 171, where a Member State does not fully comply with a judgment of the Court stating a breach of Article 171. The Commission is of the opinion that in such cases a political action is preferable to new court proceedings.[35] Also in this respect the amendment introduced into Article 171 of the EEC Treaty, might bring a change: indeed, the Court will also be empowered to impose a penalty payment. No definition of "penalty payment" exists, however, as it is contrasted to "lump sum" one may presume that for each day or each month of non-compliance the Member State might be required to pay a certain amount. Such a payment would more or less constitute a permanent threat, as long as the non-compliance continues.

(9) Until the Maastricht Treaty on European Union enters into force, the possibility of bringing proceedings against a Member State under Article 169 of the EEC Treaty and eventually to start fresh proceedings under Article 171 are the only "sanctions" available to the Community. The Treaty contains no express reference to sanctions, neither in general nor in environmental matters. It follows from Article 172 of the EEC Treaty[36] that regulations may contain provision for penalties. Article 155 (last indent) also indicates that the Council could grant the Commission "power for the implementation" of directives.[37] However, until now, environmental directives have not conferred power to pronounce sanctions.

(10) When transposing governmental directives into their national law Member States may provide for criminal, civil or administrative sanctions in case of non-compliance. In case C–68/88,[38] the Court pronounced itself on national sanctions. The Court concluded from Article 5 of the Treaty[39] that where Com-

---

[34] See pp. 377 *et seq.* above.

[35] See Commission, Seventh Report (n. 25 above) point 153 on p. 25.

[36] **Article 172** EEC: "Regulations made by the Council to the provisions of this Treaty may give the Court of Justice unlimited jurisdiction in regard to the penalties provided for in such regulations."

[37] **Article 155** EEC: "In order to ensure the proper functioning and development of the common market, the Commission shall: . . . —exercise the powers conferred on it by the Council for the implementation of the rules laid down by the latter."

[38] C–68/88, *Commission* v. *Greece*: [1989] E.C.R. 2965, [1991] 1 C.M.L.R. 31; see also Commission, Communication on Case C–68/88: [1990] O.J. C143/3.

[39] **Article 5** EEC: "Member States shall take all appropriate measures, whether general or particular, to ensure fulfilment of the obligations arising out of this Treaty or resulting from actions taken by the institution of the Community. They shall facilitate the achievement of the Community's tasks. They shall abstain from any measure which could jeopardise the attainment of the objectives of this Treaty."

munity law does not contain a specific rule on sanctions or where it refers to national legal and administrative provisions, Member States are obliged to take all necessary steps to give full effect to Community law. This may include that Member States themselves have to decide on sanctions. However, they are obliged to ensure that non-compliance with Community law is sanctioned by means of equivalent substantive and procedural conditions as similar cases of non compliance with national provisions. In any case the national measures must be effective, adequate and deterrent.

This judgment, though it is first of all concerned with criminal sanctions, is rather general. Thus, it may be of importance for environmental matters, once the details of national sanctions as regards non-compliance with Community environmental provisions are closely examined. At present, this area is entirely left to Member States.

(11) In 1990, the Commission issued the first report on the monitoring of the application of Community environmental law.[40] In its presentation, the member of the Commission in charge of environmental questions, Mr. Ripa de Meana, raised the problem whether it would not be possible to refuse financial payments—under structural funds or other sources of financing of the Community—to those Member States which do not comply with Community environmental rules.[41] In fact, the Commission has started to consider delaying or refusing payments for projects which do not fully comply with requirements of Community law. However until now, this approach has not been systematic nor has it led to any definite refusal of payment of Community funds. The potential offered by Article 7 of Regulation 2052/88 on the reform of the Community Structural Funds,[42] is by far not yet exhausted.

(12) In Cases C–6 & 9/90, the Court of Justice held that individuals are entitled to demand that the Member State make good damage which was sustained as a result of the Member State's failure to transpose a directive, provided the result to be achieved by the directive includes the conferment of rights to individuals, that these rights are identifiable on the basis of the directive and that there is a causal link between the infringment of the Member State's obligation and the damage sustained.[43] The judgment was given in a

---

[40] Commission, "Le contrôle de l'application du droit communautaire en matière d'environnement. Un premier rapport de la Commission," p–5 of February 8, 1990. The European Council in Dublin, June 25 and 26, 1990, asked for regular reports on implementation and enforcement of Community environmental legislation: [1990] 6 E.C. Bull 19 and Commission, Eighth Report (n. 25 above) p. 6.

[41] Mr. Ripa de Meana, in Annex to Commission (n. 4 above) p.8: "Ne pourrait-on pas envisager la possibilité d'exclure des sources de financement dont je viens de parler . . . les Etats Membres qui n'appliquent pas la legislation communautaire en matière d'environnement? Comme nous avons l'intention de faire dans le domaine de l'agriculture."

[42] [1988] O.J. L185/13, **Article 7**: "Measures financed by the Structural Funds or receiving assistance from the EIB or from any other existing financial instrument shall be in keeping with the provisions of the Treaties, with the instruments adopted pursuant thereto and with Community policies, including those concerning . . . environmental protection."

[43] C–6 & 9/90, *Francovich*: [1991] I E.C.R. 5357, [1993] 2 C.M.L.R. 66.

case of social policy. It remains to be seen whether in environmental cases this reasoning can be made useful.

In conclusion, it seems fair to state that efficient sanctions for non-compliance with the Community environmental law still have to be developed. "Public blame is almost the only sanction, and even that needs reception by the media in order to condemn the action."[44]

---

[44] L. Krämer, "The implementation of environmental laws by the European Economic Communities," *German Yearbook of International Law*, Vol. 34 (1991) p.9 (p. 51). See also generally on enforcement of Community environmental law: Commission, Eighth and Ninth Reports (n. 25 above); House of Lords, Select Committee on the European Communities, 8th Report 1991–1992: "Implementation and enforcement of Environmental Legislation." Vol. I and II, (London, 1992); R. Macrory, "The enforcement of Community environmental laws, some critical issues," [1992] C.M.L. Rev. 347; European Parliament, Resolution of 8 April 1992 on the implementation of Community environmental law: [1992] O.J. C125/122.

ENVIRONMENTAL CASES[1]

CASE	PARTIES	LEGAL BASIS[2]	CONTENT	DATE OF JUDGMENT REFERENCES
21/76	Handelswekerij Bier v. Mines de Potasse d'Alsace	Judicial competence; Brussels Convention of September 27, 1968 Article 177	Pollution of Rhine River by salts; competence for damages of the Court where the damage was caused or where the damage materialised	November 30, 1976 [1976] E.C.R. 1735 [1977] 1 C.M.L.R. 284
21/79	Commission v. Italy	Waste; Directive 75/439 on used oils Article 169	Financial incentives under Article 13 of Directive 75/439 for the collection and disposal of waste oils may consist in financial support or in fiscal advantages	January 8, 1980 [1980] E.C.R. 1 [1980] 2 C.M.L.R. 613
91/79	Commission v. Italy	Water; Directive 73/404 on detergents Article 169	Absence of national legal measures; environmental measures may be based on Article 100	March 18, 1980 [1980] E.C.R. 1099 [1981] 1 C.M.L.R. 331
92/79	Commission v. Italy	Air pollution; Directive 75/716 on sulphur content of liquid fuels Article 169	Absence of national legal measures; environmental measures may be based on Article 100	March 18, 1980 [1980] E.C.R. 1115 [1981] 1 C.M.L.R. 331
171/79	Commission v. Italy	Chemicals; Directive 76/769 on the restrictions on marketing and use of dangerous substances Article 169	Absence of national legal measures	February 17, 1981 [1981] E.C.R. 465
30–34/81	Commission v. Italy	Water-waste; Directives 75/439 on used oils; 75/440 on surface water; 76/160 on bathing water; 76/406 on PCB and PCT waste Article 169	Absence of national legal measures to transpose these directives	December 17, 1981 [1981] E.C.R. 3379

CASE	PARTIES	LEGAL BASIS[2]	CONTENT	DATE OF JUDGMENT REFERENCES
272/80	Criminal proceedings against Frans-Nederlandse Maatschappij voor Biologische Produkten	Chemicals; Articles 30 and 36 Article 177	Member States may request a licence for pesticide even if that pesticide is already licensed in another Member State, since environmental conditions are different	December 17, 1981 [1981] E.C.R. 3277 [1982] 2 C.M.L.R. 497
68/81	Commission v. Belgium	Waste; Directive 78/176 on waste from the titanium dioxide industry Article 169	Absence of national legal measures; internal difficulties do not justify to delay or to comply with the requirements of a directive	February 2, 1982 [1982] E.C.R. 153
69/81	Commission v. Belgium	Waste; Directive 75/442 on waste Article 169	Absence of national legal measures; internal difficulties do not justify to delay or omit to comply with the requirements of a directive	February 2, 1982 [1982] E.C.R. 163
70/81	Commission v. Belgium	Waste; Directive 75/439 on waste oils Article 169	Absence of national legal measures; internal difficulties do not justify to delay or omit to comply with the requirements of a directive	February 2, 1982 [1982] E.C.R. 169
71/81	Commission v. Belgium	Waste; Directive 76/403 on PCB and PCT waste Article 169	Absence of national legal measures; internal difficulties do not justify to delay or omit to comply with the requirements of a directive	February 2, 1982 [1982] E.C.R. 175
72/81	Commission v. Belgium	Water; Directive 76/160 on the quality of bathing water Article 169	Absence of national legal measures; internal difficulties do not justify to delay or omit to comply with the requirements of a directive	February 2, 1982 [1992] E.C.R. 193
73/81	Commission v. Belgium	Water; Directive 75/440 on the quality of surface water Article 169	Absence of national legal measures; internal difficulties do not justify to delay or omit to comply with the requirements of a directive	February 2, 1982 [1982] E.C.R. 189

Case No.	Case name	Subject	Holding	Date / Citation
96/81	Commission v. Netherlands	Water; Directive 76/160 on the quality of bathing waters	Incomplete transposal of the directive; absence of binding legal rules	June 25, 1982 [1982] E.C.R. 1791
172/82	Fabricants raffineurs d'huiles de graissage v. Inter-Huile	Waste; Directive 75/439 on waste oils; Articles 30 and 34 Article 177	Neither Directive 75/439 nor the rules of the Treaty on free circulation of goods allow a Member State to prohibit the export of waste oils to a disposal company which was licensed in another Member State.	March 10, 1983 [1983] E.C.R. 555 [1983] 3 C.M.L.R. 485
295/82	Cie "Rhone Alpes Huiles" v. Syndicat National des fabricants raffineurs d'huiles de graissage	Waste; Directive 75/439 Articles 30 and 34 Article 177	Holders of used oils must be able to deliver them to a licensed holder in another Member State	February 9, 1984 [1984] E.C.R. 575
94/83	Criminal proceedings against A. Heijn	Chemicals; Articles 30 and 36 Article 177	In the absence of Community legislation, Member States may fix limit values for pesticide residues in food even when these limit values vary from one food to the other	September 19, 1984 [1984] E.C.R. 3263
173/83	Commission v. France	Waste; Directive 75/439 on used oils Articles 30 and 34 Article 169	France has failed to comply with its obligations by excluding used oils to be exported to other Member States	February 7, 1985 [1985] E.C.R. 491
240/83	**Procureur de la République v. Association de "Défense de Brûleurs"**	Waste; Directive 75/439 on used oils Articles 30 and 36 Article 177	The protection of the environment is an important objective in the Community interest; it may justify restrictions to the free circulation of goods and the freedom of competition. The provisions of directive 75/439 are compatible with Articles 30 and 36	February 7, 1985 [1985] E.C.R. 531
187/84	Caldana	Chemicals; Dangerous substances Directive 67/548 on classification, labelling and packaging of dangerous substances Article 177	The Directive requires only to label dangerous substances, but not preparations which contain one or more dangerous substances	September 9, 1985 [1985] E.C.R. 3013 [1989] 1 C.M.L.R. 137

CASE	PARTIES	LEGAL BASIS[2]	CONTENT	DATE OF JUDGMENT REFERENCES
239/85	Commission v. Belgium	Waste; Directive 78/319 on toxic and dangerous waste Article 169	Incomplete transposal of the directive	December 2, 1986 [1986] E.C.R. 3645 [1988] 1 C.M.L.R. 248
372–374/85	Ministère public v. Traen and others	Waste; Directive 75/442 on waste Article 177	Interpretation of several rules of the directive	May 12, 1987 [1987] E.C.R. 2141 [1988] 3 C.M.L.R. 511
134/86	Commission v. Belgium	Water Detergents; Directives 82/242 and 82/243 on detergents Article 177	Absence of national legal measures	June 4, 1987 [1987] E.C.R. 2415
14/86	**Pretore di Salò v. X**	Water; Directive 78/659 on the quality of fishwater Article 000	The Directive, which was not transposed by Italy, does not cause or increase the penal responsibility of persons, who do not act in conformity with its requirements	June 11, 1987 [1987] E.C.R. 2545 [1989] 1 C.M.L.R. 71
1/86	Commission v. Belgium	Water; Directive 80/68 on the protection of groundwater Article 169	Incomplete transposal of the Directive; internal difficulties do not justify to delay or omit to comply with the requirements of a directive	June 17, 1987 [1987] E.C.R. 2797 [1989] 1 C.M.L.R. 474
247/85	Commission v. Belgium	Nature protection; Directive 79/409 on the conservation of wild birds Article 169	Incomplete transposal of the Directive. Several rules are not correctly reproduced in Belgium law	July 8, 1987 [1987] E.C.R. 3073
262/85	**Commission v. Italy**	Nature protection; Directive 79/409 on the conservation of wild birds Article 169	Incomplete transposal of the Directive. Several rules are not correctly reproduced in Italian law	July 8, 1987 [1987] E.C.R. 3073

Case No.	Parties	Subject	Nature of complaint	Date / Citation
291/84	Commission *v.* Netherlands	Water Directive 80/68 on the protection of groundwater Article 169	Incomplete transposition of several provisions of the Directive	September 17, 1987 [1987] E.C.R. 3483 [1989] 1 C.M.L.R. 479
412/85	Commission *v.* Germany	Nature protection; Directive 79/409 on the conservation of wild birds Article 169	Incorrect transposal of the Directive as regards derogations for agricultural activities	September 17, 1987 [1987] E.C.R. 3503
236/85	Commission *v.* Netherlands	Nature protection; Directive 79/409 on the conservation of wild birds Article 169	Incorrect transposal of several provisions of the Directive into Dutch law	October 13, 1987 [1987] E.C.R. 3989
208/85	Commission *v.* Germany	Dangerous substances Directive 67/548 on classification, labelling and packaging of dangerous substances Article 169	Incorrect transposal of several provisions of the Directive to German law	October 14, 1987 [1987] E.C.R. 4045
278/85	**Commission v. Denmark**	Dangerous substances Directive 67/548 on classification, labelling and packaging of dangerous substances Article 169	Incorrect transposal of several provisions of the Directive into Danish law. Possibilities of the national legislator to derogate from the provisions of the directive	October 14, 1987 [1987] E.C.R. 4069
227–230/85	Commission *v.* Belgium	Waste; Court decisions 68 to 71/81 EEC Treaty Article 171	Failure to take the necessary measures in order to comply with the Court's decisions	January 14, 1988 [1988] E.C.R. 1 [1989] 2 C.M.L.R. 797
429/85	Commission *v.* Italy	Dangerous substances Directive 67/548 on classification, labelling and packaging of dangerous substances Article 169	Incorrect transposal of provisions of the Directive into Italian law	February 23, 1988 [1988] E.C.R. 843 [1989] 3 C.M.L.R. 423
309/86	Commission *v.* Italy	Water; Directive 82/243 and 82/244 on detergents Article 169	Absence of national legal measures	March 2, 1988 [1988] E.C.R. 1237

CASE	PARTIES	LEGAL BASIS²	CONTENT	DATE OF JUDGMENT REFERENCES
252/85	**Commission v. France**	Nature protection Directive 79/409 on the conservation of wild birds Article 169	Incorrect transposal of provisions of the Directive into French law. Traditional hunting methods	April 27, 1988 [1988] E.C.R. 2243
322/86	Commission v. Italy	Water; Directive 78/659 on the quality of fishwater Article 169	Incomplete transposal of the Directive. Designation of an insufficient number of fishwaters	July 12, 1988 [1988] E.C.R. 3995
302/86	**Commission v. Denmark**	Waste; Articles 30 and 36 Article 169	In the absence of Community rules on the protection of the environment Member States may adopt such measures even where these measures restrict the free circulation of goods	September 9, 1988 [1988] E.C.R. 4607 [1989] 1 C.M.L.R. 619
187/87	**Saarland and others v. Ministère de l'industrie and others**	Nuclear installations Article 37 EURATOM Article 177 Article 150 EURATOM	Obligations to consult the Commission, before national authorisations for radioactive discharges to water are given	September 22, 1988 [1988] E.C.R. 5013 [1989] 1 C.M.L.R. 529
228/87	Pretura unificata di Torino v. X	Water; Directive 80/778 on drinking water Article 177	Interpretation of Article 10 of the Directive as regards "emergency cases"	September 25, 1988 [1988] E.C.R. 5099 [1990] 1 C.M.L.R. 716
380/87	**Enichem and others v. di Cinisello-Balsamo**	Waste; Directives 75/442 on waste, 78/319 on toxic and dangerous waste Article 177	The Directives do not prohibit local laws of certain packages in order to protect the environment	July 13, 1989 [1989] E.C.R. 2491 [1991] 1 C.M.L.R. 313
57/89R	Commission v. Germany	Nature protection; Directive 79/409 on the conservation of wild birds Articles 169 and 186	Refusal to take interim measures and to suspend work in a special protection area	August 16, 1989 [1989] E.C.R. 2849

Case	Name	Subject	Holding	Date / Citation
125/88	**Criminal proceedings against H.F.M. Nijman**	Chemicals; Directive 79/117 on the prohibition of certain pesticides; Articles 30 and 36; Article 177	Since the directive does not constitute a total harmonisation, Member States are free to prohibit the marketing of other pesticides than those regulated by the Directive	November 7, 1989 [1989] E.C.R. 3533 [1991] 1 C.M.L.R. 92
C–339/87	Commission v. Netherlands	Nature protection; Directive 79/409 on the conservation of wild birds; Article 169	Incorrect transposal of the hunting provisions of the Directive into Dutch law	March 15, 1990 [1990] I E.C.R. 851
C 206–207/88	**Vessoso-Zanetti**	Waste; Directives 75/442 on waste, 78/319 on toxic and dangerous waste; Article 177	The notion of waste includes reusable or recyclable wastes	March 28, 1990 [1990] E.C.R. 1461
C–359/88	Zanetti and others	Waste; Directives 75/442 on waste, 78/319 on toxic and dangerous wastes; Article 177	The notion of waste includes reusable or recyclable wastes authorisations to transport dangerous waste may also be issued by regional authorities	March 28, 1990 [1990] E.C.R. 1509
C–62/88	**Greece v. Council**	Nuclear energy; Article 31 Euratom; Articles 113, 130s; Article 173	The Council has correctly based Regulation 55/87 on the import of agricultural products from third countries on Article 113, Articles 130s EEC and 31 Euratom are not applicable	March 29, 1990 [1990] E.C.R. 1527 [1991] 2 C.M.L.R. 649
C–169/89	**Gourmetterie Van den Burg**	Nature protection; Directive 79/409 on the conservation of wild birds; Articles 30 and 36 EEC Treaty; Article 177 EEC Treaty	Member States may not prohibit the marketing of birds on their territory which are legally captured and marketed in another Member State	May 23, 1990 [1990] E.C.R. 2143
C–162/89	**Commission v. Belgium**	Waste; Directives 75/439 on used oils, 76/403 on PCB and PCT waste, 78/319 on toxic and dangerous waste; Article 169	Member States may not invoke internal difficulties in order to delay the complete and correct transposal of the provisions of the directives into national law (reporting requirements)	June 13, 1990 [1990] E.C.R. 2391

CASE	PARTIES	LEGAL BASIS[2]	CONTENT	DATE OF JUDGMENT REFERENCES
C–48/89	Commission v. Italy	Waste; Directives 75/442 on waste, 78/319 on toxic and dangerous waste Article 169	Internal difficulties do not justify to delay or to omit to comply with the requirements of a directive	June 14, 1990 [1990] E.C.R. 2425
C–288/88	Commission v. Germany	Nature protection; Directive 79/409 on the conservation of wild birds Article 169	Incorrect transposal of the hunting provisions of the Directive into German (regional) law	July 3, 1990 [1990] I E.C.R. 2721
C–42/89	**Commission v. Belgium**	Water; Directive 80/778 on drinking water Article 169	The directive does not apply to private water supplies. Derogations for lead may not be granted under Article 9 of the Directive	July 5, 1990 [1990] E.C.R. 2821 [1992] 1 C.M.L.R. 22
C–182/89	**Commission v. France**	Nature protection; Regulation 3626/82 on trade in endangered species Article 169	Import licences under the Regulation may not be given, where the species comes from a region where it is threatened from extinction	November 29, 1990 [1990] E.C.R. 4337
C–70/89	**Commission v. Italy**	Water; Cadmium discharges Directive 83/513 on cadmium discharges to water Article 169	Incomplete transposal of the requirements of the Directive into Italian law	December 13, 1990 [1990] E.C.R. 4817
C–334/89	Commission v. Italy	Nature protection; Directive 79/409 on the conservation of wild birds, amended by directive 85/411 Article 169	Failure to transpose the requirements of Directive 85/411 into Italian law	January 17, 1991 [1991] E.C.R. 93
C–157/89	Commission v. Italy	Nature protection; Directive 79/409 on the conservation of wild birds Article 169	The fixing of hunting periods in Italian law do not entirely comply with the requirements of the Directive	January 17, 1991 [1991] E.C.R. 57

C–131/88	**Commission v. Germany**	Water; Directive 80/68 on the protection of underground water Article 169	Failure to completely transpose the Directive into German law, by adopting in particular circular letters and legal provisions of a general nature	February 28, 1991 [1991] I E.C.R. 825
C–360/87	Commission v. Italy	Water; Directive 80/68 on the protection of underground water Article 169	Failure to completely transpose the requirements of the Directive into Italian law	February 28, 1991 [1991] I E.C.R. 791
C–57/89	**Commission v. Germany**	Nature protection; Directive 79/409 on the conservation of wild birds Article 169	Interpretation of Article 4 of the Directive. Construction of a dyke within a special protection area	February 28, 1991 [1991] I E.C.R. 883
C–59/89	Commission v. Germany	Air pollution; Directive 82/884 on a limit value for lead in the air Article 169	Failure to transpose the Directive into German law, by only adopting administrative circulars	May 30, 1991 [1991] I E.C.R. 2607
C–361/88	**Commission v. Germany**	Air pollution; Directive 80/779 on limit values and guide values for sulphur dioxide and suspended particulates Article 169	Failure to transpose the Directive into German law, by only adopting administrative circulars	May 30, 1991 [1991] I E.C.R. 2567
C–290/89	Commission v. Belgium	Water; Directive 75/440 on the quality of surface water Article 169	Failure to transpose all the requirements of the Directive into Belgian law	June 11, 1991 [1991] I E.C.R. 2851
C–300/89	**Commission v. Council**	Waste; Directive 89/428 on waste from the titanium dioxide industry Articles 100a, 130s Article 173	The Directive has a double objective, the protection of the environment and the improvement of competition conditions. The protection of the environment is capable of being ensured by Article 100a	June 11, 1991 [1991] I E.C.R. 2867

CASE	PARTIES	LEGAL BASIS[2]	CONTENT	DATE OF JUDGMENT REFERENCES
C–252/89	Commission v. Luxembourg	Waste; Directive 85/339 on liquid beverage containers Article 169	Failure to transpose the requirements of the Directive into national law. Failure to transmit waste reduction programmes to the Commission	July 25, 1991 [1991] I E.C.R. 3973
C–14/90	Commission v. France	Air; Directive 85/203 on limit values for nitrogen dioxide in the air Article 169	Failure to transpose the Directive into French law, by transposing it by administrative circulars	October 1, 1991 [1991] I E.C.R. 4331
C–13/90	Commission v. France	Air; Directive 82/884 on a limit value for lead in the air Article 169	Failure to transpose the Directive into French law, by transposing it by administrative circulars	October 1, 1991 [1991] I E.C.R. 4327
C–64/90	Commission v. France	Air; Directive 80/779 on limit values and guide values for sulphur dioxide and suspended particulates in the air Article 169	Failure to transpose the Directive into French law, by transposing it by administrative circulars	October 1, 1991 [1991] I E.C.R. 4335
C–70/88	European Parliament v. Council	Nuclear energy; Regulation 3954/87 on limits of radioactive contamination for food Articles 100a, 130s EEC Article 31 Euratom Article 146 Euratom Article 173 EEC	The regulation aims at fixing admissible concentrations for radioactive contamination in food. It was rightly based on Article 31 Euratom	October 1, 1991 [1991] I E.C.R. 4561
C–58/89	Commission v. Germany	Water; Directive 75/440 on the quality of surface waters	Failure to completely transpose the requirements of the Directive into German law, in particular by adopting administrative circulars	October 17, 1991 [1991] I E.C.R. 4983

Case	Party	Subject	Description	Date / Citation
C–192/90	Commission v. Spain	Waste; Directive 85/339 on liquid beverage containers Article 169	Failure to transpose the requirements of the Directive into Spanish law. Failure to transmit waste reduction programmes to the Commission	December 10, 1991 [1991] I E.C.R. 5933
C–33/90	**Commission v. Italy**	Waste; Directives 75/442 on waste; 78/319 on toxic and dangerous waste Article 169	Absence of waste management measures in Campania	December 13, 1991 [1991] I E.C.R. 5987 [1992] 2 C.M.L.R. 353
C–75/91	Commission v. Netherlands	Nature protection; Directive 79/409 on the protection of birds Article 171	Failure to comply with the Court judgment in Case 236/85	February 6, 1992 [1992] I E.C.R. 549
C–43/90	Commission v. Germany	Chemicals; Directive 79/831 on classification, labelling and packaging of dangerous substances Article 169	National measures to provisionally labelling dangerous substances	March 13, 1992 [1992] I E.C.R. 1909
C–45/91	Commission v. Greece	Waste; Directives 75/442 on waste; 78/319 on toxic and dangerous waste Article 169	By not taking all measures which are necessary for a safe disposal of waste and by not establishing waste disposal plans for a region in Creta, Greece has failed to respect its obligations under the Treaty	April 7, 1992 [1992] I E.C.R. 2509
C–190/90	**Commission v. Netherlands**	Chemicals; Directive 82/501 on the prevention of major-accident hazards Article 169	Incomplete transposal of the requirements of the Directive into Dutch law	May 20, 1992 [1991] I E.C.R. 3265
C–2/90	**Commission v. Belgium**	Waste; Directives 75/442 on waste; 84/631 on transport of dangerous waste Articles 30 and 36 Article 169	Member States may, based on Article 30, restrict the import of domestic waste; dangerous waste is, however, regulated by Directive 84/631 and are thus not open to national restrictions	July 9, 1992 [1992] I E.C.R. 4431 [1993] 1 C.M.L.R. 365

CASE	PARTIES	LEGAL BASIS[2]	CONTENT	DATE OF JUDGMENT REFERENCES
C–237/90	Commission *v.* Germany	Water; Directive 80/778 on the quality of drinking water Article 169	Failure to completely transpose the requirements of the Directive into German law	November 24, 1992 [1992] I E.C.R. 5973
C–337/89	**Commission *v.* United Kingdom**	Water; Directive 80/778 on the quality of drinking water Article 169	Failure to completely transpose the requirements of the Directive into British law	November 25, 1992 [1992] I E.C.R. 6103

[1] As at June 30, 1993. This list is based on the list by P. Kromarck in "Grands Arrets Communautaires–Tableaux", Jurisclasseur–Environnement, Fascicule 1110 (Paris, 1992).
Cases in bold type are discussed in detail in this book.
[2] All Articles refer to the EEC Treaty, unless otherwise stated.
See also Appendix 2.

EEC TREATY ARTICLES

Article 100a

1. By way of derogation from Article 100 and save where otherwise provided in this Treaty, the following provisions shall apply for the achievement of the objectives set out in Article 8a. The Council shall, acting by a qualified majority on a proposal from the Commission in cooperation with the European Parliament and after consulting the Economic and Social Committee, adopt the measures for the approximation of the provisions laid down by law, regulation or administrative action in Member States which have as their object the establishment and functioning of the internal market.

2. Paragraph 1 shall not apply to fiscal provisions, to those relating to the free movement of persons nor to those relating to the rights and interests of employed persons.

3. The Commission, in its proposals envisaged in paragraph 1 concerning health, safety environmental protection and consumer protection, will take as a base a high level of protection.

4. If, after the adoption of a harmonization measure by the Council acting by a qualified majority, a Member State deems it necessary to apply national provisions on grounds of major needs referred to in Article 36, or relating to protection of the environment or the working environment, it shall notify the Commission of these provisions.

The Commission shall confirm the provisions involved after having verified that they are not a means of arbitrary discrimination or a diguised restriction on trade between Member States.

By way of derogation from the procedure laid down in Articles 169 and 170, the Commission or any Member State may bring the matter directly before the Court of Justice if it considers that another Member State is making improper use of the powers provided for in this Article.

5. The harmonization measures referred to above shall, in appropriate cases, include a safeguard clause authorizing the Member States to take, for one or more of the non-economic reasons referred to in Article 36, provisional measures subject to a Community control procedure.

Article 130r

1. Action by the Community relating to the environment shall have the following objectives:

  (i) to preserve, protect and improve the quality of the environment;

  (ii) to contribute towards protecting human health;

  (iii) to ensure a prudent and rational utilization of natural resources.

2. Action by the Community relating to the environment shall be based on the principles that preventive action should be taken, that environmental damage should as a priority be rectified at source, and that the polluter should pay. Environmental protection requirements shall be a component of the Community's other policies.

3. In preparing its action relating to the environment, the Community shall take account of:

   (i) available scientific and technical data;

   (ii) environmental conditions in the various regions of the Community;

   (iii) the potential benefits and costs of action or of lack of action;

   (iv) the economic and social development of the Community as a whole and the balanced development of its regions.

4. The Community shall take action relating to the environment to the extent to which the objectives referred to in paragraph 1 can be attained better at Community level than at the level of the individual Member States. Without prejudice to certain measures of a Community nature, the Member States shall finance and implement the other measures.

5. Within their respective spheres of competence, the Community and the Member States shall cooperate with third countries and with the relevant international organizations. The arrangements for Community cooperation may be the subject of agreements between the Community and the third parties concerned, which shall be negotiated and concluded in accordance with Article 228.

   The previous paragraph shall be without prejudice to Member States' competence to negotiate in international bodies and to conclude international agreements.

Article 130s

The Council acting unanimously on a proposal from the Commission and after consulting the European Parliament and the Economic and Social Committee, shall decide what action is to be taken by the Community.

   The Council shall, under the conditions laid down in the preceding subparagraph, define those matters on which decisions are to be taken by a qualified majority.

Article 130t

The protective measures adopted in common pursuant to Article 130s shall not prevent any Member State from maintaining or introducing more stringent protective measures compatible with this Treaty.

Article 155

In order to ensure the proper functioning and development of the common market, the Commission shall:
— ensure that the provisions of this Treaty and the measures taken by the institutions pursuant thereto are applied;
— formulate recommendations or deliver opinions on matters dealt with in this Treaty, if it expressly so provides or if the Commission considers it necessary;
— have its own power of decision and participate in the shaping of measures taken by the Council and by the European Parliament in the manner provided for in this Treaty;
— exercise the powers conferred on it by the Council for the implementation of the rules laid down by the latter.

Article 164

The Court of Justice shall ensure that in the interpretation and application of this Treaty the law is observed.

Article 169

If the Commission considers that a Member State has failed to fulfil an obligation under this Treaty, it shall deliver a reasoned opinion on the matter after giving the State concerned the opportunity to submit its observations.

If the State concerned does not comply with the opinion within the period laid down by the Commission, the latter may bring the matter before the Court of Justice.

Article 171

If the Court of Justice finds that a Member State has failed to fulfil an obligation under this Treaty, the State shall be required to take the necessary measures to comply with the judgment of the Court of justice.

Article 173

The Court of Justice shall review the legality of acts of the Council and the Commission other than recommendations or opinions. It shall for this purpose have jurisdiction in actions brought by a Member State, the Council or the Commission on grounds of lack of competence, infringement of an essential procedural requirement, infringement of this Treaty or of any rule of law relating to its application, or misuse of powers.

Any natural or legal person may, under the same conditions, institute proceedings against a decision addressed to that person or against a decision which, although in the form of a regulation or a decision addressed to another person, is of direct and individual concern to the former.

The proceedings provided for in this Article shall be instituted within two months of the publication of the measure, or of its notification to the plaintiff, or, in the absence thereof, of the day on which it came to the knowledge of the latter, as the case may be.

Article 177

The Court of Justice shall have jurisdiction to give preliminary rulings concerning:

(a) the interpretation of this Treaty;
(b) the validity and interpretation of acts of the institutions of the Community;
(c) the interpretation of the statutes of bodies established by an act of the Council, where those statutes so provide.

Where such a question is raised before any court or tribunal of a Member State, that court or tribunal may, if it considers that a decision on the question is necessary to enable it to give judgment, request of the Court of Justice to give a ruling thereon.

Where any such question is raised in a case pending before a court or tribunal of a Member State, against whose decisions there is no judicial remedy under national law, that court or tribunal shall bring the matter before the Court of Justice.

Article 186

The Court of Justice may in any cases before it prescribe any necessary interim measures.

ARTICLES OF THE EEC TREATY AS AMENDED BY THE TREATY ON EUROPEAN UNION

Article 130r

1. Community policy on the environment shall contribute to pursuit of the following objectives:
   — preserving, protecting and improving the quality of the environment;
   — protecting human health;
   — prudent and rational utilization of natural resources;
   — promoting measures at international level to deal with regional or worldwide environmental problems.

2. Community policy on the environment shall aim at a high level of protection taking into account the diversity of situations in the various regions of the Community. It shall be based on the precautionary principle and on the principles that preventive action should be taken, that environmental damage should as a priority be rectified at source and that the polluter should pay. Environmental protection requirements must be integrated into the definition and implementation of other Community policies.

In this context, harmonization measures answering these requirements shall include, where appropriate, a safeguard clause allowing Member States to take provisional measures, for non-economic environmental reasons, subject to a Community inspection procedure.

3. In preparing its policy on the environment, the Community shall take account of:
   — available scientific and technical data;
   — environmental conditions in the various regions of the Community;
   — the potential benefits and costs of action or lack of action;
   — the economic and social development of the Community as a whole and the balanced developments of its regions.

4. Within their respective spheres of competence, the Community and the Member States shall co-operate with third countries and with the competent international organisations.

The arrangements for Community co-operation may be the subject of agreements between the Community and the third parties concerned, which shall be negotiated and concluded in accordance with Article 228.

The previous subparagraph shall be without prejudice to Member States' competence to negotiate in international bodies and to conclude international agreements.

Article 130s

1. The Council, acting in accordance with the procedure referred to in Article 189c and after consulting the Economic and Social Committee, shall decide what action is to be taken by the Community in order to achieve the objectives referred to in Article 130r.

2. By way of derogation from the decision-making procedure provided for in paragraph 1 and without prejudice to Article 100a, the Council, acting unanimously on a proposal from the Commission and after consulting the European Parliament and the Economic and Social Committee, shall adopt:
   — provisions primarily of a fiscal nature;
   — measures concerning town and country planning, land use with the exception of waste management and measures of a general nature, and management of water resources;
   — measures significantly affecting a Member State's choice between different energy sources and the general structure of its energy supply.

The Council may, under the conditions laid down in the preceding subparagraph, define those matters referred to in this paragraph on which decisions are to be taken by a qualified majority.

3. In other areas, general action programmes setting out priority objectives to be attained shall be adopted by the Council, acting in accordance with the procedure referred to in Article 189b and after consulting the Economic and Social Committee.

The Council, acting under the terms of paragraph 1 or paragraph 2 according to the case, shall adopt the measures necessary for the implementation of these programmes.

4. Without prejudice to certain measures of a Community nature, the Member States shall finance and implement the environment policy.

5. Without prejudice to the principle that the polluter should pay, if a measure based on the provisions of paragraph 1 involves costs deemed disproportionate for the public authorities of a Member State, the Council shall, in the act adopting that measure, lay down appropriate provisions in the form of:

— temporary derogations and/or
— financial support from the Cohesion Fund to be set up no later than 31 December 1993 pursuant to Article 130d.

Article 130t

The protective measures adopted in common pursuant to Article 130s shall not prevent any Member State from maintaining or introducing more stringent protective measures. Such measures must be compatible with this Treaty. They shall be notified to the Commission.

Article 171

1. If the Court of Justice finds that a Member State has failed to fulfil an obligation under this Treaty, the State shall be required to take the necessary measures to comply with the judgment of the Court of Justice.

2. If the Commission considers that the Member State concerned has not taken such measures it shall, after giving that State the opportunity to submit its observations, issue a reasoned opinion specifying the points on which the Member State concerned has not complied with the judgment of the Court of Justice. If the Member State concerned fails to take the necessary measures to comply with the Court's judgment within the time-limit laid down by the Commission, the latter may bring the case before the Court of Justice. In so doing it shall specify the amount of the lump sum or penalty payment to be paid by the Member State concerned which it considers appropriate in the circumstances. If the Court of Justice finds that the Member State concerned has not complied with its judgment it may impose a lump sum or penalty payment on it. This procedure shall be without prejudice to Article 170.

BIBLIOGRAPHY

Baldock, D. "The status of special protection areas for the protection of wild birds." (1992) *Journal of Environmental Law* 139.

Baldock, D.; Holzner, J.; Bennett, R; *The Organisation of Nature Protection Conservation in Selected EC Countries.* London, 1987.

Barents, R. "Milieu en interne markt." (1993) *Tijdschrift voor Europees een economisch recht* 5.

Behrens, P.; Koch, H.J. (eds.) *Umweltschutz in der Europäischer Gemeinschaft. Spannungsfelder zwischen nationalem und europäischem Gemeinschaftsrecht.* Baden–Baden, 1991.

Bennett, G (ed.) *Air pollution control in the European Communities.* London, 1991.

Bradley, K "The European Court and the Legal Basis of Community Legislation." (1988) *European Law Review* 379.

Bradshaw, A; Southwood, R; Warner, F. (eds.) *The Treatment and Handling of Wastes.* London–New York–Tokyo–Melbourne–Madras, 1992.

Breuer, R. "EG–Richtlinien und deutsches Wasserrecht." (1990) *Wirtschaft und Verwaltung* 79.

Cerana, N. Note on Case 228/87. *Pretura di Torino* v. *X* (1988) *Rivista Giuridica dell' Ambiente* 8145.

Cerana, N.; Gariboldi, L. "Sulla legitimità del divieto di vendia e uso di sacchetti di plastica e altri contenitori non biodegradabili quale rimedio preventivo alla produzione di rifiuti." (1988) *Rivista Giuridica dell' Ambiente* 821.

Coluto, O.; Coluto, S. "Protezione oggettiva e protezione soggettiva: un conflitto insanabile tra l'Italia e la Comunità europea?" (1989) *Rivista Giuridica dell' Ambiente* 145

Commission, E.C. Communication on Case 64/88 [1990] O.J. C143/3.

—— —— A Community Strategy for Waste Management, SEC(89)934 final of September 18, 1989.

—— —— Le contrôle de l'application du droits communautaire en matière d'environnement. Le premier rapport de la Commission, press release P–5 of February 5, 1990.

—— —— Information sur l'application de la directive 79/409 (Rapport 12835). Brussels—Luxembourg, 1990.

—— —— Report on the application in the Member States of Directive 82/501 of June, 24, 1982 on the major-accident hazards of certain industrial activities. COM(88)261 final of May, 18 1988.

—— —— Reports on monitoring of the application of Community Law:
First Report 1983. COM(84)181 final of April, 11 1984.
Second Report 1984. COM(85)149 final of May 13, 1985.
Third Report 1985. [1986] O.J. C220/1.
Fourth Report 1986. [1987] O.J. C338/1.
Fifth Report 1987. [1988] O.J. C310/10/1.
Sixth Report 1988. [1989] O.J. C330/1.
Seventh Report 1989. [1990] O.J. C232/1.
Eighth Report 1990. [1991] O.J. C338/1.

Ninth Report 1991. [1992] O.J. C250/1.
—— —— Report on the operation of Directive 83/189 between 1984 and 1987. COM(88)722 final of December 13, 1988.
—— —— The State of the Environment in the European Community. Overview. COM(92)23 final—Vol III of March 27, 1992.

Dewost, J.L. "Rôle et position de la Commission dans le processus legislatif, in J. Schwarze (ed.) *Legislation for Europe.* Baden–Baden, 1989, p.85.

Diez de Velasco Vallejo, M. *Aspectos jurídicos actuales de la proteción del medio ambiente en la Communidad European, y en especial, la contribución de su Tribunal de Justicia.* Granada, 1991.

Dubouis, L. "Un exemple de cooperation entre le juge administratif français et la Cour de Justice des Communautés européennes: l'affaire de la centrale de Cattenom." (1989) *Revue française du Droit administratif* 857.

Espinay, A.; Furrer, A. "Umweltschutz nach Maastricht." (1992) *Europarecht* 369.

Everling, U. "Abgrenzung der Rechtsangleichung zur Verwirklichung des Binnenmarktes nach Art. 100a EWGV durch den Gerichtshof." (1991) *Europarecht* 179.
—— —— "Umsetzung von Umweltrichtlinien durch normkonkretisierende Verwaltungsanweisungen." (1992) *Recht der Internationalen Wirtschaft* 379.
—— —— "Umweltschutz durch Gemeinschaftsrecht in der Rechtsprechung des EuGH." in P. Behrens & H.J. Koch (eds.) *Umweltschutz in der Europäischen Gemeinschaft: Spannungsfelder zwischen nationalem und europäischem Gemeinschaftsrecht.* Baden-Baden (1991), p.29.

Geddes, A. "Locus Standi and EEC Environmental Measures." (1992) *Journal of Environmental Law* 29.

Haigh, N. Manual of Environmental Policy: the EC and Britain. London [looseleaf]
—— —— (ed.) *European Community Environmental Policy in Practice. Comparative report: Water and waste in four countries. A study of the implementation of the EEC directives in France, Germany, the Netherlands and the United Kingdom.* London, 1986.

Hailbronner, K. *Umweltrecht und Umweltpolitik in der Europäischen Gemeinschaft.* Linz, 1991.

L. Hancher; H. Sevenster, Note on C–2/90 Judgment of 9 July 1992. [1993] *Common Market Law Review* 351

House of Lords Select Committee on the European Communities. 8th Report 1991–1992: Implementation and enforcement of Environmental legislation. Vols. I and II. London, 1992.

Jadot, B. Note sous Cour de Justice, arrêt du 20/9/1988 aff. 302/86, *Commission* v. *Denmark.* (1990) *Cahiers du Droit Européen* 403.
—— —— "Les objectifs de qualité de l'air au coeur d'un système d'obligations et du droit"; observations sur Cour de Justice C–361/88, *Commission* v. *Germany.* (1992) *Aménagement–Environnement* 157.
—— —— "Remous juridiques autour de la qualité de l'eau en Europe, en Belgique et à Verviers." (1990) Aménagement–Environnement 153.
—— —— Hannequart J.P.; Orban de Xivry, E. *Le droit de l'environnement.* Bruxelles, 1988.

Jans, J.H. *Europees Milieurecht in Nederland.* Groningen, 1991.
—— —— Note on Case 302/86 *Commission* v. *Denmark.* (1990) *Sociaal Enconomisch Wetgeving* 482.
—— —— Note on Case C–169/89 Gourmetterie van den Burg. Milieu en recht, (1991), 94.

Jarass, H.D. "Binnenmarktrichtlinien und Umweltschutzrichtlinien." (1991) *Europäische Zeitschrift für Wirtschaftsrecht* 530.

Juin, D. (avec A. Comolet, V. Fernandez, F. Gras) *L'application de la législation communautaire de l'environnement en France.* Tomes 1 et 2. Paris, 1992.

Kahl, W. *Umweltprinzip und Gemeinschaftsrecht. Diss Augsburg.* Heidelberg, 1993.

Kohlhepp, K.H. "Beschränkung des freien Warenverkehrs in der EG durch nationale Umweltschutzbestimmungen." (1989) *Der Betrieb* 1455.

Krämer, L. *EEC Treaty and Environmental Protection.* London, 1990.

—— —— *Focus on EEC Environmental Law.* London, 1992.

—— —— "The implementation of Community environmental directives within Member States: some implications of the direct effect doctrine." (1991) *Journal of Environmental Law* 39.

—— —— "The implementation of environmental laws by the European Economic Communities." (1991) *German Yearbook of International Law* 9.

—— —— **Kromarek, P.** "Droit communautaire de l'environnement (1987–avril 1988)." (1988) *Revue Juridique de l'Environnement* 314.

Kreutzberger, R. "Der Umweltschutz als Aufgabe der Europäischen Gemeinschaften–gleichzeitig eine Besprechung der Urteile des EUGH vom 7. Februar 1985 in den Rs 173 und 240/83." (1986) *Zeitschift für Umweltpolitik* 169.

Kromarek, P. "La Cour de Justice des Communautés européennes et l'environnement." *Jurisclasseur-Environnement.* Fasc. 1120. Paris, 1992.

—— —— "Environmental Protection and Free Movement of Goods: The Danish Bottles Case." (1990) *Journal of Environmental Law* 89.

—— —— "Grands Arrêts Communautaires–Tableaux." *Jurisclasseur-Environnement,* Fasc. 1110. Paris, 1992.

—— —— "Die Trinkwasserrichtlinie der EG und die Nitratwerte." Internationales Institut für Umwelt-und Gesellschaft. Berlin, 1986.

Langeheine, B. "Le rapprochement des législations nationales selon l'article 100a du Traité CEE: l'harmonisation communautaire face aux exigences de protection nationales." (1989) *Revue du Marché Commun* 347.

Langenfeld, C.; Schlemmer, S.; Schulte, G. "Die TA Luft–kein geeignetes Instrument zur Umsetzung von EG-Richtlinien." (1991) *Europäische Zeitschrift für Wirtschaftsrechts* 622.

Leopold, J-H.; Van den Berg, A.V. Note on Case 302/86 *Commission* v. *Denmark.* (1989) *Milieu en Recht* 113.

Lübbe-Wolff, G. "Die Bedeutung des EG-Rechts für den Grundwasserschutz." in P. Behrens-H.J.Koch (eds.) *Umweltschutz in der Europäischen Gemeinschaft: Spannungsfelder zwischen nationalem und europäischem Gemeinschaftsrecht.* Baden-Baden, 1991, p.127.

Macrory, R. "The Enforcement of Community Environmental Law; some critical remarks." (1992) *Common Market Law Review* 347.

de Malafosse, J. "Nature et liberté: les acquis de la révolution française." (1989) *Revue du droit rural* 486.

—— —— "Les usages français en matière de chasse et de pêche et le droit communautaire." (1989) *Environmental policy and law* 11.

Mastellone, C. "Prime sentenze della Corte communitaria in materia di Ambiente." (1980) *Rivista di diritto internazionale privato e prozessuale* 364.

Mertens de Wilmar, J. "Het Hof van Justitie van de EEG na de Europese Act." (1986) *Sociaal Economisch Wetgeving* 618.

Minor, J. "Environmental cases in the European Court of Justice 1991." (1992) *Journal of Environmental Law* 159.

Moe, M. *Miljøret-Miljøbeskyttelse.* Copenhagen, 1992.

Murgatroyd, C.G. "State Liability and the European Environment: Francovich, Maastricht and the question of compensation." (1993) *Environmental Liability* 11.

Pagh, P. *EF-miljøret.* Copenhagen, 1990.

Pernice, I. "Gestaltung und Vollzug des Umweltrechts im europäischen Binnenmarkt—Europäische Impulse und Zwänge für das deutsche Umweltrecht." (1990) *Neue Zeitschrift für Verwaltungsrecht* 414.

Pijnacker Hordijk, E.H.   Note on Case C–169/89 *Gourmetterie van den Burg.* (1991) *Sociaal Economisch Wegtgeving* 261.

Pillitu, P.A.   *Profili costituzionali della tutela ambientale nell'ordinamento communitario europeo.* Perugia, 1992.

Pillitu, P.A.   "Sulla "base giuridica" degli atti communitari in materia ambientale." (Note on Case C–300/89, *Commission* v. *Council*). (1991) IV. *Il Foro Italiano* 369.

Prieur, M.   *Droit de l'environnement* (2nd ed.). Paris, 1991.

Rehbinder, E.; Stewart, R.   *Environmental Protection Policy.* Berlin-New York, 1985.

Reinhardt, M.   "Abschied von der Verwaltungsvorschrift im Wasserrecht?" (1992) *Die Öffentliche Verwaltung* 102.

Renaudière, P.   "Le droit communautaire de l'environnement après Maastricht." (1992) *Aménagement-Environnement* 70.

Rengeling, H.W.; Heinz, K.   "Die dänische Pfandflaschenregelung." (1989) *Neue Zeitschrift für Verwaltungsrecht* 849.

Robinson, J.   "The legal basis of EC Environmental Law: *Commission* v. *Council*, Case C-300/89. (1992) *Journal of Environmental Law* 109.

Romi, R.   Le droit à la chasse entre l'Europe et le nationalisme." (1990) *Revue juridique de l'environnement* 367.

——— ———   *L'Europe et la protection juridique de l'environnement.* Paris, 1990.

de Saddeleer, N.   "Les conflits d'intérêt portant sur la protection des milieux naturels en droit commmunautaire." Commentaire sur la Cour de Justice, aff.57/89, Commission v. Allemagne." (1992) *Revue Juridique de l'Environnement* 351.

——— ———   "Le droit communautaire de l'environnement, un droit sous-tendu par les seuls motifs économiques?" Note sur l'arrêt de la Cour de Justice dans l'affaire C-300/89 du 11 juin 1991. (1991) *Aménagement-Environnement* 217.

——— ———   Note on Case C–62/88 *Greece* v. *Council* (1991) *Aménagement–Environnement* 149.

——— ———   Note on Case C–334/89 *Commission* v. *Italy* (1991) *Aménagement-Environnement* 91.

——— ———   "La reconnaissance du principe de proximité comme autorisant les Etats membres à interdire l'importation des déchets dont les transferts n'ont pas été harmonisés par une règle de droit communautaire dérivé: une victoire à la Pyrrhus?" Observations sur Cour de Justice, aff. C–2/90, *Commission* v. *Belgique.*

Salazar, L.   Note on Case 228/87, *Pretura di Torino* v. *X.* (1988) *Rivista Giuridica dell'Ambiente* 672.

Scherer, J.   "Umweltrecht: Handelshemmnis im EG-Binnenmarkt?" (1992) 1 *Umweltrecht in der Praxis* 76.

Scheuing, D.   "Umweltschutz durch das Recht der EG." in W. Baumann-A. Rossnagel-H. Weinzierl (eds.): *Rechtsschutt für die Umwelt im vereinigten Deutschland.* Würzburg, 1992, p. 247.

Schmidt, A.   "Transboundary movements of waste under EC law: the emerging regulatory framework." (1992) *Journal of Environmental Law* 61.

Schröder M.   "Aktuelle Konflikte zwischen europäischem und deutschem Abfallrecht." (1991) *Die öffentliche Verwaltung* 910.

Schröer, T.   *Die Kompetenzverteilung zwischen der Europäischen Wirtschaftsgemeinschaft und ihren Mitgliedstaaten auf dem Gebiet des Umweltschutzes.* Diss, Frankfurt, Berlin, 1992.

——— ———   "Mehr Demokratie statt umweltpolitischer Subsidiarität?" (Note on Case C–300/89, *Commission* v. *Council*) (1991) *Europarecht* 356.

Schult, W.; Steffens J.   "EuGH-Entscheidung zu Verpackungsvorschriften in Dänemark." (1989) *Recht der Internationalen Wirtschaft* 447.

Sevenster, H.   *Milieubeleid en Gemeenschapsrecht.* Proefschrift. Leiden, Deventer, 1992.

——— ———   "Titaandioxyde-arrest, reactie." (1992) *Nederlands Juristenblad* 419.

Simon, D.; Rigaux, A. "Les contraintes de la transcription en droit français des directives communautaires: le secteur de l'environnement." (1991) *Revue juridique de l'environnement* 269.

Somsen, H. Observations on Case C–300/89, *Commission* v. *Council.* Judgment of June 11, 1991. (1992) *Common Market Law Review* 140.

Steiling, R. "Mangelnde Umsetzung von EG-Richtlinien durch den Erlaß und die Anwendung der TA Luft." (1992) *Neue Zeitschrift für Verwaltungsrecht* 135.

Stone, C. *Should Trees Have Standing?* Los Altos, California, 1974.

Thieffry, P. "Les nouveaux instruments juridiques de la politique communautaire de l'environnement." (1992) *Revue Trimestrielle de droit européen* 669.

Tricard, D.; Buffaut, P. "L'application en France des directive 'eaux potables'." Courants (1991) 12 *Revue de l'eau et de l'aménagmement* 72.

Untermaier, J. "Des petits oiseaux aux grands principes." (1988) *Revue Juridique de l'Environnement* 460.

Von Wilmowsky, P. "Grenzüberschreitende Abfallentsorgung: Ressourcenkonflikte im gemeinsamen Markt." (1991) *Neue Zeitschrift für Verwaltungsrecht* 1.

—— "Abfall und freier Warenverkehr: Beslandsaufnahme nach dem EuGH-Urteil zum wallo-nischen Einfuhrverbot." [1992] Europaricht 414.

Vonhoff, L.J. Note on Case 302/86, *Commission* v. *Denmark* (1989) *Tijdschrift voor Milieuaansprakelijkheid* 55.

Wägenbaur, R. "The European Community's policy on implementation of environmental directives." (1990–1991) *Fordham International Law Journal* 455.

—— —— "European Community's prospects for enforcement of directives." in Ministry of Housing, Physical Planning and Environment (VROM)–United State Environmental Protection Agency (EPA) (ed.): *Proceedings of the International Enforcement Workshop, 8 to 10 May 1990, Utrecht.* Utrecht 1990, p. 173.

Weatherill, S. "Regulating the Internal Market: Result Orientation in the House of Lords." (1992) *European Law Review* 299.

Weber, A. "Zur Umsetzung von EG-Richtlinien im Umweltrecht Zugleich eine Anmerkung zu den Urteilen des EuGH vom 30.5.1991 (TA Luft) und vom 28.2.1991 (Grundwasser)." (1992) *Umwelt- und Planungsrecht* 5.

Wegener, B. "Nichtumsetzung der Trinkwasser-Richtlinien; Mitteilungspflichten." (Note on Case C–58/59, *Commission* v. *Germany*). (1992) *Informationsdienst Umweltrecht* 34.

Wijnstekers, W. *The evolution of CITES.* Lausanne, 1988.

Winter, G. "Der Säbelschnäbler als Teil fürs Ganze." (1992) *Natur und Recht* 21.

Zuleeg, M. "Comments on Article 1 of the EEC Treaty." in H. v. d. Groeben, J.Thiesing, C.D.Ehlermann (eds.) *Kommentar zum EWG-Vertrag,* (4th ed.) Baden-Baden, 1991.

—— —— "Umweltschutz in der Rechtsprechung des Europäischen Gerichtshofs." (1993) *Neue Juristische Wochenschrift* 31.

INDEX

Directive applications, legal principles—
cont.
 cultural issues—*cont.*
  practicable measures,
   harmonisation, 260
 direct-effect doctrine, 143–144, 146,
  381, 415, 418
 discretion in implementation, 111–112,
  222, 299
 EEC Treaty as legal basis, 20–36,
  392–393
  direct-effect doctrine, 143, 418
  environmental v. harmonisation
   provisions, 20–36, 296, 297, 352
  failure to fulfil, model cases, 376–383,
   394, 403, 419–420
   fines and penalties, 427–428,
    433–435
    aid, punitive suspension, 434
   fresh proceedings, enforcement,
    425–435
  interim measures, 398–407
  standards, time of implementation,
   338–339
  stricter national laws, 156, 157(n.23),
   351(n.21)
  trade relations with third countries,
   352–353
  waste in internal market, 290–301
 "effet utile" doctrine, 63–64, 141–142,
  144–145, 418
 emergency derogations, 154, 240,
  245–246
 essential objectives. *See* Essential
  objectives.
 failure to fulfil, issues, 376–396, 403,
  419–420
  enforcement. *See* Enforcement
   issues.
  fines and penalties, 427–428, 433–435
   aid, punitive suspension, 406–407,
    434
  fresh proceedings, 421, 424–435
  information requirements, 394
  infringement v. non-implementation,
   110, 121–122, 126–127
  interim measures, 398–407
 free trade. *See* Free movement of
  goods.
 fundamental rights,
  co-operation procedure, Parliament,
   24, 27–28, 32
  free trade, waste disposal, 11–12
  French administrative law and, 61

Directive applications, legal principles—
cont.
 fundamental rights—*cont.*
  information disclosure, 146
 general principles,
  drinking water, standards, 257
  EEC Treaty, Member State
   responsibilities, 429
  endangered species, trade in, 157
  environmental protection as general
   interest, 4–17
  free trade, waste disposal, 11–13, 15
  prevention/rectification of damage,
   76
 informal v. formal implementation, 110,
  111–112, 120–122, 126–127
 information disclosure. *See* Information
  disclosure; Surveillance and
  monitoring.
 infringement v. non-implementation,
  110, 121–122, 126–127
 language of transposition, 164, 165–166,
  187, 311, 316
 local measures. *See* Local measures.
 national court action, model case,
  410–421
 pollution programs, legal basis, 20–36,
  290–301
 procedural issues. *See* Procedural
  issues, directive transposition;
  Procedural issues, judicial;
  Procedural issues, E.C. legislation.
 specific subjects. *See* Standards.
 stricter measures at national level
  dangerous chemicals, 117, 332, 333,
   342–355
  EEC Treaty as basis, 156, 157(n.23),
   351(n.21)
  endangered species, trade in,
   148–159
 time factors. *See* Time factors,
  implementation and notification.
Directive applications, non-legal
 descriptors. *See also* Directive
 applications, legal principles;
 Standards.
 accidents. *See* Accidental releases of
  pollutants.
 agricultural activities and products,
  drinking water standards,
   nitrates, 245–248, 251–255, 259–264
   pesticides, 246–248, 264
   importation and marketing,
    343–355